1972

ITALIAN TRAGEDY IN THE RENAISSANCE

The University of Illinois Press, Urbana, 1965

ITALIAN TRAGEDY IN THE RENAIS- SANCE

MARVIN T. HERRICK

Preface

The preliminary work for this study was started before I began research for *Italian Comedy in the Renaissance*. When I found that our University Library did not have enough Italian tragedies of the sixteenth century I decided to postpone further reading until after I had completed the book on comedy. Meanwhile the library acquired a good collection of tragedies. Therefore I picked up where I had left off and proceeded with this companion volume.

Although it may be even more difficult to show the literary connections between Italian tragic dramatists and the Elizabethans than to show the connections between Italian comedians and the Elizabethans, I became convinced in my own mind that the *tragedia nuova* was as influential as the *commedia erudita* and the *commedia dell' arte*. I hope that the following pages will support this conviction.

More friends than I can recall have helped me in finding books and films, in preparing the typescript for the printer, and in reading the proofs. I must acknowledge special thanks to the following colleagues: Harris Fletcher, Philip Kolb, Claude Viens, and Philip Wadsworth. The following members of the staff of the University Library have repeatedly gone beyond their normal duties to assist and lighten my labors: Isabelle Grant, Rare Book Room Librarian; Suzanne Griffiths, Rare Book Room Assistant; Alma De Jordy, Consultant in Bibliography; Helen Welch, Acquisition Librarian. I owe a special debt to Rosario Armato, Benito Brancaforte, and Mario Saltarelli, who have saved me from more than one blunder in the translations from sixteenth-century Italian. Elizabeth Dulany, Assistant Editor at the University Press, has patiently borne with my many changes and insertions after the galley proofs were formed. Finally I would like to acknowledge the courtesies shown me by the Biblioteca Nazionale in Florence, the Biblioteca Nazionale Marciana in Venice, and the Biblioteca Palatina in Parma.

Urbana, 1964 MARVIN T. HERRICK

Contents

I

Tragedy in Italy Before 1500

Seneca era la stella polare di questi arditi e soli-
tari navigatori nel mar della tragedia—Apollonio

Plautus and Terence were the guides for the Italian humanists who
launched the Latin comedy of the fifteenth century and Seneca
was the pole star for the few bold mariners who ventured upon
the poorly charted sea of tragedy. There were no right comedies
and tragedies in the vernacular drama that flourished in Italy before 1500, for these medieval plays were either religious or farci-
cal, dramatizations of biblical stories, of the lives of saints and
martyrs, or dramatized episodes of peasant, bourgeois, or clerical
life. Sixteenth-century Italian drama incorporated some features of
the native popular plays, to be sure, but the most important single
factor in its formation was imitation of classical models. During
the fourteenth and fifteenth centuries there was only one classical
model for tragedy, and that was Seneca. The splendid remains of
ancient Greek tragedy, the seven extant plays of Aeschylus, seven
of Sophocles, and eighteen of Euripides, were scarcely known to
the early humanists.

In the Middle Ages and early Renaissance the identity of Seneca
was not always clear, for there were two natives of Cordova who
distinguished themselves in ancient Rome, the elder Seneca, a
rhetorician, and the younger, who wrote moral essays and trage-

dies. Some writers, such as Boccaccio, evidently thought of Seneca the moralist as a different man from Seneca the tragic poet.[1] The medieval Seneca was primarily the philosopher who wrote pithy essays on anger, on the happy life, on leisure, on tranquility of mind, on the shortness of life, and a long discourse on how to give and receive benefits. This was the "moral Seneca" that Dante found in Limbo in the company of Socrates, Plato, Aristotle, Cicero, and other ancient philosophers. This was "Senec the wise" that Chaucer repeatedly referred to.

Nevertheless, Seneca the tragedian was also known in the late Middle Ages. Dante apparently knew something about his trage- dies, for he mentioned them in his famous letter to Can Grande della Scala: "Tragedy begins admirably and tranquilly, whereas its end or exit is foul and terrible . . . as appears from Seneca in his tragedies." Moreover, there is reason to believe that there are echoes in the *Inferno* of passages from the *Hercules Furens,* the *Troades,* and *Thyestes.*[2] There is no reason to believe, however, that Dante was concerned with Seneca as a model for theater. Like Chaucer and nearly all medieval writers, Dante was evidently content to think of tragedy as a narrative form, a tale of some great man who fell from high position into misery. It will soon be shown that one of Dante's contemporaries, Albertino Mussato (1261–1329) did study Seneca the dramatist and produced the first neoclassi- cal tragedy in modern Europe that has come down to us.

Actually it must have been a rather easy step for a humanist to go from Seneca's moral essays to his plays, if the tragedies were available. The same kind of Stoic fatalism is present in both, the same kind of moralizing *sententiae,* the same kind of pithy epi- grams. The tragedies offered further attractions to men who still admired declamatory rhetoric with its emphasis on the "colors" of style. Seneca's tragic style abounded in figures of speech, in mythological allusions, and, equally if not more important for modern taste, in the brooding introspections of characters like Atreus, Medea, Hecuba, and Jocasta. Finally, the sensationalism of these Roman closet dramas, the vivid depiction of horrible deeds and black thoughts, especially the bloodthirsty revenge of

---

[1] See Paget Toynbee, "Seneca Morale," in *Giornale storico della letteratura italiana* 25 (1900), 334–338.
[2] See E. G. Parodi, "Le tragedie di Seneca e la Divina Commedia," in *Bulletino della Società Dantesca Italiana* 21 (1914), 241–252.

Atreus upon his brother Thyestes and of Medea upon her husband Jason, fascinated the Italians just as much as the sixteenth-century Italian tragedies of blood and lust and revenge fascinated French and English playwrights.

Seneca's long-winded soliloquies, the minutiae of his mythological allusions, the debates between king and counselor, and the prosy choruses, were not considered faults by people who liked long dissertations, who were eager to learn more about classical mythology, and who delighted in arguments. For nearly three centuries humanists in Italy and elsewhere regarded Seneca as the best model for tragic writers. When Sir Philip Sidney tried to find something to praise in the rude English drama of 1580 he found only one play worth mentioning, namely *Gorboduc*, which was "full of stately speeches and well sounding phrases, climbing to the height of Seneca his style, and as full of notable morality." Sidney probably knew something about the English translations of Seneca's tragedies, begun in 1559 and completed by 1581, but these highly esteemed works hardly counted as original English plays.

Long before Sidney wrote his *Defense of Poesy*, Italians were pointing out the valuable lessons in Seneca's tragedies. In 1449, Enea Silvio Piccolomini, better known as Aeneas Sylvius or as Pope Pius II, said that Seneca's tragedies "are also very profitable, but we have nothing in Latin today besides Seneca, except Gregorio Corraro, who turned the story of Memnetereus [Tereus], which comes from Ovid, into a tragedy."[3] Silvio's remark suggests two reasons why Seneca was picked as the model for tragedy, that is, his availability and his Latinity.

Seneca's tragedies, as well as his moral essays, were available in the libraries of fifteenth-century Italy. The best manuscript of the tragedies, according to classical scholars, is the *Laurentianus*, now in the Laurentian Library in Florence. The Estes, rulers of Ferrara and among the most important fifteenth-century patrons of learning and art, Lionello (1407–50), Borso (1413–71), and Ercole I (1431–1505), all bought classical manuscripts. Two of their manuscripts of Seneca's tragedies have survived, one from the library of Borso and one from that of Ercole I.[4]

---

[3] *De liberorum educatione*, in *Opera* (Basel, 1550), p. 984.

[4] See Giulio Bertoni, *La biblioteca Estense e la coltura Ferrarese ai tempi del Duca Ercole I* (1471–1505) (Turin, 1903), pp. 217, 251.

Latin, as students of history and literature know, was indispensable in medieval and Renaissance education. Moreover, it was long considered indispensable for the grandeur and splendor of both ecclesiastical and secular courts. At Ferrara, for example, Italian was the language of everyday life, French love poetry was a delight and a solace, but Latin was the language of formal discourse, of diplomacy, of solemnities and celebrations. During the fourteenth and fifteenth centuries it was well-nigh inconceivable that any courtly writer would venture upon a tragedy that was not in Latin, the language of the high style. Even Dante would hardly have tried it although he was bold enough to use the vernacular in a "comedy."

The beginnings of modern tragedy, then, were in Latin and in Italy, the cradle of all the modern arts. The writers of these early tragedies of the fourteenth and fifteenth centuries chose two kinds of arguments: (1) a story based on contemporary or recent history, (2) a story drawn from ancient Roman or Greek history, or from classical mythology. (Ancient history and classical mythology often overlap, to be sure.) I shall first examine some tragedies based on contemporary or recent history and then turn to those based on ancient history and mythology. Both kinds owed much to Seneca, but the second kind was closer to Seneca's tragedies.

MUSSATO

The earliest tragedy recorded in Italy was written about 1315 by Albertino Mussato, soldier, politician, historian, and poet. His Latin tragedy *Eccerinus*[5] dramatized actual events in northern Italy during the second half of the preceding century, specifically the career and downfall of the tyrant Ezzelino da Romano (1194–1259).

Ezzelino, a lieutenant of the emperor Fredrick II in the struggle against the papacy, won control of Verona, Vicenza, and Padua. He was wounded in battle, captured by his enemies, and died of his wounds. While he may not have been the ferocious tyrant depicted in some accounts, including Mussato's, he was certainly ruthless and cruel. Among his cruelties was the slaughter of several thousand Paduans. He became a legendary figure that fitted very well the tyrant of Seneca's tragedies.

---

[5] *Tragoedia Eccerinis*, in *Opera*, Venice, 1636. Federico Balbi brought out an Italian translation at Ivrea in 1865. Federico Doglio has included a new Italian translation by Lidia Motta in his *Teatro tragico italiano* (1960).

Mussato's drama is not precisely a history although it recalls events of thirty years or so and actually spans months and years in itself; it is an impassioned protest against tyranny that is more declamatory than dramatic. The chorus, consisting of *populus* (the common people), has a leading role. There is much moralizing; in fact, the drama is closer to a morality play than to any other kind although there are no abstract characters such as virtues and vices. The cast is relatively small, including Eccerinus, his brother Albericus, his mother, two or three soldiers, a friar, a messenger, and the chorus. There are five acts, as prescribed by Horace in the *Ars Poetica* and as the ancient Roman tragedies and comedies were soon to be divided.

The first act is a kind of prologue introducing Eccerinus, his brother, and mother. Eccerinus is arrogant, boastful, defiant of justice, defiant of the deity. When his mother, who is distressed by the actions and attitude of her son, reveals the Satanic origin of her first-born, the villain-hero is far from dismayed, but exults in his heathen birth: "O come Satan! Give me a sign that I am worthy of you!" The chorus closes the act with an ode beginning, "What madness drives you, O mortal race of men? Where are you trying to climb? Whither is ambition taking you?"

In the second act there are only two speakers, a messenger and the chorus of Paduans. The messenger, who has just come from Verona, recounts the horrors brought on that city and warns the Paduans that their turn is next: "Ah what calamities is he threatening to bring upon [your] people? Dark dungeons, fires, crosses, tortures, death, exiles, and horrible famines." In a mixture of biblical and pagan allusions the chorus appeals to Christ to take notice of the monstrous cruelties wrought by the wicked Eccerinus.

The third act has some action; at least there is some coming in and going out of characters and some debate. Eccerinus discusses plans for the war with his brother. A soldier reports the beheading of an archenemy in the piazza and Eccerinus exults. Fra Lucas comes to remonstrate with the general and to recall him to God's ways. The friar compares the tyrant with Saul, but Eccerinus refuses to accept any of his arguments. Then the messenger brings news that a strong force of exiles has captured Padua. A lieutenant confirms the report. Eccerinus rages and accuses the lieutenant of treachery as other soldiers try to calm him. The chorus takes a very gloomy view of coming events.

The fourth act is mostly narrative. The messenger gives a straightforward account of how Eccerinus was brought to bay on the Adda River, wounded, and captured. Now he is dead. The chorus rejoices and gives thanks for the downfall of the tyrant.

The last act may seem like an anticlimax added to fill out the prescribed number of five. Mussato's poem, however, is not the tragedy of Ezzelino; it is the tragedy caused by tyranny, and unfortunately tyranny did not die with the fall of this particular tyrant. The fact that tyranny did not die with Ezzelino is the "true and complete catastrophe."[6] Thus Mussato's drama remains more medieval than neoclassical, for it is closer to allegory than to classical tragedy. It is also religious, very much Christian for all its pagan allusions, and so akin to the popular *rappresentazioni sacre*.

Mussato knew Seneca's tragedies and he imitated the Roman poet, through not slavishly. The Senecan influences are clearly marked in *Eccerinus*, but they are mostly mechanical, for example, the use of chorus and messenger, the sententious rhetoric, the supernatural elements, which are nevertheless kept in the background. The Italian omitted Seneca's pagan gods and Furies. There are references to the Furies, but they are not brought onstage as is the Fury in the opening scene of *Thyestes*. There are no ghosts resurrected from the lower world to brood over the bloodthirsty deeds. Mussato was no Dante, and he did not take the big step from Latin to his native Italian, but his "tragedy" is no mere adaptation of ancient Roman drama. Like Dante's great *Commedia*, it belongs to the fourteenth century. Like Dante's great poem, it is deeply religious and, despite its Latinity, an expression of Italian life. One is tempted to conjecture that sixteenth-century Italian writers of tragedy might have produced a better drama than they did if they had followed Mussato rather than stricter imitators of Seneca.

LAUDIVIO

Over a hundred years after Mussato wrote *Eccerinus* another Latin tragedy was based on Italian history, this time on contemporary history. The *De captivitate ducis jacobi*[7] by Laudivio da

---

[6] See M. T. Dazzi, "*L'Ecerinide* di Albertino Mussato," in *Giornale storico della letteratura italiana* 78 (1921), 264.

[7] Edited by Carlo Braggio in *Giornale Ligustico di archeologia, storia, e letteratura* 11 (1884), 50–76, 111–132.

Vezzana is a dramatization of the fall of Jacopo Piccinino, a *condottiere* who served the duke of Milan, the king of Naples, and Pope Pius II. Jacopo was an able soldier. In fact, he was too able, for his masters grew afraid of him and felt obliged to destroy him. Don Ferrante of Naples engineered his death, probably with the concurrence of the pope and duke of Milan; in 1464 he lured the soldier to his castle and hired an assassin to strangle him. The author Laudivio was a humanist at Ferrara and his patron Duke Borso d'Este was a friend of Piccinino. The tragedy was prepared for a reading in the ducal palace.

Laudivio also followed Seneca but not in the same way that Mussato did. As a fifteenth-century humanist he was devoted to classical antiquity in a way that neither Mussato nor Dante was, for all their admiration of Virgil, Statius, and Seneca. Therefore Laudivio did not leave out classical mythology. Jupiter, Mars, Apollo, Mercury, Juno, Athene, Venus, Diana, Saturn, Pluto, all magic names in the early Renaissance, adorn his play, and there are numerous references to Hercules, Hector, Atrides, Sisyphus, Tityus, and Tantalus. Italy is often called by its ancient name of Ausonia. There is no Christian Heaven, but there is Olympus. There is no Christian Hell, but there are Avernus and Acheron. In his *dramatis personae* there is no Christian churchman, but there is a pagan *sacerdos* and also a soothsayer. Above them all stands the capricious deity Fortuna, who actually rules the universe, gods and mortals alike.

Laudivio did not have to be a slavish imitator of Seneca to exploit a cynical, evil atmosphere that is foreign to Mussato's Latin tragedy and foreign to the vernacular sacred drama. Italy in the fifteenth century, the century of the Visconti in Milan, of the Sforzas in Milan and Forlì, of Borgias like Rodrigo (Pope Alexander VI) and Cesare, of Don Ferrante in Naples, was teeming with treacherous plots and counterplots, with long-shot gambles for power and riches among laity and clergy. The *condottieri*, those reckless soldiers of fortune, ready to sell their swords to the highest bidder, lived on chance and served no other deity than Fortune.

The absence of Christianity makes Laudivio's tragedy different from Mussato's, and the absence of any religion makes it different from classical tragedy, including Seneca's tragedies, which are by no means devoid of religious feeling. In the tragedy of Jacopo Piccinino the planets and stars are the important influence; astrology is what shapes human destinies. It may be recalled that Charles VIII of France, who invaded Italy at the close of the century, never made a move without first consulting his astrologers. In form, Laudivio's play is closer to a *rappresentazione sacra* than to ancient tragedy, for the structure is episodic; the scene shifts from Ferrara to Naples and back again, and the elapsed time is a matter of years rather than hours. The form is more medieval than classical and the Senecan influences are still largely mechanical, such as the division into acts, the use of messenger and chorus, the declamatory rhetoric, and the trappings of Graeco-Roman mythology.

In the first act of the "Captivity of Chief Jacopo," Borso d'Este, a priest *(sacerdos)*, and the chorus speak. The scene is Ferrara, as it is in the second act, wherein a soothsayer, a messenger, and the chorus speak. The first two acts are expository, giving information about Piccinino and the political situation in Italy. In the third act the scene shifts to Naples, where King Ferdinand I (Don Ferrante) receives an ambassador who announces the approach of Piccinino. The chorus also speaks.

The action quickens somewhat in the fourth act. At least there is the excitement of a debate between Don Ferrante and Satellex, the king's adviser and accomplice. Satellex urges the immediate death of Piccinino for the good of the realm. In this debate there emerges the fifteenth-century attitude toward *condottieri*—namely, suspicion: "Beware of him who always brings war." The epigram is as pithy as one of Seneca's, but the sentiment is hardly Senecan in context. In Seneca's tragedies it is the tyrant, the king, who is dangerous to the peace of the realm. In Laudivio's tragedy there is no tyrant bent on revenge and no counselor trying to restrain the maddened ruler, but rather a king anxious to preserve the peace and a counselor who urges him to commit a treacherous crime. When Don Ferrante says that prison should be strong enough to hold the *condottiere*, Satellex replies, "A prisoner can do harm, the dead nought." When the king remarks that rulers ought to be merciful, Satellex says, "Whoever wishes to be gracious, let him retire from the court." Satellex wins the argument, as Don Ferrante doubtless hoped he would, and the death warrant is carried to the prisoner. Piccinino, who makes this one brief appearance in the whole play, receives the news stoically and offers no defense.

Laudivio's Satellex is very like the hangman (*manigoldo*) in the contemporary religious plays and his character may have been borrowed from the popular sacred drama. Actually Satellex is a combination of the medieval hangman and Seneca's counselor or trusty servant.

In the last act the scene returns to Ferrara. A messenger brings news of Piccinino's captivity and its sad outcome. Borso denounces the perfidy of Don Ferrante and of mankind in general. The chorus laments the fickleness of Fortune and brings the tragedy to a close with a maxim: "Nothing lives forever in the world; everything that is born comes to an end; only virtue remains eternal." As pointed out earlier, the nominal hero Piccinino has a very small speaking part. It is the virtuous Borso, Laudivio's patron and Piccinino's friend, who is the real hero of this curious "tragedy."

FRANCESCO ARIOSTI

A few years before Laudivio's tragedy was recited for Borso d'Este another scholarly poet in Ferrara prepared a Latin entertainment for the court. Francesco Ariosti, uncle of the great Lodovico Ariosto, wrote *Isis*, which was performed before Lionello d'Este in 1444.[8]

Isis, according to the prologue, is a "true story" (*fabula veridica*), which recounts the demise of a gay house of pleasure. Hardly a true play, it consists of a prologue, an announcement by a town crier, and two elegies. The first elegy is spoken by Carino, who laments the abandoned house of Isis, where many delightful parties used to be held. The response is spoken by Isis, who sadly explains that she has been converted by a pious man and has given up all worldly pleasures.

It may seem odd to find Ariosti's composition classified among the tragedies of the fifteenth century. From a Christian point of view the retirement of Isis would be considered a triumph of virtue and therefore a happy ending akin to comedy. The spirit of paganism, however, was growing among the Italian humanists and

---

[8] See Bertoni, *op. cit.*, pp. 178–179.

courtiers; Ovid and Seneca were becoming more admired in some circles than was Holy Writ.

VERARDI

In 1492, the *Historia Baetica*[9] by Carlo Verardi dramatized a real episode involving the conquest of Granada by Ferdinand and Isabella of Spain. In other words, this drama, like Laudivio's "Captivity of Chief Jacopo," was based on contemporary history. A year or so later came *Fernandus Servatus,* apparently first written in Latin prose by Carlo Verardi and then turned into Latin verse by his nephew Marcellino.[10] This play dramatized the attempted assassination of King Ferdinand at Barcelona in 1492.

Neither play is a tragedy. The author knew well enough that his compositions were different from classical models. In the first place he wrote in prose, the language of familiar discourse, which was often used in the Latin humanistic comedy of the fifteenth century but never in tragedy. But Verardi was not trying to write a comedy either. The prologue to the *Historia Baetica*—the prologue is in verse—states, "I do not bring the comedies of Plautus or Nevius, which you know are feigned fables; but I offer you a recent and true history." Then it goes on to say that the audience will not witness the conventional matter of tragedy, such as the wicked deeds of tyrants, royal arrogance, or intolerable pride. "Here, indeed, everything is modest and honorable, all performed by means of the best counsel, accompanied by good fortune; fidelity, good manners, and integrity are practiced; there is no place given to pride or avarice or shameless love." "Let no one demand," says the prologue in conclusion, "that the laws of either comedy or tragedy be observed here; for a history and not a fable is to be acted."

In 1492, dramatic theory and practice in Italy were somewhere between the medieval and neoclassical stages. Aristotle's *Poetics* was not yet available; Horace, the grammarians, and the rhetoricians provided the authoritative pronouncements on right drama. The sixteenth century normally accepted history as the proper basis for tragedy and fiction as the proper basis for comedy. The

---

[9] The Illinois copy is dated [Basel] 1494. The *explicit* with the colophon is dated 1492. There is a modern reprint in the *Révue hispanique* 47 (1919).
[10] See H. Thomas, "Fernandus Servatus," in *Révue hispanique* 32 (1914), 428–457.

playwrights of the Middle Ages, however, used history, or what passed for history, as the basis for nearly all plays, mysteries, miracles, moralities, and farces. "Tragedies" and "comedies" in the Middle Ages were usually narratives.

Verardi's *Fernandus Servatus* is also a history and not a *fabula*. According to the preface, "It is called a tragicomedy [*tragicocomoedia*] because the dignity of the characters and the impious violation of royal majesty seem to effect tragedy, the happy outcome comedy." Verardi's concept of tragedy and comedy had not advanced far beyond Dante's, but he was aware of dramatic form and he was trying to write a play rather than a narrative. The term *tragicocomoedia* he took from Plautus, from the prologue to *Amphytrion*. It is unlikely that he knew any of Euripides' tragedies with a happy ending. It is virtually certain that he did not know Aristotle's discussion, in *Poetics* 13, of the artistic superiority of tragedy with a single unhappy ending over tragedy with a double ending of punishment of evil and reward of virtue.

There is at least a superficial influence of Seneca in the *Fernandus Servatus*. Among the characters are the three Furies (Alecto, Megaera, Tisiphone), who incite Ruffus to murder the king. Balancing these Senecan characters, however, is St. James, who would be at home in a medieval religious play. According to Creizenach, these tragicomedies attracted some imitation in Germany; but in Italy Verardi exerted little influence.

LOSCHI

Meanwhile, and a century earlier, the second kind of Latin tragedy made its appearance in Italy, a tragedy that was not based on contemporary or recent history, a tragedy that owed little to the native religious drama, but a tragedy that used an argument from classical mythology. This important step came with Loschi's *Achilles*, which was probably written about 1390.[11]

Antonio Loschi (1365–1441), a native of Vicenza, writer, orator, and diplomat, imitated Cicero and Quintilian in his orations and chose the Trojan war for his play. Dares Phrygius, whose account of the fall of Troy was well known in the Middle Ages, was his main source, not Homer.

---

[11] See Cloetta, 2.105. The text of *Achilles* was printed at Venice in 1636, included in the *Opera* of Mussato. Loschi's tragedy is not at all in the spirit of *Eccerinus*.

Loschi's Latin tragedy is divided into five acts. The titular character, Achilles, has a small part, for he appears onstage only in the second act. There are two choruses, one Greek and the other Trojan, which sympathize with the characters speaking at the time. The author was undoubtedly familiar with the admonition of Horace in the *Ars Poetica* (193–201), that the chorus should be treated as one of the actors, that it should favor the good characters and give friendly counsel, encourage the timid, praise the simple life, justice, law, and peace. Loschi also knew Seneca's choruses.

Hecuba opens the play lamenting the fall of Troy and the death of her two sons Hector and Troilus. Paris enters and argues with his mother over the best means of retaliation. He discloses a plan to ambush Achilles in the temple and murder him, thus avenging the deaths of Hector and Troilus and appeasing their restless ghosts. The chorus of Trojans asks the gods for help against the Greeks.

Loschi's debt to Seneca is strongly marked in this first act. The pagan mythology, Hecuba's troubled visions of the ghosts of Hector and Troilus (who cannot cross Acheron until their deaths are avenged), the declamatory style of the long speeches, the epigrammatic style of the short speeches, all are characteristic of the Roman writer. A brief excerpt from an exchange between Hecuba and Paris will show the sententious manner and the arrogant attitude of his royal characters. The old queen is trying to persuade her son that any means of revenge is allowable to royalty.

Paris: Discord does not become a king.
Hecuba: Anything is allowable.
Paris: To preserve trust is the highest virtue of a king.
Hecuba: Trust dwells apart from the lofty royal house.
Paris: To overthrow the fatherland is the crime of an impious king.
Hecuba: The monarch is base who does not take revenge on the enemy.

In her contention that royalty may use any means, natural or unnatural, lawful or unlawful, to achieve its end and that the monarch should always seek revenge on his enemy, Hecuba is echoing several characters in Seneca's tragedies. Clytemnestra, in *Agamemnon* 264, who takes revenge on her husband for his philandering by cuckolding him and then murdering him, says, "There is one law for the throne, another for the private bed." Her partner in crime, Aegisthus (*ibid.* 271–272), says, "[Royal persons] believe that this is the greatest pledge of sovereignty: whatever is unlawful to others is lawful to them." Lycus, in *Hercules Furens* 400, who has usurped the throne of Thebes, says that he rules "without fear of laws." Atreus, in *Thyestes* 217–218, who plans a horrible revenge on his brother, says to his trusty servant, "Integrity, piety, and trust are private benefits; kings may behave as they please." Nero, in *Octavia* 443, tells his counselor that "the leader's greatest virtue is to destroy his enemy."

Loschi's Achilles opens the second act with a soliloquy. He addresses Cupid and not Jove, for to him, in his present state of mind, Love is the mightiest of the gods. Achilles has fallen in love with Polyxena, a daughter of Priam and Hecuba. Paris' emissary enters to greet the Greek hero, the scourge of Troy, and to urge him to marry Polyxena, thus forestalling further bloodshed and sealing the peace. Love, he says, will be the best antidote for the evils of war. The wedding party is now waiting for Achilles at the temple, so why delay? Achilles agrees to go to the temple. The Greek chorus sings of the power of love, which no one, young or old, god or mortal, can withstand.

The emphasis on romantic love in this act is neither Homeric nor Senecan; Polyxena is never mentioned in Homer, and Seneca never assigned an important role to romantic love in his tragedies. It is true that the chorus in *Hippolytus* (274 ff.) does speak of the overwhelming power of Cupid, but love here is animal passion or lust. "When Love moves them [the beasts], then the forest groans with savage uproar. Monsters of the raging sea, Lucanian bulls, Love claims all nature as his own; nothing is exempt."

It is curious to find such an emphasis on love in a tragedy of 1390, because nearly two centuries were to pass before Giraldi Cinthio was to boast that the addition of some love interest in tragedy was an improvement over the dramaturgy of the Ancients, and nearly three centuries were to pass before Corneille and Dryden were to make the same boast. Even so, the shadow of Seneca still fell over Loschi's second act, in particular the shadow of *Thyestes*. Achilles, weary of the war and drawn to the pleasanter sport of love, readily falls into the trap of reconciliation prepared by Paris. Thyestes, weary of exile and longing to see his sons' heritage secured, readily falls into the trap of reconciliation prepared by his brother Atreus. Loschi's Paris sets up his victim

for the kill just as Atreus sets up his victim. Like Seneca, Loschi
was writing a tragedy of revenge.

In the third act Hecuba reappears in soliloquy, and, as usual,
she is worrying herself sick. Now she is afraid that her sons will
be exposed to the renewed wrath of Achilles—after Paris kills him
and his ghost descends to the lower world. But she soon talks herself into better spirits by thinking of the impending death of
Hector's murderer. When Priam enters he is startled by her cheerful countenance and suspects that her mind may be affected. When
she explains, however, that Paris is about to assassinate Achilles,
he, too, rejoices in the prospect of revenge. When Cassandra, who
has just entered, foresees disaster, her mother rebukes her, bids
her rejoice, and Priam orders a general thanksgiving.

The chorus of Trojans comments on the vagaries of fate which
put man up and then throw him down. The higher the man the
readier the fall. No one is so strong but another is stronger. So
the great Achilles has been struck down by the arrow of Paris,
with the help of Apollo. The sentiments of this chorus are thoroughly Senecan, characteristic of the philosophical essays as well
as of the tragedies. Perhaps the best parallel among several is two
lines from the chorus of *Thyestes* (613–614):

> quem dies vidit veniens superbum,
> hunc dies vidit fugiens iacentem.

Ben Jonson translated these lines and used them for the conclusion
of his tragedy of *Sejanus:*

> For, whom the morning saw so great and high,
> Thus low and little 'fore the eve doth lie.

In the fourth act a Greek messenger brings details of Achilles'
death to the Greek chorus. Love, he explains, made the hero confident and unafraid, but once in the temple he was assailed by a
gang of Trojans. He put up a tremendous fight, his greatest fight,
but fell before a dart thrown by Paris. Then the Trojans hewed
his body to pieces. The Greek chorus sings of the fickleness of
Fortune.

In the last act Agamemnon laments the whim of Fortune that
has now destroyed the greatest ornament of the Greek army. His
brother Menelaus reminds him that the gods never let any crime
go unpunished, thus reminding the reader or spectator that Agamemnon has a debt of his own to pay before long. The Greek

chorus ends the tragedy with a lament over the uncertain fate of mortals, all of whom are ruled by the stars.

Loschi's *Achilles* is an advance over Mussato's *Eccerinus* in the development of neoclassical tragedy although it is not so impressive a poetic performance. Mussato's play is more moving and more expressive even though it may be less theatrical. Loschi's structure is less medieval than Mussato's, for he greatly condensed the time, curtailed the chorus somewhat, curtailed the narratives of the messenger, and put more emphasis on the dialogue. Moreover, Loschi's tragedy is neither a history play nor a morality.

Achilles is far from being good theater, however. For one thing, the catastrophe, that is, the death of Achilles, comes in Act 3 and not in Act 5. In fact, there is not much concern expressed, even by the Greeks, for the fall of the hero. The Greek messenger in the fourth act and Agamemnon in the fifth lament the fickleness of Fortune, but express no personal grief over the death of Achilles. From the Trojan point of view, and that is the prevailing one, the real hero is Paris, who is a treacherous assassin. At this early stage of tragedy in Italy, however, one could hardly expect Loschi to excel his master Seneca, and Paris is a tragic hero if Atreus is one. His Achilles, on the other hand, is hardly comparable to Seneca's Thyestes, just as there is no scene in Loschi's tragedy that even approaches Seneca's terrible banquet scene, wherein Thyestes probes his own soul as horror is piled on horror.

Cloetta calls *Achilles* the "first Renaissance tragedy," which means that it was the first tragic drama in western Europe that closely imitated the classical Senecan model and owed little or nothing to medieval mystery, miracle, or morality. As such it was an important forerunner of Italian tragedy of the sixteenth century.

CORRARO

About 1429, when he was still a student in Mantua, the Venetian Gregorio Corraro wrote a Latin tragedy entitled *Progne*. (The play was published at Venice in 1558.) Later in life, after he had entered the service of the church, the author expressed some regret over this youthful folly. The tragedy, however, must have been well received by many influential people. Aeneas Sylvius, it may be recalled, said in 1449 that Italy had "nothing in Latin [tragedy] today besides Seneca, except Gregorio Corraro."

Corraro took his argument from the celebrated story of Tereus,

Procne, and Philomela in Ovid's *Metamorphoses,* but he knew that
a play and not a narrative was demanded, so he tried to reshape
the story to fit into the framework of Senecan tragedy. He imitated
Senecan tragedy in general and the *Thyestes* in particular. According to Cloetta,[12] he wrote on the manuscript the following statement: "In this tragedy he is imitating Seneca's *Thyestes;* inasmuch
as there Tantalus is introduced coming from the lower world, so
here the Thracian king Diomedes." The influence of *Thyestes*
extends throughout the play and is especially strong in the last act.

The printed version of 1558 is not divided into acts, but the
choral odes do separate the play into a prologue and four espisodes
of varying length. The third "act," for example, is by far the long-
est. It is notable that the Italian condensed Ovid's matter of months
and years to a matter of days. The twenty-four-hour rule was not
yet in effect, of course, but Corraro made a determined if not altogether successful effort to create the illusion of a few hours passing, and the reader is almost convinced that all of the events take
place within a couple of days or so.

The prologue is spoken by the ghost of Diomedes, an ancient
king of Thrace. This is the mythical Diomedes who kept a stable
of man-eating mares until Hercules raided his kingdom and killed
him. He has been routed from his resting place in the lower world
by news of a horrible crime which demands punishment if his
native Thrace is to have any peace hereafter. The chorus of
Thracians addresses a prayer to the god of the sea that he grant
King Tereus a safe voyage home from Athens, where he has gone
to fetch his wife's sister. Cries from the harbor indicate that the
king has already arrived home.

In the second act Tereus gives thanks for a successful journey.
He is apprehensive about his wife Procne's reception of news that
he has not brought back her sister Philomela, but he hopes that
he can placate her with lies and false tears. Tereus at once discloses that he is an unscrupulous, deceitful man. When Procne
inquires about her sister, he tells her that she perished during a
storm at sea and that he buried her as soon as the ship reached
land. When Procne asks if any of the Athenian companions are still
alive, he says that old Pistus threw himself on the funeral pyre and
that the others returned to Athens. Procne is nearly prostrated by
grief and by self-reproach that she ever invited her sister to visit

---

[12] 2.157.

her. She gives orders for state mourning. The chorus laments the unexpected turn of fortune that has cast down Procne from happiness to misery and seizes the opportunity to comment on the dangers that beset all travelers who go by sea. The ode begins with a sentiment that is certainly Senecan: "No mortal joy has ever lasted long and not turned into misery."

For his long third act Corraro condensed a year of the original story into a day. Pistus, Philomela's old serving man, did not throw himself on the funeral pyre, but has arrived in the courtyard of the palace with terrible news. The nurse recognizes him and Procne comes out to question him. Pistus recounts the grisly deeds of Tereus, who had ravished Philomela and then cut out her tongue. He had tried to kill all of her attendants, but could not find the old man, who had hidden among the rocks until the ship had sailed on. Pistus' account of the violation and mutilation of Philomela follows Ovid pretty faithfully. His escape from the slaughter is reminiscent of the escape of an attendant from the slaughter of Laius and his followers by Oedipus.

After Pistus has given his terrible report Procne begins to vilify her husband: "O cunning deviser of treachery, more cruel than the Thracian Diomedes, he is truly the parent of impious blood." Now she will be revenged.

After the chorus delivers an ode to Bacchus, Procne resumes her diatribe against Tereus. Meanwhile—there is an awkward gap here, not satisfactorily covered by the choral ode—Philomela has been found by Procne's servants and released from her chains. Procne calls on the gods of the lower world to assist her revenge. She is beside herself. Then, in the best scene of the play, the nurse argues with her and tries to restrain her frenzy. The nurse warns her of the perilous obstacles that confront a foreign woman in a savage land.

Nurse: If nothing moves you, yet consider your son.
Procne: But what about my sister?

A fierce struggle rages within Procne's mind. Finally she recalls the example of Medea, who took revenge on her faithless husband Jason by killing their children. The nurse is horrified, of course.

Nurse: A mother, you will slay your only son?
Procne: He is also the son of Tereus.
Nurse: Why does the boy deserve death?

Procne: A son contaminated by his father deserves to die.

The chorus sings an ode on the corrupting influence of wealth and power with their attendant vices of greed and lust. Jupiter himself set the pattern of corruption, and few kings have honored chastity. Therefore few kings die a natural death. The poor and humble are more fortunate: "Happy the poor man, who lives on little. . . . Foul lust never crosses the threshold of the poor."

This chorus is an echo of Seneca throughout. There are numerous parallels in the Roman tragedies, the closest being in *Hercules Oetaeus* and *Octavia*. In *Hercules Oetaeus* (640–657) the chorus of attendants on Deianira, wife of Hercules, says:

How few live out their allotted span! Whom Cynthia [the moon] saw in happiness, the new-born day sees wretched. 'Tis rare to find old age and happiness in one. The couch of turf, softer than Tyrian purple, oft soothes to fearless slumber; but gilded ceilings break our rest, and purple coverlets drag out wakeful nights. Oh, if the hearts of rich men were laid bare! What fears does lofty fortune stir within! The waves of Bruttium, when Corus [the northwest wind] lashes up the sea, are calmer far. The poor man's heart is free from care; he holds cups carved from the wide-spreading beech, but holds them with hand untrembling; he eats but cheap and common food, yet sees no drawn sword hanging o'er his head! 'Tis in golden cups that blood is mixed with wine.[13]

In *Octavia* (895–898) the chorus of Octavia's friends says, "Poverty happily hides content under a low roof; lofty homes are often battered by great storms or overturned by Fortune."

The fourth and fifth acts of *Progne* are very close to Seneca's *Thyestes* in content and there are many verbal echoes as well. Medea's slaughter of her children in order to punish her unfaithful husband certainly gave Corraro important material, but it was *Thyestes* that loomed largest in his mind when he composed the climax and resolution of his tragedy.

In the fourth act a messenger brings dreadful news to the chorus. There is no explanation of how he could have discovered these horrors, which occurred in secret. Nevertheless, he tells how Procne, accompanied by Philomela, took her little son Itys to the stables, where Diomedes used to feed his horses with human flesh, and there slew him. The chorus is shocked, but it urges the messenger to continue. Whereupon he tells how Procne cut off the child's head and then, with her sister helping, minced the body for stew-

---

[13] Miller's translation in the Loeb Library.

ing and roasting. She was preparing a meal for Tereus. The chorus, possibly exhausted by the recital of horrors, contents itself with a brief comment on the enormity of the crime, which surpasses that perpetrated by Medea. "The cursed offspring of Prometheus conquers all the Furies; now there is nothing that later ages may consider forbidden."

In the last act Tereus partakes of the meal prepared by his wife and sister-in-law. Like Thyestes in Seneca's tragedy, he is vaguely troubled in both body and mind, but knows not why and tries to forget his forebodings of evil in enjoyment of the feast. This scene takes place onstage and is not reported. In fact, the last act of *Progne*, like the last act of *Thyestes*, has neither messenger nor chorus.

Procne watches her husband as he picks at his food and sips the mixture of wine and blood.

Procne: [aside] See how proudly he lolls upon his kingly throne. He is happy and he little believes that any evil can disturb his feasting. Sate your hunger with the consecrated viands. Quench your thirst with the blood of your offspring. It befits you, vainglorious man.
Tereus: Only the sight of my son can bring me my usual ease.
Procne: Only Philomela can bring me solace.
Tereus: She lies lifeless among the dead.
Procne: Your son also rests among the lifeless shades.

At this last statement Tereus looks up in startled alarm.

Tereus: Where has my son been hidden so long?
Procne: He is hidden in you.
Tereus: Where is Itys?
Procne: You will know.
Tereus: Where is he?
Procne: The ravisher who violated my sister, the beast who cut out her tongue, he who killed the companions of the virgin, that man has impiously feasted on his own son. Philomela, bring the head of the dead boy before the face of the father. Do you recognize this, father? Or do you know the sister better?

While this scene is closely parallel to the banquet scene in *Thyestes*, Corraro made some changes. For one thing, by having Procne hold back the head of Itys he sharpened the suspense. Atreus shows Thyestes the heads of his two sons on a platter before he announces, "You have feasted on your sons, an impious meal."

The appearance of Philomela, whom Tereus had left securely chained, is a shock to him almost as great as the severed head of his son. Moreover, Corraro's dialogue here is shorter than Seneca's and more brutal. Seneca's is somewhat softened by his usual devices of mythological allusion and rhetorical figures.

Tereus is now beside himself with grief and rage. He cries to Jupiter, he curses the whole world, but above all he curses himself, for he knows that it is he who brought on this horrible retribution: "I have deserved this slaughter. Do I your sire see you in this, Itys? Who may bewail my miseries enough? The father is the tomb of the son."

Procne exults in her revenge; like Atreus, she recounts all the gory details of her slaughter and preparation of the cannibal meal. Tereus is appalled by her vindictiveness: "O hands of a stepmother! What Colchian [i.e. Medea] ever committed such heinous crimes?" Tereus now wants to flee from all familiar surroundings; he would take refuge on Mount Rhodope, where the vulture of Prometheus could gnaw at his liver. Procne mockingly agrees that Rhodope is a suitable place for him since it was there that he violated and mutilated Philomela. Before he leaves he asks his wife one more question.

Tereus: What blame has the child deserved?
Procne: He has deserved to die for your guilt.
Tereus: The avenging gods be witnesses.
Procne: Rather call on the divinity of unsullied chastity.
Tereus: The Furies will hound you.
Procne: Only Itys will hound the father.

So ends Corraro's tragedy, and the conclusion is merely an adaptation of Seneca's conclusion to *Thyestes:*

Thyestes: Why did my children deserve this?
Atreus: Because they were yours.
Thyestes: Sons of the father—
Atreus: Yea, and what delights me, your very own.
Thyestes: The gods who protect the innocent be witnesses.
Atreus: Why not the gods of marriage?

. . . . .

Thyestes: The avenging gods will be present; my prayers deliver you to them for punishment.
Atreus: I deliver you to your sons for punishment.

Corraro deserves some praise for ending his play here and not carrying out the supernatural metamorphosis of Ovid, wherein Tereus became a hoopoe, Procne a nightingale, and Philomela a swallow. Doubtless he was mindful of Horace's admonition in the *Ars Poetica* (187–188): "Procne must not be turned into a bird or Cadmus into a snake. Whatever you thus show me I disbelieve and abominate." But the young Italian student was imitating Seneca rather than Ovid, for he understood the difference between theater and narrative. His play can hardly be ranked very high in European drama, but it settled Renaissance tragedy on the course laid by Loschi, and this was the course followed by tragedy during the next century and a half.

DATI

Leonardo Dati (1408–72), a Florentine humanist, whose *De amicitia* (1441) was the first attempt in Italy to adapt classical meters to vernacular poetry, wrote a Latin tragedy *Hiempsal*[14] which used an argument from ancient Roman history, from the *Bellum Jugurthinum* by Sallust. Hiempsal was cousin to the warrior Jugurtha and co-heir with him to the throne of Numidia in northern Africa. Jugurtha was an able man and very ambitious. He had Hiempsal assassinated and later captured Hiempsal's brother and tortured him to death. Then the Romans stepped in and captured Jugurtha, but only after a long and costly war.

The political situation in Dati's tragedy is similar to that in the early English tragedy *Gorboduc* and in *King Lear*—namely, the calamities inevitably brought on by dividing a kingdom. Micipsa (d. 118 B.C.) divided Numidia into three parts, leaving a part to each of his two sons and one to his adopted son Jugurtha. Like *Gorboduc*, but unlike *Lear*, *Hiempsal* is about as close to the medieval morality as it is to tragedy. The moral is the most important thing: "Ambition begot Envy, Envy begot Strife, Strife begot Treachery, with whom Want, Theft, Slaughter, Rapine follow." Yet Dati, like Sackville and Norton, had his eye on Senecan tragedy as well; he used chorus, messenger, and wise counselor, and divided his play into five acts.

In the first act, Ambition, like one of Seneca's ghosts, opens the

---

[14] See F. Flamini, "Leonardo di Piero Dati poeta latino del secolo XV," in *Giornale storico della letteratura italiana* 16 (1890), 1–107.

play. Modesty appears as a foil, and there are also real characters, one Asper and a wise counselor named Polimites (many counsels). The chorus reviles Envy and outlines the story, giving warning of the miseries in store for the reckless young Hiempsal. In the second act, Hiempsal himself is introduced arguing with the counselor. The chorus admonishes the young ruler, urging him to follow virtue instead of war. In the third act, Hiempsal talks with his brother Adherbal. Hiempsal is impetuous and choleric; he rages against Jugurtha, who, he contends, is not a legitimate heir to the throne. Adherbal tries to calm him. A prophetess foresees great sufferings for the Numidian people. The chorus again admonishes Hiempsal to restrain himself. Jugurtha appears soliloquizing in the fourth act. He justifies his projected revenge on the two brothers, who have provoked him beyond endurance. After Jugurtha leaves, Polimites and another learned man engage in a philosophical dispute. The chorus begs the gods to avert the calamity that threatens the kingdom.

In the fifth and last act *Hiempsal* becomes a morality play, though a pagan one. After the counselor and a messenger deplore the baleful portents that hang over the realm, Strife and Treachery enter. They have been summoned from Erebus by Envy. Treachery relates that Jugurtha has seized Hiempsal and cut off his head. Now Treachery proposes to fetch Want, Theft, and Rapine. Messengers come to Hiempsal's mother and other Numidian matrons to announce the sad news of the assassination. The second messenger cries, "O tempora, O mores! Is it thus that brother contrives the death of brother? When will there be any trust?" The mother says nothing. Then the moral is pointed: "Know by this what deadly and abominable misfortune can happen through Envy."

Dati's *Hiempsal* suggests that tragedy in fifteenth-century Italy was still wavering between medieval and classical forms. By the first decade of the sixteenth century, however, the learned Italian playwrights were determined to reject as models the native religious plays that they could still see performed on the street at carnival time; they were now imitating the tragedies and comedies of ancient Rome. Plautus and Terence had won in comedy, Seneca had won in tragedy, and Euripides and Sophocles were soon to become models for the most learned *letterati*.

II

Rhymed Tragedies

As has been shown in the preceding chapter, the writers of Latin
tragedy during the fourteenth and fifteenth centuries drew their
matter from both classical and native sources, that is, from Seneca's
tragedies, from Ovid's myths, from histories of ancient Greece and
Rome, from Italian history, and from the native *sacre rappresentazioni*. Writers of vernacular tragedy in the sixteenth century continued to exploit the same sources. In addition, the Italian *novelle*,
which had already suggested plots and characters to the fifteenth-
century humanists who wrote Latin comedies, now provided matter
for tragedy.

At the close of the fifteenth century and the beginning of the
sixteenth Italian poets composed a number of tragedies in rhyme.
Some of these early plays were never printed and have disappeared, but enough have been preserved to indicate the subject
matter, the dramatic forms, and the kinds of Italian verse that
were used.

Rhymed verse was the accepted medium of the early popular
drama in Italy, that is, the religious plays and farces that arose
in song. The common people liked songs and they liked rhymes.
Many learned comedies written by fifteenth-century humanists
were in Latin prose, and Italian prose appeared early in sixteenth-

century comedy, but verse was considered the proper medium for tragedy.

The favorite verse form in the popular religious plays was *ottava rima,* an eight-line stanza. Couplets and *terzine* were also used. *Terza rima,* introduced, or at least perfected, by Dante in his great *Commedia,* consists of interlocking triplets *(terzine)*—a b a, b c b, c d c, etc.—a magnificent medium for a great artist like Dante, but never very successful in plays. Nevertheless, *terzine* were used in several rhymed tragedies. *Ottava rima,* rhymed a b a b a b c c, also went back to the fourteenth century, when Boccaccio used it in his long narrative poem *Teseide.* In the late fifteenth century it became the accepted verse form for Italian romances like Boiardo's *Orlando innamorato* and Pulci's *Morgante Maggiore.* While *ottava rima* proved to be better than *terzine* for plays, it was hardly the best form for dialogue. Therefore, when the full impact of the classical revival was felt, unrhymed Italian verse, similar to the later English blank verse, was developed for both comedy and tragedy. This unrhymed verse did not become prominent, however, until the second decade of the sixteenth century, and at the close of the fifteenth century rhyme still ruled in all forms of the vernacular drama.

POLIZIANO

The earliest surviving nonreligious play in Italian is Angelo Poliziano's *Orfeo,* produced at Mantua in 1472. This work has been called the first pastoral drama and a forerunner of opera. It is about as close to tragedy as to the pastoral, and in form is closer to the medieval *sacra rappresentazione* than to classical tragedy. The author never called it anything but *favola* (fable), and an early printing at Venice (1524) called it *rappresentazione della favola d'Orfeo.* The verse form was *quasi tutta in ottava rima* ("almost all in *ottava rima").* There was no division into acts until the edition of 1772.[1]

Poliziano found his argument in the ancient myth of Orpheus and Eurydice as related by Ovid in the *Metamorphoses.* The subject, then, was pagan. The original *dramatis personae* included, besides the two lovers, Mercury (as a prologue), Pluto, Proser-

---

[1] See L. E. Lord, *A Translation of the Orpheus of Angelo Politian and the Aminta of Torquato Tasso,* Oxford, 1930.

pine, Minos, a Fury, two shepherds, a servant, a Bacchante, and a final chorus of Bacchantes. The author preserved a tragic ending: Orfeo is beheaded by the Bacchantes.

SEGNI

The *Tragedia di Eustachio romano,* by Antonio di Carlo Segni, published at Florence in 1511, was primarily another *sacra rappresentazione.* The subject matter, the martyrdom of St. Eustachius, was typical of many religious plays, which dramatized tales of saints as well as stories from the Bible. Nevertheless, the author had an eye on classical tragedy and ventured to call his play a *tragedia* although he had some misgivings about using the term. In his dedication he remarked, "I do not know if I dare call it tragedy."

Why was Segni doubtful about applying the term "tragedy" to his play? One reason, and probably the most important one, was that he wrote in the vernacular and not in Latin, which hitherto had been the language for the high style proper to tragedy. Moreover, he may have been troubled about his subject matter, which was suitable for popular religious plays but was not strictly classical history or myth. He might have got around this second difficulty by reasoning that the story of Eustachius went back ultimately to ancient Rome and was therefore a kind of classical history. At least he could have consoled himself with the assurance that his principal characters, Eustachius and Hadrian, a general and an emperor, were the exalted personages traditionally prescribed for tragedy.

At all events, Segni tried to make his play different from the popular religious plays. He provided the classical framework of five acts, each act separated by a choral ode. In the last act the chorus takes an active part in the dialogue as well. Furthermore, Segni did not eliminate the ancient pagan gods and heroes from the dialogue. All of the characters save Eustachius and his family repeatedly refer to Jupiter, Mars, Juno, *et al.,* and speak of Achilles, Scipio, Julius Caesar, and other ancient heroes. In other words, much of the atmosphere is pagan. He did not arrange his plot *ab ovo,* as did most writers of religious plays, but began in the manner prescribed by Horace, that is, in *medias res;* actually near the end, after the general had already turned Christian and just before his execution. The passage of time is not clearly defined, but the illusion of only a few hours or at most a few days is apparently intended. There is no attempt at a strict unity of place, for the scene shifts in the third act from Eustachius' home outside Rome to within the city.

The legend of St. Eustachius rests on the flimsiest historical basis and apparently did not appear before the seventh century. According to the legend, Eustachius, a Roman general under Hadrian in the second century, saw a stag with a crucifix between his horns and heard the voice of Christ bidding him give up his worldly life and suffer for His sake. Eustachius turned Christian and suffered martyrdom by being slowly baked to death inside a brazen bull.

When Eustachius first appears in the play the reader who is not familiar with the legend would be puzzled to know what troubles him, because he does not fully disclose the story of his conversion to Christianity until a climactic scene in the fourth act. During the first three acts the reader, or the audience, knows only that he has been greatly disturbed by visions and voices, that he has learned the vanity of worldly goods and worldly success, that he is debating whether or not he should carry on with the old life. His wife and two young sons share his distress and his change of heart. The chorus follows the recommendation of Horace and the pactice of Seneca: it supports good against evil and sympathizes with the hero's attempt to reform his life.

Apparently Segni had some understanding of tragic irony, that device so prominent in the best classical tragedies. For example, Eustachius' final resolution to renounce all military fame as well as all worldly goods coincides with Hadrian's offer of a great triumph in Rome. The general goes to Rome for his triumph, but is executed as a traitor. From the Christian point of view, to be sure, he wins a greater triumph in the glorious death of a martyr.

The first three acts, wherein Eustachius and his family discuss the vanities of the world and the general tries to convince the imperial ambassador and the emperor that he is tired of military glory and wishes to retire, are rather slow. The action quickens in the last two acts, however, and is arranged with some theatrical skill so that suspense is built up. The discovery that Eustachius has been converted comes in the fourth act. Standing before the temple where honors are to be heaped upon him, and face to face with the emperor, the general makes his declaration: "Now know,

Emperor, and hold it certain, that the Christian faith is true and holy." Then he relates the details of his conversion.

Hadrian is distressed by this desertion of his best general, but he takes no immediate action beyond calling a meeting of his advisory council to decide what must be done with the deserter.

In the last act the emperor has made up his mind; he believes that he must stamp out this evil lest a greater evil follow. The chorus now speaks for the first time in the midst of the dialogue: "Behold Abraham and Isaac at the sacrifice!" It is disclosed that Eustachius and his family have been thrown to the lions—offstage. The executioner reports, however, that the lions have refused to harm the Christians. Hadrian is greatly agitated and expresses his perturbation in short-line couplets instead of the usual *ottava rima*. He orders the executioner to transfer the victims to the brazen bull.

Faced with a lingering death by slow fire, Eustachius remains resolute in his desire to win martyrdom, but is shaken by the thought of the suffering that his wife and children must share with him. The family reassures him that they are as resolute as he. Thereupon Eustachius rejoices: "Today we can ascend to heaven, dying for our blessed faith."

The end is not yet, however, and the suspense continues to build up. The excutioner, who admires the general and sympathizes with him, tries to turn him from his stubborn course of self-destruction, assuring him that it is not too late to save himself and his family. Hadrian finally stops the argument and orders the execution, which takes place offstage. The chorus, in bringing the play to a close, rebukes the emperor: "They [the martyrs] are in heaven and you are in great anguish."

Segni's *Eustachio* is clearly a transitional play, standing between the *rappresentazione sacra* and neoclassical tragedy. It is closer to the religious play than to tragedy, but its classical structure separates it from the episodic medieval type; its plot is fairly close-knit, it rises to a main crisis in the fourth act, and the death scene is offstage. Moreover, the principal characters, Eustachius and the emperor Hadrian, bear some resemblance to the heroes of ancient tragedy. Segni's style is more medieval than classical, but he made an effort to give it the elevation proper to classical tragedy. There is no mixture of comedy in the play. The authors of the *sacre rappresentazioni* more often than not introduced some facetious elements into the most serious actions; but not Segni, for he was trying to write a tragedy, not a mystery.

SACCO

Another good example of the transitional play in the early six-teenth century is the *Tragedia nova intitolata Sosanna, raccolta da Daniello profeta* (1524),[2] written by a friar named Tibortio Sacco. *Sosanna* is also akin to the native religious drama, but is closer, save for its use of the vernacular, to the Christian Terence, that important body of Latin school plays using Biblical arguments but composed in imitation of Terentian comedy. Sacco used three kinds of Italian verse, *ottava rima*, short-line couplets,[3] and the new unrhymed eleven-syllable verses, the neoclassical *versi sciolti*.

The author, or more probably his publisher, called *Sosanna* a "new tragedy," but it is as much comedy as tragedy and ends happily for all but the two wicked elders who defamed the heroine. The prologue speaks of it as a "true history." If its lan-guage had been Latin, it could have been called a "tragic comedy" *(comedia tragica)*, as was Sixt Birck's *Susanna* (1537), the most popular Susanna play of the century, or it could have been called a *comedia*, as was Nicodemus Frischlin's *Susanna* (1578), the best Susanna play of the century. If it had appeared near the end of the century it would probably have been called a *tragicommedia*.

As it stands, three acts of Sacco's *Sosanna* are mainly comic and two are mainly tragic. The over-all structure is similar to that of Terentian comedy, not to that of a history that the prologue promises. In the first two acts, domestic scenes and grumbling servants are prominent. Acts 3 and 4, during which the heroine is charged and found guilty of adultery, are gloomy, unrelieved by any comic byplay. In Act 5, however, after Susanna has been exonerated and restored to her family and the wicked elders have been led offstage to punishment, the comic tone is restored. The ending resembles the ending of an ancient comedy by Plautus or Terence. Susanna's husband Joachim has sent his servant Siro— Syrus was the name of a slave in two comedies of Terence—to find out what happened to the two elders. Siro has dawdled on his errand, as usual, so the master sends another servant to find Siro. Finally he comes out to find the second servant and runs into Siro.

Joachim: Answer, Siro, are those elders dead?
Siro: Pluto has triumphed over their souls.

---

[2] Allacci lists an edition of 1524 at Venice. The Illinois copy is 1537 (Bressa).
[3] Sacco's short lines have some resemblance to the *settenarii* that Speroni was soon to introduce into tragedy.

Joachim: Pray speak plainly, and don't poetize to me; I have no wish to jest now.

Siro: It is even thus; they have just been stoned to death.

Joachim: Behold, how God punishes all wrongs.

Joachim returns to the house and Siro announces the end of the play in the Roman manner: "Farewell and clap your hands."

Is Sacco's play a tragedy or even a "new tragedy"? Hardly; and I can find no satisfactory explanation of why it was called a tragedy. It is true that in 1524, when *Sosanna* was first printed, Trissino's *Sofonisba*, the first neoclassical tragedy of the Renaissance, also appeared in print. It is also true that the medieval terms for plays, *rappresentazione, storia, mistero, miracolo, passione, essempio, festa*, were going out of fashion to make way for the classical terms *tragedia* and *commedia*. Italian dramatists at the turn of the century were eager to write new tragedies and new comedies although many of them were not yet sure what a tragedy or comedy was.

PISTOIA

Some authors of rhymed Italian tragedies turned to *novelle* for their arguments, as some of the fifteenth-century writers of Latin comedies had done. Antonio da Pistoia, or Antonio Cammelli, a sonneteer at the court of Ferrara, went to Boccaccio's romantic tale of Tancred and Gismonda in *Decameron* 4.1 and wrote *Filostrato e Panfila*, which was presented before Duke Ercole I in 1499.[4] Ercole I had encouraged the production of comedies, both those translated from Latin and original ones; but Pistoia's play was apparently the first Italian tragedy produced under his patronage. The author followed Boccaccio's plot faithfully, but changed the names of the characters, added an important character, rewrote most of the dialogue, and changed the locale from Italy to the Greek Thebes. The verse is *terza rima*.

The gist of Boccaccio's tale is as follows. Tancred, Prince of Salerno, had an only daughter, Gismonda, who married early and was soon left a widow. Since her father made no move to find another husband for her, Gismonda chose her own, a poor young serving man named Guiscardo. The two lovers met many times in secret until Tancred accidentally discovered one of their meetings

---

[4] First published at Venice in 1508. Reprinted in *Rime edite ed inedite di Antonio Cammelli detto il Pistoia*, Livorno, 1884.

in the princess' bedroom. Tancred had the young man strangled and his heart cut out. Then he sent the heart in a golden cup to his daughter. Gismonda added poison to the cup and drank it. She died holding the heart of Guiscardo to her breast.

Pistoia used the ghost of "moral" Seneca for his prologue. Demetrio, King of Thebes, opens the play proper with a Senecan discourse on the insecurity of high positions. "I believe," he says, "that a dry crust seems better to an artisan or a free peasant than does bread with fat and mellow wine to us."[5] His daughter Panfila modestly declines to debate the subject with him. Then the king begins to praise his servant Filostrato as a model young man although poor and of humble birth. After her father leaves Panfila discloses that she is in love with Filostrato but despairs of having him as her lawful husband. The chorus, apparently made up of women sympathetic with the heroine, praises the god of love: "Love, you conquer everything; you have dominion over all." Amore answers the chorus and bids them watch over the two lovers.

Filostrato is introduced in the second act. Believing that the king has encouraged him, he has already made overtures to the princess and has been invited to visit her. Then the author introduces a new character, one that was destined to become prominent in Italian comedy, a disillusioned courtier. This courtier, Tindaro, holds a grudge against the king and helps to promote the love intrigue in order to dishonor the royal family. When Filostrato shows him a letter from the princess he encourages the young man to proceed as far as he can: "This is good news, O Filostrato; love supports you well, love calls you; you are most blessed among lovers." Whether or not the author intended irony here I cannot be sure; but Pistoia was a sophisticated writer of courtly sonnets and it would be a mistake to under-rate his subtlety. A chorus of four sirens comments on the fickleness of Fortune: "Our earthly lot wavers like the sea before the wind."

The complications, as was proper in the arrangement of a Terentian comic plot, begin in the third act. The king stumbles upon the secret meeting of the lovers. The royal secretary, Pandero, announces that he has had a bad dream of two harpies who defile the palace with a pool of blood. A chorus of the three Fates sings a song, the burden of which is that everyone is born to die:

---

[5] Cf. Seneca, *Hercules Oetaeus* 640 ff.; *Octavia* 895–898; *Thyestes* 447 ff. Cf. above, p. 18.

Ciascun nasce per morire. "Virtue conquers death, and death conquers vice. Beauty, wisdom, riches, strength are of no avail to his cruel office. Whoever always serves the gods does good. Everyone is born to die."

The action reaches a crisis in the fourth act. The king is bent on vengeance and will listen to no peaceful settlement of the scandal. The secretary Pandero, who plays the role of counselor, argues with him, trying to restrain his wrath; he warns him that in seeking revenge he may make matters worse: "In this affair there is need for prudence." When confronted by the king, neither Filostrato nor Panfila asks for mercy or repents. Panfila defies her father and affirms her love for the friendless young man: "You have observed that I love Filostrato, and I always loved him, and so long as I see the sun he will be loved by me with all my heart."[6] Her speech soon wanders into wordiness, however, and is not very moving, nothing like so moving as Gismonda's speech in Boccaccio's story. The king is unshaken in his resolve to punish Filostrato. Atropus, one of the Fates, and the chorus sing a song, "Every evil is always punished."

The last act brings the death of the lovers. The execution and mutilation of Filostrato take place offstage and are reported by the secretary, whose role has been changed from counselor to messenger. The king puts the heart in a golden cup and bids a servant take it to Panfila so that she may console herself. "Then," says the king, "leave her to her woeful thoughts." Panfila receives the gift: "No sepulcher less rich, less apt, is fitting for the heart of Filostrato, for whose heart I cast off my life. [*turning to the servant*] You have brought a beautiful gift. Go back and tell my father that he has exercised great care."[7] Then she begins her lament. Her companions, waiting women and servants, comment on envious Fortune and recall that the funeral bird has sung for three nights in the garden. Panfila holds up the cup, which now has poison in it, and many a learned spectator in Ferrara must have recalled a famous line from Seneca's *Thyestes* (453), *venenum in auro bibitur* ("poison is drunk in gold"). The king arrives on the scene too late to save his daughter but in time to hear her last words. He tells the secretary to bury Filostrato with Panfila.

The secretary brings the play to a close with a moral that is

---

[6] The best part of this speech was taken from Boccaccio. See below, pp. 189–190.
[7] Here again Pistoia followed Boccaccio's wording closely.

reminiscent of the ending of a religious play: "Fathers, take care of your daughters; you have the example [here] of two rare cases." Then he asks for applause in a manner reminiscent of the ending of an ancient Roman comedy: "If this melancholy tragedy has pleased you, give the sign by clapping your hands."

Although *Filostrato e Panfila* is hardly a neoclassical play, it bears several classical features. Its structure owes much to the Ancients; more to comedy than to tragedy, for it is arranged in the Terentian order of *protasis* (exposition), *epitasis* (complication), and *catastrophe* (resolution). There is economy of time; the whole action seems to take place within a few days. The scene seems to be restricted to the royal palace and its grounds. The use of the chorus resembles the Senecan manner, but is even closer to the *intermedii* or *intermezzi* that originated at banquets and became a common feature of staged comedies in the sixteenth century. In other words, while Pistoia's *tragedia* is also a transitional play it bears little resemblance to the *sacre rappresentazioni;* it is closer to the humanistic comedies and the medieval courtly entertainments, and it is more than a little Senecan.

Filostrato e Panfila was the first Italian tragedy of love. The first English tragedy of love, *Gismond of Salerne,* was also based on the tale in the *Decameron* that Pistoia used over a half-century earlier. The gentlemen of the Inner Temple, who wrote the English tragedy in 1567-68, were even more inept than the Italian poet, for they changed the serving man Guiscardo into a nobleman, thus destroying the dramatic contrast between heroine and poor, base-born lover. They were more Senecan than the Italian; they introduced Megaera the Fury in the fourth act and labored in the choruses to reach the moral stateliness of Seneca. Cunliffe has characterized *Gismond of Salerne* pretty well in calling it a "mosaic of Boccaccio, Dolce, Seneca, and English moralizing, not very skillfully fitted together."[8] There is no evidence that the English authors knew Pistoia's play, but one wonders if they might have heard of it.

Perhaps Pistoia would have done better had he tried his hand at comedy, which was popular at the court of Ferrara. Certainly he had little bent for tragedy, because a good part of the tragic passion that Boccaccio provided in the *novella* was lost in the transfer to the stage. When Pistoia tried tragic expression he relied

---

[8] P. lxxxviii. The English prologue was based on Lodovico Dolce's *Didone* (1547). See below, pp. 167 ff.

mainly upon "O's" and classical allusions. His lyrical passages were generally more successful, as, for example, an interlude in the first act, possibly delivered by the chorus although it is not clear who the speaker is. The first three lines of this passage run as follows:

> Fior frondi arbor frutti e tener' erba,
> Zefir rinnova e la sua bella Flora,
> e canta l'rusignol l'ingiuria acerba.

Zephyr and his fair Flora revive flowers, leaves, fruits, and tender grass, and the nightingale sings of her bitter wrong.

The cynical Tindaro, essentially a comic character, has some of the most natural lines in the play. Early in the third act, for example, when the castoff courtier sees his way clear to even the score with the king, he cries, "You see that love has shown me the time and the place and the means to wreak all my revenge." Occasionally one of the other characters will speak naturally and forcefully, but never for long.

Pistoia was no Dante. He could not make *terza rima* the right vehicle for tragic emotion on the stage. Perhaps no one could, not even a Dante; but it is doubtful that Pistoia could have written a good tragedy if he had used the unrhymed Italian verse that was all but ready for poets in 1499. Nevertheless, he deserves some praise for trying and for pointing out the Italian *novelle* as sources for tragic plots. *Filostrato e Panfila* must have encouraged the development of Italian tragedy at Ferrara, which was destined to become for a time the most important center of new tragedy in western Europe.

LEGNAME

Another Italian rhymed tragedy of the early sixteenth century was even closer to the medieval courtly entertainments than was *Filostrato e Panfila*. This play was a "tragedy by Jacopo del Legname of Treviso newly composed and performed on February 17, 1517, in the great palace of the city of Treviso at the request of the magnificent and most noble Messer Nicolò Vendramin, most worthy captain and podestà of the said city."[9]

Legname mingled medieval and classical elements, putting more emphasis on the medieval. He used *terzine* for the dialogue. The choruses were varied, one composed of four peasants led by Mer-

---

[9] See Neri, pp. 10–13.

cury, another of nymphs who accompanied Cupid's chariot, another of four courtly ladies. There was singing and dancing. These choruses were used between the acts as *intermezzi*.

The only tragic element in Legname's play is an unhappy love affair. Duke Filippo is in love with Madonna Aurora, who repulses all his advances. Unable to make any progress in his suit, the duke gives way to despair and kills himself. Then Aurora repents and, full of self-reproach, dies herself.

The principal theme of the play is the perilous course of love when a coy mistress is involved. The *errore femineo* was becoming prominent in Italian tragedies. One Notturno Napolitano, author of several comedies, published a play in 1518 entitled "Tragedy of the most dangerous error in which the frail and fickle feminine sex is entangled."[10] Such subject matter, reminiscent of sonnets and *novelle*, seems better suited to romantic comedies and tragicomedies; but Italian poets were now writing "new" tragedies, and the tragic consequences of love were becoming almost as prominent as the happy consequences. Before long Renaissance playwrights were to boast that the addition of love had made modern tragedies superior to the best plays of the ancients.

FONSI

In 1520, at Siena, an important center of peasant farces, Francesco Fonsi published a *tragedia nuova* called *Despecti d'amore* ("Vexations of Love"). Cupid delivers the argument in the form of a prologue; he announces that he will show his power in bringing ruin to lovers. There are three lovers, two young men and a princess. By way of diversion, two peasants appear from time to time to entertain the court with chatter and with song and dance. There is no chorus, but the play is divided into five acts, the tragic turn of events coming toward the end of Act 4. The peasants use homely speech, though rhymed, but the serious characters use an elevated, artful style with some classical allusions. In other words, Fonsi's play is not a full-fledged neoclassical tragedy, but it is more classical than medieval.

Antiphilo is in love with Phyloti, daughter of Prospero the king. His suit has been prospering, but suddenly his mistress sends him a letter dismissing him. Then a servant named Sergio discloses that

---

[10] *Tragedia del maximo e dannoso errore in che è avviluppato il fragil e volubil sexo femineo.*

he is in love with Phyloti. He is no servant, to be sure, but the
son of a king who had heard about the great beauty of this princess and had come to her father's court to see for himself. Phyloti
returns his love. Then the rejected Antiphilo writes a letter to the
king, disclosing the whole affair. The king never receives the letter,
but he is informed of his daughter's misconduct by a loyal citizen.
Thereupon he flies into a rage and resolves to make examples of
all the lovers, who are immediately arrested. When the play ends
rather abruptly no one is dead but the lovers are doomed.

The lovers deliver either pleas or laments throughout the play.
They often become eloquent. When, in the first act, Sergio confesses to Phyloti that he has sacrificed everything for her he
becomes very persuasive.

> Tu spender facto mhai mia giovineza
> in affanni et dolor, mettendo albasso
> el mio dominio et la mia poca alteza
> In te ogni mio bene, ogni mio spasso,
> in te ciascun conforto, in te mia vita [B2].

You have made me spend my youth in troubles and pain, debasing my
power and my little pride; in you my every good, my every solace, in you
every comfort, in you my life.

When, in the fourth act, Antiphilo upbraids Phyloti and promises
to betray all, she sees that ruin is ahead.

> Misera! oime meschina, o sorte infesta!
> o cielo adverso, o mia mala ventura! [F4].

Miserable, aye-me wretched, O pernicious fate! O hostile heaven, O my
evil luck!

Sergio sees that he is also doomed, but he gallantly protests that
he has no regrets.

> Sio ti so stato servo: io non mi pento:
> sio haro morte per portarti amore
> morro felice et danimo contento [G2].

If I have been your servant, I do not repent. If I shall have my death for
loving you, I shall die happy and satisfied in mind.

The dialogue of the peasants is in sharp contrast with that of
the lovers, for they provide the comic interludes. In Act 3, for
example, Rilla and Licota entertain the court with chatter about
heifers and with song and dance. After a dance the king's brother
orders them to sing.

> *Rilla*   A dirvi el vero io so gia mezo fioco
>   ivorrei prima bere un po di vino
>   che par chio habbi nella gola el foco.
>
> *Licota*   Et io anchor vo bere un pocharino
>   et poi guicacarete tucti quanti
>   chi di tradua sara buon cantarino [E4].

Rilla: To tell you the truth, I am already about played out. I would like first to drink a little wine, for I seem to have a fire in my throat.

Licota: And I also wish to drink a sip, and then every one of you will judge which of us two is a good singer.

GUAZZO

Marco Guazzo, a historian, wrote a comedy and a tragedy on love, both printed at Venice in 1526. The comedy was called *Errori d'amore*, the tragedy *Discordia d'amore*. Both are in *terza rima*. Both are divided into five acts. The comedy has peasant *intermedii*, but the tragedy has no chorus.

The title of Guazzo's tragedy suggests a morality play, and there is a moral, but the only personification is Discord of Love, who delivers the argument in a prologue, issuing a solemn warning of the miseries that always attend her—"a thousand deceits and a thousand treacheries." She cites classical examples of women who were involved in these deceits and treacheries: Phyllis, who hanged herself because she believed that her lover Demophon had deserted her, Scylla, who was betrayed by Minos of Crete and pined away, Eurydice, and Medea.

The action of the play itself starts out like a comedy with ordinary middle-class characters involved in an amorous muddle, which normally would have been happily resolved. There are two pairs of lovers, two pert female servants, and a garrulous old man who wishes he were younger so that he might join the chase after women. This old man is the *senex* of Roman comedy, the *vecchio* of Italian learned comedy.

The two young men are getting nowhere in their courtship because each of the two young women favors the man who is not courting her. Upon the advice of a necromancer, a favorite character in Italian comedy, the men exchange clothes and identities and thereby hope to fulfill their desires. A servant girl, fearful that this exchange may alter the affections of the two women, prepares a drink that has the power of holding fast the passions already established.

The magic potion turns out badly; it poisons both of the mistresses. When the servant girl announces their deaths, one of the lovers, Pamphirio, strikes her down in a rage. When the other lover, Solonio, rebukes his friend for losing his temper and injuring the servant girl, the two begin to quarrel and end up by running each other through with their swords. Four dead! A fifth death soon follows, for the servant girl is unable to bear the remorse she feels and decides to kill herself. All of these deaths take place offstage.

Guazzo's play is a mixture of tragic violence and comic intrigue, which is strange only from the classical point of view. Such a mixture was commonplace in medieval drama, in the religious plays, for example. Evidently the author still conceived of tragedy in the medieval sense; the outcome alone determined whether the play was tragic or comic.

Guazzo was not ignorant of classical literature, however, and he made some attempt to give his play some classical qualities. References to tragic heroines of antiquity appear in the prologue. Pamphirio interlards his opening speech in the first act with allusions to the pagan gods and goddesses, especially to his patroness Venus. Pamphirio is more interested in astrology, however, than in classical mythology. Since he was born under Venus he believes that he must fall in love and keep on loving. When the old man urges him to let reason conquer appetite he replies, "I say that no one can do anything to contradict his planet." Perhaps the author meant such a sentiment to indicate tragic fate.

Aside from the prologue and the opening scenes, there are not many classical allusions in the play, and there is more teasing than torture in the first four acts. When Mirina, the servant who prepares the magic potion, expresses fear that it may prove dangerous, even deadly, another servant girl says, "It's worse than death going on as they are." But there seems to be no serious thought of death here, and the speech, whether intentionally or not, carries the spirit of comedy.

In the last act there is definitely a change of mood, as the author tried to create an air of tragedy. The second servant girl, Berinice, opens the act crying, "Cursed be Mirina and her art!" Mirina soon

enters looking utterly wretched as she faces the duty of telling
the young man about the death of both mistresses. When Berinice
reports the death of Pamphirio and Solonio, Mirina redoubles her
lamentations. Then she leaves the stage to commit suicide.

The old man, Antropeo, brings the play to a close with a lament
beginning,

> O crudel fin delle amorose pene
> Nella più bella età quatro son privi.

O cruel end of the pain of love, four are lost in the prime of life.

Some of his lines come closer to tragic poetry than do any other
lines in the play:

> Passa la nostra vita in un baleno
> Veloce più che fier fiume tra rivi
> Doi con el ferro, e dua con el veneno
> O crudel spate, o perfido liquore.

Our life passes in a lightning flash, more swiftly than the wild torrent
through its channels. Two by the sword and two by poison. O cruel
swords, O wicked drink!

Antropeo ends his discourse with an admonition to avoid the discord of love: "Think on this, and remain in peace."

Guazzo's tragedy scarcely belongs to the Senecan tradition in
Italian tragedy although its fatalism is in harmony with the imitations of Seneca. Nor was Guazzo a disciple of the "Grecian"
Trissino, whose *Sofonisba* was published two years before the publication of the *Discordia d'amore,* for his play is further removed
from the Grecian type of Italian tragedy than from the Senecan.
His concept of tragedy was more medieval than classical, his diction was medieval, yet he had picked up some of the mechanics
of classical drama, such as the division of the play into five acts
and the removal of bloodshed from the stage. Curiously enough,
he did not use a chorus, which was always a part of neoclassical
tragedy and a part of its five-act structure.

DEL CARRETTO

The writers of rhymed tragedies did not neglect ancient history and mythology, the traditional sources of Greek and Roman
tragedy. Galeotto Del Carretto, Marquis of Savona, a poet of some
prominence at the turn of the century, dramatized Livy's historical
account of events involving Sophonisba, daughter of the Cartha-

ginian general Hasdrubal. The author's dedication is dated 1502, but the play was not printed until 1546.[11]

The mechanical form of this early *Sophonisba* is mostly medieval, like that of the *sacre rappresentazioni*. It is a history, beginning *ab ovo* and continuing in a series of twenty-seven episodes, some of these very short, separated by choruses. The author used *ottava rima* in the dialogue and a variety of verse forms in the numerous choruses. Three of these choruses are in eleven-syllable unrhymed verses, *versi sciolti*, the Italian blank verse that was destined to become standard in neoclassical tragedy. Thus Del Caretto anticipated Trissino's use of *versi sciolti* in a much better known *Sofonisba* by a dozen or more years. Trissino, however, reversed Del Caretto's scheme; he used unrhymed verse in the dialogue and rhymes in the choruses. Del Caretto observed no economy of time or place; months and years pass during the action and the scene freely shifts about in Africa, Spain, and Sicily. There is obviously some influence of Seneca in the styles and sentiments of the choruses.

Del Caretto followed Livy's account, then, without any major changes. The Carthaginian Sophonisba has won over her husband Syphax to her father's side in the war with Rome. Syphax is defeated by the Roman generals Scipio and Laelius and their Numidian ally Masinissa. Rather than be captured by the Romans and taken to Rome in triumph Sophonisba takes poison. The titular character actually has a rather small role; she does not appear until halfway through the play and speaks in only four of the twenty-seven episodes. Her father Hasdrubal, Scipio, Laelius, Masinissa, and Syphax have much fatter roles.

The prologue is delivered by the tragic Muse, who endeavors to set a mood for the play about to unfold. She speaks in *ottava rima*. "I Melpomene spur myself to ring out verses with sad accents and tragic clamor, and to relate the hostile fortunes of Sophonisba, her bitter and miserable fate." She remarks that it is not "seemly that joy and gladness be here; let laughter depart, let peace depart, and only mourning, sadness, and trouble remain."

In restricting his play to gloom and sadness, Carretto was parting company with most *sacre rappresentazioni* which freely mingled laughter with tears. In other words, he was trying to follow the

---

[11] *La Sophonisba, tragedia del magnifico cavaliere e poeta Messer Galeotto Carretto*, Venice, 1546.

classical tradition. He also banished bloodshed from the stage. Sophonisba does not drink poison and die before the audience as does Panfila in Pistoia's tragedy. Here Del Carretto was probably following the prescription of Horace rather than the practice of Euripides and Sophocles, and here he was not following Seneca, whose tragedies often have death scenes.

As the prologue promises, there is much wailing and lamenting throughout the play. There is little give-and-take, no Senecan stichomythy, in the dialogue, for most of the speeches are soliloquies or formal debates. The choruses come closest to tragic expression, and the choruses are the most Senecan feature of the play. A fairly typical example is the opening of the next to last chorus:

> Tutto è dolor il danno de mortali,
> E perdasi chi sia del sangue caro.
> Tutti son fieri strali e colpi interni
> Che fanno alhor dogliose piaghe al cuore.
> Perchè la madre afflitta il caro figlio,
> Et con l' unghie ne riga il viso e 'l petto,
> Et con pianti ne fa dogliosi gridi,
> Et se potesse anchor morirne insieme,
> Il morir le saria più grata vita.

The peril to mortals is wholly painful, and the dearest blood may be lost. All cruel shafts and inner blows now make grievous wounds in the heart. The mother grieves for the dear son and scores her face and breast with her fingernails, and weeping raises doleful cries, and if she could die with him would rather be dead than alive.

There is no evidence that Trissino saw Del Carretto's play before he wrote his own *Sofonisba,* but there is a good chance that he did. Moreover, there may have been other dramatizations of the same subject in Italy, for Petrarch's treatment of the story in the fifth book of his Latin epic poem *Africa* was well known.

FALUGI

Another ancient love story, a myth rather than a historical event, was destined to become as celebrated as the unhappy tale of Sophonisba, and this was the story of Canace and her incestuous love as found in Ovid's *Heroides.* There is a play preserved in manuscript called *Tragedia di Giovanni Falugio intitulata Canace.*[12]

---

[12] See Neri, pp. 16–23.

The author, about whom very little is known, dedicated his work to Ippolito de' Medici, who died in 1535, and therefore he must have written it before this date.

This early *Canace* was written in various patterns of rhyme. It was divided into five acts with a chorus between each act. According to Neri's description, these choruses must have been *intermezzi* rather than classical choruses. One of them was made up of the three Fates, another of hunters who sang a song in praise of Diana. The author was not concerned with any economy of time, for the action covers at least nine months; in the second act Canace reveals that she is in love with her brother Macareus and by the fourth act a child has been born of the incestuous union. The scene is the island ruled by Aeolus, father of Canace and Macareus. Two Furies, Alecto and Megaera, open the play with the announcement that sister and brother are kindling with guilty love.

Falugi's tragedy is comparable to the Latin *Progne* written about a hundred years earlier by Gregorio Corraro.[13] Both plays were based on an Ovidian tale of lust, both were more or less Senecan. The author of *Progne*, it may be recalled, imitated Senecan tragedy in general, *Thyestes* and *Medea* in particular. Falugi obviously imitated Seneca's *Hippolytus;* Macareus was modeled on the young hunter Hippolytus and Canace on his love-maddened stepmother Phaedra. Corraro came much closer to classical tragedy than did Falugi, whose play evidently belongs with the other transitional rhymed tragedies we have been examining.

By 1520 rhymed tragedies were on the wane and the development of neoclassical Italian tragedy had begun. These rhymed tragedies were generally more medieval than classical, but they did bear some classical features and they did carry on the Senecan influence introduced nearly two centuries before by the Italian writers of Latin tragedy. The subject matter of these rhymed tragedies, arguments drawn from ancient history, from classical mythology, and from Italian *novelle,* was destined to be the subject matter of Italian tragedies throughout the Renaissance. The lurid love stories that some poets exploited were to become almost commonplace in the "new" tragedies. Perhaps the most important contribution of rhymed tragedy was its theatricality; all of these plays were apparently prepared for actual production on the

---

[13] See above, p. 15.

stage in Ferrara, Mantua, Florence, and other cities of northern Italy. This practical feature of Italian tragedy was to receive a temporary setback within the next few years, when learned *letterati* put the major emphasis on literary tragedy; but before the middle of the century Italian tragedies were again being acted, sometimes with conspicuous success.

III

The Grecians

Writers of Latin tragedy in the fourteenth and fifteenth centuries had little opportunity to read the ancient Greek tragedies. Seneca was much more readily available, in manuscripts and in printed texts. The first printing of Seneca's tragedies was made at Ferrara between 1474 and 1484. Then, early in the sixteenth century, printed texts in Greek of Aeschylus, Sophocles, and Euripides began to appear. Translations of Sophocles and Euripides into Latin and Italian were being printed before the middle of the century.

Aldus at Venice published the Greek text of Sophocles in 1502, all of Euripides save the *Electra* in 1503, all of Aeschylus save the *Choephoroe* in 1518. A Latin translation of Sophocles' *Antigone* appeared at Leyden in 1541 and of all seven plays in 1543 at Venice. Latin translations of Euripides' *Hecuba* and *Iphigenia in Aulis* were published at Paris in 1506, at Venice in 1507. Luigi Alamanni translated *Antigone* into Italian in 1533. Lodovico Dolce translated *Hecuba* into Italian in 1543. Several Italian translations and adaptations of Sophocles and Euripides appeared in the second half of the century and continued to appear in the seventeenth and eighteenth centuries.

A brief look at some of the translations and adaptations of *Oedipus Rex* is instructive since it will show one important direction that Italian tragedy took in the sixteenth century. Alessandro

Pazzi (d. 1530–31), whose excellent Latin translation of Aristotle's *Poetics* was first published in 1536, made an Italian version of Sophocles' *Oedipus Rex*, which was not printed, however, until 1887.[1] Bernardo Segni, whose Italian translation of Aristotle's *Rhetoric* and *Poetics* was published in 1549, also translated *Oedipus Rex* into Italian, but his version was not printed until 1811.[2] Dolce's translation of Seneca's *Oedipus* was printed in 1560. In 1556,[3] Giovanni Andrea dell' Anguillara's *Edippo* was produced and printed at Padua. This Italian version is no translation and hardly an adaptation; it is a new tragedy based on both Seneca and Sophocles' plays, but more than twice as long as the ancient models and greatly elaborated. Anguillara added numerous characters to the Sophoclean cast: Teiresias' daughter Manto (borrowed from Seneca), Oedipus' two sons (Eteocles and Polynices), Oedipus' two daughters (Antigone and Ismene) who are mutes in the Greek version, a son of Creon, a courtier, and a princess of Andros (the princess who married Polynices). Orsato Giustiniano's *Edipo tiranno*, "Sophocles' tragedy adapted in the vulgar tongue and recited with most sumptuous setting by the Olympic Academicians in the year 1585," was printed at Venice in the same year. This was the play used for the opening of the celebrated Teatro Olimpico at Vicenza. *Edipo tiranno*, "Sophocles' tragedy adapted from Greek to the Tuscan tongue" by Pietro Angelio, better known as Bargeo, was published at Florence in 1589. In the first half of the century the most popular ancient models for Italian tragedy were Seneca's *Thyestes* and *Medea*. As I shall show later on, *Oedipus* became a leading classical model by the 1580's. This rise of *Oedipus* was not solely due to Italian adaptations and translations or to the Teatro Olimpico; Sophocles was Aristotle's favorite tragic poet, and the Aristotelians more or less ruled dramatic criticism during the second half of the century.

Soon after the publication of Greek texts of Sophocles and Euripides a few learned poets began to imitate the Greeks when they composed Italian tragedies. These Grecians not only turned aside from native religious plays but from Seneca as well and tried to imitate Attic tragedy.

---

[1] See below, p. 62.
[2] See Neri, p. 96, n.1.
[3] According to Neri, p. 96, n.1. Allacci lists only two printings, one at Venice in 1565, another at Padua in the same year. The Illinois copy is Venice, 1565.

TRISSINO

The leader of the Italian Grecians was Giangiorgio Trissino (1478-1550), scholar, grammarian, critic, poet, dramatist, and courtier, the most distinguished *letterato* of his generation. Unlike many *letterati* of his time, he preferred Greek tragedy to Roman. In fact, he had a poor opinion of the pole star of tragedy in Italy; in his *La poetica* he remarked, "Those [tragedies] of Seneca that have survived are for the most part fragments of Greek matter, put together with very little art."[4]

Trissino had applied himself early to the study of Greek as well as Latin and before his death had read virtually all available Greek literature. In the dedication of his long heroic poem, *L'Italia liberata dai Goti* (1547), he declared: "It has been necessary for me to turn over nearly all the books in the Greek and Latin tongue in order to extract from them the teachings, the histories, and the doctrines, and the ornaments that I have placed in [my poem]." Thus he accurately described his own method of composition, for he wrote poetry as a scholar does: his invention was painstaking research, his arrangement borrowed from a Greek model, and his style influenced by the theory and practice of the Greeks. In the *Italia liberata,* for example, he took his argument from Procopius' history of the Gothic war in Italy, his model was Homer, and his guide was Aristotle's *Poetics.*

Thirty-two years earlier, in 1515, Trissino had completed his tragedy of *Sofonisba,* in which he had pursued a similar method; that is, he took his argument from Livy's history of Rome and his models were Sophocles and Euripides.

Aristotle's *Poetics* played a minor role in the composition of *Sofonisba* although years later the author liked to look back and find qualities in his play that fitted Aristotle's theory. When he wrote the tragedy he knew something about the *Poetics*—several references in his dedication of the printed version indicate as much—but he was not yet so familiar with the treatise as he later became. The first part of his *Poetica,* published in 1529, made little use of Aristotle, for it was largely a handbook on Italian meters and rhymes. Scholar that he was, Trissino's full comprehension of Aristotle's difficult treatise apparently had to wait for Pazzi's

---

[4] *La poetica* (1563), 13v. This Illinois copy seems to be a reprint of the 1562 edition.

good Latin translation in 1536 and Robortello's great commentary in 1548. The last two sections of his *Poetica*, published posthumously in 1562, are mainly paraphrases of Aristotle. Trissino was going over the manuscript of this latter portion of his "Art of Poetry" on the very day that his final illness struck him.[5]

If Trissino had had a good understanding of Aristotle's *Poetics* in 1513–15 and had used it as guide, he would never have chosen the story of Sophonisba in the first place, for Livy's account does not lend itself to arrangement in the complex plot employing Discovery and Reversal of Fortune that Sophocles and Euripides used in their best plays and that Aristotle admired and recommended. Many years later, in the *Poetica* (15r), which was written or rewritten just before his death in 1550, Trissino admitted that the plot of *Sofonisba* was not like that of Sophocles' *Oedipus Rex* or Euripides' *Iphigenia in Tauris*, but was like that of Sophocles' *Ajax*, which Aristotle called a "tragedy of suffering."

In the dedication of *Sofonisba* to Pope Leo X, Trissino argued that his writing in Italian instead of in Greek or Latin could not be called a defect since he wished to reach those people who had no language beyond their native tongue, and moreover that the "manners, sentiments, and discourse would not produce general profit and delight if they were not made understandable to the listeners." It looks as though he hoped he had written for the stage. If so, he must have been disappointed, for *Sofonisba* was never staged in Italy until twelve years after the author's death, when it was given a magnificent production by the Teatro Olimpico in Vicenza. Trissino had written a scholarly play, as he intended, but not a stageworthy one; he had written a play that was admired by other scholars and doubtless read by them, for there were at least ten printings of it in Italy between 1524 and 1620; but he had written a play that failed to reach the common people he mentioned in his dedication. An examination of *Sofonisba* will show why.

Trissino did not divide his play into acts, for he was following Greek models and was not concerned with Horace's prescription of five acts or with the Renaissance division of Seneca's tragedies into five acts. The scene is the city of Cirta in ancient Numidia before the royal palace of Syphax and his wife Sophonisba and

---

[5] See Bernardo Morsolin, *Giangiorgio Trissino*, p. 527.

in one episode the Roman camp outside the city. The chorus consists of fifteen women of Cirta.

Sophonisba herself "delivers the prologue" *(fa il prologo)*, which is in the Greek fashion, that is, an integral part of the play, the "first part of the tragedy, up to the entrance of the chorus."[6] The queen is not alone; her faithful companion and confidant, Erminia, is by her side.

Sophonisba's opening speech, which is in unrhymed verse, sets the tone of the whole play. As the author later remarked, it is a tragedy of suffering, emphasizing what Aristotle called *dianoia,* that is, thought. In other words, it is a talky play. Erminia always tries to console her mistress.

> *Sophonisba*   Lassa, dove poss' io voltar la lingua
> Se no là, 've la spinge il mio pensiere,
> Che giorno e notte sempre mi molesta?
> E come posso disfogare alquanto
> Questo grave dolor, che 'l cuor m'ingombra,
> Se non manifestando i miei martiri,
> I quali ad un ad un voglio narrati?
>
> *Erminia*   Regina Sofonisba, a me Regina
> Per dignità, ma per amor sorella,
> Sfogate meco pur il cor, che certo
> Non possete parlar con chi più v'ami,
> Nè che si doglia più de i vostri mali.

Sophonisba: Alas, where can I turn my tongue if not there where my thought spurs it, which day and night always troubles me? And how can I lighten somewhat this heavy grief that burdens my heart if not by expressing my torments, which I wish to relate to you one by one?
Erminia: Queen Sophonisba, queen in office but in love my sister, unburden your heart to me, for surely you could not speak with anyone who loves you more or who grieves more over your afflictions.

Sophonisba acknowledges her own great love for her loyal companion and then declares that she wants to "speak at greater length and to begin with fulsome words." She does speak at length and fulsomely; she begins with Dido and summarizes the history of Carthage from its founding to her own time, to her political marriage with Syphax, when she was already bethrothed to Masinissa, to the outbreak of war with Rome. Her narrative is interrupted from time to time by sympathetic comments from Erminia.

---

[6] *La poetica,* 12v. Cf. Aristotle, *Poetics* 12.

The queen turns to re-enter the palace as the chorus enters for the *parode* or opening chorus, which is in rhymed verse. In the *Poetica* (23v), Trissino explained that since the Greek choral passages were sung, "so it seemed proper in our tongue for me to use *canzoni* and *rime* which are most suitable for singing." He also explained in the *Poetica* (13v) that the Greek chorus was divided into three parts: "[1] *parode*, which is the first speech of the chorus; another [2] is called *stasimon*, which is the song of the whole chorus; the third [3] is called *commos*, which is the common lamentations, that are made with the help of the stage, that is, of the actors."[7] The chorus brings news that the enemy is at the gate.

Then follows the first episode, as a page enters and the play comes to life with a little give-and-take in the dialogue.

Page: Ladies.
Chorus: What do you want? Why don't you speak?
Page: I'm so tired that I have no breath to speak.
Chorus: That fellow renews my fears.
Page: Ladies, true ornament of the city of Cirta, tell me, where is the queen?
Chorus: Behold, she even now comes from the house.

The page warns the queen that he brings bad news. "O harsh exordium!" cries Sophonisba. The use of this rhetorical term *exordium* betrays the author's preoccupation with what he called *discorso*, which is more or less the equivalent of the Greek *dianoia*, the element in tragedy that Aristotle merely mentions in the *Poetics*, referring the reader to his *Art of Rhetoric*, where there is a full discussion of the processes of reasoning and arguing. In other words, Trissino emphasized the rhetorical element in tragedy.

The page tells Sophonisba that her husband Syphax is alive and well but a prisoner of the Romans. He describes the recent battle in some detail. The queen and chorus lament together in what is presumably a *commos*. Trissino used the chorus as another actor, thus fulfilling the prescriptions of Aristotle and Horace and the practice of Sophocles.

Some of the speeches in this *commos* are highly emotional, but there is no excessive use of figures, no extended similes. Sophonisba sometimes echoes the sonneteers, as, for example, when she cries,

---

[7] Cf. Aristotle, *Poetics* 12.

"My ship disarmed goes on the rocks" (1.78).[8] The chorus often uses more allusive metaphors and similes, as when it says, "I stand like a dove that sees the bird of Jove hovering over him" (1.81). Trissino's dialogue is apt to be more argumentative than lyrical.

Sophonisba fears capture by the Romans more than she fears death. The sympathetic chorus perceives the direction of her thought and argues against self-destruction. Sophonisba replies, "Our life is like a fine treasure, which ought not to be spent on base matter, nor should it shirk honorable enterprises, because a beautiful and glorious death makes our past life resplendent" (1:79). This suggestion of suicide is an anticipation of what is to come.

A messenger enters and exhorts the queen to fly, for the enemy troops are now within the walls. Then he relates "diffusely" how the Romans, led by their Numidian ally Masinissa, captured the city. At this point Masinissa himself appears.

Sophonisba, abetted by the chorus, begs the Numidian general not to turn her over to the Romans. Despite Trissino's aim to reproduce a classical tragedy, Masinissa is no more an ancient hero than Boccaccio's or Chaucer's or Shakespeare's Theseus, Duke of Athens, is an ancient Greek; Masinissa is a chivalrous knight, an Orlando rather than a Theseus. He gallantly replies to the queen's request, "There can be nothing baser than to offend women and to outrage those who are oppressed and helpless" (1.82). Sophonisba puts herself in his care with a very pretty speech. As the chorus says, words have great force when they are "sent from the heart and sweetly leave the mouth of a beautiful woman" (1.84). Masinissa promises to serve her with all his power, and he desires no reward save the sense of doing good. He assures her that he is a man of honor who always keeps his word.

Then comes the first *stasimon*, wherein the chorus sings of the evils of war and the ruin that faces the country. The only hope for the women of Cirta now lies in Masinissa.

In the second episode, the Roman general Laelius appears and questions the women of the chorus. He is as polite as Masinissa, for whom he is looking. A messenger comes out of the palace to inform Laelius that Masinissa has just married Sophonisba.

---

[8] The modern text in Doglio was not available when I wrote this chapter. The references are to the *Teatro italiano antico*, which is in many libraries.

Laelius finds it hard to believe this unexpected turn of events.

Laelius: What could induce him to make this promise?

Messenger: Love, and the sweetest words [1.94].

At the Roman's request, the messenger explains at length—most explanations in this play are at length—why and how this sudden marriage has taken place; it was the only way by which Masinissa could keep his word to the Carthaginian, the only way by which Sophonisba could escape servitude in Rome.

When Masinissa comes out of the palace he is confronted by Laelius, who asks him why Sophonisba has not been sent to the Roman camp. Masinissa tells him that the queen was formerly betrothed to him before she was given to Syphax and that now as his wife she is an ally of Rome, not an enemy. Laelius tells him that he was nevertheless unwise to marry her. Then Masinissa argues with him, pointing out that Sophonisba was never his enemy, as her husband Syphax was, but his promised wife whom he has finally been able to reclaim.

At this point Cato enters the conversation. He has been eavesdropping on the debate. Now he cautiously recommends referring the problem to the Roman commander-in-chief. Both Laelius and Masinissa agree to consult Scipio. And so ends the second episode.

In the second *stasimon,* the women pray God in his mercy to soften the heart of Scipio so that he may spare the queen and her people. This appeal to the deity, like the earlier description of the marriage ceremony, is more Christian than pagan. Again, as in his characterizations, Trissino was modernizing, either consciously or unconsciously, his ancient material. He was making his Roman characters into Italians. He was writing a new tragedy.

One would expect a good many *sententiae* in an argumentative tragedy that emphasizes *discorso,* and so it turns out. While Trissino was no follower of Seneca and he did not string together series of maxims as the Senecan playwrights were apt to do, he did use *sententiae.* But Euripides as well as Seneca was fond of philosophizing. Consequently there is more than an occasional wise saw in *Sofonisba.* A good example is Laelius' rebuke of Masinissa's ill-considered marriage: "The physician who sees that the disease needs a knife is unwise to use charms" (1.103). Scipio, the statesman, would naturally use philosophic maxims, some of them rather fatalistic, such as, "All of us who live on earth are none other than dust and shadow" (1.108). It cannot be argued that this last sentiment is more Senecan than Euripidean or more pagan than Christian.

Trissino regarded the chorus as a most important element in tragedy, as indeed it was in Attic tragedy before Euripides somewhat curtailed its importance. Therefore some of the lines most characteristic of Renaissance tragedy may be found in Trissino's choruses, in their dialogue as well as in their odes. A good example of tragic sentiment is a comment by the chorus on the Carthaginian Syphax. The thought here is in harmony with Stoic philosophy, its structure is classical in symmetry, in balance and antithesis:

> Quanto, quanto dolor, quanta pietate
> Ho del misero stato di costui,
> Che fu sì gran Signor, che fu sì ricco
> Di thesoro, e di gente, hor in un giorno
> Si trova esser prigion, mendico, e servo [1.110].

How much grief, how much pity do I have for the wretched state of that man who was so great a ruler, who was so rich in treasure and in subjects, and now in one day finds himself prisoner, beggar, and slave.

Among other echoes that might have risen in response to this sentiment was surely the well-known passage from Seneca's *Thyestes* (613–614):

> For, whom the morning saw so great and high,
> Thus low and little 'fore the eve doth lie.[9]

In the third episode, which must take place in the Roman camp, Syphax appears as a prisoner. He is naturally unhappy, but is well treated by Scipio, who is a gentleman. Scipio makes it clear, however, that Sophonisba must be taken to Rome. Masinissa defends his position by maintaining that it is honor and not lust that binds him to the queen, for she was promised to him by her father Hasdrubal. He keeps harping on the fact that Sophonisba is his wife and has been his wife for a long time, that she is as much his wife as Helen was the wife of Menelaus. Scipio replies that the case is not quite the same, since Helen was actually married to Menelaus before she eloped with Paris, and he repeats that Sophonisba now belongs to Rome along with all the rest of Syphax' possessions. Masinissa finally agrees to think it over.

The third choral ode is addressed to the god of love, imploring

---

[9] Cf. above, p. 14.

him to help the queen in her great distress. Scholars have pointed out that in this ode Trissino was imitating a chorus in Sophocles' *Antigone*, and there is certainly a strong resemblance. In *Antigone* (781 ff.) we find: "Love, never conquered in fight . . . no immortal can escape you, nor any among mortal men." And in *Sofonisba*: "Love . . . no valor avails in strife with you; not only do you make mortal men feel your golden arrows, but you mount into the heavens and humble the vaunting pride of the greater gods."

Since ancient Greek tragedy seldom made much of romantic love, it is not surprising that this particular Sophoclean chorus was singled out for imitation and elaboration. Trissino was a Grecian and yet, like most Italian poets of his time, he was writing a tragedy of love. Luigi Alamanni translated *Antigone* into Italian in 1533. When he came to this chorus he expanded it from fifteen lines to over fifty lines.[10]

In the fourth and last episode the page re-enters and talks with the chorus. He asks them to return to the queen. A maid-servant comes from the palace weeping and wailing, and, at the request of the chorus, relates in detail the suicide of the queen. Masinissa, despairing of winning over the Romans to his view, had sent a vial of poison to Sophonisba, who has just drunk it. This account of the queen's behavior, after she drank the poison, has some of the best lines in the play.

> Dapoi si volse, e trasse d' una cassa
> Un bel drappo di seta, ed un di lino,
> E disse: donne, quando sarò morta,
> Piacciavi rivoltare in questi panni
> Il corpo mio, e darli sepoltura.
> E postasi a seder sopra il suo letto,
> Sospirò forte, e disse: o letto mio,
> Ove deposi il fior de la mia vita,
> Rimanti in pace: da quest' hora inanzi
> Dormirò ne la terra eterno sonno [1.124].

Then she turned and drew from a chest a fine bolt of silk and one of linen, and said, "Ladies, when I am dead may it please you to wrap my body in these cloths and give it burial." And seating herself on her bed she sighed deeply and said, "O bed of mine, whereon I laid the flower of my life, remain in peace; from this hour forth I shall sleep the eternal sleep in the earth."

The maidservant and the chorus continue to weep and wail

---

[10] See *Teatro italiano antico* 2.182–184.

until the dying queen comes out for a last look at the sun and earth. Erminia is with her and supports her faltering steps.

Sophonisba takes a long time to die and has much to say before the end. She is concerned about her little son, two years old, whom she consigns to Erminia. Although Erminia wishes to die with her mistress, Sophonisba needs her alive to care for the child and to insure an honorable memory of the mother. Just before the end Sophonisba begins to lose her senses. Erminia holds up the child; but the mother can no longer see.

Erminia: Raise your face to this one, who is kissing you.
Chorus: Pay a little heed to him.
Sophonisba: Ah me! I cannot.
Chorus: May God receive you in peace.
Sophonisba: I go. Good-by [1.134].

Erminia breaks into prolonged lamentations and the women of the chorus take charge of the body. Then Masinissa appears, too late to see Sophonisba before her death. He gives orders for the preparation of the body and promises an escort, when it grows dark, for the funeral party's journey to Carthage.

The chorus brings the play to a close with a comment on the uncertainty of human hopes:

> La fallace speranza de' mortali,
> A guisa d'onda in un superbe fiume,
> Ora si vide, or par che si consume.

The false hope of mortals, like a wave in a proud river, now is seen, now seems to be dissolved.

What was the significance of this first "regular tragedy" of the Renaissance? What did its author contribute to modern tragedy?

For one thing Trissino opened the sources of the Greek theater and adapted the Aristotelian theories of tragedy to the Italian and thence to the European stage. When he wrote *Sofonisba* Trissino was much more concerned with imitating Sophocles and Euripides than with writing a new tragedy that would fit the recommendations of Aristotle. Years later, in parts 5 and 6 of his *Poetica*, he did adapt Aristotelian theories to Italian tragedy and tried to justify his *Sofonisba* on Aristotelian grounds. Trissino's development of a neoclassical theory of modern tragedy was similar to Corneille's in the next century; it was in part an Aristotelian apology for his own early practice.

In *Sofonisba,* Trissino freed Italian tragedy from *ottava rima* and *terza rima* and gave it blank verse *(versi sciolti),* which soon became the normal verse form for dialogue. In his *Poetica* (25r–25v) he explained why he chose unrhymed verse for both *Sofonisba* and the *Italia liberata.* Dante, he said, had found *terza rima* suitable for his great poem. Then Boccaccio, in his *Teseide,* had used *ottava rima,* which was adopted by Pulci, Boiardo, Ariosto, and others for heroic romances. Trissino had decided, however, that rhyme was not the best medium for the "matter of arms" and therefore chose *versi sciolti* for heroic poetry and for dramatic poetry. In so doing he established the formal pattern of Renaissance tragedy in Italy, and in England as well, namely, blank verse for most of the dialogue, rhyme for the choruses and for certain lyrical and sententious portions of the dialogue.[11]

Trissino was not the first to emphasize love in the new tragedy, but he certainly confirmed this emphasis. As pointed out in the preceding chapter, Del Carretto gave Sophonisba a small role in his tragedy. In Trissino's play, however, the queen is all-important and her love affair with Masinissa is what makes the play tragic. Trissino helped to establish the importance of women in Renaissance tragedy; Giraldi Cinthio's exploitation of the "cult of the feminine soul"[12] came later and owed something to the example set by *Sofonisba.*

While Trissino's tragedy is "regular" in strictly observing the unities of action and time, it did not preserve a strict unity of place. The scene certainly shifts in the third episode from the piazza in Cirta to the Roman camp. This relaxation of the unity of place was common enough in the tragedies of later Renaissance playwrights, who were more concerned with a unified single action and with a narrow limitation of time than with restricting the scene to a single spot. Nevertheless, this violation of unity of place in *Sofonisba* is curious since Trissino was a pedantic imitator of Sophocles and Euripides and considered the fixed chorus *(coro stabile)* an essential part of tragedy. Once his chorus of fifteen

[11] Unrhymed choral odes, while not numerous, were sometimes used in Italian tragedy. Del Carretto used *versi sciolti* in a few of the choruses of his *Sophonisba* (1502). See above, p. 39. After Trissino, Rucellai used unrhymed verse in the third choral song of his *Rosmunda.* See below, p. 60. Giraldi Cinthio (*Discorsi,* p. 234) cited this chorus in *Rosmunda* as proof of his contention that while rhyme was a pleasing ornament unrhymed verse could be sweet.
[12] See Louis Berthé, *J. B. Giraldi,* p. 128.

entered in the *parode,* they stayed on the stage throughout the rest of the play. It must have been awkward to represent the transfer of all these women from the royal palace to the Roman camp and back again, but apparently the author saw no way to omit the important argument between Masinissa and Scipio at Roman headquarters and the chorus had to trail along. Over a century later, the French poet Jean Mairet solved the problem.[13]

Another feature of *Sofonisba,* an obvious one it may be, should be emphasized. Although Trissino's play was not the first one based on the story of Sophonisba, it was the first important Roman tragedy in the Renaissance, and as such was the ancestor of a host of *Didos, Cleopatras, Julius Caesars,* and a good number of *Sophonisbas* in Italy, France, and England.

Some of Trissino's practices were not followed by all succeeding playwrights. For example, *Sofonisba* was not divided into five acts, but was arranged in Greek fashion as episodes and choral odes. Even so, there are actually five acts in all but name, that is, a prologue and four episodes. The better playwrights who succeeded Trissino, for example, Cinthio, Aretino, Dolce, and Groto, continued to used five acts as prescribed by Horace and as Renaissance scholars divided the tragedies of Seneca and the comedies of Plautus and Terence. Only a few followed Trissino here.

Although *Sofonisba* was completed in 1515, it was not staged in Italy until 1562. Meanwhile, about 1559, it had been translated into French prose by Mellin de Saint-Gelais and acted before Catherine de' Medici and Henri II at Blois. Later, in 1585, it was translated into French verse by Claude Mermet. There is no record of its appearance in England.

Since Trissino's tragedy was printed at least ten times before 1620, and since he was a celebrated *letterato,* it seems reasonable to suppose that *Sofonisba* exerted a considerable influence upon learned tragedy in the Renaissance. There is no questioning this influence in Italy and also in France, but in England Trissino's contribution to tragedy is all but impossible to assess. If he contributed anything to learned Elizabethans like Jonson, Marston, and Chapman, the contribution was apparently general and not specific.

In 1606, John Marston brought out his *Tragedy of Sophonisba,*

---

[13] See below, p. 56.

or the Wonder of Women, possibly in rivalry of Jonson's Roman tragedy of *Sejanus,* which had appeared the year before. Although Marston was the most "Italianate" of Elizabethan dramatists, his tragedy owed little or nothing to Trissino's play. And although the author proclaimed in a foreword that "I have not labored in this poem to tie myself to relate any thing as a historian but to enlarge every thing as a poet," he produced an old-fashioned history, which begins *ab ovo* and works its way through many scenes to the death of the "wonder of women." There is considerable violence in the play, some of it onstage. An Ethiopian slave is killed by Syphax in the third act. A Carthaginian senator is tortured to death, but offstage. Marston introduced the witch Erichtho in Act 4 and the ghost of Hasdrubal in Act 5. Syphax and Masinissa fight a duel in Act 5. So far as I can tell, there is no evidence that the English poet owed any scene or any speech to Trissino; his latest editor, Harvey Wood, cites only two verbal parallels with the Italian *Sofonisba.*[14]

It is a different story when we come to Jean Mairet's *Sophonisbe* (1634), which was no history but a thoroughly neoclassical play. In fact, it was the first French tragedy written in strict accord with the unities and the neoclassical rules. There is no doubt that the author was well acquainted with Trissino's *Sofonisba,*[15] but he made some important changes.

Mairet, like virtually all of the leading French dramatists of his time, rejected blank verse in favor of rhymed couplets. He rejected the chorus. He altered the historical accounts of Livy, Polybius, and Appian, and the plot of Trissino's play to suit his own taste and doubtless the taste of his French audience. In order to avoid the bigamous marriage of Sophonisba with Masinissa he had Syphax killed. He had Masinissa commit suicide as the final curtain closes. He reversed Trissino's treatment of the heroine's death; instead of having Sophonisba drink the poison in her bedroom and then die onstage, he had her drink it onstage and then retire to her bedroom to die. Mairet justified these alterations in a way that Trissino would have approved, that is, by authority of Aristotle; he quoted a pertinent passage from Chapter 9 of the *Poetics:* "The poet's function is to describe, not the thing that has happened,

---

[14] *The Plays of John Marston* (Edinburgh, 1938) 2.306, 308.
[15] See Charles Dedeyan's edition of *La Sophonisbe* (Paris, 1945), pp. xx ff.

but the kind of thing that might happen, i.e., what is possible
as being probable or necessary." With Mairet's *Sophonisbe* the
neoclassical theater was firmly established in France, and this
neoclassical theater owed much to Trissino and Trissino's Italian
followers.

RUCELLAI

While Trissino was writing *Sofonisba* a young kinsman of the
Medici, a nephew of Lorenzo the Magnificent, was writing another
Grecian tragedy entitled *Rosmunda*, first printed in 1525 at Siena,
but written some ten years before. The author of this second
"regular" tragedy, Giovanni Rucellai, was a friendly rival of
Trissino; the two used to climb on benches and declaim verses
from the tragedies they were composing for their own delight
and presumably for the delight of friends as well.[16] Although
Rucellai was the better poet of the two, he deferred to his friend
as the better critic and scholar and took him for his guide in
writing. He dedicated *Le api* ("The Bees"), an imitation of the
fourth book of Virgil's *Georgics*, to Trissino and inserted in the
poem a fulsome tribute to his mentor. "Without you," said Rucellai,
"my mind never created anything lofty and grand, and with you
I shall make the buzzing of bees ascend even to heaven and resound through the hollow spheres. For my love, pray, give something of the royal purple and tragic cothurnus of your mournful
Sofonisba and of that great Belisarius who, curbing the Goths,
gave Hesperia her liberty, O brightest honor of our age."[17]

Like Trissino, Rucellai imitated Sophocles and Euripides,
especially Sophocles' *Antigone*. His *Oreste* (unpublished until
1723) was an adaptation of Euripides' *Iphigenia in Tauris*. He
found the argument for *Rosmunda* in Paulus Diaconus' medieval
History of the Lombards, a source comparable to Procopius' history
of the Gothic war that Trissino used for his *Italia liberata*. The old
Gothic tale was a bloody one. Alboin, conqueror of northern Italy,
slew his enemy Cunimund and then married Cunimund's daughter

---

[16] See Rucellai, *Opere*, ed. Mazzoni, p. xviii. Mazzoni records an anecdote of
the time, which relates how Rucellai in a moment of excitement leaped on a
bench with his breeches unbuttoned. Whereupon Trissino cried, "Now you see
who wishes to compete with me, one who like a small boy doesn't yet know
how to fasten his breeches."

[17] See *Opere*, p. 5. The reference to Belisarius and the war with the Goths was
to Trissino's *Italia liberata*, which was completed some years later.

Rosamond, who nursed her revenge until Alboin was beheaded by one of her friends.

Rucellai, or the printed versions at least, did not follow Trissino's Grecian scheme of episodes, but divided his play into five acts of uneven length. He used the chorus, however, in about the same way as did his friend, and his first act is a Grecian prologue. He used unrhymed verse in most of the dialogue, with occasional rhymes. He preserved the unity of time rather carefully, but was vague about the scene, which seems to shift from Rosmunda's refuge to Alboin's camp, carrying the chorus along with it.

The resemblance between *Rosmunda* and Sophocles' *Antigone* appears in the very first speech of the heroine, who is discussing with her nurse how they may recover the body of her father from the battlefield and give it decent burial: "Now is the time that deep sleep, wearing the semblance of death, loads the earth with calm and silence, freeing with sweetest repose every man, every tame and savage animal, from the toils and care of the day; so that we are safe from the impious hands not yet dry of our blood, dear nurse, nurse and mother. Up, pray, let us return to search out the corpse of my unhappy and wretched father and to cover it with at least a little earth, since I cannot give it any other sepulcher."

The nurse tries to restrain her impulsive young mistress, but Rosmunda, like Antigone and like Sophonisba, believes that there are worse things than danger and death.

Nurse: I want you to think about keeping yourself alive.
Rosmunda: The unworthy life is much worse than death.
Nurse: The one can follow the other for you.
Rosmunda: How can I be worse off than I am?
Nurse: You can lose honor, liberty.
Rosmunda: I will not lose this without life.
Nurse: You do not yet know what death is.
Rosmunda: Death is the end of human miseries.

It seems that Rosmunda has had a dream in which her dead father appeared and asked her to give his body back to mother earth.

The chorus enters in the *parode* and in rhymed verse expatiates on the sentiment that Rosmunda has just expressed: "O happy are those of you who have adorned past life with a fine death, but wretched are they who endure harsh servitude until the very end." Then it adds a Sophoclean sentiment: "Happy is he who is not born; but more happy is that one who dies in swaddling clothes."

There is some passage of time, a few hours, between the first and second acts, for it is now dawn and the two women have buried Rosmunda's father. The chorus, which takes part in the dialogue, reports that some soldiers have already discovered the fresh grave and are now looking for the culprits. This dialogue is partly in rhyme, Rosmunda's speeches as well as those of the chorus.

An officer named Falisco orders Rosmunda to dig up the corpse, cut off the head, and carry it to Alboin. The distraught woman pleads with Falisco to have pity on her, to help her. He is loyal to Alboin, but finally agrees to do what he can for her. The chorus prays God to save their honor if not their lives.

Alboin, the conqueror, is introduced at the beginning of the third act. He is depicted as a savage barbarian, cruel and ruthless: "If any enemy still remains here, kill him and throw his body to crows, to kites, to dogs, to wolves, to bears. He who wants to rule empires, states, or kingdoms, needs above all else to be cruel, because fear is born of cruelty, and from fear is born obedience, by which one rules and governs the world."

A messenger from Falisco brings the skull of Cunimund, and Alboin gives orders to have it made into a drinking cup. The messenger adds the information that Rosmunda, in defiance of the king's orders, has buried her father. She has been taken prisoner by Falisco, who is bringing her to camp.

When Rosmunda is brought before Alboin she makes no attempt to deny her violation of the law. Like Antigone, she is proud of her defiance: "It seemed to me that I should obey the divine orders of that Lord who rules the universe rather than your decree."

Alboin's first impulse is to have the guilty woman executed; he rebukes her for her presumption and promises to give her a lesson in humility. His speech here is typical of Rucellai's style, which is usually more colorful than Trissino's.

> La superchia alterezza al fin ruina.
> Più volte ho visto un gran corsier feroce
> Nel suo veloce e furibundo corso
> Esser tenuto con un picciol freno,
> E fortissima nave in mezzo a l'onde

> Tenersi contro el gran soffiar de' venti
> Da poca fune con ritorto ferro.
> Non si conviene alla servil fortuna
> Usar superbia contro al suo Signore.

Overweening pride falls in the end. Many times I have seen a huge fierce warhorse checked in his swift and furious course by a little bridle, and the strongest ship held against a great blast of wind by a little rope with its anchor. It is not seemly for servile fortune to show pride before its lord.

Falisco reminds the king that there is no renown to be won by killing women and advises him to marry Rosmunda in order to consolidate his realm. Alboin finds this advice sound and agrees to do so. Now it is up to Falisco to persuade Rosmunda to marry her father's killer. Of course she scorns such a marriage. When the nurse urges her to reconsider she cries, "O God in Heaven, O stars, O sun, O moon! You want me to take a husband whom my eyes cannot look upon, an enemy and the destroyer of our blood? Let the earth open and swallow me before I find myself married to him."

The nurse argues that it is better to be a wife than a concubine, and, moreover, that being queen she may find a way to revenge. It is this thought of revenge that finally wins over Rosmunda, who tells Falisco, when he returns, that she accepts the proposal. The wedding is arranged for that very evening.

The second *stasimon*, that is, the ode at the end of Act 3, was unusual at the time for its verse form, which is short seven-syllable lines unrhymed, i.e. *settenarii*. These *settenarii*, rhymed and unrhymed, were destined before long to become prominent in Italian tragedy. The sentiment of this particular ode is somewhat Senecan, as the following excerpt will show.

> Simili sono i regni
> E le superba mura
> De' nostri ampli palazzi
> A' nidi de gli aragni
> E quai legati sono
> Infra tremule canne;
> Questi ogni picciol vento
> Rompe in diverse parti.

Realms and the stately walls of our spacious palaces are like the nests of spiders spun between marshy reeds; any little wind breaks these in shreds.

Almachild, a friend of the heroine's family, appears in Act 4,

He is shocked at the news of Rosmunda's marriage. But a greater shock soon follows. A maidservant enters to report the wedding ceremony to Almachild and the chorus. After describing the early part of the ceremony the servant falters, unable to continue.

Chorus: But what can it be that moves you so?

Servant: The cup was made of the skull of a dead man.

Chorus: O me, you recount a beastly thing!

Servant: Alboin, taking this horrible vessel, filled it with wine and smiling said, "Cunimund, I put a final end to our contentions and I wish to make peace with you in this frolic of drinking together." So saying he put his lips to the skull and drank most of the wine. Then, turning to Rosmunda, who had averted her weeping face so that she might not witness so horrible a thing, he said, "Behold the head of your father; drink with it, and rejoice with it." The wretched woman, forced into this position, weeping refused so noisome a drink, and the more she avoided it the more strongly he urged her with haughty and arrogant threats. Finally, having thwarted him three times, she turned with trembling hands to take the bitter cup and as many times her hands, overcome by pity, fell away. At the end, the king seized it and put it to her mouth; whereby, forced and subdued, she drank thence more tears than wine.

Chorus: O miserable marriage, O harsh fate!

The "O harsh fate" (*O duro caso*) of the last line in the quotation above points to the *O dura fata* of Seneca's *Medea* (431) and *Troades* (1056) and to the *O dira fata* of *Hippolytus* (1271). In the sixteenth century, the phrase "O cruel fates" was regarded as typically Senecan.[18]

The nurse enters supporting the fainting queen. Almachild is now determined to kill Alboin, but the nurse restrains his first impulse and urges him to proceed with caution. The chorus sings an ode that begins with a rather ambitious simile: "The sky when it is serene has no more stars, nor the great fury of the wind in tempest drives not so many waves on the shore, nor has April so many flowers or May so many green boughs, nor so many leaves fall at the start of winter, as my mind has cares."

Act 5 is very short, only seventy-five lines, and consists largely of a messenger's report to Rosmunda and the chorus on the assassination of Alboin. Almachild had disguised himself as a woman and so penetrated the enemy lines and the royal tent, where he cut off the head of the drunken king.

---

[18] See Thomas Cooper's *Thesaurus linguae Romanae et Britannicae*, London, 1565.

The chorus moralizes in a brief concluding ode on the fate of Alboin: "Let every man who rules learn from the pitiless king who lies dead not to be cruel, for cruelty is displeasing to God."

Rosmunda is no masterpiece, but it is a better play than *Sofonisba*, for Rucellai was a more original writer than Trissino and he had a better sense of the theater. Rucellai was not a great poet, but, as Mazzoni says, he was a "poetical soul and an artist always pure and sometimes perfect."[19]

PAZZI

Alessandro Pazzi de' Medici, also a nephew of the great Lorenzo, was another Grecian who followed some of the methods of Trissino; he imitated the Greek tragedians and he worked with an eye on Aristotle. Pazzi, or Paccius, became best known to posterity for his excellent Latin translation of Aristotle's *Poetics*, which was widely used by students and scholars throughout the Renaissance. He translated Sophocles' *Electra* into Latin, Sophocles' *Oedipus Rex* into Italian, the *Iphigenia in Tauris* and the *Cyclops* of Euripides into Italian, and in 1524 wrote a Roman tragedy called *Dido in Carthagine*. Is this the first Dido play written in modern times? I know of no earlier one. Dolce's *Didone* was printed in 1547. Giraldi Cinthio's *Didone* was performed at Ferrara in 1543, printed in 1583. Pazzi's *Dido* was never published until 1887, at Bologna,[20] and it was probably never performed.

Pazzi was a scholar and a good translator, but he was not so successful as a poet. His *Dido* was written for the most part in Italian hexameters, which he maintained were "more like the ancient Greek and Latin [verses], not so much in the number of syllables as in the tenuous sound that results from them." Like all Italian playwrights of the early sixteenth century, he was trying to find a verse form that would sound conversational. "It seems to me," he said, "that one should necessarily have recourse to a kind of meter not much unlike prose, in which there is nevertheless a hidden measure and poetical symmetry."[21] He probably knew what he was trying to do, but the result has baffled investigators from his own time to the present. His modern editor Solerti has been unable to find any definite pattern in his versification

---

[19] Rucellai, *Opere*, p. lxxii.
[20] In *Le tragedie metriche di Alessandro Pazzi de' Medici*, ed. A. Solerti, Bologna, 1887.
[21] Preface to *Dido*, in *Le tragedie metriche*, p. 50.

beyond a general observance of twelve syllables instead of the usual eleven in *versi sciolti*.

The opening lines spoken by the ghost of Dido's first husband, Sychaeus, are representative:

> Contro a l'eterne leggi del ceco regno
> dall' Abysso profundo venuto sono
> nel secol de i viuenti due volte poi
> ch' io fui casso del lume dell' alma vita.

Contrary to the eternal laws of the realm of darkness, twice have I come to the world of the living since I was deprived of the light that nourishes life.

Pazzi's contemporaries were apparently puzzled by his metrical experiments. Benedetto Varchi, scholar, poet, historian, dramatist, critic, author of a well-known dialogue called *L'Hercolano*, which discussed literary matters, was cautious in his criticism of Pazzi, but evidently did not approve of his versification: "Of those [tragedies] of Alessandro de' Pazzi, a nobleman and man of many letters, Greek as well as Latin, I wish to leave the judgment to others, since I am not pleased with the kind of verse nor with that way of writing without rule."[22] Varchi was himself a neoclassicist and he felt uncomfortable when there were no rules and authorities to follow.

Pazzi used no rhymes whatever in *Dido*, indicating that he was not following altogether the practice of Trissino and Rucellai. Even the choruses are unrhymed. He sometimes varied the hexameters, however, by using shorter lines.

Dido was not divided into acts, for it was a Grecian play and the author professed allegiance to Aristotle's prescriptions. The ghost of Sychaeus, Dido's first husband, delivers the prologue, which is more Senecan in spirit than Grecian. The chorus is used as an actor and its odes mark off the epsiodes. Messengers are used throughout and the old nurse of Sychaeus reports the final suicide of the heroine at the end. There is little action onstage but an excessive amount of long-drawn lamentation.

Pazzi found his argument, of course, in the fourth book of the *Aeneid*. As he himself said, the tragedy was taken *in gran parte* from Virgil but the arrangement was altered and many ornaments added. Like Trissino and Rucellai, he imitated Euripides; but

---

[22] *L'Hercolano* (Venice, 1570), p. 209.

some details are more Senecan than Euripidean, such as the ghost of Sychaeus and the use of Iarbas, King of Lydia. In Pazzi's play, Iarbas presents Dido with the head of her brother Pygmalion, who had killed Sychaeus years before in Tyre. Pazzi apparently did not share Trissino's distaste for Seneca; in his preface he mentioned the Roman tragedian, along with Aeschylus, Sophocles, and Euripides, as one of the masters of ancient tragedy. There is more than one echo of Senecan style in the play, for example, the *O durissimo fato* of the chorus (p. 133) and the *O fato crudele* of a messenger (p. 136).

Dido in Carthagine is not a good play, for its plot is ill contrived by comparison with Virgil's original story and most of the dialogue is tedious. Since it was not published in the early sixteenth century, it could hardly have been widely known. Nevertheless, it is representative of the learned Italian tragedy that set the pattern for the neoclassical theater of the Renaissance.

MARTELLI

Lodovico Martelli (d. 1531) was another, and the last, direct follower of Trissino. He left an unfinished Grecian tragedy called *Tullia* in which he combined a Roman argument from Livy with imitation of ancient Greek tragedy, specifically Sophocles' *Electra* and possibly Euripides' *Orestes* and Aeschylus' *Choephoroe* as well. The play was first published in 1533 at Rome and at Venice.

The story of Tullia is one of bloodthirsty revenge, better calculated for Senecan than for Grecian tragedy. Tullia was the daughter of Servius, an ancient king of Rome and himself a usurper. She was married to an easygoing man while her sister was married to the unscrupulous, ambitious Lucius Tarquinius, son of the former king whose throne Servius had usurped. Tullia managed to have her husband and sister done away with and then married her brother-in-law Lucius. The next step was to encourage her new husband to do away with the king her father. Servius was brutally murdered and his body thrown in the gutter. Tullia ordered her coachman to drive over the still-bleeding corpse.

Martelli treated the story freely, partly because he was aware of the Aristotelian principle that the poet should rearrange history and partly because he tried to fit Livy's characters to the ancient Greek characters of the Orestean myth. Thus Servius corresponds to Aegisthus, the queen to Clytemnestra, Lucius to Orestes, and Tullia to Electra. Of course he could not make the parallels exact since the Greek Aegisthus was the lover of Electra's mother Clytemnestra and Servius was Tullia's father. Electra, it may be recalled, revered her father Agamemnon. Martelli's version is certainly more shocking than the Greek tale.

Like Trissino and Pazzi, but unlike Rucellai, Martelli did not divide his play into acts, but marked it off in episodes and choral odes. One of the choral odes is lacking, apparently never written before the author's death. The unity of time is not so sharply indicated as in *Sofonisba* and *Rosmunda*, and the scene is vague. Martelli followed the normal neoclassical pattern of unrhymed verse for the dialogue and rhyme for choral odes, with some rhyme in the dialogue.

Lucius opens the play, speaking to his brother Demaratus. Tullia, however, delivers most of the exposition in a long speech before the *parode* of the chorus, which is made up of friends of Tullia.

In the second episode, or in the first if the opening scene is to be taken as a prologue, Tullia raves to the sympathetic chorus about her ambition, her unfulfilled desires, her impatience with the dillydallying of her husband Lucius. "O beautiful eye of day," she cries, "O cold moon, under whose circuit everything is united, end my pains, end the grief that makes me go about weeping night and day!" (3.44).[23]

Martelli's heroine is violent, impatient, single-minded, and her speech is usually violent, sometimes strong but too often tedious. She believes that she faces a dilemma: she must be an enemy to her father or an enemy to her husband. Her personal ambition puts her against her father and having taken her stand she is uncompromising—all or nothing: "Alive I will be queen, and dead nothing. Thus an end will be put to my griefs" (3.49). Her nurse urges her to be patient, to wait, to cease complaining.

In the next episode, the queen, wife of Servius and mother of Tullia, rebukes her daughter's rebellious attitude and asks her to remember the duty she owes to her parents. Tullia, like Electra, is unmoved by her mother's wishes and she calls her parents usurpers, as indeed they were. Her mother is as stubborn as she,

---

[23] Page and volume references are to the *Teatro italiano antico*.

and the two continue to wrangle. The queen finally leaves, threatening her daughter, but she is nevertheless alarmed and fearful: "I return to Servius to procure your death. Alas, my dream! O me, it grieves me much and frightens me" (3.70).

The language of this quarrel between Tullia and her mother is reminiscent of Seneca, whose influence was returning to Italian tragedy after its virtual rejection by Trissino. When Tullia cries to her mother, "Craggy Caucasus among his flinty rocks begot you, to whom Hyrcanian tigers gave fierce suck," the author was paraphrasing a famous passage in Virgil,[24] but the general tone of the quarrel is more Senecan than Virgilian. There is an allusion to the heartless behavior of Tullia in the Senecan *Octavia* (305), which may well have influenced Martelli's concept of his heroine.

Servius enters accompanied by a stranger from Corinth, who brings news of the absent Lucius; he informs the king that his son-in-law is dead. It looks as though Martelli borrowed material here from the Greek story of Merope, which became a favorite subject for Italian tragedy later in the century. Merope's exiled son disguised himself as a stranger and brought news of his own death to the usurping tyrant Polyphontes.

Tullia overhears the conversation between Servius and the stranger and is shocked by this ruin of her plan. "Alas, why should I live longer in the world? O I will kill myself with these hands! O I will go weeping through every clime, reproaching the unjust laws of Heaven, and bewailing my cruel destiny" (3.76).

In the next episode, Lucius appears in a disguise that deceives even his wife. He is carrying, so he says, an urn of Lucius' ashes. Now Tullia redoubles her complaints: "Ah me, unhappy one, ah me! Is not death less cruel than this my suffering?" (3.83). Lucius hands the urn to Tullia, who mourns over it. In fact, she works herself up to such a frantic pitch of despair that the stranger has to reveal his identity by means of a ring. He has to conceal himself from all others until the time for revenge is ripe.

When old Servius enters to greet the stranger, Lucius gives him the ashes and asks for a proper burial. His brother Demaratus is also present. Servius refuses burial and the two begin to quarrel in the liveliest scene in the play.

Lucio Se tu hai tolto a lui la patria e 'l regno,

---

[24] *Aeneid* 4.365–367. See below, p. 168.

Ben donar gli potresti sepoltura.

Servio   O superbo, o ritroso!

Lucio   O reo tiranno!

Servio   Offender me vuoi tu nel regno mio?

Lucio   I' ho di te più parte in questo regno.
            Prima che 'l Sol col dì da noi si parta,
            Avrai ne gli occhi oscura notte eterna.

Servio   E tu contra mi sei?

Demarato   Contra ti sono.
            E son fratel di Lucio: e Lucio e questo.

Servio   Così son preda, cimè, de' miei nemici?
            Così son giunto al fin de' giorni miei?

Lucio   Quest' è l' ultimo dì de la tua vita;
            Quest' è la fida spada di mio Padre,
            Ch' oggi dee far di lui piena vendetta.

Servio   Oimè, lasso, oimè!
            Oimè, lasso, oimè!

Tullia   Tratel dentro prestamente: et ivi
            Senz' udir sue parole,
            Dateli so la meritata morte.

Servio   Ahi figlia, ahi figlia cruda!

Tullia   Va, va perfido a morte
            Non padre, empio nemico [3.102–103].

Lucius: If you have taken country and reign from him, you would do well to give him burial.

Servius: O proud, obstinate man!

Lucius: O cruel tyrant!

Servius: You wish to wrong me in my own kingdom?

Lucius: I have more claim than you to this kingdom. Before the sun sets you will have dark and eternal night in your eyes.

Servius: And you are against me?

Demaratus: I am against you. I am the brother of Lucius, and this man is Lucius.

Servius: So I am the prey, alas, of my enemies? So I have arrived at the end of my days?

Lucius: This is the last day of your life. And this is the trusty sword of my father, which today is bound to bring him full revenge.

Servius: Woe is me, alas, woe is me! Woe is me, alas, woe is me!

Tullia: Drag him inside quickly, and there alone, where his cries will not be heard, give him the death he deserves.

Servius: Ah daughter, ah cruel daughter!

Tullia: Go, go, traitor, to your death. You are no father but a wicked enemy.

Lucius despatches the old man, brings his body out, and throws it in the street.

Then there may be a change of scene. The ghost of Servius rises and speaks to his widow the queen: "Ah God, dear consort, I am going elsewhere a liberated spirit, and I am parted from you by a savage, impious, reposeless death" (3.104). As the ghost leaves, the queen cries out, "Are you now my husband? O Servius, O Servius! Wait, O my Servius, that I may speak with you! He has vanished, and I can no more rejoin him" (3.105).

When Tullia and Lucius re-enter the queen turns her wrath on her daughter. Martelli was enough of a Grecian to spare his audience the actual murder of Servius and the ugly detail of Tullia's chariot rolling over the corpse. This last abomination is omitted from the play. A messenger does inform Lucius that the people have risen against him. Thoroughly frightened, Lucius appeals to Jove, and the god sends Romulus, founder of Rome, to restore order and bring peace to the realm.

The chorus ends the play with a brief ode beginning, "Too wise and happy would he be who might see the end of his days."

Martelli's tragedy is a cruder but more powerful play than Trissino's *Sofonisba*. Although some of the speeches in *Tullia* are insufferably long, there are some highly theatrical scenes which point ahead to the Italian tragedy of blood and revenge. A near-contemporary judgment of its merits and demerits may be found in Varchi's *Hercolano*. Varchi, it may be recalled, was unwilling to criticize Pazzi's *Dido* beyond disapproving of its verse form. He reported that Trissino's *Sofonisba* was highly praised by some readers, as was Rucellai's *Rosmunda,* and he said of *Tullia*, "If it had as good a soul as it has a beautiful body, it would seem to me more than marvelous, and it could stand comparison with the Greek."[25]

Varchi was a scholar and an Ancient. He was also an advocate of moral teaching in literature. His own venture into playwriting, *La suocera* (1549), was an adaptation of "The Mother-in-law" of Terence in which he turned a fine Roman comedy into a tedious series of moralizings. Apparently he did not approve of the immoral behavior of Tullia and her husband although he admired Martelli's tragic style. It must be said that Varchi hardly repre-

---

[25] *L'Hercolano,* p. 209.

sented the attitude of most Italians interested in the theater. The horrors suggested by *Tullia* were just the beginning of a reign of terror in Italian tragedy.

CRESCI

Sixty years after the death of Martelli another version of this bloody tale appeared, namely *Tullia feroce*,[26] written by Pietro Cresci, a learned poet but no Grecian. In fact, a comparison of Cresci's tragedy with Martelli's offers a good illustration of the difference between the Italian Grecians and Senecans. In the 1540's Giraldi Cinthio, as will be shown in the next chapter, had restored Seneca to the influential position he occupied in Renaissance tragedy before Trissino, and Cresci was a follower of Cinthio.

Cresci used a prologue after the Terentian pattern, that is, a detached comment on the play about to unfold. His pretentious prologue is delivered by Ambition, but there is little or no suggestion here of the Christian morality play. Ambition, thoroughly pagan, does not come from heaven or hell; she is an "Idea" and the bastard offspring of a great warrior and Emulation. Her companion is Pride, her servant Envy, her mistress Glory. She does not dwell in humble hearts and cottages, but in noble minds and palaces. She spurs the hearts of men, and women upon occasion, to the great enterprises of war and peace. She has inspired the author of this tragedy, which will recount a story of ancient Rome full of "terror and pity" and exhibiting an example of the miseries that all mortals are subject to.

The first scene of the play proper betrays the Senecan background at once, for in it two ghosts and a Fury rise from the infernal regions. The ghost of Tullia's first husband and the ghost of her sister talk about the murders already committed by Tullia and appeal for help to Alecto, who promises to avenge them. The parallel with the opening of Seneca's *Thyestes* is obvious, and the scene may owe something to Cinthio's *Orbecche* as well.

As dawn breaks the infernal visitors retire, leaving behind them the stench of sulfur and pitch. The first mortal character to appear is an old servant of the king. He is seeking the royal counselor, because the king has had a nightmare in which he saw a monstrous serpent give birth to a young serpent that immediately devoured its mother.

---

[26] *Tullia feroce, tragedia di Pietro Cresci Anconitano*, Venice, 1591.

Cresci's action follows about the same track that Martelli's does, but he put more emphasis upon the old king and deleted the role of the queen. He added a counselor, a favorite character in Senecan tragedy, and introduced an Oriental magician to support the supernatural atmosphere.

Cresci's chorus is not Grecian; it is used only at the end of each act except the last, wherein it takes a small part in the dialogue. It delivers rhymed odes on man's greed for power, on fickle Fortune, and on the uncertainty of mortal life. The ode on sleep at the end of the second act is not bad. Cresci was a better lyric poet than dramatist. The dialogue, usually stilted, is mostly in unrhymed verse. The chorus uses some unrhymed verse in the dialogue of the last act. Senecan echoes abound, including a paraphrase of two celebrated lines in the *Thyestes* that have already been cited several times—"He who had a living body in the morning is often a forlorn spirit and ghost by evening."[27]

The big scene in "Tullia the Cruel" is 5.4, wherein a messenger reports the assassination of the old king. Cresci's *nuntio* is patterned after Seneca's and probably after Cinthio's, but he is more tedious and more pedantic than his prototypes in *Thyestes* and *Orbecche*. The climax of his narration—he speaks to the old nurse and the chorus—is Livy's episode that Martelli deliberately omitted, namely, Tullia's driving her chariot over the dying body of her aged father. According to Cresci's *nuntio*, the horses, as though moved by a pity that their driver never felt, stopped short of the prostrate figure in the gutter. The old king, wounded and exhausted, stretched forth his bloodstained hands to beg mercy of his daughter; but Tullia lashed the team with her whip and forced them forward. "The wheels broke the luckless limbs, mangled the fainting and weary flesh, smashed the unhappy bones, and (O what terror!) miserably demolished the body of the king in a trice." The royal blood spurted over the gilded ornaments of the chariot and stained the spotless white robe of the driver.

In the last scene (5.5), which is somewhat anticlimactic, the old servant who opens the play reports more horrors to nurse, chorus, and messenger. It seems that Tarquin and Tullia have dragged the mangled body of the king over the rough cobblestones and thrown it into the Tiber.

---

[27] "Quem dies vidit veniens superbum/hunc dies vidit fugiens iacentem" (*Thyestes* 613–614).

The reign of the Grecians in learned Italian tragedy was short, being all but eclipsed by Giraldi Cinthio, who respected Trissino and the ancient Greek dramatists but preferred Seneca. The influence of Trissino and his followers was to reappear, however, later in the century, in such tragedies as Giusti's *Irene* (1579), Massucci's *Costanza* (1585), Torelli's *Merope* (1589) and *Tancredi* (1597).

IV

Giraldi Cinthio's Theory of Tragedy

Although Grecian tragedy in Italy never attracted many followers, it left its mark on the theater, and few Italian plays written after Trissino, Rucellai, and Martelli were much like the earlier rhymed tragedies. The *letterati* were succeeded by more practical dramatists, but the pattern evolved by the Grecians was unchanged save for certain modifications, many of them minor. In other words, Euripidean and Sophoclean models and the Aristotelian "rules" remained in force throughout the sixteenth century, sharing authority with a revival of Seneca, whose influence had never wholly disappeared even among the Grecians.

The leading tragic dramatist in the middle of the sixteenth century was Giraldi Cinthio of Ferrara. Poet, teacher of philosophy and rhetoric, protégé of Ercole II, Cinthio wrote plays and organized theatrical entertainments for the ducal court. He was not a Grecian although he respected the ancient Greeks and enjoyed the lectures of Vincentio Maggi on the *Poetics* of Aristotle. Maggi, or Madius, was the scholar who brought out the second modern commentary on Aristotle's celebrated treatise in 1550.[1]

Cinthio did not admire Trissino as a poet; at least he disap-

---

[1] Madius and Lombardus, *In Aristotelis librum de poetica communes explanationes,* Venice, 1550.

proved of the *Italia liberata,* which he thought imitated the vices rather than the virtues of Homer. He thought better of *Sofonisba* and awarded its author the honor of being the first to "bring tragedy from the Tiber and Ilissus to the waves of the Arno."[2] Moreover, he praised Trissino for introducing unrhymed verse into Italian tragedy. On the other hand, he maintained that the "customs and manners of the Greeks were not suitable for the man who would write about Roman matters."[3] Although Cinthio admired the *Oedipus Rex* of Sophocles, doubtless influenced here by Aristotle's preference, he did not share Trissino's poor opinion of Seneca. On the contrary, he considered the Roman the greatest of all the ancient tragedians: "In nearly all his tragedies (as it seems to me) he surpasses in prudence, in gravity, in decorum, in majesty, in sentiments all the Greeks who ever wrote, although in style he could have been more temperate and correct than he is."[4] And again, in comparing Seneca with Euripides, he said that "good judges would set him above Euripides if he had had as pure Latin as Euripides had Greek, because no one who judges rightly would not give him the victory in majesty, in feeling, in observation of character, and in liveliness of sentiments."[5]

Therefore Cinthio returned to emulation of Seneca. He also returned to the theater; he did not write primarily for scholars but tried to please the audience at the court of Ferrara. Although there is no record that all his plays were actually produced on the stage, he always wrote with production in mind. As Neri[6] says, his *Orbecche* (1541) was the first Italian tragedy *regolare e rappresentata,* that is, the first Italian tragedy composed according to the neoclassical rules and produced on the stage. Trissino's *Sofonisba* (1515) was not seen on the stage until after the author's death, and the other Grecian tragedies were written for readers rather than for spectators.

In devising this neoclassical tragedy that appealed to a more or less popular audience, Cinthio modified some of the practices of the Grecians. Some of these modifications probably evolved in

---

[2] *La tragedia a chi legge,* appended to *Orbecche.* See *Tragedie* (1583), p. 134.
[3] *Discorsi* (1554), pp. 179–180.
[4] *Discorsi,* p. 220.
[5] *Discorsi,* p. 262.
[6] P. 59.

actual rehearsals, coming as a result of trying out the play on a stage. Other modifications were the result of Cinthio's own interpretations of Greek and Roman theory and practice, that is, his study of the plays of Sophocles, Euripides, Seneca, and Terence, and his study of the critical treatises of Aristotle, Horace, and Donatus. I mention Terence and his fourth-century commentator Donatus because, as will be shown, a considerable amount of comic theory and practice entered Cinthio's theory and practice of tragedy. Above all, while he accepted the ancient writers as guides, he was determined to modernize ancient material, for he put his sixteenth-century audience first; if ancient theory and practice seemed to run counter to modern taste, then ancient theory and practice were sacrificed. The prologue to *Altile* (c. 1541) declared that the author was going to fit his business to the "age, the spectators, and the subject matter never touched before by either ancient or modern poet." Furthermore, "he holds it as more than certain that if the ancient poets were here now they would seek to satisfy these times, these spectators, and this new subject matter." It is more than likely that Cinthio found assurance for his modern stand in the numerous statements of Italian authors of the "new comedy." The comic dramatists, beginning with Ariosto, had been proclaiming their independence of the Ancients for some years before 1541.

There is no lack of critical material in the writings of Cinthio, for he was a critic as well as a poet and was always discussing dramatic theory in his prologues, in *La tragedia a chi legge* ("Tragedy to Whomever Reads") appended to *Orbecche,* in his Apology for *Didone,* and in the more systematic essays of his *Discorsi.* The last-named treatise was not published until 1554, but parts of it were undoubtedly written some years before that date. We can find in his critical writings discussions of nearly every important consideration of tragedy. Specifically I propose to examine his criticism of the following: The Five-Act Formula, The Prologue, The Chorus, The Proper Number of Actors, The Use of Messengers, Soliloquies, Death Scenes, The Role of Spectacle, *Deus ex Machina,* The Right Style for Tragedy, The Function of Tragedy, Tragic Characters, Historical Plot *vs.* Fictitious Plot, Tragedy with an Unhappy Ending *vs.* Tragedy with a Happy Ending, The Dramatic Unities.

THE FIVE-ACT FORMULA

Cinthio rejected the Grecians' arrangement of a play into pro-logue, episodes, and choral odes and returned to the Roman five acts. Like most men he was able to rationalize his personal likes and dislikes and to quote authority to suit his own purpose. If Aristotle suited him and Horace did not, he followed Aristotle and rejected Horace. In deciding upon five acts he followed Horace and the Romans instead of the Greeks: "I admit that the Greeks did not use this device, because with them the stage never remained empty since the chorus was always there, as appears manifest by the authority of Aristotle and in the Greek plays that have escaped the damage of time. But I hold it certain that in this feature the Romans saw things better than the Greeks, for it is not at all likely [verisimile] that great and lordly persons would want to treat actions of great importance, such as happen in tragedies, amidst a multitude of people, even if these were servants."[7] The use of five acts, as Cinthio conceived them, made it possible to clear the stage from time to time of riffraff and so preserve the privacy and dignity proper to the great actions and grave deliberations of noble characters. In other words, the Romans, in his judgment, preserved the *decorum* of tragedy better than did the Greeks and the arrange-ment into separate acts favors this *decorum*.

Cinthio actually chose the arrangement of five acts in Terentian comedy as explained by Donatus. He believed that a good tragedy, like a good comedy, should consist of separate *prologue, protasis* (exposition), *epitasis* (complication), and *catastrophe* (resolution), the whole arranged in five acts. "The first [act]," he said, "contains the argument. In the second the matter of the argument begins to be directed toward the end. The obstacles and perturbations come in the third. The fourth begins to offer means of redressing the afflicted. The fifth brings the welcome end with a just resolution of the whole argument." This pattern holds for comedy, to be sure, "but change the details, as they ought to be changed, and it can also serve for tragedy."[8]

An important advantage of the Roman scheme, according to Cinthio, lay in the welcome breaks between the acts, which could

---

[7] Apology for *Didone* (1583), p. 141.
[8] *Discorsi*, p. 255.

be filled with music and so offer recreation to the spectators. The new Italian comedy from its beginning made use of musical *intermedii* or *intermezzi,* and Cinthio was well aware that the people liked such entertainments.

THE PROLOGUE

Donatus' analysis of Terentian comedy included a prologue as well as *protasis, epitasis,* and *catastrophe,* and Cinthio favored the Roman prologue over the Greek. Consequently his prologues were not part of the plot, that is, the first scene of the tragedy, but separate explanations of the play about to unfold or critical remarks on drama in general or on the play in particular. His prologues were always impersonal, never spoken by characters from the play, never a ghost or Fury or goddess although these supernatural persons might appear in the action.

THE CHORUS

Cinthio modified the Grecian pattern of the chorus considerably. In the first place, he rejected the *parode* or opening chorus. It may be recalled that in Trissino's *Sofonisba* the chorus was a fixed chorus, a *coro stabile:* once entered in the *parode,* it remained on the stage throughout the whole performance. Cinthio retained the *coro stabile* after a fashion, but confined its use to odes at the end of each act. I confess that it is not clear to me how and when this chorus entered and left the stage; but it is certain that Cinthio often cleared the stage of all save the main actors and their close associates, such as a servant or a nurse. He often used a *coro mobile* in the dialogue, usually in a scene of lamentation with one or more of the principal characters; that is, in a *commos.* When the chorus took part in the dialogue only one member spoke.[9] In the odes at the close of each act all members of the chorus spoke or sang together. Cinthio conjectured that the ancient *commos* was somewhat like a Moorish dance, and pointed to the first chorus of Seneca's *Troades* as an illustration. He did not say that his own *commos* was like a Moorish dance, but he insisted upon a mobile chorus for this part of the play.

Cinthio made most use of the chorus in his first tragedy, *Orbecche.* In this play, the chorus takes part in the dialogue toward

---

[9] See *Discorsi,* pp. 229–231.

the close of Act 3, and Act 4 is virtually an extended *commos,* wherein a messenger and a member of the chorus lament together. A semi-chorus appears in the second scene of Act 5, the only instance of such a chorus in Cinthio. The semi-chorus was seldom used in Italian tragedy.[10]

In *Altile,* another early play, the chorus is almost as prominent as it is in *Orbecche* and a good part of its fourth act is also a *commos. Didone* has three *commoi,* but here the chorus does not take so prominent a part as in the two earlier tragedies. The chorus participates in the dialogue of three scenes in *Epitia,* and one of these scenes (3.4) is a *commos.* The *coro mobile* appears only briefly in *Cleopatra, Euphimia,* and *Selene,* and not at all in the *Antivalomeni* and *Arrenopia.* The *coro stabile,* the fixed chorus, which was not actually a fixed chorus in Cinthio, closes each act in all nine tragedies. In all save one play, *Arrenopia,* the choruses are made up of women sympathetic with the heroine. In *Arrenopia,* however, the chorus consists of Irishmen from Limerick, probably because the heroine is disguised as a man until almost the very end.

THE PROPER NUMBER OF ACTORS

In his Apology for *Didone,*[11] Cinthio remarked that he had been censured for using too many speaking roles. Here again he parted company with the Grecians, who had imitated ancient Greek tragedy, which limited the speaking parts to three, that is, three speakers in one scene. Cinthio used twenty speaking parts in *Didone,* but there are never this many engaged at one time. All of his tragedies have fairly large casts, running from a dozen speaking characters to twice as many.

Cinthio justified this departure from classical practice by maintaining that the larger number of tragic characters increased the "regal majesty of the action . . . specially when kings of various nations appear with their courts." "I know," he said, "that in the time of the most illustrious lord your father, your Excellency [Ercole II] saw how unhappily that comedy turned out which was represented with only five interlocutors, and with what tedium (although the argument was pleasing) it was carried out to the

---

[10] Marguerite Little, in an unpublished doctoral dissertation, "Some Italian Elements in the Choral Practice of *Samson Agonistes*" (University of Illinois, 1946), discusses the semi-chorus.

[11] Pp. 148–149.

end, for the spectators were bored by seeing and hearing the same
persons all the time."

THE USE OF MESSENGERS

It must not be supposed that Cinthio changed all the practices
of the ancient Greeks and the Italian Grecians, for he retained
many ancient devices more or less intact, when they suited his purpose. He believed, for example, that the messenger who reports
death and suffering was one of the most important characters in
tragedy. In the role of the messenger there arise "all the horror
and compassion which are the pith of the plot, and it ought to be
made great with every kind of speech that is fitting."[12] Cinthio's
model here was principally Seneca, whose messengers often have
the finest speeches in the tragedy, that is, the speeches best calculated to arouse pity and horror. "Hence he [the messenger], as
though smitten with fury, cannot help uttering great words full of
the horror he has in his mind, and he ought to amplify in narration the wretched and horrible mishap by showing the actions, the
wailings, the words, the cruelty, the desperation, the manner in
which the wretched victim fell."[13]

Cinthio believed that the messenger in the performance of his
Orbecche succeeded in doing all that a messenger in tragedy
should do: "It seems to me that I still feel the earth tremble under
foot, as it seemed to tremble then, when he [the actor] represented
the messenger with so much horror that seemingly he incited the
mind of every spectator to horror and compassion and they all
remained amazed."[14]

SOLILOQUIES

Any poet who favors extensive use of messengers can hardly
object to the soliloquy, and Cinthio used soliloquies freely. In keeping with his theory that tragedy should be majestic, aloof from the
vulgarities of common life, he contended that no actor save the
prologue, who was not involved in the plot, should ever address
the audience directly, for contact with the audience would destroy

---

[12] *Discorsi,* p. 265.
[13] *Discorsi,* p. 265.
[14] *Discorsi,* p. 279.

the verisimilitude of the play. The actor should speak to himself "as if there were no spectators."[15]

It seems paradoxical at first sight, but Cinthio apparently wanted his tragedies to be regal and majestic and at the same time natural in the sense that the actors should behave as though they were at home in the privacy of familiar surroundings. Cinthio's style was often highly rhetorical, but he apparently did not want his actors to be oratorical. He anticipated the techniques developed by the picture-frame stage of naturalistic drama and yet he believed in the soliloquy and made extensive use of it.

DEATH SCENES

Since Cinthio assigned so much importance to the messenger's report of death and suffering, one might expect that he would favor the Greek custom and Horace's recommendation of keeping all death scenes offstage. Not so, however, for the heroine in *Orbecche* kills herself onstage and the author justified the deed by ancient authority. "It is not so remarkable," says Tragedy, "that I should depart from the laws of the Venusine [Horace] and wish that her strong hand should dispense her own death with cold steel in view of the audience,"[16] because Aristotle allows deaths onstage. It is true that "murders on the stage," along with tortures, woundings, etc., are mentioned in *Poetics* 11; but Cinthio was probably following the practice of Seneca, who more than once showed violent death on the stage. Cinthio believed that elaborate, highly colored reports of death scenes were very effective in tragedy but he was not averse to showing death onstage as well.

THE ROLE OF SPECTACLE

Aristotle regarded spectacle, that is, scenery and costumes, as the least artistic quality of tragedy. Cinthio professed to agree with Aristotle that the *apparato* does not belong to the art of the poet, but he regarded a magnificent scene as essential to complete success in the actual performance of a tragedy, and he strove to have his own productions well mounted and richly costumed. He believed that costumes were an important part of the scene, especially

---

[15] *Discorsi*, p. 280.
[16] *Orbecche* (1583), p. 132.

the dress of characters from distant lands. He knew that his spectators delighted in exotic costumes and this awareness of public taste may have dictated, at least in part, his own choice of exotic locales for his plays. *Didone* and *Cleopatra* are laid in Carthage and Alexandria, conventional locales for Roman tragedies; but most of the other tragedies are laid in places far from Italy. The scene of *Orbecche* is Susa in Perisa. *Altile* is laid in Damascus, the *Antivalomeni* in London, *Arrenopia* in Limerick, *Euphimia* in Corinth, and *Epitia* in Innsbruck. The prologue to *Altile* proclaimed: "Behold, spectators, behold the royal chambers, the proud and lofty palaces of those rulers whom you will see appear today to give you high delight."

DEUS EX MACHINA

Aristotle frowned upon the use of any mechanism outside the plot for resolving a tragic action. Horace condemned the use of a *deus ex machina* unless the untying of the knot of complications was worthy of a god's hand. Cinthio pointed out that while Horace did condemn the intervention of a god Aristotle was not opposed to the introduction of gods on the stage except in the resolution of the plot.[17]

Cinthio himself used gods, goddesses, and supernatural agents in four of his nine tragedies: Nemesis, Furies, and a ghost in *Orbecche;* Venus in *Altile;* Juno, Venus, Cupid, Mercury, and Fame in *Didone;* Juno in *Euphimia.* He was careful, however, to avoid any use of supernatural agents in the final solution of the plot except in *Altile,* wherein Venus does have a hand in the resolution. He was a devout believer in verisimilitude and his theory of drama was essentially realistic. Moreover, as he developed his tragedy with a happy ending, which was actually tragicomedy, he made less and less use of supernatural machinery.

THE RIGHT STYLE FOR TRAGEDY

Cinthio had much to say about the style of both tragedy and comedy. He accepted the traditional prescription of a lofty style for tragedy and the impropriety of introducing any vulgar or comic speech into tragic dialogue. Moreover, he accepted intact the pattern of tragic diction set by Trissino, namely, rhyme for the cho-

---

[17] Apology for *Didone*, p. 138.

ruses and occasionally for the "moral and passionate parts"[18] of the dialogue, unrhymed verse for most of the dialogue. He believed that verse, unrhymed or ryhmed, was the only medium proper to drama, both tragedy and comedy. Italian playwrights had been using prose for comedy; but Cinthio disapproved.

Although Cinthio welcomed any device to heighten the majesty of tragic representations and regarded a lofty style as normal for tragedy, his eagerness to make his plays stageworthy and his worship of verisimilitude actually led him to tone down much of his dialogue to a more familiar, conversational pitch. Moreover, he condemned bombast and excessive ornament in dialogue. He was especially concerned with the danger of preciosity in speech, such as, "Thus the billows of my conceits, issuing from the fountain of my heart and entering the sea of your profound virtue, lose their straight course in the waves of your praises."[19] This "Spanish" mode of speaking, he maintained, had corrupted Italians, and it should be avoided, for the meaning should always come first. He knew that Aristotle, in both the *Poetics* and *Rhetoric*, had insisted upon clarity as the essential quality of any good style. Cinthio's own tragic style became simpler as he turned from affairs of state to domestic situations, as he turned from tragedy with an unhappy ending to tragedy with a happy ending.

THE FUNCTION OF TRAGEDY

The proper function of tragedy was of concern to Cinthio, as it was to all Renaissance critics, and he went through the usual procedure necessary to reconcile Aristotle's tragic *catharsis* with the "teach and delight" of Horace. Moreover, he accepted "admiration" or the "marvelous" that Robortello, Minturno, and other Italian scholars had added to the pity and fear of the tragic function. The laments of tragedy, said Cinthio, "ought to induce wonder [*maraviglia*], pity, and horror."[20] Cinthio was both an Aristotelian and a Horatian, but he emphasized the didactic function, which is present in Aristotle only by implication. Cinthio honestly believed, apparently, that tragedy was a powerful instrument for inculcating good morals; he believed with Trissino and other contemporaries

[18] *Discorsi*, p. 234.
[19] *Discorsi*, p. 270.
[20] *Discorsi*, p. 283.

that the function of tragedy, and indeed of all good poetry, was to induce the reader or spectator to flee vice and follow virtue.[21] The prologue to *Cleopatra* stated his position accurately: "[Tragedy] imitates royal actions with that gravity, with that decorum, whence pity and horror arise, purging mortal minds of vice and making them desire only virtue."

The whole tragedy of *Cleopatra*, according to the prologue, was designed to teach a valuable lesson in the behavior of human beings in general, of rulers in particular: "Here, spectators, you will see how empires and treasures and other human endowments are of little use when pleasure prevails over virtue, pleasure that draws man out of himself. Delights and pleasures that are outside the common rule of reason wage greater war on empires than do many squadrons of armed enemies. He only reigns long who takes the light of reason for his guide. He who knows how to command himself knows how to rule." The moral here probably owed something to Seneca, whose good characters repeatedly warn rulers of the consequences of violent, irrational behavior. In the *Troades* (358–359), Agamemnon says to Pyrrhus, "No one rules long by unrestrained force; temperance endures." In the *Hercules Furens* (739–743), Theseus says: "He who rules temperately, though lord of life, keeps blameless hands; he who respects reason and rules his realm mildly and without bloodshed shall measure long stretches of happy life." Seneca (the character) in *Octavia* (471–491) points to Augustus as the model ruler, whose virtuous and long reign was finally rewarded by elevation to divinity. Seneca's good characters are no less emphatic in their condemnation of idle pleasure and lust, which inevitably lead to ruin. Notorius examples of people who paid with their lives for unrestrained lust are Phaedra in *Hippolytus* and Agrippina in *Octavia*.[22]

TRAGIC CHARACTERS

Cinthio's theory and use of characters in tragedy were fairly conventional save for the frequent introduction of young unmarried women on the stage. He agreed with most critics of the Renaissance that tragic characters should be noble, better still, royal. He accepted Aristotle's recommendation that the best tragic character

---

[21] See *Discorsi*, p. 285.
[22] See *Hippolytus* 177 ff.; *Octavia* 137 ff., 257 ff.

should be a man neither all good nor all bad, a man like Oedipus, who sinned but was ignorant of having sinned. Spectators, argued Cinthio, believe that Oedipus suffers too much for his errors and consequently feel both pity and fear for him. Decorum, that is, the preservation of correct behavior and speech in dignified characters, should always rule.

Cinthio's innovation, or what he believed to be an innovation, was the free use of young maidens on the tragic stage. The theory behind this move was suggested by Roman comedy, which always played a part in his theory and practice of tragedy. His argument[23] may be summarized as follows.

Terence, said Cinthio, was more careful than Plautus in keeping honest young women offstage lest they come in contact with pimps, courtesans, and parasites who take part in ignoble actions and use lascivious speech. There is no indecorum, however, in introducing a "royal virgin" on the tragic stage, where most of the characters are noble and the speech is sublime even when it is about love.

Comedy does not exhibit the loves of great ladies like Phaedra and Clytemnestra (who are nevertheless evil). Such evil loves suit tragedy, not because these women arouse pity and fear for their own plight, but because their evil actions make their victims suffer and so arouse pity and fear for the victims. Nevertheless, it is proper to introduce the honest loves of honest maidens in tragedy, certainly in tragedy with a happy ending, if the royal maiden does not talk about her passion to her lover or to a go-between, but laments to herself as though she were in the privacy of her own room. Therefore Cinthio ventured to introduce such amorous maidens in his *Antivalomeni* ("Changelings").

According to Berthé,[24] Cinthio practiced *le culte de l'âme feminine* more than did Boccaccio and as much or more than did any of his contemporaries. The principal characters in his tragedies are always women; women gave the title to every one of his tragedies save the *Antivalomeni,* and the best characters in the last named are women. We have seen that women had dominant roles in Italian tragedy before Cinthio, in Trissino's *Sofonisba,* Rucellai's *Rosmunda,* Pazzi's *Dido,* and Martelli's *Tullia,* but Cinthio was apparently more conscious of emphasizing the role of woman. In

---

[23] *Discorsi,* pp. 271–276.
[24] *J. B. Giraldi,* p. 128.

part at least, he was glorifying the Renaissance ladies that he met at the court of Ferrara.

Women were often important in ancient Greek tragedies, and in Seneca's tragedies, to be sure—Medea, Antigone, Phaedra, Iphigenia, Hecuba—but Aristotle had remarked in *Poetics* 15 that "it is not appropriate in a female character to be manly or clever." Again Cinthio ventured to depart from Aristotle in the interests of Italian verisimilitude. It is true that the great ladies of Ferrara enjoyed virtually the same social, moral, and intellectual station that men occupied. Consequently it was no indecorum in Cinthio's *novelle* and plays for a great lady to be manly in the sense that she be highly intelligent and even brave and chivalrous, well trained in arms and horsemanship. Arrenopia, for example, and Philene (in the *Antivalomeni*) could assume the disguise of a knight and carry it off as well as could most gentlemen. It was not inappropriate for a Renaissance countess or princess to be clever, and some of Cinthio's ladies were more than clever, for they were as wise, resolute, and resourceful as the best of men.

The dedicatory epistles written by Cinthio's son, Celso Giraldi, for the 1583 edition of the tragedies were not altogether conventional courtly eulogies; with some reason Celso maintained that his father consciously patterned his heroines upon the ladies of the ducal court. Tragedy, who addresses the reader of *Orbecche*, suggests that the feminine characters in this play owed much to a living model:

Nor should it appear strange to you that the ladies I have in my company are wiser than some deem proper for them, because in addition to the light which a woman, like a man, has from reason, the great wisdom that resides in that sublime and remarkable lady, whose high and royal name I keep secret within me with the highest reverence and the highest honor, can make evident to every honest judgment not only how much worth a gentle woman can have in herself, but that in prudence and in discretion (if the envy of others be banished) she can match any wise man in the world.[25]

HISTORICAL PLOT *vs.* FICTITIOUS PLOT

The most significant change that Cinthio made in the pattern of tragedy that Trissino had left him was in promoting a feigned argument in place of a historical argument. The Greeks had almost

---

[25] *Orbecche*, pp. 131–132.

always found their tragic stories in history or in quasi-historical legend and myth. So had Seneca. So had the early Italian writers of tragedy. The traditional prescription for tragedy that had come down to the Renaissance from Horace and from the grammarian Donatus was that while comedy was based on a fiction tragedy was usually based on history.

Cinthio was perfectly acquainted with this traditional prescription:

And although the plot may be common to both comedy and tragedy, some nevertheless wish that the plot of tragedy be taken from history and the plot of comedy feigned by the poet. . . . I hold, however, that the tragic plot, like the comic, can be feigned by the poet; moreover, that Aristotle, as judicious in this matter as in any other, grants it in more than one place in the *Poetics*, and after him Comulo [Donatus?] among the Latins, saying that the plot of comedy is feigned and tragedy is often taken from history, shows that it is not always necessary to take it from history.[26]

It was Aristotle who gave Cinthio the principal classical authority for using a feigned plot in tragedy. In *Poetics* 9 Aristotle does remark that as comedy developed, its authors abandoned the method of the old iambic lampooners, namely, imitating the actions of particular persons, and began to invent their plots and characters. Tragic poets, he says, continued to use history, but sometimes invented characters, and "there are some [tragedies] without a single known name, e.g. Agathon's *Antheus*, in which both incidents and names are of the poet's invention; and it is no less delightful on that account."

Certainly Aristotle did not condemn the feigned plot in tragedy, but he implied that the normal and approved procedure among the ancient Greeks was to take tragic arguments from the traditional stories, because historical events are regarded as possible and the possible is convincing.

In two of his Italian tragedies, namely *Didone* and *Cleopatra*, Cinthio followed the traditional practice. For the other tragedies, all seven of them, he used feigned arguments, actually arguments from the *novelle* in his own *Hecatommithi*.[27] He eagerly seized the loophole that Aristotle had left for the feigned plot in tragedy.

---

[26] *Discorsi*, pp. 208–209.

[27] *Orbecche* was based on *Hecatommithi* 2.2, *Altile* on 2.3, *Selene* on 5.1, the *Antivalomeni* on 2.9, *Arrenopia* on 3.1, *Epitia* on 8.5, *Euphimia* on 8.10.

In discussing the difference between ancient and Italian heroic poetry he remarked that Boiardo and Ariosto feigned their plots while Homer and Virgil based theirs on history. As for tragedy: "Aristotle, in his *Poetics,* speaking of tragedy, which is very like heroic compositions inasmuch as it imitates illustrious actions, and giving the example of Agathon's *Flower,* points out that feigned plots are more pleasing since they are not known."[28]

Cinthio's interpretation of *Poetics* 9 is pretty free; his changing of Aristotle's phrase "no less delightful" to "more pleasing" is hardly justified. Such a change, however, suited his purpose, for he believed that his own feigned plots were more pleasing to his audience than were the shopworn stories from history. Apparently *Orbecche* was more successful than were *Didone* and *Cleopatra.* Therefore he modified the traditional theory of tragedy and contended that the feigned plot was not only equal but superior to the historical plot. He assembled a variety of proofs and illustrations to support his contention, as will be shown in the next section.

TRAGEDY WITH AN UNHAPPY ENDING *vs.* TRAGEDY WITH A HAPPY ENDING

Cinthio's defense of the feigned plot was closely involved with his promotion of tragedy with a happy ending. Here again he ran into Aristotle and here again he sidestepped Aristotle's recommendations.

In *Poetics* 13, Aristotle recognized the existence and the popularity of tragedy with a double ending, like that of Homer's *Odyssey,* "an opposite issue for the good and the bad personages." While admitting that audiences preferred such an ending, with its reward of virtue and punishment of evil, he nevertheless condemned such plots as artistically inferior to the plot with a single tragic outcome because the pleasure of the double outcome is not that of tragedy but belongs more properly to comedy, "where the bitterest enemies of the piece [e.g. Orestes and Aegisthus] walk off good friends at the end, with no slaying of anyone by anyone."

Cinthio faced the problem squarely, but found a way around it in his belief that the tragic plot should have much in common with the comic plot and that the writer of tragedy could, and should, emulate the artistry of Terence:

---

[28] *Discorsi,* p. 12.

Even if double tragedies [*tragedie doppie*] are little praised by Aristotle (albeit some think otherwise), double plot is nevertheless very praiseworthy in comedy, and has made the plays of Terence succeed marvelously. I call that plot double which has in its action diverse kinds of persons of the same social class, as two lovers of different sagacities, two old men of different temperaments, two servants of opposite manners, and other such characters, as may be seen in the *Andria* and in other plays by the same poet, where it is clear that these similar persons of dissimilar manners give the greatest comeliness to the knotting and untying of the plot. And I believe that if this be well imitated by the good poet in tragedy also, and the knot so made that the untying does not create confusion, it will succeed no less acceptably than it does in comedy, always saving the reverence due to Aristotle. If there have been some who have favored this faction and have held another opinion than that of Aristotle, they are not to be blamed, in my estimation, especially if the tragedy has a happy ending which conforms closely to the ending of comedy and therefore can be similar to comedy in its imitation of the action.[29]

Cinthio agreed with Aristotle that the complex plot, with its startling discoveries and reversals of fortune, is far superior to the simple plot, and believed that since tragedy with a happy ending is more likely to be complex because of its double plot it may well be better than tragedy with an unhappy ending: "Such tragedies prefer intricate knots and when double are more praiseworthy than those that end unhappily, for the latter are much better single [*semplice*] than double."[30]

Cinthio agreed with Aristotle that a tragedy should always arouse pity and fear. (He actually preferred "horror" or "terror" to "fear.") Aristotle rated tragedy with a single unhappy outcome over tragedy that rewards the virtuous and punishes the wicked because the former better arouses pity and fear. Cinthio maintained, however, that pity and terror are not wanting in a good tragedy with a happy ending, which is the "more pleasing to the spectators for ending in gladness."[31] Moreover, Cinthio was not satisfied with Aristotle's argument that the popular audience prefers a happy ending to a tragic one because of human weakness. At all events, the audience was the final arbiter for Cinthio, and he believed that his own *tragedie di lieto fin* were successful.

Continuing his defense of tragedy with a happy ending, Cinthio

---

[29] *Discorsi*, pp. 214–215.
[30] *Discorsi*, p. 224.
[31] *Discorsi*, p. 220.

said, "In this kind of tragedy, the disclosure [*cognitione*] or, as I wish to call it, the recognition [*agnitione*] of persons has a special place, for by this recognition those who aroused horror and compassion are snatched from perils and from death." In other words, there may be just as much pity and terror in a plot that ends happily as in one that ends unhappily. The test of tragedy is the presence of these tragic emotions and not necessarily the ultimate death of hero or heroine. In both kinds of tragedy there should be tears, misery, suffering, and there may be death. Tragedy with an unhappy ending may arouse more terror than does one with a happy outcome, but the latter may arouse more pity. Cinthio went so far as to suggest that terrible tragedies were better calculated for closet dramas than for the stage, where plays with a happy ending always please the spectators. "Nevertheless," he said, "the events in these less terrible plays ought to arise in such a way that the spectators are suspended between horror and compassion until the end, which leaves everyone consoled after a happy resolution. And this holding of the spectator in suspense ought to be so managed by the poet that one does not always stand in the dark, but the action ought to go on unraveling the plot bit by bit so that the spectator sees himself guided to the end but remains doubtful that it can succeed."[32]

The last quotation above may be called Cinthio's prescription for a stageworthy play, either tragedy or comedy, and he tried, often with indifferent success, to follow it. It is a pretty good prescription, nevertheless, for a successful play, and it must have exerted a considerable influence in the Italian theater, and in other theaters of western Europe as well.

So far as I know, Cinthio never used the term "poetic justice," but he became a zealous advocate and practitioner of plays that rewarded virtue and punished vice. He soon gave up "terrible tragedies" like *Orbecche* and turned his hand to *tragedie di lieto fin* or, as he sometimes called them, *tragedie miste* (mixed tragedies). He did so in the face of Aristotelian disapproval and in defiance of Seneca's practice. Seneca, it may be recalled, was his principal classical model, favored by him over Sophocles and Euripides.

Cinthio freely admitted that Seneca never used a happy ending in his tragedies. "Nevertheless," he said,

---

[32] *Discorsi*, p. 221.

I have composed some in this pattern, such as *Altile, Selene,* the *Antivalomeni,* and others, only to serve the spectators and to make the plays succeed better on the stage, and to conform to the fashion of our times. Although Aristotle may say that this is to serve the ignorance of the spectators and the other faction has its defenders, I have held that it is better to satisfy him who has to listen with something less excellent (if Aristotle's opinion be accepted as better) than to displease those for whose pleasure the play is brought on the stage with a little more grandeur; because it would bring little enjoyment to compose a play a little more praiseworthy and then have it irksome when acted.[33]

The audience was always the supreme arbiter for Cinthio, higher than Sencea, higher than Aristotle.

The capricious cruelty of fate was a factor in ancient Greek tragedy and even more important in Senecan tragedy, wherein the phrase "cruel fates" was virtually a motto. Cinthio managed to circumvent the cruel fates, at least in his *tragedie di lieto fin,* by showing that the goddess Fortune might work both ways; she could suddenly raise up as well as suddenly cast down. The prologue to *Epitia* argued that the "mutability of Fortune makes the human state so doubtful and so uncertain that often those matters that seem secure arrive at the place where despair rules everything, and, on the contrary, those matters in which there lay no hope arrive in the end at the place where he who was sad becomes joyful."

In medieval times, before the revival of the ancient theater, the fall of princes was the traditional subject matter for tragedies in narrative form. In the Renaissance, royalty was generally accepted as the most fitting state for tragedy, and Cinthio agreed. He maintained, however, that princes do not always fall, that royal characters do not have to come to grief. "Royal plots," said the prologue to *Arrenopia,* "are not so condemned to tears and vexations that the griefs and burdensome miseries cannot have a merry and happy ending, turning grief into joy." In this particular tragedy with a happy ending the author put his main emphasis upon jealously, which was a prominent passion in serious comedy as well as in tragedy and tragicomedy.[34]

Finally, Cinthio justified his preference for the happy ending in tragedy on moral grounds as well as on its appeal to the public.

---

[33] *Discorsi,* pp. 220–221.
[34] Della Porta, one of the leading writers of serious comedy, made much of jealousy. See my *Italian Comedy in the Renaissance* (Urbana, Ill., 1960), pp. 200–201.

He believed that an exhibition of virtue rewarded and vice punished was instructive as well as delightful. The prologue to
Euphimia promised a wholesome lesson: "A noble queen, married
to a cruel husband, has suffered rough usage and torments from
him but has never slackened in the love she bore him. Constant
and firm, like a rock fronting the waves, she has withstood the fury,
the rages, the vexations of this evil man. Here, at the end, she will
have reward for her trust, and the ungrateful man punishment for
his misdeeds." God does reward the virtuous, as the final chorus of
Arrenopia proclaims: "Divine justice comes no less to the innocent,
and if sometimes the gentle soul falls into affliction, it ought always
to hope that God, with joyful and fortunate moderation, will change
irksome pains to benefits, that no cruel chance can prevail against
the Ruler of the Celestial Court."

THE DRAMATIC UNITIES

Without actually calling them such, the sixteenth-century Italians
formulated and put into practice the dramatic unities of action,
time, and place. A rather belligerent champion of "new" comedy
and "new" tragedy, Cinthio nevertheless accepted the classical
structure and the Aristotelian doctrines that enjoined the three
unities.

Although Cinthio defended the multiple actions in the Italian
romances, for example in Ariosto's *Orlando furioso*, and contended
that a double plot was right for tragedy as well as for comedy,
he never questioned the merit of a unified whole in poetry. In other
words, he took unity of action for granted, although he believed
that classical unity was not the only kind. The best kind of unity
of action, he believed, was that achieved by the "skill" *(ingegno)*
of the poet in a highly involved plot which had an ingenious resolution. His admiration for an intricate plot led him to call the *Andria*
of Terence the best of all ancient comedies and to place Ariosto's
dramatic masterpiece, *La Lena*, below the *Cassaria*, which is by
no means so good a play. The latter, in Cinthio's opinion, was the
"most comely and the most artful" of Ariosto's comedies; the *Lena*
was inferior because it has a "single argument where the *Cassaria*
is double."[35] His admiration for an intricate plot led him to praise
the *Oedipus Rex* of Sophocles, to increase the number of actors

---

[35] *Discorsi*, pp. 213–214.

in Italian tragedy, and to introduce secondary or parallel love affairs in his own *Antivalomeni* and *Epitia*.

Spingarn[36] has asserted that the first reference to the unity of time in modern literature is in Cinthio's *Discorsi* (pp. 205–206), where the author says that a good playwright "feigns the passage of time in his action as the length of one day or a little more." If dates of publication are considered, however, Cinthio must yield precedence to Francesco Robortello and to Bernardo Segni. In 1548, Robortello's comment on Aristotle's phrase "within a single circuit of the sun" *(Poetics* 5) argued that an artificial day of twelve hours is meant.[37] Segni, whose Italian translation of the *Poetics* was printed in 1549, differed with Robortello, arguing that a natural day of twenty-four hours is meant.[38]

It is not clear how many hours were in Cinthio's "one day or a little more"; but he took great pains in his own plays to compress the action within the limits of hours rather than days. Sometimes, as in *Arrenopia*, this drastic condensation of time forced him to use more narrative cutbacks than seem advisable for good theater. But Cinthio liked messengers and since he was determined to preserve a strict economy of time he made such characters bear the burden of extensive exposition and narration.

The unity of place was not formulated until Castelvetro did so in his commentary on Aristotle's *Poetics*, first published in 1571.[39] While the neoclassical Italian playwrights nearly always tried to preserve economy of action and time, they were not so much concerned with unity of place. They had observed that the setting of ancient Roman comedy was invariably a street and that the setting of ancient Greek and Roman tragedy was usually a place before the entrance to a palace, but even the Grecians did not solve the problem of reducing the setting of an Italian tragedy to a single scene.

Cinthio was not exceptional among the Italian tragedians; he sought unity of action and narrow limits of time in his tragedies but paid no attention to limiting the scene, at least in the printed versions, beyond such directions as "the scene is in Susa, royal city

---

[36] *A History of Literary Criticism in the Renaissance* (New York, 1924), p. 91.
[37] *In librum de arte poetica explicationes* (Florence, 1548), pp. 49–50.
[38] *Rettorica e poetica d'Aristotile tradotte di Greco in lingua vulgare fiorentina* (Florence, 1549), p. 290.
[39] See *Poetica d'Aristotile vulgarizzata, et sposta* (Basel, 1576), pp. 534–537.

of Persia" and "the scene is in Damascus, royal city of Syria." The locale of *Arrenopia,* for example, is "Limerick, noble city of Ireland"; but it is hard to believe that all the forty-two scenes in this play, ranging as they do from domestic household to military camp, were confined to one place. Cinthio liked sumptuous settings for his tragedies; but I cannot determine just what these were or whether they were single or multiple. Apparently it remained for the French, in the next century, to establish a strict unity of place, that is, a single setting, one room or one courtyard.

Cinthio was a Modern and not an Ancient; he believed that modern poets should be free to develop a new poetry which would naturally be different in many ways from the poetry of ancient Greece and Rome. His modernity is best seen in his defense of the Italian *romanzi*[40] that Minturno and others compared unfavorably with Homeric and Virgilian epic poems, basing their judgments on Aristotelian doctrines as well as on comparisons with the ancient models. Cinthio was also a Modern in his theory and practice of tragedy, but here he was willing to concede more to the Ancients than he was in his discussion of the Italian romances. He never liked to oppose Aristotle and Horace, Sophocles and Seneca, and he always tried to reconcile his own theory and practice with these ancient critics and models. Nevertheless, as I hope I have shown, he was always willing to sacrifice the support of the Ancients if ancient poetry and criticism did not fit the taste of the contemporary Italian audience.[41]

---

[40] See *Discorsi,* pp. 1–198.
[41] P. R. Horne's valuable study, *The Tragedies of Giambattista Cinthio Giraldi* (Oxford, 1962), came to my attention too late for me to make proper use of it. I have not found any serious disagreement between his interpretation and mine.

V

Giraldi Cinthio's Practice

ORBECCHE

In 1541 Cinthio staged a dramatization of one of his own *novelle* (*Hecatommithi* 2.2) at his own house in Ferrara. His patron Ercole II was in the audience. Apparently acting, scenery, and music were all good and the performance was a success. It was so successful, in fact, that an encore was called for and printing of the play followed in 1543, in Venice. From 1543 to 1594 there were no less than nine printings of *Orbecche*.

The ducal court of Ferrara had been enjoying comedies for half a century when Cinthio's first venture into tragedy appeared. His prologue called attention to the differences the audience would find between this play and the comedies they were accustomed to. There would be no crafty tricks played on old misers in *Orbecche*, no ready wit to raise laughter, no amorous embraces of young lovers, but "tears, sighs, anxieties, troubles, and cruel deaths." These lamentable sights and sounds, however, would be somewhat softened since they would not take place in happy Ferrara but in the far-off city of Susa in Persia. The first act could hardly have proceeded very far before the learned members of the audience recognized imitation of Seneca, particularly imitation of the *Thyestes*.

The first scene of *Orbecche* introduces the goddess Nemesis, who

discourses on the divine retribution that inevitably comes to the
wicked, and to the good as well when they fall into error. Sometimes, says Nemesis, it is difficult to understand the workings of
divine justice: "O silly people, you who scarcely see what is before
your eyes, do you wish to pass judgment on almighty God? O
mad presumption! Nothing proceeds without infinite order." Now
an evil tyrant is going to find out that he cannot escape retribution,
for the Furies are ascending from the dark abyss.

The Furies enter and report to Nemesis, who orders them to
punish Sulmone, King of Persia, and his wicked court, to see to
it that Sulmone and his daughter Orbecche suffer pain and death.
The Furies promise to obey.

> Assai fatt' è; veloci omai tornate
> A le case di Dite, ai regni oscuri,
> E accelerate il passo, che l'aspetto
> Vostro non può soffrir terra, nè cielo.
> Ecco che 'l Sol si oscura, e da ogni parte
> Fuggono da la terra erbette e fiori,
> E lasciano le frondi, e i frutti i rami,
> E tutto 'l mondo vien pallido e nero.

That is enough. Now return quickly to the halls of Dis, to the dark realms,
and quicken your pace, because neither earth nor sky can tolerate your
presence. Behold, the sun is darkened, and on every side plants and flowers shun the earth, blossoms and fruits drop from the boughs, and all the
world becomes wan and black.

This speech contains echoes of a chorus in *Thyestes* (789 ff.), and
the whole scene sets the dark tone of the play about to unfold.
The appearance of a ghost in the next scene further emphasizes
the parallel with the first act of Seneca's tragedy, wherein the ghost
of Tantalus, goaded by a Fury, warns of the horrors about to be-
fall the house of Atreus.

The ghost of Selina, bearing a torch, rises from Tartarus, spurred
by desire for revenge. (Years before, her young daughter Orbecche
had innocently informed her father that the queen was sleeping
with her first-born, a son. Sulmone had killed both mother and
child.) Now the queen's ghost predicts that when Sulmone, his
daughter, his son-in-law, and his grandchildren arrive in hell
the terrible sufferings of Tantalus, Ixion, and Sisyphus "will seem
to them a pleasure and a toy." She knows what is going to happen
and as she leaves she says, "At least I carry this satisfaction with
me, that before the sun plunges today into the waves they will

also come to the Tartarean shore to endure with me eternal torment." This speech also promises that the author of the play will preserve a strict economy of time.

The chorus of Persian women closes the first act with a rhymed ode to Venus, the goddess who first brought love and hope into the world.

The mortal characters are introduced in the second act, which continues the exposition. Cinthio had not yet worked out his adaptation of *prologue, protasis, epitasis,* and *catastrophe* from Terentian comedy, for the first act of *Orbecche* is very like the prologue of Grecian tragedy, but he was probably thinking about it by now. He was already using the detached prologue borrowed from Roman comedy and he had already curtailed the role of the chorus.

The heroine Orbecche opens the second act lamenting to herself and to her nurse. "Alas, how brief are our own pleasures! Tears always dwell next to laughter!" When urged by the nurse to give the cause of her grief, the princess explains that only yesterday her father had ordered her to marry the king of Parthia. As the nurse knows, Orbecche has been secretly married to Oronte for four years and has two children. The nurse tries to comfort her with assurances that some remedy will be found. After philosophizing at some length on the inconstancy of human affairs, the nurse meets Oronte and bids him join his wife, who is anxious to speak with him.

Oronte first appears in 2.3, wherein Orbecche tells him the alarming news of the king's decision. Oronte has a sanguine nature and feels sure that they can win over the king, but Orbecche knows better; she knows her father's cruel nature and she reminds her husband of the fate that befell the late queen. Oronte remains hopeful, however, that the king may have outgrown his wrathful temperament and he suggests that they enlist the aid of Malecche, the royal counselor and an honest man.

After Oronte leaves, Orbecche delivers her first soliloquy. "I tremble," she says, "like the duck who sees the fierce hawk hovering to devour her." She knows that her father will never accept a poor man like Oronte for a son-in-law. "The world values nothing but gold. Virtue herself goes poor and naked. Alas, the foolish judgment of the erring multitude! Alas, the grievous error that dims mortal eyes!" And there is nothing she can do about it. What could any woman do? "Whereas every animal on earth, no matter how ignoble, is born free (a gift that ought to be prized more than life), we, alas, we are born to chains, to shackles, ah me, to ever-enduring servitude" (2.4).

The chorus closes the second act with a gloomy ode. It begins with a classical simile that owes as much, perhaps, to Sophocles as to Seneca.

> Come corrente rio sempre discorre,
> E non è mai una medesma l'onda,
> Ma fuggendo la prima, la seconda
> Succede, e un' altra a questa;
> Così il viver mortal nostro trascorre,
> E non siamo oggi quelli,
> Ch' jeri eravamo, e presta
> Più che saetta, da nascosto viene
> La debole vecchiezza e in bianchi velli
> Accompagnata da dolenti pene.

As a running stream flows and no wave is ever the same, the first one hastening, the second following, and another after this; so our mortal life runs, and we are not today what we were yesterday, and swifter than an arrow, and secretly, feeble old age in its white fleece comes, accompanied by wretched afflictions.

The *epitasis* (complication) begins with the third act, which is unusually long and largely devoted to a debate between counselor and king. This debate is reminiscent of Seneca, whose tragedies usually contain at least one such wrangle between a headstrong tyrant and a wise counselor. In this instance the very texts of Malecche's lecture to Sulmone were probably inspired by Seneca's famous essay on wrath, "the most hideous and frenzied of all the emotions." These two texts are: (1) anger is "closed to reason and counsel," (2) "virtue alone is lofty and sublime."[1] The good counselor's purpose in delivering his long lecture is to prevent the king's taking vengeance on his daughter and son-in-law while he is still enraged. Seneca's recommendation was "the best remedy for anger is delay."[2] When he delivers the soliloquy that opens Act 3, however, Malecche takes as gloomy a view of the future as does Orbecche, for he has little hope that the king will listen to reason. He steps aside as the king enters.

In the next scene (3.2), Sulmone appears in a great rage; he

---

[1] *De Ira* 1.1.2, 1.21.4.
[2] *De Ira* 2.29.1.

has just found out about his daughter's secret marriage. (A maid-servant has betrayed the secret.) Now he is studying a revenge proper to such heinous treachery. Malecche moves forward and the debate begins. The situation is very like that in Seneca's *Octavia*, wherein Seneca (the character) tries to restrain the blood-thirsty Nero, and very like that in *Thyestes*, wherein an attendant tries to restrain the bloodthirsty Atreus.

When Malecche advises Sulmone to show mercy, the king answers that he has no intention of swallowing such an affront. "Do you, Malecche, want me to see that white is black and that manifest evil turns me to good?" Malecche rises to eloquence: "To give pardon to him who deserves punishment, and even in anger (which is an enemy to prudence and also to counsel), to show discretion, a proper sense of value, piety, mercy, this indeed I do not esteem the work of an invincible king, but of a man who can be likened to God."[3]

Sulmone listens politely. Next Malecche argues that Oronte is no traitor since he has behaved like an honorable man in marrying Orbecche instead of betraying her. Moreover, if Oronte is not of noble birth he is nevertheless a virtuous man. Malecche believes that virtue alone is true nobility. He maintains that Orbecche also believes this, for she "preferred a man of low station but of royal soul to a king who had a great empire and the heart of a vulgar man."

Sulmone: Can I, peradventure, make an eagle out of a dove, or a fierce lion out of a mouse?
Malecche: Yes, Sire, you can if it pleases you.

Then the counselor appeals to the king's natural affection for his own blood, for his grandchildren as well as for his beloved daughter. Suumone grants the reasonableness and sincerity of his counselor. "But," he says, "if I then turn my heart to this injury I become wholly embittered, and especially against Oronte, who has wantonly done me such an injury." The king's attitude may owe something to the father in the story of Gismonda[4] as well as something to Seneca's Atreus.

Malecche then shifts to a political argument, pointing out that the Parthians have been Persia's enemies and will be her enemies

[3] Cf. Seneca's *Octavia* 471 ff.
[4] See above, p. 31.

again, that Oronte may be trusted to serve the kingdom well. At last Sulmone professes to be convinced; he hands Malecche a ring which he is to give to Oronte as a pledge that the son-in-law will be the king's successor. Furthermore, Sulmone asks that his daughter and grandchildren be summoned, for he intends to honor his whole family. The counselor is delighted at this unexpected success and hurries away to fetch Oronte.

The next scene (3.3) shows, of course, that the counselor's eloquence has been wasted on the king, who now reveals his true intentions in a soliloquy. "Does foolish Malecche in his dotage think that he can get around my mind with his speeches and tricks, that I ought not to show the traitor the import of this injury?" Like Atreus, Sulmone is determined to wash his hands in the blood of his betrayer, and in the blood of his offspring as well. Like Atreus, he resolves to inflict a punishment so cruel that it will be a lesson to all the world.

But what about Orbecche? Sulmone decides to spare his daughter's life. "If I kill her," he says, "it would put an end to her pain; because death to one who is wretched is not punishment but the end of punishment and anguish." No, his daughter shall live to see the corpses of her children and husband, and she will envy the dead. There is an echo here of the ghost's prophecy in the first act. Having made this terrible decision, the king feels much relieved, so that he easily dissembles his wrath when Orbecche and her husband return to the stage.

Malecche, Oronte, and Orbecche join Sulmone. The chorus also enters at this point, and the leader has a few lines in the scene. The two children are probably present, too, but there is no indication in the text that they are. Oronte is happy, as is the good counselor. Orbecche, however, is still troubled: "I fear the hook under the bait and the gall in the sweet." Both Oronte and Malecche try to reassure her, but she still trembles with anxious foreboding.

Sulmone receives the three graciously and tells them that he has forgiven any injury. The leader of the chorus interjects a few congratulatory rhymes. The king asks Oronte and his two sons to accompany Tamule and Allocche into the palace, where all may partake of a feast and where the "victims for the altars" are to be sacrificed. Then the king, Orbecche, and Malecche leave the stage.

Oronte is left, with his sons, musing on the happy reversal of

his hardships. Allocche and Tamule, minions of the king, summon
Oronte inside. Tamule remarks in an aside, "See how man errs;
he thinks that he will be content and he goes to his death."

The nurse and the chorus unite in an ode celebrating the happy
turn of fortune for the princess. This ode is not in conventional
rhymes, but the last word in each line of the first six-line stanza
is repeated in the following five stanzas, though not in any regular
pattern. The last word in each stanza, except the last stanza, is
repeated at the end of the first line of the following stanza, form-
ing a link between stanzas.

The fourth act is short. It is essentially a *commos* in which a
messenger and the chorus join in lamentations for horrible deeds
done within the palace. The whole act is an adaptation of the
fourth act of Seneca's *Thyestes*, wherein a messenger describes
Atreus' butchery of his nephews to the chorus. Cinthio was very
proud of this act; the narration of the messenger was most effective, he believed, in arousing a sense of horror in the spectators.[5]

When the messenger first enters he is all but paralyzed by the
horrible events he has just witnessed. When urged by the chorus
to explain, he replies that he cannot, no, not if he had a thousand
tongues. He doubts that they can bear to hear what he has seen,
"which is so piteous that it ought to darken the moon and the
sun in the sky." Nevertheless, he begins his narration:

> Giace nel fondo di quest' alta torre
> In parte sì solinga, e sì riposta,
> Che non vi giunge mai raggio di Sole,
> Un loco dedicato a' sacrifici,
> Che soglion farsi da' Re nostri a l'Ombre,
> A Proserpina irata, al fier Plutone;
> Ove non pur la tenebrosa notte,
> Ma il più orribil' orrore ha là sua sede.
> Quivi Sulmon fatt' ha condurre Oronte
> (Oronte miser, che pensava omai,
> Che fosser giunti al fin gli affanni suoi)
> Da due, che d'improvisso l'avean preso,
> Mentr' egli ragionando il tenea a bada;
> E venuto il Re poi ne l' alta torre,
> Con le sue proprie mani 'l prese, e disse:
> "Ti voglio far mio successor del regno,
> Oronte, in questo loco." E questo detto,
> Pigliar gli fe' le braccia a que' malvigi,

---

[5] See above, p. 78.

> Ch' ivi l'avean condotto, e ambo le mani
> Gli fe' por sopra un ceppo, e da le braccia
> Levogliele il crudele in due gran colpi
> Con un grave coltello, e dopo alquanto
> Trattosi a dietro prese in man le mani,
> Le porse a Oronte, a lui dicendo: "Queste
> E lo scettro che t' offro, a questo modo
> Ti vo' far Re. Come ne sei contento?"

At the bottom of this high tower, in a part so solitary and so remote that no ray of the sun ever reaches there, lies a place devoted to sacrifices which our kings are wont to make to spirits, to angry Proserpine, to savage Pluto; where not only gloomy night but an even more horrible horror has her seat. Here Sulmone had Oronte (wretched Oronte, who now thought that his sufferings had reached an end) conducted by the two who had unexpectedly seized and held him as he was idly talking. And the king then came to the high tower and took him by the hands and said, "Oronte, I want you to be my successor to the realm in this place." So saying, he made those evil men who had brought him there take him by the arms and put both of his hands on a chopping block, and he severed the hands from the arms in two great strokes from a heavy knife, and afterwards, withdrawing somewhat, he picked up the hands and offered them to Oronte, saying, "This is the scepter that I offer you, and this is the way I wish to make you king. Now are you satisfied?"

In *Thyestes*, Atreus butchered his nephews in a gloomy vale, haunted by ghosts and funeral deities. Cinthio transferred the locale to a haunted dungeon. He fell far short of Seneca's messenger in building up the dark horror of the scene, but he tried.

The messenger continues his narration. Hapless Oronte, he says, defied the tyrant to strike his neck, his breast; but Sulmone only smiled in answer. Then, seizing the two little boys, the king bound one of them hand and foot, butchered him, and threw his body down at the father's feet.

At this point the women of the chorus dissolve in tears and the leader cries, "Alas, into what great pain has this joy that Oronte had in his heart changed, when the wicked king feigned to pardon him and the daughter! I have not a marrow of my bones nor a fiber of my blood that does not shudder. But what did Oronte in this doleful case?"

Oronte, says the messenger, threw himself on his knees, raised his bleeding stumps, and begged the king to spare the other child who was himself pleading for mercy. "Ah me," cries the messenger, who has now thoroughly worked himself into his part, "my heart bursts, words and voice fail me, in merely thinking of the violence,

GIRALDI CINTHIO'S PRACTICE   101

of the fury of this wicked man." But he rallies and continues.
"After the little boy went to Oronte, Sulmone followed him as a
dog burning with rage follows a timid deer through the woods."
Then, despite the frantic pleas of the mutilated father, despite the
tears that flowed from the image of savage Pluto and from the
very walls of the dungeon, the pitiless king struck down father
and son together.

The chorus relaxes after this bloody climax of horror. But, as
the messenger says, death did not put an end to this monstrous
cruelty. After ordering his serving men to throw the corpse of
Oronte to the vultures and dogs, Sulmone put the head and hands
in a silver vessel and covered them with a black silk veil. Then,
stripping the bodies of the two children but leaving the daggers
sticking in them, he put the two small corpses in silver vessels,
and carried the lot to his royal chamber.

In an ode closing the act the chorus takes what comfort it can
in the eternal order that holds fast despite the wicked deeds of
men and in the belief that the supreme Ruler will dispense justice. "Wicked one, just vengeance awaits your broken trust."

The fifth and last act is long and tediously talkative, as was customary in Cinthio's plays. The king is unrepentant; in fact, he
complacently reviews the salutary example he has given his court
of upholding the royal honor. He again shows that the advice of
his counselor has made no impression on him. "A good king ought
always to be terrible," he says, echoing the sentiments of Atreus,
Nero, and other tyrants in Seneca's tragedies. And he adds, "The
crown and hatred are like two brothers." His two minions applaud
him. "What," says Tamule, "does Malecche know about this? He
has been brought up in idleness among women, and he measures
you by his own craven heart."

Tamule: Invincible Sire, I say, and I shall always say, that the remedy
for outrage is revenge, and cruel death and spilled blood are manifesta-
tions of royal souls. And who ought to do it if kings do not?
Sulmone: It is not otherwise [5.1].

Next comes an episode reminiscent of the tragedy of Gismonda.[6]
The king orders Tamule to fetch his daughter, for he wishes to
give her a wedding present. Even the brutal Tamule hesitates to

---

[6] See above, p. 31.

carry out this order; but Sulmone drives him off the stage and moves to a corner to wait for Orbecche's entrance.

Orbecche, her nurse, and a semi-chorus (probably of ladies in waiting) enter. Orbecche is still uneasy, for she has no trust in fickle Fortune and she knows that Tamule is an evil man who never brings good news. Moreover, she has had a bad dream, in which she saw a fierce eagle attack two snow-white doves and their brood. The nurse tries to comfort her, but Orbecche considers the dream a warning from the gods.

Sulmone sends everyone away except his daughter and ceremoniously presents a silver vessel covered with a black silk veil. Some fearful premonition holds Orbecche back. Her father urges her to lift the veil.

Sulmone: The gift, wicked daughter, that your feigned love for me has earned.
Orbecche: Ah, miserable me, ah wretched one!
Sulmone: And your broken trust.
Orbecche: O me, forlorn.
Sulmone: And the regard for our honor.
Orbecche: O cruel sight, O grievous state!
Sulmone: It is such as you deserve.
Orbecche: Alas, that the sharp knife had now pierced me! O me!
Sulmone: You deserved this.
Orbecche: O me, you should at least have had pity on the children.
Sulmone: Pity has no power where the injury is so outrageous.
Orbecche: O me, I were rather dead than to see such a thing!
Sulmone: You see that satisfaction, traitress, that you gave to your father [5.2].

Orbecche draws the knives from the bodies of her two children, presents one to her father, and begs him to strike her in the breast. Sulmone, however, is content now and wishes to become reconciled with his dear daughter. "Now put down the knives," he says, "and enter with me into the house, where you may give me a clear sign that you would have peace." Orbecche drives a knife into his breast.

Sulmone roars for help, but the only people who answer his cries are some that would be least likely to come, namely, the frightened ladies of the semi-chorus. Arrived on the stage they stand helpless as the princess cuts the royal throat with the second knife. The king dies crying for pity. While the semi-chorus comments on the gruesome scene, Orbecche cuts off her father's head and then his hands. The semi-chorus is appalled by such fury in a woman, but is forced to acknowledge that the cruel king deserved just what he got. "No one offers a more pleasing victim to God than that of a wicked tyrant such as this man was." Orbecche carries the severed head and hands into the palace.

Orbecche returns to the stage. "Now," she cries, "rejoice, traitor, in your misdeeds. Go on, rejoice more than any cruel Scythian, more than any wild beast, in your pride and in your violated trust. You, pitiless one, are sated with my innocent blood, and I am sated with your guilt, but for a reason more just." Then, in much the same manner that Thyestes uses after he learns that he has feasted on his own children,[7] Orbecche cries,

> O Sol, che solo il mondo orni et illustri,
> Perchè nonti fuggisti allor dal Cielo,
> Che quest fier Tiran, ch' or per me giace,
> Commise così sozzo e orribil atto? [5.3].

O Sun, who alone adorns and brightens the world, why did you not flee from Heaven when this fierce tyrant, who now lies fallen by my hand, committed so foul and horrible a deed?

The nurse and the ladies in waiting can only gaze in awe at such heart-rending grief, putting in an occasional word of sympathy.

Orbecche now prepares to join her husband and children. She holds up one of the bloody knives. Then, despite the cries of the women, she plunges it into her heart. The nurse clasps her mistress, kisses her, and tries to coax some spark of life into the body. Finally, realizing that Orbecche is indeed dead, she promises to give a decent burial to her and her family and to have the body of the king thrown to the vultures and wolves. The chorus—it looks as though the regular chorus has now joined the semi-chorus— delivers a short closing ode on the fleeting happiness of mortals.

As Neri says, Orbecche was the first Italian tragedy that was "regular" and at the same time successfully staged.[8] The author himself was well satisfied with the productions. He was especially pleased by the fine performances of the actors who played Orbecche, Oronte, and the messenger, and he was gratified by the response of the audiences. "Not only the newcomers," he said, "but those who had come every time could not contain their sighs

---

[7] See *Thyestes* 1035 ff.

[8] P. 60: "la prima tragedia regolare e rappresentata."

and tears."[9] *Orbecche* became the standard for measuring other sixteenth-century tragedies. Some years later, Benedetto Varchi reported that Giraldi had the reputation of being the best of the tragic poets. "I well know," he said, "that when *Orbecche* was recited in Ferrara it pleased marvelously, according to what was reported to me by the two cardinals Salviati and Ravenna, who attended the performance."[10]

DIDONE

For his next tragedy Cinthio turned to a traditional source, Roman history. As the prologue acknowledges, the author followed Virgil's story. He followed it not only in plot and characters but in speech; many of Cinthio's lines are paraphrases of the *Aeneid*, some of them almost literal translations into Italian. Consequently *Didone* is the only play of Cinthio, save one comedy and a pastoral, that owes very little to Seneca. Even the supernatural characters, Juno, Venus, Cupid, Mercury, and Fame, came from Virgil.

Since Cinthio was enough of a classicist to preserve the economy of the ancient playwrights, he reduced the events of Virgil's argument to a single day and restricted the scene to the royal palace in Carthage. Moreover, he found no opportunity in this play to use the Terentian double plot that he later adapted to tragedy. *Didone* has even less action than does *Orbecche*, and it has more monologues; no less than twelve of the twenty-six scenes are soliloquies.

Juno, still smarting from the insults offered her by the Trojans, opens the play with a soliloquy. She is soon joined, in the next scene, by Cupid and Venus. The third scene of the first act is a soliloquy by Venus, who has Jove and destiny on her side and is determined to thwart Juno's evil designs on her protégé Aeneas.

The heroine is introduced in the fourth scene, engaged in conversation with her sister Anna. It is dawn. Dido is debating what she should do. Should she forget her dead husband Sychaeus and marry the Trojan visitor who has won her heart? Will Aeneas marry her?

The next scene, the last in the first act, is a soliloquy by Dido, in which Cinthio, aided by Virgil, tried to dramatize the conflict

---

[9] *Discorsi*, p. 210. Cf. p. 279.
[10] *L'Hercolano*, pp. 208–209.

in the heroine's mind. The memory of her late husband troubles her and she laments the inability of mortals to foresee good and evil. "But these our senses, which present the forms, are often deceived by false appearances, and images spring up in the mind in lying specters, so that we are blind to colors as moles are to the sun." Cinthio liked soliloquies and he took great pains with them. The following figure, although already trite in 1542, is nevertheless effective and represents the author's better efforts. Dido exclaims,

> Stò come nave, che da vari venti
> Combattuta è nel mare, e quinci e quindi
> E non scorga a qual via debba piegarsi,
> Per torsi da tempesta e gire al porto [1.5].

I stand like a ship at sea that is assailed here and there by divers winds, and it descries not which way it ought to take to avoid the tempest and make port.

The chorus of Carthaginian women closes the first act with an ode on the instability of worldly possessions.

Anna opens the second act with a soliloquy. She fulminates against the folly and lies of the soothsayers, with their absurd reading of birds' entrails and their gloomy predictions. The soothsayers have predicted evil consequences if Dido marries Aeneas; but Anna favors the match. In the *Aeneid*, Venus sends Cupid disguised as little Ascanius to inflame the Carthaginian widow with love for Aeneas. Cinthio, presumably in the interest of better verisimilitude, of greater realism, substituted Anna for the god of love.

Aeneas is introduced in the second scene of Act 2, accompanied by the faithful Achates. Aeneas is weary from travel. Italy, his destined goal, seems remote, and the comfortable, luxurious life at Carthage is tempting. Anna encourages him to settle down while Achates tries to rouse his ebbing courage and ambition. Throughout the play Achates tries to counteract the influence of Anna, persistently nagging at Aeneas to leave Carthage and fulfill his destiny and the destiny of his son and heir Ascanius.

The gloom of the unfavorable auguries deepens when a messenger from the neighboring king Iarbas adds to the alarm felt by the Carthaginians as they watch the growing intimacy between their queen and the Trojan exile. A priest tells the messenger to reassure Iarbas that Dido will remain true to the memory of her dead husband.

The second choral ode contrasts the perils and evils of ambition with the honorable state of virtue.

Virgil's goddess of fame, adorned with many eyes and ears, opens the third act with a soliloquy. Cinthio used Fame as a messenger to report the consummation of the love affair between Dido and Aeneas. The goddess promises to reveal their secret to all the world.

Aeneas is now happy and contented; but Achates will not let him remain so, again reminding him of the duty he owes to his offspring, of the danger he runs of forfeiting eternal fame while lingering in Dido's court. Aeneas stubbornly resists all arguments, however, until Mercury arrives with orders from Jove. Mercury exhorts Aeneas to bestir himself, to be gone before the next sunrise:

> Leva ogni indugio, e non ti fidar punto
> Ne l'amor di Didon, perchè le donne
> Mobili e varie son per lor natura [3.2].

Give over every delay, and trust not in the love of Dido, because women by their nature are fickle and variable.

This scene is among the better ones in the play, for Aeneas appears to be deeply moved by the decision forced upon him by divine command. "Achates, I am beside myself; a cold sweat and a sudden fear run through my bones." But Achates is unrelenting. Finally, and reluctantly, Aeneas gives orders to gather the crew.

After more talk, including soliloquies by Aeneas, by a crewman, and by a maidservant of Dido, the Trojans make ready to sneak away before daylight. The maidservant informs Dido of what is going on.

Dido: Have you perhaps seen this ungrateful, this cruel, this faithless Trojan?

Servant: I have not seen him, your Majesty.

Dido: He should be at the port. I wish to go there.

Servant: This sort of thing is not worthy of you, your Majesty.

Dido: O me, love has made me do much worse.

Servant: If you have committed one error for love, don't commit two [3.7].

Dido and the chorus lament in a *commos.*

The chorus closes the third act with a Platonic ode in praise of mortals who do not forget their divine origin. Poor Dido has forgotten, for now she is mad.

Aeneas is still fretting over his troubled conscience when the fourth act opens. Achates advises him to leave without seeing Dido. The episode is another realistic interpolation by Cinthio, and with it the play comes to life again.

Achates: It would be better to get away and then make the excuse for your departure in a letter full of love.
Aeneas: I could never, Achates, be so discourteous [4.1].

Before Aeneas can make up his mind what to do Dido finds him and proceeds to upbraid him. The beginning of her tirade is virtually a paraphrase of Virgil:

> Dissimulare etiam sperasti, perfide, tantum
> posse nefas tacitusque mea decedere terra? [*Aeneid* 4.305–306].

> Anche, infedele,
> Sperato hai con fittion poter coprire
> Tanta sceleratezza, e del mio regno
> Tacitamente uscir? [*Didone* 4.1].

False one, did you hope that you could cover so great a villainy with a lie, and leave my realm in silence?

Cinthio could not hold the pace, however, for he could not rise when Virgil rose to greater heights of poetry. Virgil's Aeneas thus describes the dream that visits him at night:

> me patris Anchisae, quotiens umentibus umbris
> nox operit terras, quotiens astra ignea surgunt,
> admonet in somnis et turbida terret imago;
> me puer Ascanius capitisque iniuria cari,
> quem regno Hesperiae fraudo et fatalibus arvis [4.351–355].

> As often as the night obscures the skies
> With humid shades, or twinkling stars arise,
> Anchises' angry ghost in dreams appears,
> Chides my delay, and fills my soul with fears;
> And young Ascanius justly may complain,
> Defrauded of his fate, and destined reign [Dryden].

Cinthio's Aeneas says:

> Giamai la terra
> Non copre l'humid ombra de la notte,
> Che con turbata imagine il mio padre
> Nel sonno, con terror, non mi riprenda,
> E il conoscermi fare ingiuria espressa
> Al mio unico figliuolo, Ascanio caro,
> Col levargli d' Italia il bel paese,
> A lui fatal, molto me preme, e afflige.

The moist shades of night never cover the earth but in my dream the troubled image of my father checks me in terror, and the knowledge of the fatal injury I am doing to my only son, dear Ascanius, in depriving him of the beautiful country of Italy, wrings me much, and afflicts me.

Thanks to Virgil, however, this is a pretty good scene. Dido, supported by the chorus, continues to reproach Aeneas, and Achates continues to stiffen his resolution. Aeneas tries in vain to convince the queen that he is not an ungrateful scoundrel. Finally, Dido sends him away.

After a lamentable soliloquy by Anna—"Miserable me, how miserable is that person who becomes wise through savage accident!" —Dido, Anna, and the women of the chorus join in lamentations. Dido is now determined to die. She sends everyone away to prepare for the mourning and launches into another soliloquy (4.4) that is based on Virgil.

The chorus closes the fourth act with an ode addressed to Nature, who appears to be a mother to all animals save naked man. To man Nature is a stepmother, and his only recourse is to reason.

A maidservant opens the last act with a soliloquy describing the distraught queen before the funeral pyre. Then Dido, who is bent on suicide, curses Aeneas and his venture. Anna is still feeling guilty for her part in promoting the unhappy love affair and she is now troubled by a terrible sight she has just witnessed by the river. She saw a wolf, feigning pain from a thorn in his foot, approach a shepherdess for help. When the girl stooped to remove the thorn the wolf seized her and tore her to pieces. This sight must be an omen of ruin.

A messenger enters to report dismal news to Anna, an old nurse, and the chorus. "O lofty court, O proud court, to whom Juno queen of heaven promised the empire of all the world, have you not now been led from the most sublime degree of happiness to the abyss of sorrow?" (5.4). As usual with Cinthio's messengers, he is so overcome by grief that he is reluctant to speak; but Anna insists on hearing his news, so he tells her that Dido has killed herself. His report follows Virgil's account pretty closely.

The dying queen is carried onstage for the final death throes. Cinthio here abandoned the violence of *Orbecche* and returned to the practice recommended by Horace. Anna hangs over her sister, begging her to speak. The dying queen does speak a last word, *Oimé, oimé!* Anna seizes the bloodstained sword, Aeneas' sword, and tries to stab herself; but the nurse and the women of the chorus restrain her until she faints.

The chorus delivers a brief concluding ode on the instability of Fortune and the cruelty of love, of which Dido is a wretched example.

Evidently *Didone* was not so well received as was *Orbecche*, and the author wrote an Apology to answer adverse criticisms raised by the Grecians. Most of these answers have already been dealt with in the preceding chapter on Cinthio's theory. In saying that Cinthio's play was an advance on Pazzi's *Dido* we are scarcely praising it. Cinthio was not yet so discouraged, however, that he abandoned Roman tragedy.

CLEOPATRA

Cinthio's *Cleopatra* was commissioned by Ercole II. It was probably the first *Cleopatra* on the Renaissance stage although it was not the first to be printed.[11] *Didone* was a somewhat slavish dramatization of the fourth book of the *Aeneid*. *Cleopatra* was an equally slavish dramatization of Plutarch's life of Antony. In both plays, Cinthio reduced the passage of time to one day and restricted the scene to a royal palace. Then he replaced narrative and dialogue by monologues and dialogues. Of the thirty-seven scenes in his *Cleopatra* fifteen are soliloquies.

Cinthio followed the same procedure in *Cleopatra* that he did in *Didone*, but he encountered more difficulty in the second play. Since he followed Plutarch's narrative faithfully but restricted the passage of time to less than twenty-four hours, he was forced to lose Antony early in the second act. Then he had to prolong the dying of his second principal character, Cleopatra, for nearly three more acts. Cinthio opened his action at approximately Act 4, Scene 10 of Shakespeare's *Antony and Cleopatra*. Consequently he was hard pressed to provide enough matter to fill up the later acts. He tried to solve the problem by composing debates and lamentations. The debates are mostly between Octavius, Maecenas, and Agrippa, who repeatedly argue over the best way of capturing the queen alive so that she may be brought to Rome in triumph (2.5,

---

[11] Allacci listed ten *Cleopatras* and one *Marc' Antonio e Cleopatra* in Italy between 1550 and 1725. Cinthio's play was printed in 1583.

3.3, 3.8). Cleopatra also argues with Octavius. The lamentations are provided by Cleopatra, her women, and the chorus. It must be admitted that the play grows tedious, more tedious than *Didone*, which is too long.

Any Renaissance play about Cleopatra must inevitably be compared with Shakespeare's masterpiece, and the result of such a comparison will scarcely be flattering to Cinthio. It should be pointed out, however, that other Renaissance treatments of the subject, such as Jodelle's *Cleopatre captive* (1552), Garnier's *Marc-Antoine* (1578), Samuel Daniel's *Cleopatra* (1594), will hardly come off any better than Cinthio's in a comparison with *Antony and Cleopatra*.

Shakespeare used his source material from Plutarch in two ways: he turned some passages in North's translation into verse and he developed certain hints from Plutarch into poetry. Cinthio had the same opportunities, but he usually failed to capitalize on them. A few illustrations will demonstrate the different results attained by the two poets.

Perhaps the most celebrated passage in Shakespeare's play is Enobarbus' description of the first meeting between Antony and Cleopatra on the river Cydnus, the passage beginning,

> The barge she sat in, like a burnished throne,
> Burned on the water. . . .

As every student of Shakespeare knows, these luscious lines are mostly poetic paraphrases of North's translation.

Cinthio also made use of the same description, but he brought it in rather casually as though he failed to recognize its poetic possibilities. One of Cleopatra's companions brings the bad news that many soldiers are deserting Antony and going over to Octavius, who is at the gates of Alexandria. The *famigliere* cries,

> O quanto fu infelice,
> Perchè quel dì, che con la nave d'oro
> E coi remi d'arengto, e con le vele
> Di porpora n'andasti a Marco Antonio,
> Ornata sì, che simigliavi proprio
> Vener che Baccho a ritrovare andasse [2.2].

O unhappy was that day when you went to Mark Antony in a golden ship with silver oars and purple sails, and you so bedecked with ornaments that you resembled Venus herself going to meet Bacchus.

Plutarch gave no details of Antony's reaction to Cleopatra's running away from the naval battle beyond remarking that the Roman
cried out against the betrayal. Shakespeare seized the hint and
created a fine tragic outburst:

> All is lost!
> This foul Egyptian has betrayed me. . . .
>   Triple-turned whore! 'tis thou
> Hast sold me to this novice. . . .
> O sun! thy uprise shall I see no more;
> Fortune and Antony part here; even here
> Do we shake hands. All come to this? The hearts
> That spanieled me at heels, to whom I gave
> Their wishes, do discandy, melt their sweets
> On blossoming Caesar; and this pine is barked,
> That overtopped them all. Betrayed I am.
> O this false soul of Egypt! [4.10].

Cinthio merely made Antony revile fickle Fortune and fickle Cleopatra:

> Fortuna, oimè, Fortuna, oimè, dove hai
> Condutto hor Marco Antonio? . . .
>   O Cleopatra iniqua,
> O malvagia, O infedele, O scelerata,
> Per te, per te io, che ponea terrore
> A tutto il mondo, horo son dato in forza
> Al mio nemico [1.5].

Fortune, O me, Fortune, O me, where have you led Mark Antony now?
. . . O wicked Cleopatra, O lewd, O faithless, O villainous, for you, for
you I, who brought terror to the whole world, now have yielded all to
my enemy.

Sometimes, when Cinthio did try to develop a hint from Plutarch, he made the mistake of doing too much, of making his character say too much. For example, when the nurse tells Antony that
Cleopatra is dead, and that she died for him, he drops his abuse
of the queen and feels a resurgence of his former love: "Ah, Cleopatra, where have you gone? Your hand did not give you death,
but mine. Ah, alas, and my hand, O my Cleopatra, will also give
me my death" (1.6). Shakespeare's touch here was perfect:

Antony	Dead, then?
Mardian	Dead.
Antony	Unarm, Eros; the long day's task is done,
	And we must sleep [4.12].

Cinthio was not a gifted poet, but it must not be supposed that he always bungled in his dramatization of Plutarch. Sometimes, often in soliloquies, he struck a natural tone that brought his play alive. He was almost invariably more successful in unpretentious lines than in the big speeches. For example, Cleopatra's remarks on the loss of her lover seem appropriate: "Thus at one stroke I have lost Mark Antony and the kingdom. But I do not grieve for the kingdom; I grieve more to have lost Mark Antony than if I had lost a thousand thousand kingdoms" (1.3). Cleopatra's mourning in the second act is sometimes forced, but certain passages are better than others, such as, "You, Mark Antony, were my life while you were alive, and you, ah, alas, will also be my death. I wish that that sword which opened the road to your soul would open it to mine, to join me to you. You, cruel, savage sword, that pierced my lord's side, will you now be merciful in piercing my heart?" (2.3). There is a studied conceit here in the idea of opening the road to the hereafter, but it is less studied, less trite, than some, such as the cry of the nurse in the next act: "O court, formerly the chamber of every pleasure, even so you are now the lodging of every sorrow" (3.5).

In fairness to Cinthio it cannot be said that he indulged in a large number of shopworn conceits. There are not many like "O eyes, no eyes, but fountains fraught with tears"[12] in his tragedies, and Ben Jonson would not have found him the readiest target for his satirical thrusts at tragic bombast.

The most lifelike speeches in Cinthio's plays are apt to come from humble characters, from servants and soldiers. In *Cleopatra*, a captain and a eunuch usually sound like living men. One of the better passages in the play is a conversation between a maidservant and the eunuch.

Eunuch: Why do you weep?
Servant: I weep for our misfortune. Miserable me.
Eunuch: What is this great misfortune?
Servant: In drawing forth the sword from Mark Antony's side his soul went out with the blood. Whence he died.
Eunuch: Would he had died the first day he came to the kingdom [2.2].

In sharp contrast with *Orbecche*, there is little or no Seneca in *Didone*. The supernatural characters in the second tragedy, even

---

[12] See *Every Man in His Humor.* And see below, p. 297.

the talk about fortune and destiny, all had a basis in the *Aeneid*. In *Cleopatra*, however, Cinthio returned to his favorite classical model although Plutarch's full argument gave him no opportunity to indulge in any full-scale imitation of Seneca's tragedies. The most prominent Senecan feature in *Cleopatra* is the running debate between Octavius, Maecenas, and Agrippa. Maecenas is the good counselor who tries to restrain Octavius from committing violence and cruelty, who tries to make him fit the picture of Augustus in Seneca's *Octavia* (472 ff.). "I will say," Maecenas declares, "and I believe I speak the truth, that he who wields his power with modesty and piety shows clearly to everyone that he is worthy of empire" (2.5). One of the eunuch's speeches is thoroughly Senecan: "I have often seen in this my short life that the higher Fortune raises someone to the summit of her unstable wheel the more disdainfully she makes him fall, and our Queen of Egypt and the Roman Mark Antony now offer a clear example of this. Ah, how true it is that no one is blessed while he lives" (2.2).

CINTHIO'S TRAGEDIES WITH A HAPPY ENDING

Didone and *Cleopatra* were important contributions to the development of Roman tragedies in the Renaissance, but they were not successful on the stage. Therefore Cinthio abandoned Roman history and returned to the source of his first tragedy, *Orbecche;* he returned to his own *novelle*. He wrote six more tragedies, all of them "mixed tragedies" *(tragedie miste)* or "tragedies with a happy ending" *(tragedie di lieto fin)*, all dramatizations of *novelle*. He never wrote another tragedy with an unhappy issue for the principal characters, that is, for the heroines. In *Epitia*, for example, he even changed the plot of his own *novella* to insure a happy ending.

Cinthio did not like the term *tragicommedia*, but he was willing to accept it for his own plays if the public insisted. The prologue to *Altile* stated: "But if you don't like it to have the name of Tragedy, you can call it at your pleasure Tragicomedy (since our language does use such a name), the outline of which has conformed to Comedy—after troubles it is filled with gladness." He liked to think of *Altile* and the new plays that followed it as comparable to the *Ion, Orestes, Helen, Alcestis,* and *Iphigenia* of Euripides. Although he developed the double plot from Terentian

comedy in these *tragedie di lieto fin,* he never inserted comic matter. In other words, he adapted the structure of comedy, especially
the cheerful denouement, to *Altile* and succeeding plays, but he
excluded facetious scenes, clownish characters, vulgar speech, and
jokes.

Perhaps Cinthio would have done better had he written comedies,[13] for he could write plain dialogue pretty well, but he admired tragedy and he wished to become a tragic poet. At the
same time he wished to please his public at Ferrara. Therefore,
despite his preference for Seneca over Euripides, he composed
"*Altile, Selene,* the *Antivalomeni,* and others, only to serve the
spectators and to secure a more pleasing effect on the stage and to
conform more closely to the fashion of our time."[14] The fashion of
the late sixteenth century, thanks to Cinthio, became tragicomedy.
Guarini, author of the famous *Pastor fido,* for example, derived
much of his theory and practice of tragicomedy from Cinthio's
tragedie di lieto fin. Cinthio's happy ending, his increased emphasis on a complicated plot, his increased emphasis on romantic
love, his decreased emphasis on an elevated style, all encouraged
Guarini and others to write tragicomedies.

I have discussed Cinthio's tragedies with a happy ending in another place[15] and therefore will pass over his last six plays briefly.
The best of them, in my judgment, is *Epitia,* which maintains suspense pretty well throughout the last two acts. There is even some
convincing motivation of character in the portrait of the heroine
during the last act. Here Epitia is depicted as struggling within
herself to decide between revenge and mercy. The governor of
Innsbruck, named Juriste, had betrayed Epitia and repudiated his
promise to save her brother from execution on a charge of adultery.
Now Juriste has also been sentenced to die for violating the imperial edict against adultery. Only Epitia can save him, and she
does save him, but not until she has been beseiged by pleas from
her sister, her aunt, the captain of justice, and from the emperor
himself. Even these powerful advocates cannot break her stubborn
resolve to see her betrayer die as her brother has died, until the
captain reveals that he substituted the corpse of another con-

---

[13] He did write one comedy, the *Eudemoni,* early in his career, but it was not
published until 1877.
[14] *Discorsi,* pp. 220–221.
[15] *Tragicomedy* (Urbana, Ill., 1955), pp. 67–92.

demned prisoner for her brother's when he delivered the body at
her house. Epitia is overjoyed by this miraculous reversal of fortune and when she learns that the emperor will set aside the death
sentence against her brother, on condition that he marry the girl
he seduced, all thoughts of revenge vanish and she agrees to save
Juriste by marrying him.

Epitia illustrates nearly every feature of the tragedy that Cinthio
sought to develop. It has a double plot (two cases of seduction).
Its threats of death keep the reader or spectator in doubt, full of
pity, torn between anxiety and hope, until the very end. It makes
extensive use of discoveries and reversals of fortune. It emphasizes
the role of women in courtly life of the sixteenth century. It has
an exotic setting in Innsbruck.

Arrenopia might be mentioned, for it has Cinthio's most attractive heroine, who represents a popular romantic type found in
many Renaissance comedies and tragicomedies. Arrenopia, who
goes through most of the play disguised as a young knight, is active,
spirited, brave, well trained in warlike exercises, yet kind and loving, and withal highly intelligent, wise beyond her years. The
Antivalomeni is even closer to romantic comedy and tragicomedy.
Its complex Terentian plot provides two love affairs, both opposed
by a tyrannical father but both brought to a happy issue by startling
discoveries in the last act.

Giraldi Cinthio made several important contributions to Renaissance tragedy. He established a kind of standard form for neoclassical tragedy. He encouraged the writing of Roman tragedies. He
established the Italian tragedy of blood and revenge. He established tragedy with a happy ending, which ultimately became
tragicomedy. He assisted the introduction of romantic love into
European tragedy. He exploited exotic settings for his plays.
Finally, he encouraged the development of a more realistic, more
conversational style in tragedy.

Trissino and fellow Grecians worked out a neoclassical form of
Italian tragedy in imitation of Sophocles and Euripides. Cinthio
modified this Grecian form; he reduced the role of the chorus until
it served mainly as an entr'acte, returned to Senecan practices, and
adapted the Terentian five-act formula to tragedy.

Although Cinthio's Roman tragedies were unsuccessful on the
stage, they encouraged Italians and other Europeans to use Roman
history for plots. Consequently many *Didos, Cleopatras, Julius*

Caesars, and *Sophonisbas* appeared in Italy, France, and England.

The celebrated and influential Italian tragedy of blood and revenge stemmed principally from Cinthio's *Orbecche.* In this play, which is largely an adaptation of Seneca's *Thyestes,* Cinthio popularized the qualities that were copied by many succeeding playwrights in Italy and England: ghosts stalking the stage, shocking scenes of violence onstage and lurid descriptions by messengers of shocking scenes offstage, tragic complaints against fickle Fortune, sententious speeches by wise counselors, lamentations and moralizings by the chorus. In other words, Cinthio revived Seneca in tragedy and insured his reign for the next two generations.

Since the emphasis on love in Cinthio's plays has already been discussed, I shall merely remind the reader that eight of his nine tragedies were named for women in love and the ninth, the *Antivalomeni,* actually exploits romantic love more than does any one of the others.

Cinthio sought exotic settings for all of his plays, and this practice undoubtedly influenced his followers throughout western Europe. In England, for example, Elizabethan and Jacobean tragedies more often than not had exotic settings. Of Shakespeare's tragedies only *Lear* and *Macbeth* had native locales; the others went to Troy, Athens, Rome, Alexandria, Elsinore, Venice, Cyprus, and Verona. Webster, Middleton, and Beaumont and Fletcher also chose foreign scenes.

Cinthio probably wished to master an elevated speech worthy of comparison with that of his principal mentor Seneca. He tried it in *Orbecche,* but with indifferent success. He was always able to write fairly convincing conversation for his humble characters, for his soldiers and servants, and gradually he turned to a quieter, more conversational style for his principal characters. This change in style, which appears prominently in his *tragedie di lieto fin,* exerted a considerable influence upon the writers of tragicomedy. Guarini, for example, was carrying on the work of Cinthio when he characterized the style of his own *Pastor fido* as the best kind for tragicomedy:

> In the *Pastor fido* the verse is not turgid, not noisy, not dithyrambic. Its periods are not prolonged, not short, not intricate, not hard, not difficult to understand; they need not be re-read many times. Its figures of speech are taken from significant qualities, from proper and not from remote qualities. Its diction is clear but not low, proper but not vulgar,

figurative but not enigmatical, beautiful but not affected, sustained but not inflated, pliant but not languishing; and, to conclude in a word, such as is not remote from common speech and yet not close to that of the common herd; it is not so elaborate that the stage abhors it nor so vulgar that the theater condemns it, but rather it can be played without trouble and read without labor.[16]

Such, at all events, was the aim of both Cinthio and Guarini, and the fact that neither poet actually attained this theatrical style does not destroy the importance of their ideal.

---

[16] *Compendio della poesia tragicomica,* in *Opere* (Verona, 1737–38) 3.428.

VI

Speroni's *Canace*

Although Giraldi Cinthio's *Orbecche* was not the first Italian play of blood and revenge, it certainly established a pattern for Renaissance tragedy, and imitations of it soon followed. One of these imitations was *Canace*, by Sperone Speroni, a *letterato* of Padua, famed as a philosopher and orator, and, like many another Italian dramatist of the sixteenth century, something of a pedant. Speroni composed his tragedy in 1542 and read it to the Accademia degl' Infiammati in Padua. It was first printed in 1546, reprinted in 1550, 1562, 1566, and 1597.[1] There was no printing of the unfinished prologue and no division into acts until the revised 1597 edition at Venice. Apparently the author never did write the choruses for the ends of Acts 1 through 4; but there are brief appearances of the chorus in the dialogue of Acts 4 and 5.

Canace, as it appears in the 1597 edition, prepared after the author's death in 1588, is arranged in the Cinthian pattern, not in the Grecian. There are five acts, each divided into scenes (unnumbered), with "chorus missing" *(choro manca)* at the end of each act save the last.

All of the action presumably takes place before the palace of

---

[1] Illinois has all of these save the 1562, including two printings of the first edition in 1546, one at Venice and the other at Padua. The text in the *Teatro italiano antico* is often different from the sixteenth-century printings.

Eolo between morning and evening. Speroni avoided the awkward
lapse of time in Falugi's earlier version by beginning his play on
the day that Canace's child is born. The versification is neither Trissino's nor Cinthio's, but Speroni's own peculiar scheme, namely,
seven-syllable lines interspersed with some five-syllable and eleven-
syllable lines. In other words, he reversed the usual practice of
tragic poets before him by emphasizing short lines and using the
traditional *endecasillabi* sparingly. He had his reasons for such
unconventional practice, and we shall examine these reasons later
on. He used rhyme frequently but irregularly. Since the choruses
are missing, we can only conjecture that these would have been
all in rhyme.

The incomplete prologue, missing until the 1597 edition, is
spoken by Venus, who directly addresses the audience. A fair
sample of her speech goes as follows:

> State attenti, e pensate d'ascoltare
> Non filosofo errante,
> Ne fallace oratore,
> Ma le parole sante
> D'una mente divina,
> Del terzo ciel reina,
> Madre e Dea dell' Amore.

Be attentive and imagine you are listening not to a rambling philosopher
nor to a deceitful orator, but to the sacred words of a divine intelligence,
queen of the third heaven, mother and goddess of Love.

Apparently Venus is about to launch a solemn warning about the
overpowering force of love.

The play proper opens with a ghost, the ghost of Canace's nameless infant, who had been strangled at birth and thrown to wild
beasts by his grandfather Eolo. The ghost's chief complaint, however, is against Venus, who had sought a cruel revenge for the
mistreatment of her protégé Aeneas. (Eolo, ruler of the winds, had
wrecked the Trojan fleet bound for Italy.) Another complaint is
that Lethe, who mercifully destroys the memory in adults when
they descend to the lower world, has spared him and he now suffers
miseries that he knew nothing about during his short life on earth.
These lamentations are interrupted by the entrance of Eolo. As
the ghost retires to hell he delivers a grim warning for his grandfather: "Watch and hear and wait, because sweet paternal love
will soon be turned to harsh and cruel hate, whereby wretchedly

blind he will weep eternally." The parallel here with the opening of Cinthio's *Orbecche* is obvious.[2]

Eolo is in a cheerful mood, for a festival of the winds is being held; but his good humor is soon dampened by the royal counselor, a Senecan character, who distrusts prosperity and feels sure that some god or goddess must be planning trouble for his master. "O light and vain joy that relies upon winds! O fleeting mirth, O unstable wealth, if it comes and goes with the winds!"

At this point the first chorus was supposed to deliver an ode.

In the second act, Deiopea, wife of Eolo, enters with her waiting woman. The queen has been troubled by bad dreams in which Venus threatened her, and now she fears for her twin children, Canace and Macareo. The *cameriera*, in a soliloquy, expresses her distrust of fortune, which is a natural enemy to human happiness.

Macareo, who enters next, is also gloomy and fearful. The waiting woman adds to his uneasiness by telling him about his mother's bad dreams. After the woman leaves he admits to his servant that this news confirms his growing awareness that the love affair with his sister is not a "mortal malady, but was a celestial compulsion that conquered and extinguished our every virtue." He realizes now that he has been involved in a dreadful crime and given his father reason to inflict the most severe punishment.

Canace's nurse enters to inform Macareo that his sister is even now in the throes of childbirth. Macareo admits that all he can do is to confess to his father and then kill himself. The nurse rebukes him for deserting his sister, who will never be able to survive his death. Then, in another Senecan soliloquy, the nurse curses her parents who forced her to exchange a humble roof for service in the royal palace, to exchange peace and quiet for turmoil and grief.

The act closes without a chorus.

The heroine Canace first appears at the beginning of Act 3. She faces a tragic dilemma:

> O Giunone Lucina,
> O Dea de' parti, Dea
> De' nascenti mortali;
> Finalmente una volta
> Ponga fine a miei mali
> La tua bontá infinita.
> Certo è, tu il sai: questa infelice salma

---

[2] See above, p. 94.

> Non è men grave all' alma
> Ch' al corpo afflitto e stanco:
> Con lei ho poco andare
> A morirmi d' affanno
> O palesar mia colpa e mia vergogna.

O Juno Lucina, O goddess of childbirth, goddess of newborn mortals, once and for all may thy infinite goodness put an end to my pains. Surely, as thou knowest, this unhappy burden is no less heavy on the soul than on the weary and tormented body; I can do little else than kill myself in despair or publish my guilt and my shame.

The situation here is dramatic and pretty well expressed. Canace is now thinking of her child as much as of herself; torn by both fear and pity, she forseees the wretched fate of both child and mother.

> Ma a cui nasci infelice
> Figliuol mio? a cui nasci?
> A cui ti partorisco?
> D' augei preda, e di cani,
> Nascere veggio a pesci,
> Partorirò infelice
> Le tue membra innocenti,
> Et io 'l veleno e 'l ferro
> Aspetto, se la vista pauroso
> Del fiero padre, armato
> Di minaccie e di sdegni,
> Non mi basta a morire.

Why, my unhappy child, are you born? Why are you born? Why do I deliver you? I see you born to be the prey of birds and dogs, I, miserable, shall deliver your innocent limbs to fishes, while I await poison or steel, if the fearful sight of my cruel father, armed with threats and hate, is not enough to kill me.

The nurse urges Canace to hide; but there is no place to hide that Eolo will not find sooner or later. Moreover, Canace now has no wish to live. Nor does she want the child to live, a "monster, a dishonor to our times, an eternal testimony of wicked love." The nurse counters with an admonition to think of the innocence of the child and to think of her brother.

The first and second scenes of Act 3 are the best in the play. The style is pretty direct and fairly simple in most passages. When the author did resort to figurative language here he was apt to use metaphors reminiscent of Italian love poetry. The following speech of Canace, near the end of the second scene, is one of the better examples.

> Ora ovunque si trovi, o nel profondo
> Del mare, o presso al porto,
> La debil navicella
> Della mia stanca vita,
> Poco poss' esser lunge
> Dal fin d' ogni mio affano.

Now, wherever the frail vessel of my weary life is, either in the depth of the sea or near to port, I cannot be far from the end of all my trouble.

The queen, Deiopea, makes another appearance as the anxious mother. The nurse tries to pacify her. Canace's condition is still a secret to all save the nurse; but now Macareo's servant has to be taken into confidence, for he is part of the nurse's plan to conceal the newborn infant. The baby will be hidden in a basket of flowers that is being carried to the altar of Juno.

Again the chorus is missing at the end of the act.

Act 4 of *Canace* is rather better than most of Cinthio's fourth acts, which are usually static debates and monologues. The chorus takes a small part in the dialogue here; it has to listen to the dismal reports of messengers. Perhaps it stays onstage throughout the whole act, but there are no directions to indicate either entrance or exit.

The servant brings bad news:

> O misera Canace!
> Misero Macareo! O infelice
> Parto innocente! O misera e infelice
> Questa casa real, figli, parenti,
> Nipoti, servi, serve, huomini, e Dei!
> Chi peccò, chi è innocente,
> Chi sarà tormentato,
> Chi tormenterà altrui,
> Chi sente e chi non sente,
> Mortali et immortali
> Infelici egualmente!

O wretched Canace, wretched Macareo! O unhappy, innocent offspring! O wretched and unhappy this royal house, children, parents, grandchildren, menservants, maidservants, men, and gods! Who sinned, who is innocent, who will be tormented, who will torment others, who feels and who feels not, mortals and immortals alike unhappy!

The servant messenger tells the chorus that all is discovered. He gives a circumstantial report of how the baby cried out in the basket and so betrayed the secret to the king and court.

Then, in the second scene, Eolo is shown with his counselor.

This Senecan scene is comparable to the second scene in the third act of *Orbecche*, wherein the royal counselor vainly tries to appease the wrath of Sulmone, who is bent on punishing his daughter and her family.[3] Eolo is beside himself with rage and hate; he can think of nothing but revenge. The counselor tries every argument he can muster to restrain his master and to arouse compassion in him. The following exchange, which is Senecan and Cinthian, is typical.

Eolo: In such a case the less compassionate the revenge the more just it will be.

Counselor: Justice cannot be the enemy of compassion.

Eolo: Here it would be impious to have compassion.

Counselor: Signor, do not forget yourself and turn God; and as you are king so you are also a father.

Eolo: Do you want license from the gods for my children to be impious and wicked?

Counselor: This no; but I would like to think that resentment and the desire for revenge were only faults of us mortals, not sins of the gods.

The king hands the counselor a knife and orders him to mix some poison with wine, then to send both knife and jug to Canace and her nurse. He will have the infant strangled and its body thrown to the wolves, dogs, and crows.

In the next scene, Deiopea, overwhelmed by the disaster to her children, begs the king's minister not to carry out the order for the death of Canace. She is soon joined by the king, who listens unmoved to her pleas. She reminds him that Venus is actually responsible for the incestuous love that has blighted the twins because the goddess is still angry with him for harrying Aeneas. She reminds him of other victims of the goddess—perhaps Speroni was here anticipating adverse criticism of his play—Circe, Medea, Pasiphaë, and Byblis (who also fell in love with her brother). She reminds him that Jupiter himself married his own sister (Juno). Finally she collapses in a swoon, and the king leaves her to the care of the waiting woman.

Macareo and his servant open the last act. The young prince has been unable to learn anything about his sister, but he fears the worst from his father. These fears are soon realized when the king's minister, now taking the role of messenger, reports in detail the death of Canace. Macareo prepares to kill himself.

---

[3] See above, p. 97.

In the second scene of Act 5, Eolo returns to his senses. Now that it is too late he wishes that he had followed the advice of his counselor. Now his own blind rage appears to him a greater evil than the sin of his children. He hopes that Macareo is still alive; but this hope is sunk by the servant, who makes a formal announcement: "King, my master, he who was formerly your son has died twice today; once from the news of his sister's death, and another time from this same sword, still hot with his blood."

Now Eolo laments the death of son, daughter, and grandchild. He grieves the more because he himself is immortal and so denied the solace of death. Some of the lines here are worth quoting as typical of the Italian tragic style that carries echoes of Seneca.

> Spegnete, venti,
> Quella face infernale
> Di Megara e d' Aletto, che riluce
> Pur in forma di sole,
> E ingombra il sol di sì odiosa luce.
> Che parlo? dove sono?
> Debbo sempre dolermi
> Senza saper giamai di che mi doglia?
> Nova furia celeste,
> Peggior dell' infernale,
> Arde il mio regno e d' ogni ben lo spoglia.
> Ingiustissima Dea,
> Madre, com' altri dice,
> D' amor, ma, com' io provo,
> Madre d' odio e di sdegno.

Winds, quench that infernal torch of Megaera and Alecto which shines in shape of the sun and impedes the hateful light of the sun itself. What am I saying? Where am I? Must I always grieve without ever knowing what afflicts me? A new celestial fury, worse than the infernal, burns my realm and strips it of every good. Most unjust goddess, mother, as other men say, of love, but, as I feel, mother of hate and malice.

Eolo ends his complaint with a curse on the descendants of Aeneas. The chorus brings the play to a close with a brief promise that this curse will be carried out.

While *Canace* is hardly a good tragedy, it attracted much attention at the time of its composition and throughout the second half of the century, for it touched off a critical controversy that explored the whole theory of neoclassical tragedy. This controversy, which started as attack and defense of *Canace*, continued until it embraced tragedy in general and many particular tragedies, ancient and contemporary.

The quarrel over *Canace* was actually an extension of the quarrel over Cinthio's *Didone*. In large part it was another battle between Ancients and Moderns. The Grecian enemies of Cinthian tragedy maintained that *Didone* violated Aristotle's prescriptions for tragedy, that its division into acts and scenes was not in accord with Greek practice, that it offended decorum, that it did not square with the best classical model of tragedy, namely, the *Oedipus Rex* of Sophocles. Cinthio answered these objections in an Apology, and his answers have already been incorporated in an earlier chapter (IV) on his theory.

It is possible, even likely, that the instigator of the Grecian attack on *Didone* was Bartolomeo Cavalcanti, a follower of the "learned Trissino"[4] with one important difference; he did not share Trissino's distaste for Seneca, but admired the Roman tragedian almost as much as did Cinthio. It seems virtually certain that Cavalcanti was the author of the *Giuditio sopra la tragedia di Canace e Macareo,* which circulated in manuscript until 1550, when it was printed at Lucca. This treatise is one of the important critical documents of the century, for it explores almost every current theory of dramatic composition. It is of special interest, of course, for the study of tragic theory in the sixteenth century.

The *Giuditio* is a dialogue, with several speakers expressing diverse opinions, but the chief speaker is a learned Florentine who is a Grecian for the most part and who must be the author's mouthpiece. Cavalcanti, then, was an Aristotelian and an upholder of ancient models, Sophocles, Euripides, and Seneca. For him Horace was a secondary authority who had to yield precedence to Artistotle when the two ancient critics were in disagreement. For example, Cavalcanti agreed with Cinthio,[5] with whom he sometimes disagreed, that although Horace forbade Medea to kill her children onstage, Aristotle allowed "murders on the stage" and Seneca did show Medea killing her children before the public.

---

[4] See *Giuditio* (1550), 32v. I am assuming that Cavalcanti was the author of the *Giuditio* that attacked Speroni's *Canace*. In this essay (13r), Trissino is represented as reluctant to criticize Speroni's play, but, when pressed, does say that such evil subject matter can not be used in tragedy to arouse pity and terror.

[5] See above, p. 79.

Although Cavalcanti was an Aristotelian, his critical procedure owed less to the *Poetics* than to the conventional rhetorical scheme of invention, arrangement, and style.

The *Giuditio* begins with a sweeping condemnation of *Canace* as no true tragedy because the author "had not pondered Aristotle's *Poetics* very diligently" (2v). Then it proceeds to illustrate in detail what is wrong with Speroni's *inventio, dispositio,* and *elocutio.*

According to Cavalcanti, Speroni erred in his choice of argument, for he picked a story of evil persons whose fall from happiness to misery cannot arouse pity and terror, which constitute the *fondamento della tragedia.* It is true that Oedipus committed incest with his mother Jocasta; but in Sophocles' play, which Aristotle rightly judged a paragon among tragedies, both Oedipus and Jocasta sinned unwittingly and therefore do arouse pity and terror. It is true that Orestes and Electra, in Spohocles' *Electra,* do evil in killing their mother Clytemnestra; but neither one of them is an evil person, for both are "middling characters, that is, they are between good and evil, and therefore (as Aristotle says) deserving of compassion: they are evil for causing the death of their mother, but are good in avenging their father" (5r). Furthermore, the author of *Canace* is most reprehensible in yielding to the vice of modern times and making his characters try to evade the responsibility of their own wicked behavior. In the third act, Macareo excuses himself for the crime of incest by attributing it to an uncontrollable impulse that seized him and drove him to it. Cavalcanti emphasized the *impeto fatal,* but conveniently omitted Macereo's earlier explanation, in the second act, that his sin was "not a mortal villainy, but was a celestial force that conquered and extinguished every virtue in us"—an allusion, well understood by the audience, to the supernatural influence of Venus, before whom all mortals were helpless. Cavalcanti would not even allow that Canace's baby arouses pity and terror, "because the wickedness of his parents stains all his innocence" and he does not compensate for the abomination of his birth by performing good deeds, as does Sophocles' Antigone, whose death is worthy of compassion (8v–9r).

Cavalcanti found the arrangement of Speroni's play ill contrived, full of irrelevancies, and a violation of the rule that the stage should never be left empty. The detached prologue—the opening scene of Act 1, wherein the ghost appears, was considered a prologue— goes against the best practice of the Greeks. The author violated verisimilitude, confounding past and future, in introducing the ghost of Canace's child before it was born. More serious, perhaps, was the author's ill-advised tampering with his ancient source, that is, Ovid's poem. In Ovid's story, Aeolus sends his daughter a knife; Speroni added poison. Speroni also departed from his source in introducing the death of the nurse, which is doubly wrong because she is a base-born character unworthy of tragedy, according to Aristotle's definition. The author of *Canace* ignored Aristotle's advice to keep supernatural machinery out of the plot.

Speroni's play, according to Cavalcanti, offends the decorum of tragedy throughout in both characterization and style. In the second scene of Act 1, Eolo indulges in unseemly tittle-tattle about his children. The counselor does not speak in a manner worthy of a wise man. The first scene of Act 3 violates both decorum and verisimilitude; here Canace talks in public about the child she is about to bear. Even in comedy it is not seemly for middle-class women to lament the pangs of childbirth, but it is much worse for a princess to do so in tragedy. "Immortal God . . . did he not know that these things full of ugliness are only laughable?" (21v). The next scene, in which Canace reveals her shame to the nurse, is of the same kind, unworthy of tragedy.

Speroni's versification was subjected to detailed analysis and condemnation in the *Giuditio*. Cavalcanti was willing to allow some short lines in a vulgar (Italian) tragedy, but not many and not throughout the whole play. *Versi rotti* (broken or shortened verses), he conceded, are suitable for expressing overpowering grief or pain. The author of *Canace*, however, reversed the approved practice; instead of inserting a few short lines among the usual full-length lines *(endecasillabi)* he used a few long lines among many short lines. And he used far too much rhyme. Many short lines and much rhyme are unsuited to a *rappresentazione* (dramatic performance). (Neoclassicists in Italy, especially the Grecians, had only contempt for the rhymed *rappresentazioni sacre* of the popular drama.) Trissino had provided the best model *(Sofonisba)* in the vulgar tongue, and he had shown that unrhymed, full-length verses *(versi sciolti)* are best for tragedy. Trissino's *versi sciolti* correspond to the Greek iambics that Aristotle recommended for dramatic poetry because they are closest to conversation. When another speaker challenges this statement by pointing out that *versi sciolti* are not verses at all since they do not have the iambs, trochees, anapests, dactyls, and spondees of ancient Greek and

Latin poetry, Cavalcanti's spokesman, the Florentine, explains that Italian verse does have, or should have, a regular number of syllables which bear accents and that it is not rhyme that makes poetry.

Another member of the company in the *Giuditio* suggests that writers of tragedy should go a step further and write in prose, which is even closer to conversation than is unrhymed verse. But the Florentine disagrees, and on the basis of Aristotelian authority. Aristotle says that verse does not make a writer a poet, who must be first of all a maker of plots, but Aristotle does not recommend prose for tragedy. Moreover, Seneca has shown how much verse can add to the majesty and splendor of tragedy.

Cavalcanti accepted the traditional doctrine that the tragic style should be serious, dignified, and elevated, free from obscurity, free from frivolity, free from any excess. He found many examples of bad tragic style in *Canace*, and one of the worst in the opening of the second act, when the queen talks to her faithful waiting woman.

> Ben puoi securamente
> Spatiare a tua voglia
> Per entro a miei secreti
> Tu, la cui fede ha seco ambe le chiavi,
> Onde sì serra et apre
> L' arbitrio del mio core.

You can confidently enter into my secrets as you wish, for your loyalty holds both the keys whereby my heart's will is unlocked and open.

This, says the Florentine, is not the speech of a noble queen, for it is a "figure of extreme affectation, and of a false and vicious art, without any light of nature"; it represents the worst vice in writing, which is "to reveal art and bury nature" (41v). And, he adds, "He who seeks praise for his writing ought to flee the affected fads of speaking more than sailors flee rocks in the sea."

According to Cavalcanti, verisimilitude and decorum and the laws laid down by Aristotle and Horace are the best guides for a good writer, who must always avoid extremes. Boccaccio's *Decameron* provides good examples of natural speech and the poetry of Petrarch shows how serious matter may be expressed without bombast or preciosity. Among the Ancients, Sophocles and Euripides show how dignity and majesty may be expressed naturally.

For all this good advice on concealing art and following nature, on avoiding the extremes of bombast and puerility, Cavalcanti's final judgment on the art of writing betrays his Grecian limitations. "I tell you," says the Florentine, "that it is better to earn the praise of ten or fifteen judicious men than to gain the favor of the whole mob" (54v). Here speaks the disciple of Trissino, who wrote plays for scholars, who earned the praise of scholars, but who failed to reach the public. The author of *Canace* failed to earn the praise of scholars, at least of the Grecian scholars, but he tried to fashion a play that would appeal to the public. He failed here, too, it may be, but the remedy for his failure hardly lay in the prescriptions of Cavalcanti and ten other "judicious" men.

Apparently Speroni did not answer the *Giuditio* until after it was published in 1550. Then he wrote his *Apologia contra il Giuditio fatto sopra la Canace*, and later on expanded his defense to six lectures. The *Apologia* and *Lettioni* were not published, however, until 1597, together with the revised edition of *Canace*.

Speroni's *Apologia* is only twenty-five pages long, perhaps hurriedly written and left incomplete. He did not try to answer all of Cavalcanti's objections, but he did argue that his play was true to the laws of Aristotle. *Canace*, he maintained, since it was based on an old story familiar to readers from school days, was calculated to bring a pleasure similar to that brought by a painting of things we know and love. This argument echoes Aristotle's comparison of the tragic poet with the portrait painter, Horace's *ut pictura poesis*, and Plutarch's "speaking picture."

Speroni argued that his plot fulfilled Aristotle's requirements, because it has not merely one but two reversals of fortune leading from happiness to misery and arousing pity and terror. Canace and Macareo are not all evil, but, as Aristotle recommends, between good and evil. Moreover, both are young and their destruction is brought on by love. There is ancient authority for such characters involved in similar events—for example Amnon's ravishing of his sister Thamar (2 *Samuel* 13) and Byblis' despairing love for her brother (Ovid's *Metamorphoses*). Dante, as all know, had a special place in hell for incontinent lovers and he felt a special compassion for such unfortunates.

Speroni (pp. 154 ff.) sought support for his peculiar versification in Dante's Latin essay *De vulgari eloquentia*, which he interpreted to suit himself. For example, he evaded the explicit statement in the fifth chapter of the second part that the eleven-syllable line (the line that Dante himself used in the *Commedia*) is superior to all others in stateliness, but he played up Dante's recommendation of a mixture of *endecasillabi* with *heptasillabi* and *pentasillabi* for certain poems. This was the mixture that Speroni used in *Canace*. Furthermore, Dante did remark that some writers have begun a poem in the tragic style with a line of seven syllables. Speroni supported his choice of *heptasillabi,* or *settenarii,* as they came to be called, as the principal verses in his tragedy by Aristotle's statement that iambs are better for dramatic poetry than the stately hexameters used in epic poems. In other words, he convinced himself, or tried to, that the Italian *heptasillabi* correspond to Greek iambs while the *endecasillabi* correspond to Greek hexameters.

Why did he not use more *pentasillabi* in *Canace,* since these are even simpler than *heptasillabi?* Because, said Speroni, the shorter line is not so measured and harmonious as that of seven syllables and therefore not so seemly for the tragic style. On the other hand, *endecasillabi* are too measured and too heavy for natural conversation.

Speroni expanded his defense in the *Lettioni,* adding no important new arguments but showing a more independent attitude toward Aristotle, an attitude comparable to that of Cinthio, who always put the audience first, even ahead of Aristotle. In other words, Speroni here became something of a Modern. In the second lecture, for example, while still maintaining that his Canace and Macareo are between good and evil, he ventured to assert, contrary to Aristotle's judgment, that pity and terror may also be felt for evil characters. If the punishment of a great sinner is too harsh, if he loses his immortal soul, then compassion may be felt for him. In the *Inferno,* Dante felt pity for Ugolino (whom he found buried in ice and gnawing the neck of his deadly enemy, Archbishop Ruggieri), because the count, traitor that he was, suffered so horrible a punishment on earth as well as in hell. (Ugolino, it may be recalled, was shut up in a tower and forced to watch his sons and grandsons starve to death.)

Speroni also tried to justify his *Canace* as fulfilling Aristotle's requirement of a single complex plot. He no longer claimed that Canace and her brother fall from happiness to misery because of a discovery; they are already in great trouble when they first appear in his tragedy. Their father Eolo, however, does fall from happiness to misery when he discovers that his children have committed incest. Therefore the tragedy of Eolo is unified and complex (containing discovery and reversal of fortune). Eolo is a good tragic hero, too, because his downfall is brought on by the error he had made in harrying Aeneas, the pet of all-powerful Venus. If Speroni could not justify his tragedy as true to Aristotle's rules in one way, he could justify it in another, and here he was no different from most Italian critics of the century, Ancients and Moderns alike.

Other critics became involved in the controversy over *Canace*, both friends and enemies of Speroni. Giraldi Cinthio apparently replied to Seproni's defense in a letter that was never published.[6] Although Cinthio was presumably Speroni's friend, he could not accept the author's defense of *Canace* and condemned the tragedy as defective in Aristotle's requirements for plot and characters.

Years later, in 1590, after Speroni was dead, another friend, Faustino Summo, did the author of *Canace* no better service. Summo, one of the most uncompromising Aristotelians of the century, in his essay on the "wrangle between Signor Speron Speroni and the *Giuditio* published against his tragedy of Canace and Macareo," started out to refute the *Giuditio*, and presumably to defend the *Apologia* and *Lettioni*, but he soon came to the conclusion that "neither the one nor the other lacks defects." The principal defect of both authors in the dispute was that the "rules of Aristotle in the *Poetics* . . . are understood and interpreted wholly contrary to the intent of the author" (p. 2). Summo had studied the *Poetics* in Madius' edition and commentary published in 1550. Summo was a Grecian, a follower of Trissino.

Cavalcanti, like Cinthio, had taken Aristotle's phrase "murders on the stage" (*Poetics* 11) as license to exhibit death scenes. Cavalcanti had objected to Speroni's changing some details of the Canace story as he found it in Ovid. Cavalcanti, like Cinthio, had ventured to assert that Aristotle condoned tragedies with a happy ending. Summo found all of these arguments misguided. In the first instance, Cavalcanti had been led astray by the practice of Seneca, whom the best judges do not rank so high as Sophocles and Euripides. The quibbles over changing details of the source for *Canace* are wrong, for Aristotle calls attention to the freedom of the poet, a creator, as compared with the fact-bound historian. The third argument was especially offensive to Summo, who found Aristotle

---

[6] See Weinberg, pp. 926–928.

distinctly preferring the unhappy ending in tragedy because it
is more artistic. Summo, in fact, would not allow that the happy
ending had any place in a true tragedy.

Passing on to Speroni's defense, which he carefully summarized,
Summo was forced to conclude that the author of *Canace* had also
misinterpreted Aristotle. Speroni's attempt to prove that Canace
and her brother are not actually wicked and his attempt to show
that evil characters can evoke pity and fear are failures. Carnal
love between brother and sister is wicked and scandalous, as all
the most illustrious authors of antiquity affirm, and a drama based
on such love cannot be a tragedy in the true Aristotelian sense.
Summo rejected the example of Ugolino in Dante's *Inferno*, because
Ugolino's wretched plight is so unusual, so far removed from
common experience, that it is unsuitable for the drama.

Summo's attack on the *Giuditio*, and on *Canace* as well, provoked
a reply from Giovanni Battista Liviera,[7] a disciple of Cinthio and
author of a tragedy, *Cresfonte* (1588). Liviera may have intended
to answer Summo's unfavorable judgment of *Canace*, but he
became so preoccupied with defending the happy ending in
tragedy, particularly the happy ending of his own tragedy, that he
forgot about Speroni and Cavalcanti.

Liviera, then, diverted attention from *Canace* to the increasingly
popular *tragedia di lieto fin*. Faustino Summo was vexed by the
attempts of Giraldi Cinthio and his followers to promote what Aristotle called an inferior art form, and he turned his attention to the
quarrel over tragedy with a happy ending and its offshoot, the
quarrel over Guarini's pastoral tragicomedy, *Il pastor fido*. Summo
condemned both *tragedia di lieto fin* and tragicomedy.[8] In the
lively and prolonged controversy between the Grecians and the
followers of Cinthio and Guarini, Speroni's *Canace* was all but
forgotten; it was not reprinted after 1597 until the publication
of the author's *Opere* in 1740. And apparently no other Italian
dramatist ventured to revive the story.

Although no succeeding playwright wrote another *Canace*, and
although Speroni's was not a good play, it exerted a considerable
influence upon Italian tragedy in the second half of the century.
We find it repeatedly held up as one of the leading models, along

---

[7] *Apologia . . . contro l'eccell'te Sig. Faustino Summo Padovano*, Padua, 1590.
[8] In *Discorsi poetici*, Padua, 1600.

with *Sofonisba, Rosmunda,* and *Orbecche.* It was especially influential in introducing modifications of the verse forms in tragedy. Apparently Italian playwrights who followed Speroni found his short lines (the *heptasillabi* or *settenarii*) attractive, and most tragedies published after 1546 contained many short lines in highly emotional passages.

VII

Roman Tragedies

Italians of the Renaissance liked to think of themselves as the
heirs of ancient Rome, and the writers of tragedy were naturally
attracted to subjects from Roman history. Although Trissino was
a Grecian, he turned to Livy's history of Rome for his *Sofonisba*.
After Trissino, Alessandro Pazzi wrote "Dido in Carthage," Martelli
wrote *Tullia,* Giraldi Cinthio a *Didone* and a *Cleopatra.*

Cinthio preferred Roman history to Greek, and Roman tragedy
to Greek tragedy. In fact, he thought that Trissino had spoiled a
good subject in *Sofonisba* by putting it in Grecian form; he would
have done better, said Cinthio, if he had put aside the Grecian
manner in favor of the Roman, which is grander, more majestic.[1]
Seneca, it is true, usually chose Greek subject matter,[2] but he
wrote as a Roman, and Cinthio preferred his tragedies to those
of the Greeks; he believed that his *Troades,* for example, preserves
the lofty decorum of tragedy better than does Euripides' play about
Hecuba.[3]

Cinthio, then, encouraged the writing of Roman tragedy in Italy.
At the same time, however, his *Orbecche,* based on one of his own

---

[1] See *Discorsi,* p. 261.
[2] *Octavia* is the only play in the Senecan canon that is based on Roman history.
While it is not now ascribed to Seneca, the sixteenth century took it to be his.
[3] *Discorsi,* p. 262.

novelle, proved to be more successful on the stage than did *Didone* and *Cleopatra.* Consequently, Cinthio abandoned Roman history and wrote romantic tragedies. And since he found that the public liked romantic tragedies with a happy ending, he wrote tragicomedies. The followers of Cinthio, therefore, had two roads to follow, that is, Roman tragedy or romantic tragedy. After Cinthio, Roman tragedies continued to appear, but not in the large numbers that the early direction of Italian tragedy indicated.

ARETINO'S *ORAZIA*

Pietro Aretino, the great satirist, author of five comedies and a Roman tragedy, was neither a Grecian nor a follower of Giraldi Cinthio. In fact, Aretino liked to scoff at the neoclassical rules and literary plays. The prologue to his comic masterpiece, *La cortigiana* ("The Courtesan"), was in part a manifesto of independence: "If you see the characters enter on the stage more than five times, don't laugh, because the chains that hold the mills on the river would never hold the madmen of today. Moreover, don't wonder if the comic style is not observed as ordinarily required, because we in [modern] Rome live in another manner than that of [ancient] Athens." Nevertheless, he did not throw away all the rules, and his plays were not quite so revolutionary as he implied. The plots of his comedies were not very different from the routine plots of other learned comedies in the sixteenth century; they reflected the practice of Plautus and Terence and the Italian followers of Plautus and Terence. The structure of his tragedy, *Orazia,* was essentially neoclassical, although he did not imitate Senecan bombast and he eliminated the soliloquy. He preserved a strict economy of time and place, for example; all of the action occurs within a day and on a street in Rome. The author had to maneuver his action in a rather unnatural way to preserve this unity of place; he had to report scenes that took place in the forum and he had to move the continuance of the trial from the forum to this particular spot where the heroine was killed and where the action started. He divided his tragedy into five acts with a chorus at the end of each act. He used a detached prologue. The prologue and choruses are in rhyme, the dialogue in unrhymed eleven-syllable verses *(versi sciolti).*

Orazia, which was written in the early 1540's, first printed in

1546,[4] was based on the quasi-historical account of the Horatii in Livy.

According to Livy, the war between Rome and her neighbor Alba was settled by each king's choosing three young warriors to fight to the death; the Horatii brothers from Rome, the Curiatii brothers from Alba. Two of the Horatii were killed early in the fight and all three of the Curiatii were wounded. The remaining Horatius managed to separate his opponents and dispatch them one by one. Then he returned to Rome in triumph. There he met his only sister, Horatia (Celia in Aretino's play), who was betrothed to one of the Curiatii. This young woman was all but prostrated by the death of her Alban lover, and her lamentations so enraged Horatius that he plunged his sword into her body, crying, "Begone to your betrothed with your untimely love, since you have forgotten your brothers, both living and dead, since you have forgotten your country. So may every Roman woman go who mourns an enemy."[5] This shocking deed called for punishment, so the king summoned an extraordinary court of duumvirs (special magistrates) who found the killer guilty. Horatius appealed to the Roman people. The father of Horatius, who had now lost all his children save one, implored the people to show mercy. The sentence was changed from capital punishment to expiation by walking under a yoke or beam with covered head. The sister Horatia was buried where she fell.

Aretino followed Livy's argument without any significant deviation and added no new matter until the last act, when he introduced a *deus ex machina* in the form of Jove's voice, ordering the Romans to stop their bickering and fulfill the ends of justice. Learned contemporaries of Aretino must have objected to this departure from the ancient source and to this disregard of Aristotle's advice to avoid using any outside mechanism to resolve a tragic plot. Actually such a device was unnecessary—in Livy's account the Romans solved their legal problem without any help from the gods—but Aretino probably introduced it for theatrical effect. In other words, with the exception of the *deus ex machina*, Aretino let Livy take care of the plot and concentrated on expanding the dialogue and developing the motivations of the leading characters.

---

[4] I have used the modern text in *Teatro di Pietro Aretino*, Lanciano, 1914, comparing it occasionally with that of the 1549 printing. Doglio (pp. 129–219) now offers a modern text.

[5] Livy, 1.26.

On the whole, Aretino performed his task well, though, ironically enough, he might have done better had he discarded some of the neoclassical rules he professed to despise. His only violation of the strictest rules was allowing Orazio to kill his sister on the stage, and, as we have seen, sixteenth-century Italian critics did not all agree to accept Horace's ban on death scenes. As it stands, *Orazia* is too often debate instead of drama.

The title of the play suggests that the author intended to write the tragedy of Horatia; but Aretino did not subscribe to Cinthio's "cult of the feminine soul," and Celia's part is all over before the end of the third act. Publio, father of the family, is certainly the leading character and a worthy protagonist of tragedy, for he is torn this way and that by love of son, love of daughter, love of country, and love of justice. Moreover, the chorus, playing the traditional role prescribed by Horace and practiced by Seneca, sympathizes with Publio, who is a righteous man. Aretino himself, in the dedication of the play to Pope Paul III, said that his aim was the "story [*istoria*] of the Orazi and the Curiazi." Probably the most satisfactory interpretation is that *Orazia* is the tragedy of a noble family of ancient Rome.

The prologue is delivered by Fame, who assures the spectators that she has not come from "infernal horrors," nor from the Elysian fields, but is merely revisiting Rome, which now, under the rule of Paul III, is greater and more beautiful than ever before. Aretino used the prologue to glorify Rome and to compliment the pope, the emperor Charles V, and Francis I of France.

Publio, father of the Orazi, opens the play and provides most of the exposition. Since Aretino renounced soliloquies, doubtless because he considered them unnatural, he provided a faithful companion (Spurio) for Publio, so that the exposition is all in dialogue. There are no soliloquies in the play, offering a sharp contrast with the practice of Cinthio, who, it may be recalled, considered the soliloquy an important part of tragedy and took great care in composing them. Although Aretino rejected the soliloquy, he retained the neoclassical economy of time and place and therefore could not dispense with messengers. He did not call these necessary couriers *nuntii*, however, but provided ordinary characters to report offstage events. Thus the head priest informs Publio of arrangements for the fight and one Tito reports its outcome. Spurio reports the proceedings of the trial in the forum and the duumvirs inform

Publio of its outcome. In the last act, the family nurse tells Publio about the offstage suicide of Celia's maidservant, who could not survive her beloved mistress. Even so, messengers are less prominent in *Orazia* than they are in the usual Senecan tragedy. The third act, which has more dramatic action than does any other, and which culminates in the killing of Celia, has no messenger and needs none.

Aretino's *coro di virtù per intermedi* was used, as the phrase suggests, in the manner of the *intermedii* or *intermezzi* of comic performances in the sixteenth century; that is, it closes each act or operates between the acts. Nevertheless, the chorus of *Orazia* was also used in the Senecan manner, for it offers moral comments on action and characters. Aretino sharply curtailed the length of the choruses. He compensated for this shrinking of the chorus by introducing the *popolo Romano*. The Roman populace in *Orazia* was used as an actor, and a rather important actor, too, for it has the final decision in Orazio's appeal to set aside the duumvirs' sentence of death by hanging. Aretino's *popolo Romano* is not a theatrical mob like the citizens in Shakespeare's *Julius Caesar*, with various members crying out from time to time. Apparently Aretino's *popolo* comes onstage as a body, but its members do not speak in unison or separately; a single spokesman, using the first person, carries on all the dialogue, which often becomes lively as the arguments between the spokesman and Publio or Orazio grow heated. Aretino's *popolo* is virtually the same thing as a chorus taking part in the dialogue. It may be recalled that Cinthio and other tragic dramatists often made a similar use of the chorus in the fourth and fifth acts, but not to the extent of Aretino's populace and not to such good dramatic effect.

It is hardly necessary to give a detailed summary of the action in *Orazia* since it follows Livy's account in outline. Aretino worked hard to dramatize the narrative. One important feature of his technique was to provide at least one big scene, a climactic scene, in each act. This technique became common enough in the next century, in the English tragedies and tragicomedies of Beaumont and Fletcher, for example; but I have not observed it in Italian tragedy before Aretino.

The big scene in the first act is between Celia and the nurse, wherein the distraught young noblewoman finds herself facing a hopeless dilemma: if the Orazi lose the fight, all Romans (Celia included) become slaves to Alba; if the Orazi win, then Celia loses her betrothed, whom she always speaks of as her "husband."

> Ma io, io, se Roma vince, perdo
> il marito dolcissimo e i cognati,
> e vincendo Alba, qual vincer potria,
> oltre il dominio della libertade,
> dei fratelli privata mi rimango.
> Or chi provò giammai fortuna iniqua,
> che la sorte mia dura in parti agguagli?

But I, if Rome wins, I lose the sweetest husband and his relatives, and if Alba wins, as it could win, besides my loss of liberty, I remain bereft of brothers. Whoever felt fortune so evil that it could match, even in part, my hard lot?

The dutiful nurse urges her mistress to be patient; but Celia has already gone too far, for she feels that she is already united with her betrothed. "And if he dies," she cries, "I also will die, and I will live if he lives." As she works herself up to a frenzy of despair she imagines that she already sees the glowing torches of the Furies.

In the second act Publio is so distressed by the pitiful sight of his daughter that he almost forgets the perilous state of his sons.

> *Celia*   Padre, o padre?
> *Publio*   Figlia cara, o figlia, e perchè questo?
> *Celia*   Amor legge non ave.

Celia: Father, O father?
Publio: Dear daughter, O daughter, and why this?
Celia: Love has no law.

Publio does his best to reason with her, reminding her that Rome must come before private individuals, that she can always find another husband but never other brothers. Celia replies, "I revere you, father, and I say to you that in the fall of my beloved brothers two parts of me fell, but in the fall of my noble husband I myself fell; for wives live with the life of their husbands, and die with the death of them." Then she collapses in a swoon.

In the third act, the climax comes swiftly, and, unlike most Italian tragedies, with few words. The sight of his moaning, unkempt sister enrages Orazio and he grasps her by her hair.

Celia: O my husband, he who took you from me sends me to you!
Nurse: Such was her fate!
Orazio: And so be it!

Then Orazio buries his sword in her breast.

It must be confessed that the staging here is not altogether clearly defined. Orazio orders everyone to move back before he draws
his sword. Since the actual blow that kills Celia is described by
her maidservant, it is possible that the deed is done behind other
characters on the stage, out of sight of the audience. Was Aretino
bothered by the well-known pronouncement of Horace that Medea
must not kill her children in public?

Paraphrasing Livy, Orazio delivers a brief admonition to the
corpse of his sister: "Away to your husband, who waits for you on
the bank of the Lethe, away, mad one, who has forgotten your
dead brothers, the one who lives, your country, and all else. So
may anyone end that ever dares to weep over the death of our
enemies." The *popolo Romano*, which makes its first appearance in
this third act, cannot condone such an outrageous deed. Turning
to the father, the spokesman says, "Publio, surely for my part, I
cannot say which is the greater in your double-dealing son, the
honor he has had against the enemy or his shame in taking the
life of this beautiful and loving sister."

The fourth act of sixteenth-century Italian tragedy is often dull,
as it usually is in Cinthio's plays. Aretino tried to provide a big
scene here, and he succeeded rather better than did his contemporaries.

The duumvirs bring Orazio to the very spot where Celia died
and tell Publio that his son has been found guilty. Publio debates
with them, but they stand fast and order the lictor to bind the
prisoner. Publio desperately hangs on, still pleading for a justice
tempered with mercy. Again he fails to move the duumvirs. Again
the lictor steps forward with his cord. Then Orazio cries out, "I
appeal to the people!"

The fifth and last act, which is nearly all a debate or quarrel
between the surviving Orazi and the Roman populace, rises to
two climaxes. The first is reached when Publio, who has been
arguing that the youth of his son should be an extenuating factor,
dramatically reminds the people that Orazio has been the savior
of all Rome.

> Perchè se vincitrice Alba di Roma
> restava in cotal dì, non rimanea
> qui pietra sopra pietra; andando il tutto
> in rovine ed in ceneri, elevando
> l' una città con il cader dell' altra.

Because, if Alba had remained the victor today, not a stone would be left upon a stone here, all going to ruin and ashes, the one city rising with the fall of the other.

Finally the *popolo* relents:

> Io assolvo,
> Orazio, te, e ciò faccio e dispongo,
> oltre la pietà, che ho del tuo buon padre,
> per meraviglia della tua virtute,
> non per giustizia della causa inerme.

I acquit you, Orazio, and I do this, beyond the compassion that I have for your good father, because of admiration for your courage, not because of the justice of your unsupported appeal.

Orazio is ordered to cover his head and walk under the yoke.

But the play is not over, for Orazio stubbornly refuses to be so humiliated. The people are just as stubborn as he is, so the contention is renewed. Thereupon the whole action is resolved by the voice of Jove—"Orazio, bow your head to the yoke."

The tragedy ends with a fatalistic, mildly Senecan comment from the chorus, that the patient man who accepts whatever fate bestows is the only man to win contentment in the end.

Orazia differs in several ways from Italian tragedies preceding it. The abolition of the soliloquy and the drastic reduction of the chorus were significant, but more important, aesthetically, were the author's characterization and style. Aretino tried to make his leading characters behave and speak as normal human beings rather than puppets or monsters mouthing high-sounding sentiments. Cinthio, in some of his tragedies with a happy ending, for example *Epitia* and *Arrenopia,* humanized the characters to some extent; but Aretino went far beyond him. As Neri says, "*Orazia* has, then, its own inner life."[6]

Publio, patriot, leading citizen, father of a family, is a well-drawn character; he has to resolve a great inner conflict, and he resolves it. Orazio, in my judgment, is more remarkable, for he comes to life much more vividly than does his father although he appears only occasionally onstage and never talks much when he does appear. While Aretino scoffed at literary models, he used them when they suited his purpose, and I suspect that Orazio was influenced by the classical Achilles, both the character in the *Iliad* and the brave, arrogant, lawless Achilles that Horace rec-

---

[6] P. 86.

ommended in his *Ars Poetica*. Aretino modified this classical model by emphasizing the extreme youth of Orazio. Moreover, he added a complexity that Horace did not recommend; Orazio is arrogant and yet modest, stubborn and yet generous, cruel and yet kind.

The first glimpse the reader has of the young hero is in the messenger's report of the fight. While Tito does justice to Orazio's skill and courage, he also shows another side of his character: "But being no less worthy of praise for having pity on his unhappy enemy, whom he saw spent and vanquished at his feet, our warrior, in a voïce devoid of pride, said sorrowfully, 'O wretched brother-in-law, it is not obstinate hatred or enmity, but love of country, that requires me to kill you. Now pardon my vengeance, for I have already pardoned your cruel offense in killing my brothers.' " Aretino surely built up this gracious side of Orazio for dramatic contrast with his subsequent cruelty to his sister.

Publio repeatedly stresses the youthful, impulsive nature of his son, arguing that Orazio has not yet learned to control his passions.

> La Gioventù debbe scusare Orazio,
> quanto ch' egli abbia pur commesso errore.
> La Gioventù furor della Natura,
> che in l' esser suo un caval fiero sembra,
> dai legami disciolto in un bel prato,
> che in sè ritroso la giumenta vista
> nei campi aperti, alza su i crini folti,
> le nare allarga e la bocca disserra,
> fremita, ringe, calcitra e vaneggia.

However great the wrong he may have committed, youth ought to excuse Orazio. The impetuous youth of Nature, which in his being is like a fierce, unruly stallion let loose in a fine meadow; when he sees a mare in the open fields he raises up the thick hairs, dilates his nostrils, and opens his mouth, rages, snarls, kicks, and runs riot.

Popolo Romano objects to this argument on the ground that if Orazio were always such an easy prey to passion, he would have lost the fight, while, on the contrary, in his mortal combat with the Curiazi he displayed the judgment and craft of a mature man. And so it goes throughout the last three acts of the play; Orazio is a contradictory but lifelike character.

Aretino's tragic style is as revolutionary, if not more so, as his portrayal of characters. He all but abandoned the high-pitched rhetoric of Senecan drama, with its swarms of mythological allusions, long-drawn-out lamentations, and lugubrious complaints

about cruel Fortune. The nurse is the only character who broods
over the miseries of life, and she never raves. Her remarks addressed
to Publio and Spurio in the third act run as follows:

> Il non nascerci è gran felicitade,
> e gran beatitudine, se presto
> chi ci nasce si muor, che stato alcuno
> di quiete no ha chi vive in terra.
> S' abiti le città, l' ambizione
> ognor ti noia, se nei boschi stanzi,
> delle fere hai commercio; s' altri servi,
> vendi te stesso, se domini altrui,
> compri la invidia e te la movi contra;
> s' hai prole, hai cura, se non l' hai, tormento.

Not to be born is great happiness, and he is blessed who dies soon after
he is born, for no one who lives on earth is at peace. If you live in cities,
ambition often frets you; if you live in the forest, you must deal with
wild beasts; if you serve others, you sell yourself; if you rule others, you
purchase envy and incite it against you; if you have offspring, you have
anxiety; if you have none, torment.

The sentiment here is perhaps more Sophoclean than Senecan.[7]

When Tito informs Publio that Orazio is the winner of the fight,
the old man cries:

> E perchè non gli Orazi? adunque un solo;
> un solo adunque avrà il trionfo? ovvero
> tutti gil altri son morti? Tito, dillo,
> dillo a me senza indugio, chè per Dio
> non mancherò d' esser quell' uom ch' io debbo.

And why not the Orazi? Only one then; then only one will have the triumph? Are all the others dead indeed? Tito, tell me, tell me without
delay, because with God's help I shall not fail to be that man I ought
to be.

Sometimes the stoical Publio fails to maintain full control over
his feelings and bursts out in figurative language that may suggest,
somewhat mildly, Senecan rant. There is such a moment in the
fourth act, when the duumvirs order the lictor to bind Orazio.
Then Publio cries out: "What do I hear? What do I see? Stand
back a moment, lictor. Even Hyrcanian tigers, even the dragons
of Lybia would do me the favor I ask."[8] Such outbursts, however,
are not frequent, nor long sustained.

---

[7] Cf. *Oedipus at Colonus* 1224 ff.
[8] The "Hyrcanian tigers" are Virgilian. See below, p. 168.

Once in a while the language of narrative passages in *Orazia* is fairly elaborate, and in a conventional manner. Tito's blow-by-blow report of the fight, for example, sounds more like the approved elevated style of neoclassical tragedy than do most passages in the play.

> Onde incontrarsi e dier di petto insieme
> con quel tuon, con quel suon, che tona e sona
> il ciel e il mar, se le procelle e i nembi
> e del mare e del ciel turban la pace.

Whence they rushed together breast to breast with that thunder, with that uproar with which sky and sea thunder and resound when storms and clouds disturb the peace of sea and sky.

It should be pointed out, however, that in this rather long speech of over 150 lines, there is not a single mythological allusion of the type that Seneca and his Renaissance disciples favored. Furthermore, Tito does not moan, weep, and break down, unable to continue, as Cinthio's messengers often do.

Bertana calls *Orazia* "by far the most notable and respected of all the [Italian] historical (and perhaps nonhistorical as well) tragedies of the sixteenth century."[9] But apparently Aretino left no disciples in tragedy, unless Maffio Veniero[10] be counted as one, and his salutary reforms went virtually unheeded. Perhaps the satirist's unsavory moral reputation made his serious work suspect; more likely, fellow Italians in the sixteenth century preferred Senecan rhetoric and the romantic, exotic spectacle of Cinthian tragedy to the severe re-creation of ancient Rome in *Orazia*. At all events, Ben Jonson's English dramatizations of Roman history, *Sejanus* and *Catiline,* are closer to *Orazia* in spirit and style than are other Italian tragedies of the Renaissance.[11] The motto from Martial[12] on the 1605 title page of *Sejanus*—"You will not find Centaurs or Gorgons or Harpies here; our page smacks of man"—fits Aretino's play as well as it fits Jonson's.

---

[9] P. 75.

[10] See below, p. 258. A brazen reprint (almost word for word) of *Orazia* appeared in 1604 at Venice under the title *Amore della patria* and attributed to Giuliano Goselini. A new prologue, spoken by Fame, was added.

[11] In his preface to *Sejanus,* Jonson admitted that his tragedy was "no true poem, in the strict laws of time . . . as also in the want of a proper chorus." He explained that he could not present correct tragedy on the London stage with any hope of popular success.

[12] *Epigrams* 10.4.9–10.

CLEOPATRA PLAYS

There were four *Cleopatras* printed in Italy during the sixteenth century. The first written was Cinthio's, which was not printed, however, until 1583. Then came one by Alessandro Spinello, which was performed at a carnival in Venice, printed in 1550.[13] Then came another by Cesare de' Cesari, printed at Venice in 1552, and finally Celso Pistorelli's *Marc' Antonio e Cleopatra,* printed at Venice in 1576.

The Cleopatra in Spinello's play is not the one associated with Caesar and Antony, but an earlier queen who lived at Thebes. As the prologue says, "I do not mean that Thebes which Amphion encircled with stately and lofty walls, sounding his sweet and sacred lyre, but that which the cruel tyrant Busiris reared so proudly in Egypt." The prologue gives more than a hint of the cruelty and bloodshed to be exhibited in this corrupt city of horrors; in fact, the tragedy promises to be another *Thyestes.*

Spinello's dialogue is in unrhymed *endecasillabi* and a good many *heptasillabi* or *settenarii,* though the author did not favor the shorter line so much as did Speroni in *Canace.* The chorus of Theban women, friends of the queen, speaks in rhyme. And the chorus has a prominent role with many lines. The sentiments throughout the play are Senecan, but there is no particular emphasis on mythological allusions.

The nurse—there is almost invariably a nurse—expresses a typical sentiment in her soliloquy near the end of the first act.

> Ahi; quanto ciechi son del lume vero
> Color che cercan Regni, imperi, e stati,
> Per viuer vita più lieta, e tranquilla.
> Ma non san poi che sempre portan seco
> Timor, sospetto, dubbio, affanni, e doglie,
> E per un poco di finta dolcezza
> Che porta il regnar seco gustan poi
> Il più de la lor vita molto amaro [10r].

Alas, how blind to the true light are they who seek kingdoms, empires, and states in order to live a happier and more peaceful life. But they do not know that these things always bring with them fear, suspicion, doubt, suffering, and grief, and that for a little false sweetness which ruling brings with it they will taste much bitterness during most of their life.

Astrology, which had long been prominent in tragedies written

---

[13] The dedication reads 1540, but this date must be a mistake.

by Italians, is more prominent in Spinello's play than is mythology; "cruel stars" and "cruel fate" abound. The author used rather more Senecan stichomythy than did some other contemporary play-wrights, and this ancient device at least enlivens some of the long debates.

The heroine is a victim of her brother's cruelty. Ptolemy, Cleo-patra's younger brother, who is also her husband, had poisoned his older brother (Cleopatra's older brother and former husband) in order to gain the throne. Now he has thrust out his sister-wife in favor of their daughter. Consequently Cleopatra is now living as a beggar outside the royal palace. One of her chief complaints is present poverty compared with former luxury, and she repeatedly bewails fickle Fortune.

A priest has the role of good counselor. He accuses the king of being tyrannical rather than kingly, warns him that his lust for power and wealth and his neglect of justice, prudence, fortitude, honesty, temperance, and religion can lead only to disaster. But Ptolemy, who is a thoroughgoing villain, like Atreus, like Nero, refuses to listen, for he dislikes to be reminded of anything save power and pleasure. The priest is often tedious, but he can be pithy upon occasion, and he sums up the situation in three lines:

> Ahi, secol tristo, ahi, maladetta etade,
> In cui la verità non ha più loco,
> Ma sol l'adulatione, e la bugia [29v].

Alas, knavish age, alas, cursed times, in which the truth no more has a place, but only flattery and lies.

This is a perfect Senecan sentiment for a good counselor.

The fourth act culminates in a Thyestean meal. The messenger, reminiscent of the *nuntius* in *Thyestes*, more reminiscent of the *nuntio* in Cinthio's *Orbecche*, is highly emotional, so worked up that he can scarcely speak of the horrors he has witnessed. As usual, however, he manages to give the chorus a long circumstan-tial report. The drunken king had risen from a great feast, con-ducted his young son (Cleopatra's son) to a secret room in the palace and there killed him with a knife, then ordered the servants to carry the child's body to the kitchen and prepare a supper for the queen. Even as the messenger is finishing his report a servant comes from the palace bearing a covered dish to the queen's quarters. The horrified chorus tries to stop him, but he is afraid to disobey the king's orders.

Revenge comes in the last act. Cleopatra complains about the latest indignity inflicted upon her: "I ate and swallowed, and now I hold the very flesh of my dear little son in my belly" (40v). The queen, who speaks of herself a little earlier as the "sepulcher of my own son," may be echoing the cry of Tereus in Corraro's fifteenth-century *Progne*, "The father is the tomb of the son";[14] but the common source for both writers was the last scene in *Thyestes*.

Now Cleopatra emulates Medea; she determines to punish her husband-brother. "Great cruelty," she cries, "ought to be avenged with greater cruelty" (42v). She summons a faithful servant and asks him to gather stout helpers and kill the king in his drunken revels, then set fire to the banquet hall. Before long a bloodstained messenger brings news that her wishes have been fulfilled. The trusty servant has lost his life in the shambles of the hall, but the tyrant is dead.

Cleopatra tells her daughter what has happened and confesses that she has already taken poison. She leaves the daughter to the care of the nurse and says farewell to the chorus. Then she dies: *Mi parto, a Dio.* The play ends in frantic lamentations from all the women and a brief ode from the chorus beginning, "Let every tyrant learn from this crude example [*crudo essempio*] to live a life full of virtue."

In sixteenth-century Italy *crudo* could mean "cruel" as well as "crude" or "unripe"; but Spinello's tragedy is certainly rather "crude." It offers a mirky specimen, however, of blood and revenge, of the type of Italian tragedy that was destined to capture the imagination of English dramatists in the next generation. The fact that it was performed at a Venetian carnival—the author speaks of this public performance in his dedication—testifies to the common people's relish for such exhibitions.

Cesari's *Cleopatra* follows the same argument that Cinthio used, but the author penalized himself even further by opening the play after Antony's death. Cinthio lost Antony early in the second act and had to prolong the queen's dying for nearly three long acts.

[14] See above, p. 20.

Cesari had to provide a dirge for five acts, broken only by occasional appearances of the Roman Octavius, called Caesar Augustus in the play.

Cleopatra is already a prisoner when the lamentations begin. Her fortunes have already sunk to their lowest ebb and her only desire is to avoid being taken to Rome to be exhibited in triumph. One of her servants states the basic motif of the tragedy in a soliloquy at the beginning of Act 3: "The greatest affliction of Cleopatra is that she cannot die." She does die, however, in the last act. The chorus of Alexandrian women tells a servant that they found her lying dead, an asp curled around an arm. Octavius is enraged that the queen has foiled his plans for a triumph, but he is a Renaissance gentleman and therefore makes the best of it. He orders a decent burial for Cleopatra with her beloved Antony.

The scene, of course, is Alexandria, but it is not clear that it remains in the same spot throughout the five acts. The chorus of women closes each act with an ode, some of these pretty long, and also takes a prominent part in the dialogue. There is a semi-chorus of Roman soldiers, which appears briefly in the last act to talk with Octavius. When engaged in dialogue, both chorus and semi-chorus speak in unrhymed verse, usually in short lines *(settenarii)*. The choral odes are in rhyme. There are only three soliloquies, but some of the speeches in the dialogue are unconscionably long. Senecan sentiments are fairly prominent—there is much talk about "cruel Fortune"—but the style is tedious rather than bombastic.

Celso Pistorelli's *Marc' Antonio e Cleopatra*, published at Verona in 1576, is a learned, dull play. The author was not a Grecian though he was a fellow townsman of Trissino, but he consciously followed *Sofonisba, Rosmunda, Orbecche, Canace,* and the "stately and learned offspring" of Lodovico Dolce.[15] He also mentioned Aristotle, Sophocles, and Euripides in his dedication. His principal model, however, was Cinthio. He evidently borrowed some of his versification from Speroni or Dolce, mingling a good number of seven-syllable lines *(settenarii)* with the conventional eleven-syllable *versi sciolti*.

Pistorelli's tragedy is mostly a tedious repetition of Cinthio's *Cleopatra* with some additions, namely, more characters and more

---

[15] See dedication of the 1576 edition. For Dolce's tragedies see below, pp. 159–177.

bloodshed. He introduced Cleopatra's two sons and gave them speaking parts: Caesarion, whose father was Julius Caesar, and Antillo, whose father was Antony. The chorus of Alexandrian women plays a prominent role; it has far more lines than does any other character in the play, taking part in the dialogue during every act and closing each act with an ode. The following extract from a speech of the chorus in Act 3 (28r) is typical of the author's labored attempts to be poetical. Here the chorus is arguing that the Greek spoilers of Troy were not so numerous

> Come son questi qui nemici nostri,
> Che sembran tanti Lupi
> Intorno ad' una Agnella,
> Per divorarla Ingordi
> E stracciarla con denti a brano a brano,
> Se ben' a la lor gola
> Fia poco cibo, e a la insatiabil fame
> Breve diletto e gioia.

as are these our enemies here, who seem to be so many wolves surrounding a lamb, greedy to devour her and tear her to pieces, although she may make but scant meal for their gullet and brief delight and joy to their insatiable hunger.

Pistorelli was not skillful in adapting Roman history to the stage. He made even less use of Antony that did Cinthio. The great Roman appears only in the opening scene of the first act, wherein he delivers an exposition of past events to Eros, and then briefly in Act 2, again with Eros. The two famous lovers never meet on the stage. Octavius has a more prominent part than does Antony. Cleopatra spends most of her time in lamentations, grieving with or at the chorus and her waiting women. Messengers are kept busy throughout the play, and especially in the last two acts when the deaths occur. Antony's death is reported at the beginning of Act 4. In Act 5, the nurse gives a detailed account of Cleopatra's death, asp and all. A page reports that Octavius has had Antillo executed. Then a tutor (bailo) reports that Caesarion has been beheaded. The tragedy seldom comes to life since it is mostly narrative and elegy. There is one tolerably convincing scene in the last act between Octavius and his counselor, who are discussing what is to be done with the Egyptian captives. The counselor tells the emperor that one Caesar in the world is enough. Octavius rather likes young Caesarion, his kinsman, but this advice makes him think, and he says, "You have put strange thoughts in my heart, and already it seems that my ship is between Scylla and Charybdis, and is about to drown. Come with me, and we will speak further of this" (46v).

PESCETTI'S *IL CESARE*

Although neoclassical Italian tragedy began in 1515 with a Roman tragedy, that is, the *Sofonisba* of Trissino, and several *Cleopatras* and *Tullias* soon followed, there was no play about the greatest Roman of all until near the end of the century. In 1594, *Il Cesare* by Orlando Pescetti was published at Verona. According to Allacci, there was a second printing of the play at Viterbo in 1604.

Pescetti was a fairly prominent scholar and critic who was involved in two major literary quarrels during the second half of the century. In 1588 he entered the controversy over Ariosto and Tasso on the side of the Moderns, maintaining that Ariosto's poetry compared favorably with Virgil's.[16] Later he contributed a defense of Guarini; his *Difesa del Pastor fido* (1601) was in answer to Faustino Summo's attack on tragedy with a happy ending and pastoral tragicomedy.

Pescetti allied himself against the strict classicists, but, like most of the Moderns in Italy, he wanted Aristotle on his side. Like Giraldi Cinthio before him, he argued that Aristotle approved tragedy with a double ending, that is, reward for the good characters and punishment for the wicked. He demanded verisimilitude in the drama. His own conception of verisimilitude, however, was of a special kind, not simple realism, but a poetic verisimilitude that did not exclude the marvelous or supernatural.

You should know, then, that poetic verisimilitude is not that which happens most of the time (like the rhetorical), because it must also be marvelous, and how could it be so if it happened often? It is not the things that happen often but those that happen rarely which produce the marvelous, those things we believe have happened sometimes, or can happen, although they could not actually happen; for there are things possible but not verisimilar, just as, on the contrary, there are things impossible but verisimilar, and these are what, according to the doctrine of Aristotle, the poet should most often choose.[17]

Although written for the defense of tragicomedy, this restate-

---

[16] See Weinberg, pp. 1048–51.
[17] *Difesa del Pastor fido* (Verona, 1601), pp. 168–169.

ment of Aristotle's preference of a probable impossibility over an improbable possibility was Pescetti's credo for tragedy, and his *Cesare* illustrates his theory pretty well. The prologue, which consists of a dialogue between Venus, Mars, and Jove, introduces the marvelous or supernatural at the very outset. Brutus opens the first scene with an address to the ghost of Pompey,[18] and the scenes following, most of them, swarm with portents, divinations, dreams, and prodigies of nature.

Cesare fits the author's tragic theory in another way, for it is not strictly speaking a tragedy with an unhappy ending, unless Caesar is regarded as the hero. Shakespeare's *Julius Caesar* also offers some difficulty since Brutus seems at first sight to be the tragic hero; but it can be argued that the spirit of Caesar broods over the last two acts, in which Brutus is scarcely heroic. Dante, a monarchist, introduced Brutus into Italian poetry as an arch-villain doomed to the lowest pit in hell; but republicanism in the fifteenth century had rehabilitated the ancient Roman, for the glory of the Roman Republic before the Caesars was cherished in thought if not always in deed among all northern Italians. At all events, Pescetti made Brutus a hero, as Shakespeare, a loyal subject of a strong monarchy, did not, and his Brutus triumphs over the tyrant Caesar and restores liberty as did his illustrious ancestor (Lucius Junius Brutus), who drove out the wicked Tarquin. The most satisfactory interpretation of *Cesare* is to call it a tragedy with a happy ending.

Pescetti's principal historical source was Appian's account of the civil wars in Rome, but he also made extensive use of Plutarch's lives of Julius Caesar, Brutus, and Antony. He must have known the earlier Latin *Julius Caesar* by the French scholar Muretus; his play, in fact, is an expansion and elaboration of this very short Latin tragedy, with, however, two important changes: the Italian poet omitted Caesar's ghost introduced by Muretus near the end, but began with Pompey's ghost. There is no good evidence that Pescetti knew Jacques Grévin's *César* (1560), though he could have read it. Grévin's French tragedy was also an expansion and elaboration of Muretus' short play.

Pescetti's play is intolerably long and windy. Since there is little physical action onstage, declamation is the principal feature; the

---

[18] Pescetti doubtless borrowed Pompey's ghost from Lucan's *Pharsalia*. He did not use Caesar's ghost (from Plutarch) as did Shakespeare.

characters deliver speeches at each other and at the audience, and
some of these speeches run well over fifty lines. The dialogue and
soliloquies are mostly in unrhymed *endecasillabi*, as might be
expected, but there are a good many shorter lines as well, the
heptasillabi or *settenarii* that Speroni favored in *Canace* and that
Spinello and Cesari also used. Unfortunately for the reader, there
is relatively little give-and-take in the dialogue, and only one passage of Senecan stichomythy, which comes in the second scene
of the last act, wherein the chorus tries to console Calpurnia,
who refuses to be consoled. The choruses—there are four of them
(Roman matrons, ladies of the court, citizens, soldiers)—speak in
rhyme. A chorus delivers a short ode at the end of each act, sometimes at the end of a scene within an act, and the ladies of the
court take part in a dialogue with Calpurnia in the fourth act and
again in the last act. There is no indication of any special place
for the scene, which presumably remains the same throughout the
five acts. The passage of time is brief, for the action begins a few
hours before the assassination of Caesar and ends with the rioting
following the assassination.

Pescetti's prologue not only introduces the important supernatural element but also connects the death of Caesar with the
history of ancient Italy and Rome. Venus, the mother of Aeneas,
is in tears because the last of her mortal descendants, Julius Caesar,
is doomed to die a shameful death. Mars indignantly demands an
explanation from Jove; but the ruler of the gods is asleep. Venus
says, "He is grown old, O Mars; he no more sees nor hears than if
he were blind and deaf and witless." Jove is not so far gone, however, and he soon wakes up to explain that he plans to treat Caesar
as he treated Hercules, to whom he brought strife from cradle to
grave, but finally immortalized. So he will do for Julius, who
"tomorrow will shine resplendent in heaven."

This investing of Julius with divinity seems to contradict my
earlier contention that Caesar is not the hero of the tragedy. I can
only say that the action proper is inconsistent with the prologue,
that the Caesar of Acts 1–5 is shown as an arrogant dictator who
deserves his mortal end. Pescetti, it is true, offers no convincing
political argument in favor of liberty and the republican form of
government, but he does show Brutus as a man of high moral purpose and Caesar as a tyrant.

The style of *Cesare* is representative of Italian tragedy in the second half of the century although there is less emphasis on Senecan features, on bombast loaded with mythological allusions, for example, than in some plays. Not that Pescetti broke away from Seneca, as did Aretino in *Orazia,* for there is more than enough bombast in *Cesare.* Plutarch's characterization of Antony's oratorical style often fits Pescetti's style: "He [Antony] used a manner of phrase in his speech called Asiatic, which carried the best grace and estimation at that time, and was much like to his manners and life; for it was full of ostentation, foolish bravery, and vain ambition." Shakespeare sometimes adopted the Asiatic style in *Julius Caesar,* as in Marullus' fine speech about Pompey in the very first scene, but he also provided plenty of contrast by means of realistic, colloquial speech, much of it in prose. Pescetti rarely succeeded in writing easy, natural dialogue and, of course, never used prose.

The clearest example of Senecan style in *Cesare* comes where we would expect it, in a messenger's report of the assassination in the last act. Pescetti's messenger is more than a little reminiscent of the *nuntius* in *Thyestes* and of the *nuntio* in Cinthio's *Orbecche.* A few lines will illustrate the likeness.

> O Sole e tu riluci, e non t' inuolui
> In tenebrosa notte? e puoi vedere
> Opre sì fiere, e empie? e puoi dar luce
> A sì spietati mostri? O terra, o terra,
> Che non t' apri, e inghiotti
> Nel tuo più cieco, e cauernoso Abisso
> Huomini sì maluagi? [p. 119].

O sun, are you shining and not wrapped in gloomy night? Can you look upon deeds so savage and wicked, and can you give light to monsters so cruel? O earth, O earth, why do you not open and swallow men so evil into your darkest and hollowest pit?

Sometimes the sentiment of Italian speeches is Senecan but the style is not especially so, as in Calpurnia's tirade in the third scene of Act 2 (p. 54).

> Ahi che le Signorie, gli imperi, e i regni
> Altro non son, ch' un ben fiorito prato,
> Che cela sotto ogni suo fiore un angue,
> Altro non son, ch' un sontuoso, e lauto
> Conuito, ou' ogni cibo, ogni beuanda,
> È d' assenzo, di fele, e di veleno
> Mortifero condita; altro, ch' un vago,
> E rubicondo pomo, ch' entro il verme

> Hà, che 'l marcisce, che 'l corrompe, e rode.
> Io mille volte più contenta, e lieta
> viuea nella priuata, e bassa sorte.

Alas, states, empires, and kingdoms are no other than a fine flowery
meadow that conceals a snake under every flower, no other than a
sumptuous, abundant banquet, where every food, every drink is sea-
soned with wormwood, with gall, and with deadly poison; no other than
a lovely red apple that has a worm inside, which rots it, corrupts it, and
devours it. I would live a thousand times more content and happy in a
private and humble station.

Typical of Pescetti's formal dialogue, or monologue, is Brutus'
opening address to the ghost of Pompey:

> Magnanim' Ombra, ecch' io ti seguo, ecch' io
> M' accingo all' alta impresa, a che m' esorti.
> Oggi o del sangue del crudel Tiranno,
> O del mio spargerassi il terren sacro.
> Oggi o vendicarò l' empia tua morte,
> E riporrò la patria in libertade,
> Overrotti a trouar, douunque sei.
> Oggi a Roma farò conoscer, ch' io
> Degno nipote son di quel gran Bruto,[19]
> Che di questa Città cacciando i Regi
> Alta vendetta, e memorabil feo
> Del barbarico stupro di Lucrezia.

Noble-minded spirit, behold, I follow you, behold, I gird myself for the
high enterprise to which you call me. Today I shall sprinkle the sacred
ground with the blood of the cruel tyrant or with my own. Today I will
either avenge your impious death and restore liberty to the fatherland
or join you, wheresoever you are. I shall make Rome know that I am
a worthy descendant of that great Brutus who drove out the kings
and wrought eminent and memorable revenge for the barbaric rape of
Lucretia.

Although Pescetti did not use so great a proportion of short lines
in the dialogue as did Speroni, he often wrote highly emotional
speeches in short lines or in a mixture of long and short lines. In
a long speech, wherein she expresses her fears for the life of
Caesar, wherein she sees her husband's body broken and bleeding,
Calpurnia works herself to such a pitch that she breaks into a
lament in short lines, beginning,

> O Sole, o Luna, o Stelle
> Erranti, e fisse, o cieli,

---

[19] Lucius Junius Brutus, who led the insurrection that drove out Tarquin and
royalty from Rome.

> E tu notte del mio
> Affanno consapeuole,
> Che con le negre penne
> Riporti il sonno, e i sogni . . . [p. 45].

O sun, O moon, O wandering and fixed stars, O heavens, and you, Night, privy to my trouble, you that with black wings bring back sleep and dreams. . . .

At the beginning of Act 5, Brutus announces the death of Caesar in a mixture of long and short lines:

> Cittadini, il Tiranno ha col suo sangue
> Pagate le douute
> Pene, e ha soddisfatto
> All' anime di tanti huomini illustri,
> Che son, per colpa sua, giti sotterra.
> Omai libera è Roma,
> Dalle nostre ceruici è scosso il giogo.

Citizens, the tyrant has paid the penalties he owed with his blood, and has given satisfaction to the souls of many excellent men who fell to earth because of him. Now at last Rome is free and the yoke is shaken off from our necks.

In my judgment, the most natural, most lifelike dialogue in *Cesare* is in the second scene of Act 2, wherein Portia assures her husband Brutus that she will have no life on earth if he loses his life in any rash enterprise.

Brutus: If you love me, you ought to comfort me in my desire.
Portia: I wish nothing more than to satisfy you.
Brutus: And I, who live, wish, so far as it pleases the All High Ruler, to reclaim you from Heaven.
Portia: That cannot be true, if you love me.
Brutus: Why not?
Portia: Because, if you love me, you cannot wish me harm.
Brutus: I wish you harm in wanting you to live?
Portia: You wish me torment, hell, in wanting me to live when you are dead.

Another convincing scene is the fifth in Act 4 (pp. 108–110). Here Brutus and Cassius wriggle in an agony of apprehension while Popilius Lena, who knows about the conspiracy, talks confidentially with Caesar. Plutarch provided the material for this good scene. Shakespeare[20] handled the material more economi-

---

[20] *Julius Caesar* 3.1.1–27.

cally, without sacrificing dramatic suspense; but Pescetti's treatment is not much inferior.

Is there any connection between the Italian *Cesare* (1594) and Shakespeare's *Julius Caesar* (c. 1599)? This question roused a mild flurry among Shakespearean scholars in the early part of our century, but, so far as I know, editors and critics since that time have ignored the possibility that the English playwright might have known something about the earlier Italian play.

In 1910, Harry Morgan Ayres[21] cited a parallel or two between the Italian and English tragedies, but offered no solution. Three years later, G. Sarrazin[22] gathered together more parallels between *Cesare* and *Julius Caesar*. In the same year, Alexander Boecker[23] published a monograph in which he made a detailed comparison of the two plays and cited parallel after parallel in plot, characterization, and diction. Boecker convinced himself at least that Shakespeare must have been influenced in some way by Pescetti; either he had seen the Italian play or one of his learned friends, possibly Ben Jonson, had called his attention to it.

It must be admitted that some of the parallels fished forth by Boecker can hardly be explained by common sources, such as Plutarch, Appian, or the earlier plays on the subject by Muretus or Grévin. At least one of these parallels is so striking that it is worth reviving.

In the third scene of Act 1 of *Cesare*, Cassius argues that Antony, a dangerous man, ought to be killed along with Caesar; but Brutus, who thinks of himself as a high-minded patriot and no assassin, rejects the proposal, assuring Cassius that Antony will cause no trouble after Caesar is gone.

> *Bruto*   Col troncar della testa all' altre membra
>   Troncasi ogni vigore, ogni possanza.
>
> *Cassio*   Nell' Idra ou' una testa si troncaua,
>   Iui ne rinascean subito sette [p. 27].

Brutus: In cutting off the head from the other members all strength, all power is cut off.

Cassius: In the Hydra, where one head was cut off, immediately seven heads were reborn there.

---

[21] "Shakespeare's *Julius Caesar* in the Light of Some Other Versions," in *PMLA* 25 (1910), 215.
[22] "Shakespeare und Orlando Pescetti," in *Englische Studien* 46 (1913).
[23] *A Probable Italian Source of Shakespeare's Julius Caesar*, New York, 1913.

In *Julius Caesar* (2.1.163–167) we find the following:

Cassius   Let Antony and Caesar fall together.
Brutus   Our course will seem too bloody, Caius Cassius,
          To cut the head off and then hack the limbs,
          Like wrath in death and envy afterwards;
          For Antony is but a limb of Caesar.

Plutarch was doubtless responsible for the basic situation, namely, the conspirators' belief that Antony should also be killed and Brutus' refusal on the grounds of honor. But the figure of speech here, that by cutting off the head the limbs will also perish, is not in Plutarch.

Pescetti could have found a suggestion for head and limbs in the figure of roots and trunk that Muretus[24] used, and after him Grévin.[25] Hydra might have been suggested to Pescetti by Muretus, or Grévin, for Cassius refers to Hercules' cutting off the heads of Hydra in the last act of the Latin *Julius Caesar* and in the last act of the French *César;* but the old myth was well known. There is no mention of Hydra in Shakespeare's *Julius Caesar.*[26]

I am not insisting, with Boecker, that there must have been some connection between the Italian *Cesare* and the English *Julius Caesar,* but I am not altogether satisfied that there could not have been any connection. A negative can hardly be proved, but present-day Shakespeareans may be right in ignoring Pescetti.

It may seem odd that the sixteenth-century Italians did not write more Roman tragedies than they did, since the beginnings of Italian tragedy were largely Roman. There were more Roman tragedies in the century than I have indicated, but I have not been able to find many more. Of these others, three are worth mentioning.

Paolo Regio's *Lucretia* (Naples, 1572), based on the celebrated rape in ancient Rome, is a conventional neoclassical play that owes much to Cinthio and Seneca. Alecto the Fury and a ghost are promi-

---

[24] *Cassius*   Perimatur ergo ab infimis radicibus
               Ne quando posthac caesa rursum pullulet.
    Brutus   Latet sub uno tota radix corpore [Act 2].
[25] *Cassius*   Si seroit-ce bien faict, arrachons la racine
               Avecque le gros tronc de tout' ceste vermine.
                              [*Théâtre complet*, Paris, 1922, p. 28.]
[26] Professor T. W. Baldwin suggests that Shakespeare may be drawing upon himself in the figure of head and limbs. In *3 Henry VI* 5.1.41 and in *Titus Andronicus* 1.1.186, the body is spoken of as useless without the head, that is, the body politic cannot function without the ruler. The basic proposition of the metaphor was a commonplace.

nent characters. Fortune and the stars seem to rule, but justice will prevail in the end, when Collatine and Lucius Brutus solemnly swear to drive out the wicked Tarquin and bring a republic to Rome. In an epilogue, "Tragedia to the Reader," the author admits that he has departed from the strict *stil tragico* in allowing two days of action, in having the heroine kill herself onstage, in the loose arrangement of scenes, and in introducing ghosts, Furies, and gods. But he maintains that he scorns slavish imitation of the Ancients.

Bongianni Gratarolo published two tragedies at Venice in 1589, namely, *Astianatte* and *Polissena,* which are Roman in the sense that they dramatize events in the lives of Aeneas' Trojan relatives and in their Senecan-Cinthian form. Signorelli's *Storia critica de' teatri antichi e moderni* (vol. 5, Naples, 1813) praised both plays but admitted that they were inferior to their Senecan models. So they are, and they are inferior to their Cinthian models as well.

VIII

Dolce's Tragedies

Lodovico Dolce (1508–68), born in Venice, educated in Padua, was what the Italians call a *poligrafo,* that is, a writer of nearly everything—poems, plays, essays, dialogues, biographies, commentaries, and many translations. He was a literary hack, but a learned one, and occasionally he wrote pretty well. He is of importance to the student of English literature since he was one of the few Italian dramatists whose direct influence on English drama can easily be established. The authors of *Gismond of Salerne* (1567) used Dolce, and the first "regular" tragedy in English, Gascoigne's *Jocasta* (1566), was mostly a translation of Dolce's *Giocasta.*

Between 1540 and 1550, Dolce wrote five comedies, some in verse and some in prose. All of these were "new" comedies, but all save two—*Il ruffiano* ("The Pimp"), which the author said was "taken from the *Rudens* of Plautus" but was actually cribbed from Ruzzante's *Piovana,* and *La Fabrizia,* which was original—were modernizations of ancient Roman comedies. Dolce used the same technique in his "new" tragedies, only two of which, *Didone* (1547) and *Marianna* (1565), were original; the rest were adaptations or translations of Seneca and Euripides. Thus *Thyeste* (1543) was *tratta da Seneca, Hecuba* (1543), *Giocasta* (1549), *Ifigenia* (1551), and *Medea* (1558) from Euripides, and *Le Troiane* (1566) from both Seneca and Euripides. In 1560, Dolce published an Italian translation of all ten of Seneca's tragedies. His collected *Tragedie,* including *Didone* but omitting *Marianna,* and including all of his adaptations save the *Troiane,* appeared in 1566.

THYESTE

The most slavish of Dolce's adaptations is *Thyeste,*[1] which is scarcely more than a paraphrase of Seneca's play. Dolce turned Atreus' confidential servant into a royal counselor but preserved the role. There is no concluding chorus in the Latin *Thyestes,* but Dolce added a short appeal to God by the chorus, asking that the tyrant's monstrous deed be punished. In his translation of *Thyestes,* as in all his translations of Seneca, the Italian poet used mostly short unrhymed seven-syllable lines *(heptasillabi* or *settenarii).* In the adaptation, he favored the long line of eleven syllables, which had been used by Trissino and Cinthio, but inserted some *settenarii.* The choruses, as usual, were mostly in rhyme.

HECUBA

Hecuba, Dolce's first adaptation from Euripides, is fairly typical of all his other Euripidean tragedies. The Italian poet preserved the Greek plots, making only minor changes, such as omitting characters or, more often, adding characters. In his *Hecuba,* for example, he left out Agamemnon, who has a prominent role in the original play, but more than made up for this omission by expanding the Italian version to about 2,500 lines. Euripides' *Hecuba* has 1,295 lines.

Apparently Dolce did not adapt from the Greek but used an intermediary Latin translation. More often than not he stayed fairly close to Euripides' dialogue, but he did not, or could not, follow all the choruses so faithfully. Euripides' tragic choruses are rich in concrete imagery and allusion. Dolce's Italian versions are usually tame and flat by comparison, and he often substituted Senecan fatalism for Euripidean lyricism. Sometimes he also changed the original dialogue to conform to the more familiar Senecan sentiments. Euripides' Hecuba, in her first speech, which is an impassioned one, implores the gods to spare her remaining children, Polydorus and Polyxena. Dolce's Hecuba, in her first speech, cries, "Shall I lament, ah, alas, wicked Fortune or the stars? This

---

[1] Not to be confused with Dolce's translation, as they often are.

one is false, and those turn now good now evil, as fate is fixed
for each mortal. Tell me, what remains to be done to me?" This
sentiment may have been borrowed in part from Hecuba's speech
in Euripides' *Troades* (98 ff.) and from Hecuba's speech that opens
the first act of Seneca's *Troades*. Certainly the Italian Hecuba here
is more Senecan than Euripidean.

Trissino and Cinthio tried to modernize their ancient material.
Trissino, for example, turned Masinissa and Scipio from a Numidian and a Roman into Renaissance courtiers. While Dolce was
usually following an ancient Greek or Roman model pretty closely,
he also sometimes modernized. When Hecuba quarrels with
Odysseus in Euripides' play she grows very angry and upbraids the
Greek chieftan in strong terms: "Art thou not caitiff proved then
by these plots?" (250).[2] In Dolce's *Hecuba* this passage comes out

> Questa non pare a me, Signor, cortese,
> D' un animo gentil risposta degna.

This does not seem to me, gracious lord, an answer worthy of a noble
mind.

GIOCASTA

Dolce's *Giocasta* is over 2,700 lines long. The original *Phoenissae*
of Euripides has 1,766 lines. The English *Jocasta*, by George Gascoigne and Francis Kinwelmersh, is approximately the same length
as the Italian version that they followed.[3] Dolce again kept the
original plot but made even more changes than he did in *Hecuba*.
He added a prologue of the detached kind used by Cinthio. He
inserted more Senecan elements than he did in *Hecuba*, for he
evidently thought of this tragedy as akin to *Thyestes;* the concluding lines of the prologue are: "But behold the queen [Jocasta].
O sun, hide your rays as you did once before at the dreadful table
of King Thyestes, so that you may not see the impious slaughters
which are bound today to fill the earth with blood."[4] It is true
that the *Phoenissae* is the most sensational, the most "Senecan"
of all the extant tragedies of Euripides.

---

[2] I have used Way's translations (Loeb Library) for all the quotations from
Euripides.
[3] *Jocasta: a Tragedie written in Greeke by Euripides, translated and digested
into Acte by George Gascoygne and Francis Kinwelmershe of Grayes Inne, and
there by them presented, 1566.* Gascoigne translated Acts 2, 3, and 5, Kinwelmersh 1 and 4, but from the Italian, not from the Greek.
[4] The English poets omitted the prologue, substituting the "order of the dumb
shows and musics before every act."

In this second adaptation from Euripides, Dolce doubtless felt more confident of his literary powers and he ventured to comment on his own style. The prologue remarks: "If the author does not fully attain the lofty style that fits tragic poems, he assures you that in this age no one else among many has overtaken us." In other words, the author believed that he had done as well here as Trissino, Rucellai, Cinthio, and Speroni, the four tragic dramatists whom he regarded as the leaders in Italian tragedy.[5] Cinthio was Dolce's principal model among the native playwrights.

One change that Dolce made was transforming Euripides' humble slave (paidogogus) into a Venetian bailo (tutor) and expanding some of his speeches into sententious Senecan harangues. (Gascoigne and Kinwelmersh kept the Venetian character, calling him simply Bailo.) In the third scene of Act 1, Bailo says to Antigone:

> Fanciulla, io ti vorrei (sasselo Iddio)
> Recar qualche conforto: ma non posso
> Darti quel ben ch' i' non possedo ancora.
> La cagion, ch' Eteocle e Polinice
> Conduce, come intendi, all' odio e all' armi,
> È troppo grande: e già per questa molti
> Hanno senza alcun fren rotte le leggi,
> E sottosopra le Città rivolte.
> Troppo, figliuola mia, troppo possente
> È il desio di regnar, nè ben comporta
> Chi solo è in Signoria di aver compagno.

Kinwelmersh's somewhat loose translation is:

> Daughter, God knowes how willing I would be
> With sweete reliefe to comforte thy distresse,
> But I cannot impart to thee the good
> Which I my selfe doe not as yet enjoye.
> The wailefull cause that moves Eteocles
> With Polynice to enter civil warres
> Is overgreat, and for this onely cause
> Full many men have broke the lawes of truth,
> And topsieturvie turned many townes.
> "To gredie (daughter), too too gredie is
> Desire to rule and raigne in kingly state."
> Ne can he bide that swaise a realme alone
> To have another joynde with him therein.[6]

---

[5] See the prologue to *Marianna* below, p. 170.
[6] Cunliffe, pp. 166–169. For the sake of convenience I shall use the edition of *Giocasta* and *Jocasta* in Cunliffe's *Supposes and Jocasta* (Boston, 1906).

The particular echo of Seneca in this speech is, as Kinwelmersh translated it, "Too greedy is desire to rule and reign in kingly state," which is almost a translation of *regno pectus attonitum furit* ("their hearts are mad with lust for kingship") in *Thebais* 302. This sentiment repeatedly appears in Seneca's tragedies and must have been familiar to most Renaissance schoolboys.[7]

Dolce modified the Euripidean choruses considerably. The original Greek chorus is made up of Phoenician maidens from Tyre who were trapped in the besieged city of Thebes while on their way to Apollo's shrine at Delphi. Dolce's chorus is made up of Theban women, possibly fifteen in number, the English chorus of "four Theban dames."

But Dolce's changes were not always consistent. Sometimes he found the Greek chorus, or rather the Latin version of it, too complicated and contented himself with simplifying it. On the other hand, he was apt to expand and embroider some fairly simple passages. He often followed the same procedure in the dialogue. For example, the chorus in *Phoenissae* 355–356 says to Jocasta:

> Mighty with women is their travail's fruit;
> Yea, dear the child is to all womankind.

Dolce's version:

> Amor non è che s' appareggia quello
> Che la pietosa madre ai figli porta;
> Il qual tanto più cresce, quanto in essi
> Scema il contento, e crescono gli affanni.

Gascoigne's version:

> There is no love may be comparde to that
> The tender mother beares unto hir chyld:
> For even somuche the more it dothe encrease,
> As their griefe growes or contentations cease.[8]

Even more striking is Dolce's expansion of one line to seven. Way's version of Euripides:

Polynices: 'Twas night: to Adrastus' palace-porch I come [413].

Dolce's version:

> Era sparito in ogni parte il giorno,

---

[7] See *Octavia* 144 (*regni cupido*); *Thebais* 664; *Hippolytus* 542–543; *Hercules Oetaeus* 604 ff.
[8] Cunliffe, pp. 194–195.

> E la terra adombrava oscuro velo;
> Quand' io, cercando ove alloggiar la notte
> Dopo lungo cammin, stanco pervenni
> A una picciol loggetta che congiunta
> Era di fuori alle superbe mura
> Della ricca città del vecchio Adrasto.

Gascoigne's version:

> The shining day had runne his hasted course,
> And deawie night bespread hir mantell darke,
> When I that wandred, after wearie toyle,
> To seke some harbrough for myne irked limmes,
> Gan fynde at last a little cabbin, close
> Adjoyned faste unto the stately walles,
> Where king Adrastus held his royall towres.[9]

At the conclusion of the *Phoenissae* the chorus raises a short prayer to the goddess of victory, asking for victory in the dramatic contest at Athens.

> Hail, revered Victory!
> Rest upon my life; and me
> Crown, and crown eternally!

Dolce substituted eleven lines of Senecan sentiment for this prayer, which, to be sure, would not have made much sense in Italy in 1549. The gist of this last chorus in *Giocasta,* in Gascoigne's words, is "How fickle 'tis to trust in Fortune's wheel."

Occasionally Dolce either failed to understand Euripides or deliberately ignored the sense of the original. For example, in the *Phoenissae,* Antigone, when bullied by Creon into accepting his son for a husband, rebels and says that if she is forced to marry Haemon she will kill him on the wedding night: "That night shall prove me one of Danaus' daughters" (1675). It is hard to believe that Dolce missed this allusion to the myth of Danaus' fifty daughters (all of whom save one slew her bridegroom on the wedding night), for there is an allusion in his *Marianna* to Hypermnestra, the only daughter that spared her husband's life. Yet Dolce's translation is all but meaningless. The Latin translation of Euripides in 1541 by Dorotheus Camillus (Rudolphus Collinus) was correct: "Nox utique illa ex Danaidis me habitura est una."[10] The

---

[9] Cunliffe, pp. 204–205. It is true that this speech incorporates further Euripidean dialogue between Polynices and his mother, but not much.

[10] The Illinois copy of the 1541 translation is defective, and I quote from the 1550 (Basel), which seems to be a reprint.

Italian line came out "Io seguirò lo stil d' alcune accorte," which was hardly improved by Gascoigne's "I will ensue some worthie womans steppes."[11]

IFIGENIA

Dolce's adaptation of *Iphigenia in Aulis* suffers more, perhaps, than do his other Euripidean tragedies because of his failure with the choral odes, which are very beautiful in this play. The Italian poet could do little with the first great ode (164–302), contenting himself with seventy-four lines of the usual lamentation over tyranny and the horrors of war. Nor did he do much with the beautiful ode to Aphrodite, beginning

> O well for them for whom the Queen
> Of Love shall temper passion's fire,
> And bring fruition of desire
> With gentle pace and sober mien [543–546].

Dolce's version, at the close of Act 2, begins

> Donne voi ben vedete,
> Che non si trova in terra
> Stato felice alcun sotto la Luna.

Ladies, you see, indeed, that no one on earth is happy under the moon.

MEDEA

Dolce expanded *Medea* somewhat, adding a Cinthian prologue which discusses the differences between comedy and tragedy, maintaining that it is easier to move laughter with an old miser, a young prodigal, a flattering parasite, a crafty pimp, and an ungrateful servant than to move sadness with a just king, a tyrant, and a faithful counselor. He added a counselor to the original cast.

Dolce usually played up the sensational scenes in Euripides, making them more Senecan. In the famous scene wherein Medea kills her two little sons, however, Dolce followed the Greek poet rather closely.

In Seneca's play, Medea kills one son onstage, climbs to the housetop and kills the other little boy, then throws both bodies down at the feet of their father, Jason. In Euripides' play, Medea kills the children offstage, but the audience hears their pitiful cries for help. Dolce merely expanded the Euripidean original, giving

---

[11] Cunliffe, pp. 400–401.

the boys more lines and starting the scene outside the doors of the palace.

One Son: Ladies, where can we flee from the hands of our cruel mother so that she may not kill us?
Other Son: I, wretched one, do not understand it, but I well see, I see that we are both dead.
Chorus: Ah, wretched children, come to us, for we will do all that women can do to save you.
Medea: Women, get back, each of you. [*turning to the boys*] You most wicked seed, do not think to escape.

The children continue to beg for mercy as Medea takes them inside. Then the audience hears more cries.

One Son: [*from within*] Alas, savage mother, alas, merciless, this blow is enough to take away my life without wounding me again.
Other Son: O wretched brother, I will soon bear you company. Mother, open my breast; O cut this wretched throat with your knife. Aye-me!
Chorus: O wicked woman! Why do I say woman? You are rather iron itself; if you had been made of flesh, at that name of mother you would have burst breast and heart.

TROIANE

Le Troiane was produced with fine scenery, music, and *intermedii* at Venice in 1566. Dolce made several changes in the ancient material. He used Menelaus, who is in Euripides' *Troades* but not in Seneca's; Agamemnon, who is in Seneca but not in Euripides; Polyxena, who is in neither the Greek nor Latin tragedy. (Polyxena is in Euripides' *Hecuba.*) Dolce followed Seneca rather more than he did Euripides.

The *intermedii* are of interest to the student of the theater because they were not common in Italian tragedies though more or less required in productions of Italian comedies. Dolce carefully explained that the Ancients did not use *intermedii*, but relied on the chorus for between-the-acts entertainment. There were four *intermedii* for the *Troiane*, all of them rather short: (1) Trojan mourners; (2) Pluto and "some ghosts of slain Trojans"; (3) Neptune and fellow sea-gods; (4) Venus, Cupid, Vulcan, Juno, Athene, Mercury.[12]

---

[12] I have used the 1593 (Venice) edition. There was an earlier printing in 1567.

DIDONE

Dolce's first original tragedy was *Didone* (1547), which clearly owes much to Cinthio's earlier version. Both Italian dramatists followed the *Aeneid*, of course, and Dolce remarked in the *argomento* that here he was basing a tragedy on fiction rather than on history: "The subject is taken from the feigned story by Virgil and not from the truth of history." In other words, he accepted Cinthio's contention that fiction is as good a basis for tragedy as is the traditionally prescribed history.

Although Dolce was a follower of Cinthio, he departed from the earlier play in several ways. One of these differences appears at the very beginning, in the prologue, which is spoken by Cupid "in form of Ascanius." Here Dolce followed Virgil more closely than did Cinthio, who omitted Cupid disguised as Ascanius and made Anna encourage Dido to fall in love with Aeneas. Moreover, Dolce's version promised to be more of a tragedy of blood and revenge than was Cinthio's *Didone*. Cupid announces, "I do not feed on ambrosia, as do the other gods, but on blood and tears." Then he adds, "I want the new city [Carthage] to be bathed in her [Dido's] blood, and her desperate and cheerless soul to descend wailing into the dark abyss. I want her demise to carry with it other tears, other deaths; and women, maidens, old men, and defenseless children to go a prey to swords and flames, and palaces and houses to be sacked." Cupid wants to promote these horrors to get revenge for both "past and future injuries" that cruel Juno has brought, and will bring, to Aeneas.

The play proper follows the path of Cinthio's with only minor variations. Dolce, perhaps influenced by Speroni's *Canace*, which he evidently admired, used a good many short lines along with the conventional long lines. He omitted Fame, whom Cinthio introduced at the beginning of his third act, but added the ghost of Sychaeus at the beginning of his second act. Dolce made Anna hang herself at the close of Act 5, whereas Cinthio made Anna try to kill herself but fail.

Both Dolce and Cinthio admired and imitated Seneca, but in *Didone* Cinthio stayed pretty close to Virgil. Dolce, on the other hand, was more apt to depart from Virgil and inject Senecan sentiments. Dido's complaint in 4.1, for example, sounds more like

Seneca than Virgil: "I feel the stone that burdens Sisyphus on my back and the vulture that feeds on Tityus in my heart, and placed by the fountain with Tantalus, I see fruit and water slipping from me, whereby I have more hunger and thirst. Then the wheel of Ixion at every revolution raises me to the peak of my torments."

Sometimes Dolce borrowed from both Virgil and Cinthio and then added an echo of Seneca, as in Dido's denunciation of Aeneas (3.7):

> Sciocco è chi crede, che vi fosse madre
> La santa, e gentil Dea madre d' amore,
> Et la paterna di voi stirpe scenda
> Da Dardano; anzi in duri e freddi sassi
> Caucaso istesso, od altro horrido monte
> De la nivosa Sythia vi produsse,
> Et vi diede le Tygri Hyrcane il latte.

Cinthio wrote in his *Didone* 4.1:

> Ahi disleal, non ti fù madre mai
> Venere Dea, nè da Dardano venne
> Mai la tua stirpe; ma da gli aspri sassi
> Del Caucaso nascesti, e da le poppe
> Havesti il latte de le Tigri Hircane.

Virgil wrote in *Aeneid* 4.365–367:

> Nec tibi diva parens, generis nec Dardanus auctor,
> Perfide; sed duris genuit te cautibus horrens
> Caucasus, Hyrcanaeque admorunt ubera tigres.

Christopher Marlowe's English version, in his *Dido, Queen of Carthage* 5.1.156–159, will serve pretty well as a translation of all three passages:

> Thy mother was no goddess, perjur'd man,
> Nor Dardanus the author of thy stock;
> But thou art sprung from Scythian Caucasus,
> And tigers of Hyrcania gave thee suck.

All of the mythological allusions in these four speeches came from Virgil except the allusion to Scythia. Dolce's "snowy Scythia" (*nivosa Sythia*) certainly smacks of Seneca, for example, of *ursae frigidum Scythicae genus*[13] and *sub axe frigido pontus Scythes*.[14]

---

[13] *Hercules Oetaeus* 40.
[14] *Hercules Oetaeus* 1251. And cf. *ibid.* 335–337. But Ovid may have provided the reference to icy Scythia, along with Seneca. See *Metamorphoses* 2.224, 8.788; *Heroides* 12.27; *Epistulae ex Ponto* 1.3.37. Ovid was also fond of tigers and upon at least one occasion, in a letter to a "Traitorous Friend" (*Tristia* 1.8.37–44), combined Scythia with a nursing tigress.

Marlowe may have taken his "Scythian" from Seneca or Ovid; there is no good reason to believe that he knew Dolce's play.[15]

Sometimes Dolce merely rearranged speeches in the earlier play or assigned them to other characters. For example, in the last scene of Act 1, Cinthio's Dido says:

> Stò come nave, che da vari venti
> Combattuta è nel mare, e quinci, e quindi,
> E non scorga a qual via debba piegarsi,
> Per torsi da tempesta, e gire al porto.

In the second scene of Act 2, Dolce's Aeneas says:

> Et stò, si come combattuta nave
> In mezzo l'onde da diversi venti,
> C' hor da quel lato, hor da quest' altro inchina.

And I stand like a ship assailed by divers winds in the midst of the waves, a ship that yields now to that side, now to this.

In this his first original play, Dolce tried hard to reach a high level of poetry. Occasionally he certainly rose above the common level of Italian tragedy. Dido's speech in the very first scene, when she is happy in her new-found love, is a fair sample of the author's better efforts.

> A me parea, ch' io fossi
> In un bel prato herboso,
> Ove un fiume correa di puro argento.
> E appresso a me sedea
> Questo mio cuore e alma,
> Coronando i mie crini
> D' una ghirlanda verde,
> Ch' egli tessuto havea con le sue mani.
> Et meco compartia dolci parole
> Con si soavi accenti,
> Ch' acquetavano i venti.

It seemed to me that I was in a fine grassy meadow where a river of pure silver ran, and this man, my heart and soul, sat near me, crowning my hair with a green garland that he had woven with his own hands. And he gave me sweet words in tones so soft that the winds were hushed.

Dido's long soliloquy at the beginning of Act 5, which owes much to Virgil, is perhaps the best poetry in the play. The following excerpt, in which the heartbroken queen is addressing "cruel love," will illustrate:

---

[15] I have noticed only one close parallel: both Dolce and Marlowe made Anna commit suicide at the end.

> Ho potuto ingannar l' astuto Iarba,
> Et città fabricar nel suo terreno,
> Ho potuto frenar genti superbe,
> Et non temer di mille armate squadre;
> Ma già non ho potuto da tuoi colpi
> Coprirmi, ne schermir, ne far difesa.

I have been able to deceive crafty Iarbas and build a city on his land, I have been able to curb haughty tribes and defy a thousand armed companies; but I have been unable to shield myself, to fend, to put up any defense against your blows.

MARIANNA

Dolce's second original tragedy, and certainly his best one, was based on Josephus' *Ancient History of the Jews*. The villain is the Herod who slaughtered the innocents, the celebrated tyrant of the mystery plays. Josephus not only provided the outline of the story but suggested the characterization of the king, who was "sweltered and devoured in his passions." The ancient historian showed Herod as torn between love and hate for his wife Miriamne: "So much was his mind traveled between love and hatred, that when as oftentimes he desired to punish the woman's pride, his heart by love's mediation failed him in the enterprize."[16]

There are two Cinthian prologues to *Marianna*. In the first, Tragedy, dressed in a dark gown and holding a scepter and naked sword, speaks. Tragedy was born, she says, not among private citizens, but among princes, kings, and emperors. She promotes no merry sports, as does Comedy, "but pain and tears, representing the gloomy and mournful deaths of tyrants, or of just kings oppressed by hostile Fortune, or of queens." She professes a modest reluctance to put her present play on the same level with *Sofonisba*, *Canace*, *Orbecche*, and *Rosmunda*, but she feels some complacency when she recalls the kind reception given her earlier productions, such as *Ifigenia*, *Giocasta*, and *Didone*. Today the audience will find "no haughty words or weighty epithets, but smooth discourse and pure, easy speech." The audience will see "hate and love, disdain and jealousy struggling together in the heart of Herod, and him condemning to death his mother-in-law, his wife, and his children, and then later repenting, as happens to him who makes too hasty judgments."

The second prologue is a dialogue between Pluto and Jealousy.

---

[16] See Thomas Lodge's translation, in *Works* (London, 1640), p. 397.

The god of the lower world has come to fetch the tyrant who will destroy himself with jealousy and rage. Jealousy will gladly obey the summons of Pluto and fill every vein of Herod with her deadly poison. "My every joy," she says, "my every joy is to bathe myself every hour in the blood of others."

Marianna, the queen, opens the first act on a sinister note with an appeal to the Furies.

> O fiere, sanguinose empie sorelle,
> Vendicatrici de gli humani oltraggi,
> S' è ver quel, che di voi si legge e scrive,
> Spiccatevi da' crini un de' serpenti,
> E spargete per tutto di veneno
> Il mio dolente et angoscioso petto.
> Ingombratemi, a guisa di Medea,
> Di disdegno, di rabbia, e di furore:
> E questa regal casa, alta, e sublime,
> Oggi ripiena sia tutta di sangue.[17]

O savage, bloody, and evil sisters, avengers of human outrages, if what one reads and what is written about you is true, pluck one of the serpents from your locks and fill my aching and tormented breast with poison. Load me, like Medea, with scorn, rage, and fury, and let this lofty royal house be filled with blood today.

Marianna tells her nurse that she is weary of the cruelties practiced by her tyrannical husband, who, among other outrages, has killed her grandfather and is about to kill her brother. She has had a dream in which her bloodstained brother warned her to beware of Herod. The nurse, as usual in such tragedies, argues with her, insisting that Herod still loves her. The queen retorts that cruelty can have no place in true love.

Then Soemo, the captain of the guard, enters to warn the queen that Herod has become so fearful that he suspects everyone of plotting against him. The captain is exceeding his duty, but he urges the queen to dissemble. Marianna, however, is modeled upon Sophonisba and Rosmunda; she is a great lady who never stoops to any vulgar trickery. She replies to Soemo:

> Leale e vero amico, il Ciel m' ha dato
> Così intrepido il cor, l' animo grande,
> Che finger io non sò, nè dir menzogna:
> Nè di letitia posso ornar il volto,
> Quando gravedolor m' affligge l' alma [1.2].

---

[17] I have used the text in the second printing of 1593 (Venice) and that in the *Teatro italiano antico* 5.

Loyal and true friend, Heaven has given me such a fearless heart, such a great spirit, that I know not how to feign or lie; nor can I deck my countenance with joy when great grief vexes my soul.

Soemo: It is prudent, Queen, to flee death.

Marianna: Not to abide in a shameful life.

Soemo: In this case, you ought to follow the custom of the mariner, who makes use of divers sails for divers winds.

The last scene in the first act is a soliloquy by Soemo, who is much troubled, for he knows that Herod is thinking of killing all suspects, including members of his own family. The chorus of women friendly to the queen prays God to protect their mistress and punish the king.

Herod is introduced in the second act. He is confiding in his sister Salome; he tells her that he now fears both his wife and his cupbearer. Salome assures him that his wife has already tried to corrupt the cupbearer and that his mother-in-law, Alessandra, is behind the plot.

Herod summons the cupbearer and bullies him until the man confirms what Salome has said. But Herod wants proof. (Apparently he trusts his sister no more than he trusts any other person.) He summons the queen. Marianna denies that she has any design on his life. The cupbearer repeats his confession. Marianna says that he lies. Thereupon the cupbearer admits that Salome had forced him to accuse the queen.

Now Herod summons the queen's eunuch and commands him to tell everything he knows. "I will not only pardon you," says Herod, "but I will give you moreover a reward so great that you would not have to envy any man. On the other hand, if you keep silent, and the truth is told to me by another tongue, you know that fire, halter, crosses, and wheels, together with a thousand thousand other tortures, will be light punishments compared with those I will make you feel in all your limbs." Thus encouraged, the eunuch throws suspicion upon Captain Soemo.

The chorus, which has already appeared briefly in the second scene, or so the stage directions indicate, closes Act 2 with Senecan sentiments on the evil behavior of tyrants.

After a short opening scene, in which Marianna, her mother, and the chorus try to console each other, the third act shows Herod in a towering rage. He accuses Marianna of adultery, of planning to poison him, and of excessive pride. Marianna denies every charge, but Herod refuses to listen to any explanations. The royal counselor, in the traditional manner, urges the king to curb his wrath, to think before he acts, to proceed slowly and justly.

The debate between Herod and his counselor is reminiscent of scenes in Cinthio's *Orbecche,* wherein the good counselor tries to restrain Sulmone, who is intent on punishing his daughter and her family.[18] Herod cries, "As he who has no children cannot judge the love and affection of a father, so he who has suffered no outrage cannot judge how much it weighs. I am offended in my personal honor and the offense is manifest. And should I not give vent to the passion that my heart feels in a worthy and memorable revenge?" (3.2).

Herod then calls Soemo and accuses him of adultery with the queen. Soemo protests that he is as guiltless as the Hebrew Joseph or the Greek Hippolytus. Herod again flies into a rage and condemns the captain to death: "I could make our people stone you, and have you torn by dogs, or hanged on a stake, or put on a cross, or give you some other harsh punishment. Such a death would be fit and just. But out of humanity I wish to have you beheaded today. This is my sentence" (3.3). As he leaves, Soemo says to the king, "Herod, as I shall die innocent, so may the great God make you never see yourself content or happy in your own children."

Herod now becomes calmer as doubts begin to torture him. He wants to live without these terrible suspicions that turn him against everyone; he wants above all to live secure in the love of Marianna. The counselor assures him that the queen is certainly innocent.

The chorus asks God to destroy this tyrant and relieve his oppressed subjects. "You may hope, afflicted people, to escape these perils, for as every day comes to an end so death relieves you of every tyrant."

The first messenger—there are three of them in the play—appears at the beginning of Act 4. "Oh, why do not I, miserable one, have wings that could raise me high above the earth so that I might no more see trace or sign of this wicked castle?" Soemo has been executed, and the messenger is bringing the captain's head, heart, and hands to the king.

---

[18] See above, p. 97.

When Herod enters, the messenger delivers a detailed report of the execution, for the king wants to savor every drop of blood. Soemo, says the messenger, went to his death protesting his innocence and denouncing the tyrant. The severed head, as it fell, cried out three times "I die innocent." Herod remarks that he has been too kind to the traitor. As for what his subjects may think, Herod, like Nero,[19] has only contempt for *hoi polloi:*

> L'ignoranza è cagion ne la vil turba
> Di sciocchi affetti, e di giudicii falsi.
> Nè cosa è più volubile e leggera
> Di quel, ch' è il volgo, e temeraria e pazza.
> E sovente quel, ch' oggi li dispiace,
> Doman gli aggrada, e sommamente il prezza;
> Onde di lui far non si deve stima [4.2].

Ignorance is the cause of silly feelings and false opinions in the vile mob. Nothing is more fickle and light, more harebrained and foolish, than the common people; and often that which displeases them today is acceptable and greatly esteemed tomorrow. Therefore one ought to pay no heed to them.

When Marianna enters, Herod offers her a precious gift—the basin containing the severed remains of Soemo—and gloats over her revulsion and grief.[20] Marianna upbraids him for his scandalous cruelty and tells him that now she prefers death to life. Herod becomes more enraged, but says that he will be merciful since he once loved her, still loves her; she may choose her own way of dying. Marianna replies:

> Io torno a dir, ch' ogni cruda morte
> A me più cara fia,
> Che star in vita teco
> Nimico di giustizia, e di pietate.
> E se me fai la grazia, ch' io ti cheggio,
> Donna non morì mai di me più lieta [4.3].

I say again that any cruel death will be dearer to me than life with you, you enemy of justice and pity; and if you grant me the boon I ask, no woman ever died more gladly than I.

In her last appearance on stage, Marianna, like a true heroine of tragedy, rises to the occasion; she becomes stronger and calmer. In fact, this last appearance of Dolce's heroine is comparable to

---

[19] In Seneca's *Octavia.*
[20] Cf. *Orbecche* 5.2 above, p. 102.

the great scene in the fourth act of John Webster's masterpiece, the *Duchess of Malfi*, wherein the noble Duchess defies her brothers, her executioners, and death itself.

After Marianna leaves, the nurse pleads once more with the king to spare her. The oldest boy begs his father to spare her. So does the younger boy. Herod shouts at them that they are not his sons, but Soemo's, and then gives the order for the execution of Marianna, Alessandra, and the two "bastards." The counselor urges the king to revoke this order and warns him that he will soon repent of his injustice. Herod stands fast.

The chorus again asks God to rid the city of this mad tyrant. "If, Father, you wish to punish your weary people for some sin, punish us, Lord, lest innocent and royal blood perish."

The last act begins with a *commos*, lamentations by the nurse and chorus. Then Herod appears sober and thoughtful: "O how easily do our thoughts change! And who would have believed that my harshness would have softened so soon and become such that I repent and grieve for my cruelty, which has driven me to condemn to death those most dear to me? And above all I grieve for my Marianna."

Herod has already sent a messenger to revoke the death sentence, but fears that it is too late. A messenger soon informs him that it is too late. Marianna and her mother have been beheaded, the two boys strangled.

Another messenger gives a circumstantial account of the executions. Marianna, he says, had to watch her mother die and then her sons. Just before he was strangled, the younger child spoke thus to his mother, who stood immobile, as if carved of marble:

> Madre,
> A Dio piace, ch' io mora, et a me piace;
> E sì come io ne moro volentieri,
> Così morite voi salda e costante,
> Perche l' anime nostre ascenderanno
> Ove salir non suole alcun tiranno,
> Nè alma iniqua e di peccati lorda [5.3].

Mother, it pleases God that I die, and it pleases me, and as I die willingly so do you die firm and constant, because our souls will ascend where no tyrant is wont to climb, nor any soul evil and foul in sin.

Marianna died as her little son would have her die, bravely and with dignity. Her last words were addressed to the executioner:

E tu, se vuoi
Questo mio petto aprir, eccolo ignudo:
(E si squarciò con man la vesta) ovvero,
Se brami di svenarmi, ecco la gola.
E se questa non vuoi, nè quella morte,
Ma dispartir dal busto a me la testa,
Ecco ch' io piego obbediente il collo.

And you, if you want to open my breast, behold it bared; (and with her hand she tore aside her robe) or, if you wish to bleed me, here is my throat. And if you do not want me to have this or that death, but to cut off my head, behold, I obediently bow my neck.

At last Herod feels the full impact of his jealous rage and madness, for he knows that he alone was responsible for the tragedy. "I do not have to lament me of Fortune, because I myself was my own evil instrument." He does realize, however, that his sister Salome had deceived him and he determines to punish her. But most of all he thinks of his wife: "Ah, my Marianna, where are you now? How can I remain alive without you alive?" He knows that he has lost her forever, that he can never join her after death, for he is not going where she is.

The chorus ends the play with a short ode.

Vedete, egri mortali,
Come l' ira è cagione
D' incomparabil mali.
Però non vi lasciate uscir di mano
Il fren de la ragione,
Se poi doler non vi volete in vano;
Che questo acuto sprone,
Voi trasportando a precipizii tali,
Vi guasti ogni opra, ogni consiglio sano.

You see, weak mortals, how wrath is the cause of incomparable evils. Therefore do not let the reins of reason drop from your hand, if you do not want to grieve in vain; because this sharp spur will transport you to such a dangerous pitch that every labor and every wholesome counsel will be confounded.

Marianna is Dolce's masterpiece, and it is among the best Italian tragedies of the sixteenth century.[21] Aretino's *Orazia* is a

---

[21] The Herod who slaughtered the innocents was a favorite character in the mystery plays and for that reason, perhaps, was not much used by the learned writers of tragedies in Italy. The other Herod, who became involved with John the Baptist, was also well known, and it would be surprising if no learned

better play and Cinthio's *Orbecche* is perhaps as good a play; but neither Aretino nor Cinthio created so impressive a tragic character as Dolce's Herod, who is the most believable tyrant among all the Italian descendants of Seneca's Atreus, Hercules, and Nero. Marianna is a tragic heroine comparable to Orbecche and Rosmunda, better drawn than Sofonisba or Canace or Cinthio's Cleopatra. If Dolce had enjoyed the same freedom of movement on the stage that the Elizabethan Webster enjoyed in his *Duchess of Malfi*, if the Italian had not been restrained by Horace and the neoclassical rules from showing the actual death scene of the heroine but instead had to assign this scene to a messenger's report, Marianna would indeed be comparable to the great Duchess. But Dolce did not enjoy such freedom, and moreover, even at his best, he was not the poet that Webster was at his best. Therefore the Italian critic Rébora could say with justice, "Ah, why on earth can no Italian tragedy in seven centuries of national literature boast of a scene so pathetic, so intensely human, so exquisitely poetical as this of the death of John Webster's Duchess of Malfi?"[22] Dolce's *Marianna* came about as close as any.

The diction of *Marianna* is also notable. The author promised, in his second prologue, that there would be no extravagant language, and, for a follower of Seneca, he kept this promise surprisingly well. The best speeches of Marianna and Soemo, even the ravings of Herod, are kept within the bounds of nature. Dolce had little or no lyrical gift, but he was a good rhetorician. Here again the influence of Cinthio was probably at work. Dolce's progress in tragic diction was parallel to that of Cinthio; both dramatists, as they continued to write tragedies, tried to make their characters speak less like Roman *declamatores* and more like Italian men and women, albeit Italian kings and queens, dukes and duchesses.

---

dramatists used his story. Giambattista Marzii did; his *Herodiade* was published at Florence in 1594.

Marzii sought the *stile tragico* and wrote a conventional play in the Cinthian manner. It starts with the ghost of Herod's earlier wife, who was discarded in favor of Herodias. Now the ghost seeks revenge. The whole first act is devoted to supernatural characters. The high spot in the main action is the dance by the princess in Act 4, followed by the reward of John the Baptist's head, which is brought onstage by a messenger in the last act.

[22] P. 205.

IX

More Blood

Rosmunda and *Orbecche*, especially the latter, set examples for tragedies of blood and revenge, and there were numerous disciples of Rucellai and Cinthio during the second half of the sixteenth century. Perhaps Italian playwrights would have written tragedies of blood without the encouragement of their leader Cinthio, for, as we have seen, the Thyestean banquet, the savage rape of Procne's sister, the incest of Canace, and the brutal punishment of Gismonda by her father Tancred had already been dramatized before the 1540's. Followers of Cinthio continued to use these same tales of horror and they found new ones in Ovid, Boccaccio, and ancient history. Seneca's *Thyestes* continued to be the favorite ancient model, followed by *Medea*, but was challenged by *Oedipus*. Lodovico Domenichi,[1] a friend of Dolce and also a *poligrafo*, translated Corraro's fifteenth-century *Progne* into Italian *versi sciolti* and rhymed choruses. Giralamo Parabosco published a *Progne* in 1548. Luigi Groto evidently wrote a *Progne* which has been lost.[2] There was a *Gismonda* in 1569 and three tragedies entitled *Tancredi* between 1588 and 1614. There was only one *Canace* after Falugi's play (c. 1530), but Speroni's exerted a very considerable influence, not only in encouraging the use of short lines *(settenarii)*

---

[1] *Progne, tragedia*, Florence, 1561.
[2] See Neri, p. 105.

in emotional passages but also in abetting an interest in the tragic effects of romantic love and incest.

PARABOSCO'S *PROGNE*

Girolamo Parabosco, novelist, playwright, musician, wrote eight comedies, some of which were better than average and one of which, *Il pellegrino* ("The Pilgrim"), coined the name of the famous braggart soldier in the *commedia dell' arte*, namely, Capitan Spavento (Captain Fear). Bertana calls his one tragedy *miserabilissima*. While I do not propose to defend *Progne* as a good play, I do not find it quite so bad as that; in fact, there are occasional sparks of feeling and a little poetry scattered throughout dreary stretches of lamentations, narratives, and moralizings.

There is no evidence that Parabosco paid any attention to Corraro's Latin version, but, like, Corraro, he omitted Ovid's metamorphosis of the leading characters into birds and substituted a more realistic ending. He spared his audience the sight of Tereo dining on the flesh of his child, but provided blood enough and revenge enough. In the last act, Progne sends her husband a covered basket containing the "thing most dear to her and that he loves most in the world." When Tereo lifts the cover he finds the head of his little son. Thereupon, after the proper lamentations, he stabs his wife, who falls dead on the stage.

Parabosco tried to humanize the grief-maddened queen, and the various stages leading to her Medea-like decision to kill Itys (since this was the only way she could get revenge for the outrage done to her sister Philomela) are portrayed with some understanding of human nature. Shortly after Progne learns the truth about her sister from an old woman, and before she has decided what she must do, the prattling of the little boy pierces her to the marrow, as though she already sensed what the outcome must be. "Hush, sweet son," she cries, "close your mouth now, for your sweet talk redoubles my grief."[3] In the fourth act, after she has killed the child, her remorse seems convincing: "No drop [of blood] fell from you, son, that was not a knife that passed through my heart" (25r).

Such glimpses of humanity are not numerous, however, and the play piles up the usual horror upon horror in long-winded

---

[3] *La Progne, tragedia nova* (Venice, 1548), 20v. This scene is in the third act.

narrations by messengers, usually female messengers. The nurse
is typical; like Cinthio's messengers, she is both horrified and
fascinated by the horrors she recounts. "Prepare tears, ladies, to
make a lake," she cries. Then:

> Veduto ho donne mie tal crudeltate
> Ch' io temo d' ingannarmi, e non affermo
> Che non sia stata visione, o sogno:
> Tanto prendo stuppor, che la pietate
> Hoggi non m' habbia fuor di vita tratta [22r].

Ladies, I have seen such cruelty that I fear I deceive myself and I am
not sure but it was a vision or a dream. I am much amazed that pity
has not deprived me of my life today.

The nurse spares the ladies of the chorus no detail. As Progne
pressed the knife against his breast, the child cried out, "Sweet
mother, what are you doing? Why do you kill me?" And then,
says the nurse, "turning to give her another kiss, alas, he gave up
the ghost" (23r).

Neri, who is much kinder to Parabosco than is Bertana, finds a
certain sweetness in the lamentations of the queen and chorus. I
might add that there is a certain moralizing in the choruses, which
was proper enough, however, in the sixteenth century. The following extract from a chorus at the close of Act 2 might have been
written by almost any Italian imitator of Seneca and Sophocles.

> Che l' huom quand' egli è nato
> Iscritto nella fronte il bene, e 'l male
> Porta di giorni suoi:
> Nè d' alcun tempo poi
> Il calcitrar gli vale,
> Ch' ogni rimedio, ogni riparo humano,
> Contra colpi del cielo è scarso, e vano [14r].

When man is born he carries the good and evil of his days inscribed on
his brow; nor does protest avail him at any time thereafter, for every
remedy, every human defense against the blows of heaven is feeble
and vain.

CESARI'S *SCILLA*

Cesare de' Cesari, author of a mediocre *Cleopatra*,[4] dramatized
the ancient myth of Nisus and his daughter Scylla. According
to Ovid's version in the *Metamorphoses*, when Minos of Crete
besieged the Greek city of Megara, he attracted the attention

---

[4] See above, pp. 147–148.

of Scylla, daughter of the king, Nisus, and she fell desperately in love with him. She knew that Megara was protected by a magic purple lock of hair on her father's head, so she cut off the lock, thus insuring the fall of the city and the death of her father. Minos, however, was so revolted by this unfilial conduct that he repudiated the maiden. Whereupon she was turned into a bird. Her father was turned into a sea-eagle and he pursued his daughter over the waves.

Cesari's *Scilla* is not a good example of the tragedy of blood; but I have included it in this chapter because the original story has bloodthirsty possibilities similar to those in the Procne myth and because it also emphasizes the cruel pangs of unrequited love. Cesari's Scilla starts the play with a confession to her nurse that she is suffering all the agonies of love, and the last chorus is addressed to Amore, "cause of all our ills."

The situation of Scilla, caught between duty to her kind father and fascination for the enemy warrior, is essentially dramatic and has appeared in hundreds of plays. Cesari recognized the drama here, but he was unable to capitalize on it. Apparently he was influenced by the Dido plays and also by *Canace*. He did little more, however, than string together laments, declamations, and narratives. The poetry, such as it is, is usually more lyrical than dramatic. The chorus of maidens has a major role, and consequently the tragedy is mostly an extended *commos*. There is also a semi-chorus of Cretan soldiers that has a prominent part in the last act.

Girolamo Ruscelli (d. 1566), another *poligrafo*, praised Cesari's tragedy for its arrangement and versification.[5] It is true that the author tried to make his plot conform to the best neoclassical practice. For example, there is a turning point at the close of Act 3, when Scilla sends the keys of the city to Minos by a trusty servant. From then on a tragic outcome is more or less inevitable. But Cesari lacked invention. He had only a short tale from Ovid at hand and he was unable to fabricate any further complications beyond the already hackneyed device of giving Niso a bad dream, wherein he saw his loving daughter turn against him and betray him. The good old king cannot believe that there is any truth in such a nightmare and Scilla's actual betrayal comes as a shock

---

[5] See *Scilla* (Venice, 1552), 3r.

to him. Seeking verisimilitude, Cesari had his heroine throw herself from a cliff. The news of his daughter's death crushes the old king, who begs the Cretan soldiers not to prolong his life. The soldiers pity the old man, but they are under orders from Minos, so they lead him offstage and cut off his head. The brokenhearted nurse crawls away to die of grief.

As to the versification that Ruscelli praised, it is typical of Italian tragedies after Speroni's *Canace;* that is, it abounds in short lines and has much rhyme. Some of Scilla's soliloquies are not bad, though the text of 1552 could be better. An illustration from Act 4 is representative, and I have tried to make sense of it in English.

> Giusto, e pietoso ciel, che de' mortali
> L' opre riguardi; o cielo,
> So ch' io pecai a l' amorevol padre
> Tendendo occulti inganni;
> Ma vedi hor ne' miei danni
> Signor, quel che tu sai,
> Che Amor è cieco, perche il lume invola
> A un' infelice cor, quand' il suo strale
> Con piaga aspra, e immortale
> L' affligge si, ch' ei non pur resta cieco,
> Ma ancor senza di lui
> Afflitta e sola [35v].

Just and merciful Heaven, you who are concerned with the actions of men, O Heaven, I know that I sinned against my loving father in harboring dark deceits; but you see now, Lord, in my peril, what you know, that Love is blind, for he steals the light from an unhappy heart, when his arrow with bitter and immortal wound vexes her so that not only does he remain blind but even [she] without him [remains] comfortless and lonely.

GROTO'S *DALIDA*

Luigi Groto, *il Cieco d'Adria,* the blind poet and orator from the town of Adria near Venice, wrote tragedies, comedies, pastorals, and at least one mystery play *(rappresentazione sacra).*[6] In the dedication of his first comedy, *Emilia* (1579), he remarked that his blindness had encouraged melancholy and consequently a bent for tragedy, of which he had already given proof in *Dalida* and *Hadriana.* Earlier, in the dedication of *Dalida* (1572), he explained that his affliction had driven him to seek other than normal means

---

[6] *Lo Isach, rappresentation nova,* Venice, 1586.

of producing children, that Dalida was a daughter, a young woman lacking the gorgeous trappings of the Rosmundas, Canaces, and Didos, but dressed in plain linen and wearing her own face. Groto's modesty was not altogether frank, for he tried to surpass in tragic horror all the heroines of Rucellai, Cinthio, Speroni, and Seneca. And his play became influential, even outside Italy.[7]

The scene of *Dalida* is exotic, the city of Bactra in far-off Bactria, that ancient province between Persia and India.[8] Groto preserved an economy of time, but left the scene uncertain. His versification was conventional, *versi sciolti* and *settenarii*, with some rhyme. It is a long play of 4,000 lines or so. His principal model was *Orbecche*, but the ghost of Thyestes was standing at his shoulder. The prologue informs the reader that he must not expect a comedy or pastoral. He, however, who "comes prepared to listen to laments, tears, and deaths, sit still and be silent, because today the fulfillment of his wish may perhaps be enough." For most readers *Dalida* is more than enough.

The first act of Cinthio's *Orbecche* has only supernatural characters, Nemesis, the Furies, and the ghost of the dead queen Selina. The first act of *Dalida* is also devoted to supernatural characters. In the first scene, the ghost of Moleonte, deposed king of Bactria, talks with Death, who appears as a skeleton carrying a scythe. Death greets the royal ghost respectfully, remarking that he has just arrived in time for a "horrendous slaughter," and is now completely at his service.

Death: Now command what you wish. Do you want me to make a sweep with my scythe and leave the Bactrian land empty of men and animals? *Moleonte:* I do not wish such. But to reveal in brief the occasion that drives me to indignation and revenge. . . .

Then follows the exposition, which actually is brief. Candaule, nephew of Moleonte, had usurped the throne and married Moleonte's daughter (Dalida) although he already had a wife

---

[7] William Alabaster's *Roxana*, acted at Cambridge about 1592, was a Latin version of *Dalida* which attracted some attention. It was printed in 1632.

[8] Groto may have found a suggestion for the plot of *Dalida* in Herodotus (9.108–113), in the story of Xerxes and his brother Masistes, Viceroy of Bactria. Xerxes coveted Masistes' wife, arranged a match between her daughter and his son, then switched his affection to the daughter. When Xerxes' wife, the queen, found out what was going on, she summoned Masistes' wife, cut off her breasts, nose, ears, and lips, and cut out her tongue. Masistes fled to Bactria, but was intercepted by Xerxes' troops, who killed him, along with his sons.

(Berenice). There have been two children by Dalida, none by Berenice. Now the ghost wants revenge; he wants the nephew dead and also those "evil offspring who can call their mother both mother and aunt." And he wants his daughter dead, for she has dishonored both her father and herself.

In the next scene (1.2), Moleonte delivers a violent outburst against his daughter:

> Ah figlia, non già mia, ma d' Acheronte,
> Ingrata, dishonesta, ov' è l' Amore,
> Che a tuo padre mostravi? v' la pietade
> Ch' eri tenuta a i genitori tuoi?

Ah daughter, not mine indeed but Acheron's, ungrateful, unchaste, where is the love you showed your father, where the piety that you held toward your parents?

He sees a way to revenge, namely, to make the queen, Berenice, jealous: "Lybia has no fierce lion, Hyrcania no savage tiger, that can equal the fury of a woman incensed by jealousy." When Death re-enters with Jealousy (dressed as a Fury) Moleonte makes his request. "Work it, O Jealousy, so that there is not enough steel, not enough poison, not enough fire to glut her [Berenice's] jealous mind against her wicked, adulterous consort and my daughter his whore, and those incestuous, adulterous offspring" (1.3).

The chorus of women delivers a rhymed ode that views the situation with alarm. Groto followed the practice of Cinthio; he made little use of the chorus in dialogue until the fourth and fifth acts.

Candaule the king is introduced in the second act talking to his secretary, Besso. So far only the secretary knows about the king's secret life with Dalida. It is soon revealed that Besso, who is in love with the queen, is planning to betray this secret, and he does betray it, bringing the queen up to date on the love affair and handing over a letter to Dalida from Candaule. At this point Jealousy re-enters to offer her services, and Berenice begins to lay her plans.

> O figlie horrende de la trista sera,
> Che a l' opre humane, e ree gastigo date,
> Tu Tisifon, tu Aletto, e tu Megera,
> O quante alme dannate
> Ne l' inferno habitate
> A me venite, e d' una rabbia fera,
> D' un disperato, e ardente cor mi armate [2.3].

O dreadful daughters of gloomy night, who punish evil deeds of men, you Tisiphone, you Alecto, you Megaera, O as many damned souls as inhabit hell, come to me and arm me with savage rage, with a desperate and burning heart.

Besso has a key to Dalida's house and he promises to help the queen get her revenge.

Berenice is determined to emulate, and to surpass, Clytemnestra and Rosmunda: "Rage, do not abate, run, grow, multiply, shine, boil, blaze! Behold I open my breast to you and offer you my heart. You, Berenice, venture every great trial, nor fear any villainous undertaking. Let my eyes be dry, my hands bold, viperish, dragon-like, rocklike; let nothing bend nor sway me save wrath" (2.5). The chorus, appalled, calls on the gods to punish the treacherous Besso.

In the third act, the familiar good counselor appears, and his good advice to the king has the same result that all good advice to tyrants has, that is, nothing beyond fine words. Groto used a favorite device of his own in some of the counselor's arguments, namely, topical allusions to distinguished Italians. Later on, in his comedy *Emilia,* he did the same thing; there he introduced allusions to the war between Venice and Turkey.

Dalida makes her first entrance in the third scene of Act 3, which is a domestic scene obviously built up for contrast with the blood and torture that follow. Apparently mother and children have been brought to the city. Dalida is still grieving over the loss of her parents and is beset with premonitions of disaster. For one thing, she has had a vision of a fierce tiger tearing her two children to pieces and charging her. Groto introduced a little family dialogue here.

Boy: Mother?
Dalida: Son?
Boy: What trees are those?
Dalida: They are the lofty banners of this city.
Boy: Why do you sigh so when you speak? Mother? Mother, ah me, why are you crying?
Dalida: I cry because I can't help it [3.3].

The counselor again tries to bring the king to reason, but Candaule has another worry on his mind now: the old nurse has informed him that his supposedly faithful secretary is having an affair with his supposedly faithful queen. Candaule is a Senecan tyrant, maintaining that laws are made for other people, that a king makes his own laws. Now he decides to poison Berenice. Jealousy is operating again. The chorus closes the third act with an ode to the green-eyed goddess: "Incurable are her wounds."

The horrors, as was proper in the neoclassical tragedy of the sixteenth century, begin in Act 4, which is comparable to the fourth act of *Orbecche* and of *Thyestes*. A messenger enters beside himself with horror. The chorus listens with groans and tears as he unfolds the gory account of Berenice's revenge.

The queen, in the ironical manner of Sulmone in *Orbecche*, had received Dalida courteously, then had led her to a dungeon in the castle, where she was stripped and bound. "Dalida," said Berenice, "this is the place and this is the time where and when to provide your nuptials. These funeral lights are the marital torches. Since roses, lilies, and myrtles are lacking, cypress will be used. To honor you I wish to be the bride's matron; let Mercury be the patron and escort you to the bridal bed with his golden wand. Hyman, who when called was busy with other affairs, will send Death in his place. He has sent the nuptial knot on ahead, and you already feel it clasping you. The bridegroom whom you await this evening is the great Pluto" (4.1).

The messenger is proceeding with his narrative when he is interrupted by the entrance of Moleonte's ghost, who has come to share the horrors, actually to revel in them.

After beating her rival with iron rods until a shower of blood fell, Berenice freed one of her hands and forced a knife into it, saying, "Behold I hand over to you the scepter; now bring justice to your incestuous offspring." Then, guiding the helpless hand of Dalida, Berenice proceeded to cut the wailing children to pieces. (The ghost relishes every drop of blood and commends the ingenuity of the queen.) When the maddened queen finally cut the throat of the little girl, Dalida herself put an end to the suffering of the boy. Then Berenice, crying, "Accompany your children who go before, O Dalida, and your bridegroom who will come after," drove the knife through her left breast until the point snapped on the shoulder blade. The ghost is in a rapture of admiration: "You wish to please me well, and you wish to show that your coming is very different from that of the three Furies in bringing tragedies into the world" (4.2).

The messenger's tale is not yet done. Berenice, he says, removed the hearts, cut up the bodies, and handed over the parts to the seneschal with orders to have them cooked. The three heads she placed on platters of gold. The messenger now leaves to invite Candaule to supper.

When Berenice next comes onstage she is triumphant:

> Hor son donna, hor son forte, hor son Reina,
> Meritamente hor la corona porto.
> Si fa cosi a ribatter con fortezza
> Da se l' ingiurie. Imparino i mariti
> Ad esser fidi a le lor fide spose [4.3].

Now I am a woman, now I am strong, now I am Queen, now I wear the crown worthily. This is the way to repay injuries with interest. May husbands learn to be faithful to their faithful wives.

Her revenge is not yet complete. She tells the chorus of the treat she is preparing for Candaule; it will surpass the feasts of Tantalus, Tereus, and Thyestes, for she is going to add poison to the viands. Thereupon an argument in Senecan stichomythy ensues between the queen and the chorus. Candaule appears, ready for supper.

Act 5 is similar to the last act of *Thyestes* and the Procne plays although the actual banquet is not shown. Candaule has already supped. Berenice presents the heads on the golden platter.

Candaule: What compassionate hand comes to pluck out my eyes?
Berenice: I wish you had as many as Argus had [5.1].

When Candaule asks what has become of the other remains, Berenice replies that she has given them the most excellent burial: "Is not your belly a worthy sepulcher? Was not my castle a worthy kitchen for their limbs? Were not these hands worthy ministers of a just slaughter?" The king is overwhelmed by the enormity of the crime. "Now," he cries, "if I want to bury my children it is necessary to bury myself alive. If I want to light the pyre for my wife it is necessary to burn myself." He begs Berenice to kill him. She informs him that it is not necessary, for she has already poisoned him. Then Candaule informs her that she has also been poisoned.

In the next scene (5.2), Candaule dies onstage, cursing Berenice and begging the counselor to bury him with the heads of Dalida and the children. The counselor does what he can to ease the death throes. "Take comfort, Sire, for you will soon leave this wayward world, where birth is pain, living is travail, and death a necessity." In the last scene, a damsel reports the death of Berenice to the chorus, which moralizes on the uncertainty of human existence.

TANCRED AND GISMONDA

Girolamo Razzi, writer of comedies, one of which, *La Cecca,* is the liveliest drama in the sixteenth century of student life, wrote a tragedy called *Gismonda* (1569).[9] Although the author had a good ear for conversational speech and more than a little wit, he was not at home in tragedy. He might have done better, perhaps, had he merely rewritten Pistoia's rhymed tragedy of *Filostrato e Panfila,* which was arranged as a Terentian plot with the choruses treated as *intermezzi.*[10] Like Pistoia, he followed Boccaccio's tale closely, but, unlike Pistoia, he began not *ab ovo* but in *medias res.* In other words, he was influenced by Cinthio and Speroni and arranged the action as a classical tragedy. His chorus of Salernian women has the role of another actress and takes a prominent part in the dialogue. He tried to bolster the rather brief story with supernatural elements, a ghost, dreams, and dismal auguries. He introduced a faithful *cameriera,* who serves as Gismonda's confidante and takes the action into her own hands at the end in order to gain some revenge for the cruel treatment of her mistress; she sets fire to the palace and burns it to the ground.

Razzi's tragedy has a prologue in which he used the familiar device of a spirit rising from hell. His ghost is a woman who had been damned for love, and she foretells the outcome of the action about to unfold: "I come today among the living to see in others what I see in myself, an unhappy and dismal ghost in my greenest and loveliest years; and to predict a bloody and miserable death for two happy lovers, happy now but soon most unhappy."

Gismonda opens the play talking to Eugenia (the *cameriera)* and the chorus. She has had a bad dream in which she saw her lover Guiscardo attacked by two fierce mastiffs that tore out his heart.

---

[9] One of Razzi's contemporaries, apparently inspired by *Gismonda,* dramatized a similar tale from Boccaccio. The result was *Sormonda* (Venice, 1569) by Bartolommeo Tanni (Tommaso Giuseppe Farsetti), a professed Grecian but an imitator of *Thyestes* and *Progne* along with *Gismonda.* The heroine Sormonda sups on the heart of her lover. Before she commits suicide, she remarks appropriately enough, "He could not have a worthier sepulcher."

[10] See above, pp. 29–33.

Tancred first appears in Act 2, philosophizing on the uncertain state of mortals. Guiscardo is happy in his love; he and Gismonda have been carrying on their secret affair for some time. Before the second act is over, however, Tancred has discovered their secret and has had Guiscardo arrested. Eugenia has a nightmare in which a ghost tells her to flee the palace in Salerno, for it will soon be swimming in blood.[11]

Thanks to Boccaccio, the meeting between Tancred and Guiscardo in Act 3 is pretty well done. The best lines are transcribed almost verbatim from the *Decameron*. The third character on the stage is Fulvio, the king's confidant.

Tancred	Tu hai ben fatto, Fulvio.
Fulvio	In fatti egli non può tener le lachrime;
	Oh come egli l' amava.
Tancred	La mia benignità, Guiscardo, verso
	Te, non ha meritato il grave oltraggio,
	E la vergogna, che hai nelle mie cose
	Fattami, e, che ho vist' io con gl' occhi proprii.
Guiscardo	Amor può troppo più,
	Che voi nè io possiamo [p. 30].

Tancred: You have done well, Fulvio.

Fulvio: Indeed, he cannot hold back the tears. Oh, how he loved her.

Tancred: My kindness toward you, Guiscardo, has not deserved the grievous outrage and shame you have done to me and mine, and what I have seen with my own eyes.

Guiscardo: Love has more power than you or I.

A quotation from the *Decameron* (4.1) will show Razzi's debt to Boccaccio.

"Guiscardo, la mia benignità verso te non avea meritato l'oltraggio e la vergogna la quale nelle mie cose fatta m' hai, sì come oggi vidi con gli occhi miei."

Al quale Guiscardo niuna altra cosa disse se non questo: "Amor può troppo più che nè voi nè io possiamo."

When Tancred rebukes his daughter for taking a low-born lover, Gismonda speaks frankly to him, and here again Boccaccio provided the most natural lines.

Egli è vero, che io ho amato, et amo,
Et amerò Guiscardo
Quanto io viverò, ch' homai fie poco [p. 34].

---

[11] Cf. *Filostrato e Panfila* above, p. 30.

It is true that I have loved, do love, and will love Guiscardo so long as I shall live, which henceforth may not be long.

Boccaccio wrote: "Egli è vero che io ho amato e amo Guiscardo, e quanto io viverò, che sarà poco, l' amerò."[12]

Generally the style of Razzi's *Gismonda* is undistinguished. The author tried to pump up emotion by repeated complaints about the tyranny of love, but the results were commonplace. The following extract from the short choral ode at the close of Act 2 is typical.

> O folli, e ciechi Amanti
> Come spesso vi trae del senno fuore
> L' empio Tiranno Amore?
> Si che voi non vedete
> Quel, che sempre dinanzi a gl' occhi havete?

O foolish and blind lovers, how often does the wicked tyrant Love take away your discretion, so that you do not see what is always before your eyes?

Il Tancredi by Federigo Asinari, Count of Camerano, published at Bergamo in 1588, went beyond earlier versions in scope and ostentation. The author, obviously influenced by Cinthio, tried to build up the tale into a majestic spectacle. He expanded the cast to include a captain of the guard, a counselor, and a priest. Almonio the captain is a cruel man, the villain of the play. The counselor is the wise man that tries in vain to restrain the prince, who has been influenced by the brutal soldier. Asinari kept the trusty maidservant added by Razzi, and used a nurse to boot. He added a new complication to the domestic crisis, namely, a projected marriage of Gismonda to the king of Sicily. This political move forces Tancred's hand when he discovers his daughter's affair with Guiscardo. Asinari tried to make the tragedy more Senecan than the earlier versions. The chorus in Act 4, having listened to the messenger's account of Guiscardo's death, cries: "Day once joyful, now more ominous than any other, for are you not darkened as when Thyestes saw the cruelty of Atreus? This deed was not less deserving than that one of being hidden in gloomy night" (40v).

Asinari's prologue introduces a priest and the ghost of the Duke of Capua, Gismonda's first husband. The ghost has been aroused by jealousy of his widow's new lover, Guiscardo, and he seeks revenge

---

[12] Cf. Pistoia above, p. 31.

for the insult to his memory. Although the ghost does not appear in the play proper, Gismonda is aware of his presence. Early in the action she says, "I seem to see the sad image of my dead Duke wrapped in a dark cloud, and it threatens a cruel end to my sweet renewed desire" (8v).

Asinari's style is usually pompous, often full of classical allusions. Only occasionally, when the author was imitating Boccaccio or the stichomythy of Seneca, are the speeches pithy and natural. The following outburst from Gismonda in the third act is about as good as any. The princess has been berating her father for carrying out the letter of the law in Salerno, that is, royal blood can only be mated with royalty. Guiscardo, already doomed, is present.

> Trahate dunque voi per farne stratio
> Colui, che vostra libertade, e vita
> Col proprio sangue suo difese? O Sole
> Fuggi dal Ciel, non apportar più lume
> A quest' ingrato secolo [27r].

Are you gathered, then, to massacre this man, he who defended your life and liberty with his own blood? O Sun, flee from Heaven, no more furnish light for this ungrateful age.

Some of the scenes between Tancred and Almonio are lively, but they are mostly derivative, imitations of earlier Senecan exchanges between tyrant and counselor. Tancred makes a great show of respecting the laws of the state.

Almonio: But what is this power that presses him [the prince]?
Tancred: The laws have power to bind him and unbind him.
Almonio: The prince is not subject to the laws.
Tancred: He is either subject to the laws or he is a tyrant.
Almonio: The prince is himself laws to his [subjects] [14v].

Guiscardo is the most convincing character in the play. At least he is not so stuffy as Tancred or Almonio or the good counselor, and he speaks as a man might speak in his predicament. Even so, the brightest spot in his answer to Tancred is another echo of the familiar line from Boccaccio: "Love is more powerful than these your laws or you or I" (26v).

Pomponio Torelli, author of the next *Tancredi*, which went through at least three printings between 1597 and 1605, was a disciple of Aristotle and a Grecian. He chose the subject of his first, and best, tragedy, *Merope* (1589),[13] because Aristotle, in *Poetics* 14, had praised the tragic situation in Euripides' *Cresphontes*[14] as the best in Greek tragedy, "where Merope, on the point of slaying her son, recognizes him in time." According to the author's dedication of *Tancredi* to the duke of Urbino, he chose the story of Tancred and Gismonda because it fitted Aristotle's requirements for a good tragedy and because it had already been successfully treated by three illustrious predecessors, Boccaccio, Girolamo Razzi, and Asinari, Count of Camerano.

One does not have to proceed far into Torelli's long, tedious play to perceive that he owed much to his immediate predecessor Asinari. He kept Almonio as the villain. He kept the good counselor and increased his part. He kept the nurse, but omitted Gismonda's *cameriera*. He added a comrade of Guiscardo. There is no messenger by name, but a page performs the function of one. Torelli omitted the ghost in Asinari's prologue and he omitted a prologue, probably because Grecians did not favor the Senecan-Cinthian type of prologue. Since he approved of Asinari's attempt to elevate the story above a domestic quarrel, he increased the trappings of state and

---

[13] *Merope* is a tragedy with a happy ending *(tragedia di lieto fin)* although Torelli was a Grecian and no follower of Cinthio. There is a detailed account of this play, and of two earlier Merope plays (Cavallerino's *Telefonte* and Liviera's *Cresfonte*), in my *Tragicomedy*, pp. 101–121.

In addition to *Merope* and *Tancredi*, Torelli wrote two other tragedies, *Il Polidoro* (1605) and *La Vittoria* (1605). He also wrote *La Galatea* (1603), which is a pastoral tragedy recounting the sad fate of the shepherd Acis, beloved of the nymph Galatea but brutally slain by the jealous Cyclops Polyphemus.

Antonio Cavallerino may well deserve more attention that I have been willing to give him, for he was a competent versifier and as good a dramatist as many I have discussed. Neri maintains that Cavallerino is important for his experiments in tragic verse. He illustrates what he calls *quinta rima* (a b c b a, c d e d c) from some dialogue in Cavallerino's *Rosimonda regina* (1582). The curious reader may be interested in a variation (a b c b a c, c d e d e f) that appears in the Act 4 chorus in *Il Conte di Modona* (1582). A stanza will illustrate this last scheme.

> O Nume delle stelle, alla cui luce
> Ogn' altra si scolora,
> O cuor del Ciel, ch' in un sol giorno miri
> I Sabei posti là sotto l' Aurora,
> E l' Ibero, ch' a noi la sera adduce,
> Altrui forse il mattino, e ne' tuoi giri. . . .

Cavallerino's *Ino* (1583), which, like *Telefonte* (1582), used an argument from Hyginus' handbook of fables, is more conventional in its versification.

[14] The *Cresphontes* is lost, but a summary of the argument survived in Hyginus' handbook.

the discussions of politics, adding a new character, the president of the senate of Salerno. He raised Guiscardo from a low-born youth to a prince disguised as a simple knight.

Torelli's *Tancredi* is arranged in a Grecian form comparable to that of Trissino's *Sofonisba*. There are no divisions into acts and scenes, but there are five episodes separated by choral odes. The chorus is male, made up of knights of Salerno, friends of Guiscardo but loyal to the prince. It is a *coro fisso*, like Trissino's; after it enters at the conclusion of the first episode it stays on the stage until the end, often taking part in the dialogue and listening sympathetically to the long series of debates, complaints, and reports of offstage violence. The verse form is mainly *versi sciolti*, with the choral odes in rhyme. The author made some concession to the new fashion, however, and introduced some *settenarii* in highly emotional speeches that come late in the play.

Torelli not only made it clear that only one scene is used but he compressed the time more than did his predecessors. When his play opens, Tancred has already discovered the affair between his daughter and Guiscardo. Consequently the action is largely wrangling over what is to be done with a situation that is embarrassing the state of Salerno. Wranglings, complaints, and lamentations, words, words, words! It seems that the characters will never stop talking.

The good counselor tries to calm Tancred's indignation at the lovers' disruption of his political plans, which apparently bothers him as much as does the insult to his royal honor. "As for the seriousness of this fault of theirs," says the counselor, "it is a fault of youth, a fault of love, which always finds pardon in a noble [*gentil*] heart" (p. 17).[15] The clergy and the senate add more complications to the solution of the problem, so that the prince becomes more and more reluctant to commit himself to any action. The tough captain, however, stands fast; he says, "If you got rid of Guiscardo soon, you would see these false specters vanish like shadows" (p. 47). Finally Tancred accepts Almonio's advice and gives an order in one of his few straightforward speeches:

Va tosto a la prigione, e fa troncare
Il capo di Guiscardo, e Sergio paggio
Il cor me porti in una coppa d' oro [p. 66].

Go quickly to the prison and have Guiscardo's head cut off, and let the page Sergio bring me his heart in a golden cup.

---

[15] *Terza editione* (Parma, 1605).

There is no swift rush to the catastrophe after this turning point, however; there are well over a thousand more lines of repentance, recrimination, lamentation, and long reports of death. The tragedy comes to a quiet close with Tancred's intimating that he will become a hermit and with the chorus reminding the spectator that "these are the hopes and this is the fruit of immoderate love."

Since Torelli was a Grecian, he presumably preferred Euripides and Sophocles to Seneca. There was hardly any escape from Seneca, however, for the sixteenth-century playwright, and the tale of Tancred and Gismonda seemed made for Senecan tragedy. Its climax, when Gismonda pours poison in the golden cup holding her lover's heart, must have sounded like an echo from *Thyestes* 453: *venenum in auro bibitur* ("poison is drunk in gold"). At all events, Torelli, like Asinari, certainly thought of *Tancredi* as akin to *Thyestes*. After Sergio the page delivers a detailed report of Guiscardo's execution, the chorus of knights cries, "Alas, what new Atreuses, what new Thyesteses this unhappy age still produces!" (p. 77).

Although the third *Tancredi*,[16] by Ridolfo Campeggi, lies beyond the scope of this study of sixteenth-century tragedy, a brief description of it will show that it was typical of seventeenth-century Italian plays, most of which were imitations of earlier works.

Campeggi carried on the changes made by Asinari and Torelli; that is, he also tried to elevate the tragedy to the plane of Seneca and the ancient Greeks. He kept Torelli's chorus of Salernian knights. For Captain Almonio he substituted a simple soldier, actually a messenger who reports the brutal killing of Guiscardo. He kept the good counselor. He added a Sicilian ambassador and a special emissary of the Sicilian king. He relegated Guiscardo to an offstage character, but also built him up to a noble prince. He increased the emphasis on the pathetic, sentimental tone that both Asinari and Torelli had adopted.

As for tragic style, Campeggi's play scrarcely suffers by comparison with earlier versions although its author was even more long-winded than Torelli. In my judgment, some lines in Campeggi's *Tancredi* are rather better than any written by his predecessors when they ventured beyond Boccaccio. The death of Guiscardo, as reported by the soldier to the chorus, is pretty well done.

---

[16] *Il Tancredi, tragedia*, Bologna, 1614.

Il ferito Signor, c' homai sentendo
Ne le viscere offese
I Messi de la morte,
Languidamente disse;
Misero; se dovea
Esser di ferro la mia fera Morte;
Deh fosse stata almeno
Di ferro ostile, e non di ferro amico [pp. 53–54].

The wounded gentleman, who now felt the messengers of death in his injured breast, spoke faintly, "Unhappy me, if my cruel death had to be by the sword, alas, would that it had been by the sword of an enemy and not by the sword of a friend."

And one of Tancred's late speeches to the chorus has some merit although it is an echo of the Senecan manner.

Ecco il vostro Tancredi (O Cavallieri)
Prence il Mattino, e Prigionier la Sera,
Padre al Meriggio, e senza Figli al Vespro;
Serbato dal furor d' empia Fortuna [p. 143].

Behold your Tancred, O knights, prince at dawn and prisoner at eve, father at noon and childless at sunset; cherished by the fury of evil Fortune.

TURCO'S *CALESTRI*

Carlo Turco, a *letterato*, author of a comedy *(Agnella)* that went through two printings in 1558 and 1585, wrote a tragedy called *Calestri*, first printed in 1585 but finished at least twenty-five years before.[17] Apparently the author was influenced to some extent by the Tancred-Gismonda story, but he changed the setting to the Orient, either Persia or Arabia. Turco was a classicist, though not a Grecian, and his tragedy is carefully constructed on the approved classical pattern. There is only one scene in each act, and the unities are carefully preserved. There is even a *catastasis* in the last act, that is, a sudden turn-around or back eddy in the action wherein the tragic descent halts for a moment, offering some hope for a better outcome, only to plunge again to the gloomy *catastrophe*. There are two choruses, one of men, another of women. The chorus of women takes part in the dialogue.

The *Prologo et Argomento* introduces a ghost and Morpheus, god of sleep, who provide the background of the tragedy and

---

[17] *Calestri, tragedia nuova*, Venice, 1585. A printed letter from Paolo Manutio, thanking the author for sending him the tragedy, is dated May 7, 1560.

indicate the direction the action will take. The ghost of Selambria explains that she was once the empress. When her husband left to wage war on the Medes she fell in love with her brother-in-law, Hisitaspo, and bore him a son. The two guilty lovers did away with Hisitaspo's wife and then poisoned the emperor on his return. Hisitaspo became emperor and married Selambria. Ten years passed, and a daughter, Calestri, was born. Then the emperor poisoned Selambria and took a third wife, who brought with her a son named Anazarbo. Morpheus assures the ghost that all of these crimes will be punished before another sunset.

The first act is devoted to the great warrior Anassarco from Egypt, who has secretly married the princess Calestri. Now he is fretting over a dream in which a tearful woman appeared in a cloud and informed him that she was his mother who knew that the emperor was planning to marry Calestri to his stepson Anazarbo. The second act is devoted to Calestri, who confides in her nurse that she is being forced to marry Anazarbo. The third act of this neatly constructed play is the best written, in my judgment, and offers one of the best dialogues of the sixteenth century between good counselor and tyrant. The emperor asks what punishment is proper for a traitor. When the counselor replies, "All the punishments that can be thought of are not enough," Hisitaspo informs him that Anassarco has secretly married Calestri. Since Anassarco is a great favorite with all, the counselor begins to temporize, advising the emperor to proceed slowly, to control his indignation, and to remember that there is a higher judge of these matters: "You ought to know, most excellent Emperor, that all those who hold realms and empires in the world are lieutenants of the King of Heaven and render account for their every deed" (D2v). And he reminds Hisitaspo that the "wise, the great, the noble, the strongest, all commit greater madnesses for love than does the lowest rabble" (D3r). As usual in such cases, the tyrant agrees to accept this good advice and has no intention of following it.

In Act 4, the inevitable messenger appears, first to inform the chorus of women that Anassarco has been poisoned and then to present Calestri with the golden cup that held the poison. Before Calestri can recover from the shock, her father and stepmother inform her that she must marry Anazarbo at once. After some protest the princess pretends to yield to parental authority.

Saurania: Dear daughter, you may be sure that I will never neglect anything to content you.
Calestri: And I shall never be ungrateful to you [E7r].

In the last act Calestri's handmaid, Aspasia, takes the role of messenger, bringing dismal news to the chorus.

> Non basta il Nilo, o il Gange,
> Non l' Indo, o la Dannoia,
> A lavar piaghe tante,
> Che fan di sangue questa casa un lago [F1r].

There is not enough Nile or Ganges or Indus or Danube to wash so many wounds, which make this house a lake of blood.

She proceeds with her report. Calestri was married to Anazarbo, and after the new couple feasted and danced in the great hall they retired. Shortly after midnight Calestri's maid summoned the empress, who ran half-dressed to the bridal chamber, where she found her son stretched on the bed in a pool of blood and Calestri standing by with a bloodstained sword in her hand. After the proper exchange of vituperation and lamentation, Calestri cut her stepmother's throat and thrust her body on the bed. Then she addressed her sword: "Now that I have offered the victims I owed to my dear husband it is time that I cut the thread of this frail life" (F4v). By the time the emperor arrived there were three corpses in the bedchamber.

Now it is time for the emperor to make his lament and to acknowledge that he should have followed the advice of the good counselor. Even in this dismal collapse of the royal family the counselor does what he can to comfort his master: "He who bears his miseries patiently does what befits a liberal soul; he takes arrogant fate in stride and seeing good and evil fortune always presents an invincible countenance" (F7v). At this point a trusty servant enters, the man to whom the emperor's son was entrusted years ago. This man reports that the son is well and has become a great warrior. The emperor begins to live again and a glimmer of hope appears. After a brief account of the young prince's exploits the servant says that he now calls himself Anassarco. Now all is blacker than before as lamentations are renewed and the emperor leaves the stage to kill himself.

Turco's tragedy is certainly no worse than the average Italian tragedy of blood and it has certain advantages over most of its

rivals. For one thing it is compact; there are no rambling monologues that go on and on. Although all the killings are offstage,
as was proper in the strictest neoclassical tragedy, the action does
move steadily to climax and resolution. There is little excessive
verbiage in the dialogue, which is almost natural at times, at
least as natural as the conventional tragic style of the century
permitted. Turco, however, was no Aretino; he was content to
follow the path of Trissino, Cinthio, and Speroni.

VALERINI'S *AFRODITE*

Adriano Valerini, a well-born, well-educated poet from Verona,
became a leading actor in both the *Gelosi* and *Uniti* companies of
the *commedia dell' arte*. In 1578 he published a neoclassical
tragedy entitled *Afrodite*.[18] Like the authors of the Tancred-
Gismonda plays, Valerini combined a love story with blood and
revenge; in fact, he increased the emphasis on romantic love
and the emphasis on blood as well. He doubtless knew Groto's
Dalida and he must have known *Orbecche* and some of Cinthio's
tragicomedies.

Although *Afrodite* is another tragedy of blood, no better and
no worse than the average, it has some interesting features. Possibly because of the author's familiarity with comedy, and possibly
because he knew Cinthio's theory, he arranged his plot in the
Terentian pattern. There are two love stories that are developed
in parallel, finally coming together in the last act, after one of
the lovers is dead. The first action is resolved in Act 5, the second
action in Act 4, as was proper in neoclassical comedy and tragicomedy. The author turned what could have been a comedy or
tragicomedy of love intrigues into a tragedy of blood.

There is no prologue for *Afrodite*, but the first scene is devoted
to the ghost of Adonis, Cupid, and Scorn. The ghost explains that
the king of Paphos in Cyprus, a city specially devoted to the
worship of Aphrodite, has desecrated his (Adonis') temple by
turning it into a theater. Therefore, "to avenge such a serious outrage, I have come to disturb the peaceful ease of this profane
king and his sons." Adonis has enlisted the aid of Cupid and of

---

[18] *Afrodite, nova tragedia,* Verona, 1578. This is perhaps the first play written
by a member of the *commedia dell' arte*.

Scorn, "that monster by whom Love is conquered." Cupid promises to inflame the young queen and her two stepsons and Scorn promises to madden the queen's *cameriera*.

In the next scene, the king's first son, Tirintio, discloses that he is in love with his stepmother. When the royal secretary enters, Tirintio confides in him. After dutifully advising the young man to suppress all illicit desires, the secretary agrees to secure the help of Orifile, the *cameriera*.

The second action, the love affair of the second prince, Polinnio, and Afrodite, daughter of a priest, is introduced later in the first act.

The chorus of Paphian women is used in the conventional way; it takes part in some of the dialogue and delivers rhymed odes at the close of each act. Dreams and auguries are prominent throughout the early half of the play.

The first complications are projected in the second act, when the king, the royal counselors, and the Athenian ambassador discuss arrangements for the marriage of the two Paphian princes with two daughters of the king of Athens. A crisis arises in the third act, when the queen, Arete, who returns Tirintio's affection although nothing improper has yet occurred, confides her secret to Orifile, who promises to help her. But Orifile has no intention of acting the bawd, for she is already Tirintio's mistress. She appeals to Scorn:

> Santo, et amico Sdegno, ecco ch' io t' apro
> Le porte del mio Cor, tu scaccia Amore
> Dal loco, ove sedea, ponti in sua vece,
> Guidami tu, fa, ch' al mio Re palesi
> Con parole si ardenti il suo disnore,
> Ch' a i duo malvagi Amanti dia la morte [p. 21].

Dear, blessed Scorn, behold I open the doors of my heart to you; drive out Love from the place where he was seated, put yourself in his stead, guide me, bring it about that I may reveal his dishonor to my king in words so fervid that he will bring death to the two wicked lovers.

When Afrodite, who is Polinnio's mistress, learns from her father that both the princes are going to marry, she decides to kill both her lover and herself. "To kill only myself," she says, "would be small correction for the fault committed today."

Bloodshed and death advance in the fourth act. The king

has been told by Orifile that his wife and first son are living in incest. Although his counselors advise him to forgive both son and wife, he is bent on revenge.

In the last scene of Act 4, an overwrought messenger describes Afrodite's punishment of her lover. She had bound him hand and foot as he lay sleeping on her bed, then waked him and cut out his tongue as he tried to cry "Afrodite" but could get no further than "Afro——." Then, upbraiding him for his treachery, she cut off his arm and "plucked out both the lights [eyes] of wretched Polinnio, who heaved a sigh from the heart instead of words" (p. 32).[19] The messenger says that he left before the death of the prince, for he could bear no more.

The chorus, disobeying Horace's admonition that it should support the good, give wise counsel, and control the passionate, exults in this triumph of a wronged woman.

> Il torre ad una Vergine l' honore
> Con lusinghe, e con frode
> È cosi grav' errore
> Che scancellar si deve con la morte,
> Per ciò degna di lode,
> Più che di biasmo è questa invitta Donna [p. 32].

To rob a virgin of her honor with flatteries and fraud is so serious an error that it ought to be erased with death, and therefore this indomitable woman is more worthy of praise than blame.

A Senecan messenger in the last act tells the chorus that the king took his wife and elder son to the temple of Aphrodite, where he offered them a golden cup of wine. They drank. Then the king informed them that the wine was poisoned. Again "poison is drunk in gold."[20] The next scene (5.2) is very romantic and pathetic. Arete and Trinitio, both of them dying, come onstage to make their farewells. The queen admits that she loves her stepson—"not to love you I must needs have been a stone, a stump, or some other unfeeling thing"—but maintains her innocence of any unchaste act. She dies on the stage. Tirintio carries her body to the temple

---

[19] There is an interesting parallel between this gory Italian scene and the first scene of Act 5 in Beaumont and Fletcher's best play, the *Maid's Tragedy*. In the English scene, the royal mistress Evadne ties the king to his bed as he sleeps, wakes him, upbraids him for his sins, then stabs him to death. The motivation behind Evadne's deed is quite different, however, from that behind Afrodite's.

[20] Cf. above, p. 194.

to place it in a tomb and to "breathe my last breath in her bosom" (p. 38).

Orifile now confesses her duplicity to the king; she admits that her accusation of incest was unfounded. And now the king repents, blames himself for the unjust death of wife and son, resolves to abandon the throne, but remembers to send Orifile to the hangman. The royal tale of woe is not yet done. Afrodite now tells the king her story and presents him with the head of his younger son. Then she stabs herself. The admiring chorus cries, "The wretched woman pierces her chaste breast with the steel. O indomitable and generous heart that lodges within! Alas how much blood that wound pours forth, but it sheds more praise and glory than blood" (p. 42). The despairing king is left begging for death. His last wish is: "May some wild beast moved by pity come to tear me to pieces with teeth or claws, and may his body be a sepulcher for my body."

CESARE DELLA PORTA'S *DELFA*

In the last two decades of the century, the tragedies of blood tended to become more bloodthirsty, more shocking, more melodramatic, for the playwrights tried to outdo Cinthio, Speroni, and Groto. The results for the most part were uninspired imitations of *Orbecche, Canace,* and *Dalida,* with tiresome repetitions of cruel tyrants, persecuted royal ladies, and the inevitable good counselors, faithful nurses, trusty servants, soldiers, and sympathetic choruses, not to forget the ghosts. The tragic language became more tragic in the sense of more wailful and more deranged; classical allusions increased and the figures of speech became even more extravagant.

A poor play but a good illustration of this tendency is Cesare Della Porta's[21] *Delfa,* printed at Cremona in 1587 but written some twelve years before. In his dedicatory epistle, the author says that he became so discouraged when he compared his heroine with Rosmunda, Orbecche, Adriana,[22] and other royal ladies that he put his work away. According to his printer, Christoforo Draconi, there was a demand for the tragedy and so it was taken out of storage and published. Most readers will probably agree that the author's first critical reaction was sound. Nevertheless, *Delfa*

---

[21] Not to be confused with the admirable Neopolitan playwright Giambattista Della Porta.

[22] See below, p. 213.

is no worse than some other tragedies that have been noticed.

In his prologue the author speaks modestly enough. "He knows that he lacks the art of Sophocles. . . . He also knows, and confesses it, that this his tragedy is not rich in the profitable and wise sentiments with which Seneca embellished his Medea, Octavia, and his other daughters, with almost too many pearls and jewels." Moreover, he admits that his Delfa "surrenders to Sofonisba, Cleopatra, Altea,[23] Dalida, Rosmunda, Adriana, Canace, Gismonda, Orbecche, and the other royal sisters of the great Cinthio's daughters." His principal model was Orbecche. In fact, Delfa is mostly an imitation of Cinthio's first tragedy, with only one alteration, namely, substituting a wife for a daughter. Even the scene is the same: the city of Susa in ancient Persia.

At the beginning of the first act the ghost of Armilla promises to rival the horrors of Oedipus, Thyestes, and the mad husband of the unhappy Ino.[24] Armilla had lost her life and kingdom to Soffi and his first wife Delfa and now she seeks revenge. Delfa is her daughter.

When the action proper opens we find that Soffi the king has

---

[23] In Altea (Venice, 1556), by Bongianni Gratarolo. Altea is the ancient Althaea, mother of Meleager. She cursed her famous son and brought about his death when he slew her brothers after the great Calydonian boar hunt.

Gratarolo's tragedy was written in versi sdruccioli (unrhymed dactyls), which were often used in early Italian comedy but almost never in tragedy, partly because Cinthio disapproved of them. Gratarolo justified his use of sdruccioli because he believed that they corresponded to the iambs of Greek and Latin dramatic verse and because, according to Aristotle's rules, they were fit for the majesty of tragedy. Gratarolo was anxious to conform to the best classical practice. His play, however, is a dull, learned imitation of the Cinthian tragedy of revenge, and his sdruccioli are monotonous and unnatural. The following is a sample from the first act. Diana is talking with Nemesis and Envy.

> Tu dei saper che Meleagro il Prencipe,
> Figliuol de l'empia mia nemica publica;
> Moglie d' Eneo, che la Provincia domina,
> Per liberar da quella fiera i popoli,
> Ha messo in punto una caccia mirabile;
> Dove invitati son tutti i notabili
> E famosi Baron, c' habbia la Grecia.

"You should know that Meleager the prince, son of my impious open enemy, the wife of Oeneus who rules the province, in order to free the people of that wild beast has arranged a wonderful hunt, to which all the notable and famous lords of Greece have been invited."

Two other tragedies by Gratarolo, Astianette and Polissena, are better done although scarcely notable. See above, p. 158.

[24] Ino's husband was Athamas. See Ovid's Metamorphoses 4.

rejected Delfa and married Altilia, who is far from happy since she lives in constant terror of the first wife's jealousy. The king is somewhat apprehensive, too, and when Delfa returns to the court his first impulse is to have her executed. He feigns magnanimity, however, and after his good counselor has delivered an exhausting moral harangue offers to receive his first wife and to "honor" her and her young son. He does receive his first family graciously, telling Delfa that he will make amends and restore the knot of Hymen. He also wants to give her a present, but first he must appease the gods.

> Guiderò io in palagio il mio figliolo,
> E al sacrificio, c' hor preparo a Giove
> Per questa nostra rinovata gioia,
> Egli sarà presente, e meco insieme
> Offerirà la vittima a l'Altare [p. 83].

I shall conduct my son into the palace and to the sacrifice which I am preparing for Jove because of this renewed happiness of ours; he will be present and together with me will offer the victim before the altar.

Any reader familiar with earlier Italian tragedies is well prepared for Soffi's soliloquy in the next scene. "The proper virtue of a king is to be rigorous in giving punishment for the trespasses of others." Then he adds, "I enter the palace to prepare such a horrible sight for her that she the fool will likely envy the dead" (p. 85).

The fourth act is a slavish imitation of the fourth act of *Orbecche*. A messenger gasps out the story of Soffi's slaughter of his son. A little later the messenger returns with the present for Delfa. Of course there is consternation when the mother uncovers the silver vase and finds the head and mutilated body of her child. She and the nurse indulge in an extended outburst of lamentations in *settenarii*.

The fifth act ends in a shambles, the only real shambles that I know of on the neoclassical Italian stage. As we have seen, Italian tragic dramatists were inclined to respect the Horatian dictum banning blood and violence from the public view. The tables are now turned on the cruel king, but the heroine is not allowed to enjoy her revenge. First, a *cameriera* reports the death of the second wife, Altilia, and the subsequent madness of the grief-stricken king. Soffi himself appears onstage in a fit; he falls senseless to the ground, blood gushing from mouth, nose, and ears. In the finale, two soldiers, who believe that Delfa and her nurse are responsible for the king's collapse, strike the two women. Although Soffi, who now shows some spark of repentance, commands the soldiers to stop, the wounds are fatal. The king dies, Delfa dies, and the nurse dies. The good counselor is left in charge of the realm. The chorus of women delivers an admonition which under the circumstances might well apply to the author as well as to his reader: "Learn, O mortals, to regulate the passions."

The worst faults of *Delfa* are the faults of most tragedies of blood and revenge, that is, excessive verbiage, too many hackneyed classical allusions, and strained figures of speech. A typical example of Della Porta's style is the *cameriera*'s description of Altilia's grief. The queen's grief is excessive and the maid's account of it is expressed in excessive comparisons. Restraint was a classical virtue seldom imitated by the Italian writers of tragedy.

> Poscia tal volta un Etna di sospiri
> Trahendo dal profondo del suo core,
> Il pianto, che parea perle, e cristalli,
> Di furto s' asciugava [p. 108].

Then sometime drawing an Etna of sighs from the depth of her heart, she furtively wiped away the tears that seemed to be pearls and crystals.

DECIO'S *ACRIPANDA*

Antonio Decio must have known Turco's tragedy, for his unconscionably long play has a plot similar in several details to that of *Calestri*. *Acripanda* was first printed in 1591,[25] reprinted in 1592, 1610, 1617, and then in 1809 in volume 9 of the *Teatro italiano antico*. In the opinion of some historians, Decio's play is the most revolting of all Italian tragedies of blood, but it is inferior to Groto's *Dalida* as drama and scarcely more bloodthirsty.

Acripanda has no prologue, but the first scene introduces the ghost of Orselia, who has risen from hell to witness revenge for her murder. "But what do I see? This is the palace, the abode of Tantaluses and Atreuses, foul sink of loathsome vices, temple of discord, open school of error, refuge and lodging of guilty women, asylum of infamous men. Behold still the window of the room within which stood my marriage bed, where Ussimano, cruel king, cruel husband, dealt me naked this wound . . . only to be united to this new wife."

Ussimano, the king of Egypt, now has two young children by

---

[25] According to Allacci. The Illinois copy is marked Venice, 1592.

his new wife Acripanda. His son by his first wife (the ghost) had grown up in the court of his grandfather, the king of Arabia, had inherited the throne, and is now attacking Egypt. Acripanda is unhappy, for she has had a dream about a wolf that devoured two little lambs and she is sure that the wolf signifies the king of Arabia. She thinks of herself as another Philomela, doomed to a shameful death. Later on she compares herself with Cleopatra, Sofonisba, and Lucretia. The chorus of Memphian women console her as best they can.

The second act, although far too long, like all the other acts, is dramatic in the sense of building up an approaching disaster. Acripanda, who keeps hearing voices and seeing visions, waits in an agony of fear. "Blood, blood, and revenge went clamoring" (2.2). All of the auguries are bad. And the first bad news comes by messenger in this act: the Egyptian army has been routed and Ussimano is running home to Memphis.

The exposition is strung along through the first three acts in seemingly endless discussions and narratives. There is much philosophizing from a garrulous counselor. What appears to be good news is brought by an Arabian messenger in Act 3, namely, that the enemy king is willing to talk peace. He wants Acripanda's two children as hostages, however, and the queen reluctantly permits the emissary to take the little boy and little girl to the enemy camp.

At the very beginning of Act 4 two small ghosts come to visit Acripanda.

> Noi siam l' anime nude
> De' tuoi fidi gemelli,
> Che vederti bramiamo
> Prima, ch' al ciel saliamo.

We are the naked souls of your devoted twins, who wish to see you before we mount to heaven.

Their bodies, they explain, lie on the bank of the Nile, victims of the treacherous king of Arabia.

The queen's servant, who fills in what was omitted by the twins, comments in traditional style on this not altogether unexpected turn of events.

> Hor dove io son? son tra le selve Hircane
> O tra i monti di Scithia? o tra l' orrende
> Rupi son io del Caucaso gelato?
> Esser non puote, ch' in Egitto io sia.

Where am I now? Am I among the Hyrcanian forests or the mountains of Scythia? Or am I among the horrendous crags of icy Caucasus? It could not be that I am in Egypt.

He has been an eyewitness to the slaughter of the children and he recounts every shocking detail. He tells the mother that the severed arms were wrapped in a linen cloth and given to him to present to the queen. Acripanda insists on opening the blood-stained bundle.

> Ch' io non vi riconosco,
> E quand' io bacio, e palpo
> Qualche lacero membro,
> Non so se palpo e bacio
> Qualche membro, che sia
> Parte di te, figliuolo,
> O di te parte, o figlia;
> E non posso distinti
> Pianger là il filgio, o la figliuola quivi [4.3].

I do not recognize you, and when I kiss and touch some mangled limb I do not know whether it is part of you, my son, or part of you, O daughter; and I cannot distinguish to mourn for my son there or for my daughter here.

The last act is a series of dismal reports to the chorus, which itself is in terror of the approaching hordes of barbarous soldiers. A damsel brings news that Acripanda is dead; she had leaped into the tomb after the remains of her children were buried. Ussimano mourns for his dead. Then he has to witness the corpse of Acripanda carried through the streets amid the taunts of the enemy soldiers. The Arabian king appears to triumph over his father and to pay his respects at the grave of his mother (the ghost of the first act). The play ends in fire and blood, with the sack of Memphis and the slaughter of its inhabitants. The chorus concludes that worldly riches and glory pass in a moment, like "dust, arrow, smoke, cloud, shadow, air, or wind."

MANFREDI'S SEMIRAMIS

The climax of the Italian tragedy of blood may be illustrated by Muzio Manfredi's Semiramis, printed at Bergamo in 1593 but probably composed about ten years earlier.[26] Manfredi was a

---

[26] This tragedy should not be confused, as it apparently was confused by Al-lacci, with the same author's La Semiramis boscareccia (Bergamo, 1593), which is a pastoral based on the famous queen's first love affair with Mennone (On-nes), a general under the Assyrian king Ninus.

successful courtly poet, a writer of madrigals, and his tragedy was
evidently well received and highly regarded. No less than forty
commendatory poems, one by Torquato Tasso, were appended
to the printed version of 1593. The gist of most of these poems,
some in Latin, more in Italian, is that Manfredi had restored
ancient tragedy in the theater and had recaptured the eloquence
of ancient Athens and Rome. Several authors went so far as to
say that the Italian poet had surpassed Euripides, Sophocles, and
Seneca.

Manfredi's plot was based on the semi-mythical history of the
fabulous warrior-queen who succeeded her husband Ninus as
ruler of Assyria and founded the city of Babylon. The scene is
Babylon at the close of Semiramis' career. Ninus has been dead
for some time, and their only son is now grown.

Manfredi's principal model was Cinthio's *Orbecche*, but he also
borrowed from Speroni's *Canace* and probably from Groto's *Dalida*.
When the play proper opens, Semiramis is confiding in her waiting woman Himetra that she plans to wed her son Nino. Himetra
tries to dissuade her from incest, but the queen maintains that
such a match would strengthen the empire and that lust plays
no part in it. She orders Himetra to start preparations for a double
wedding, for she intends to match her chief general, Anafarne,
with a young woman named Dirce. The first choral ode, by the
chorus of Babylonian women, is addressed to Amore.

The second act introduces Nino and Dirce, who have been
secretly married for seven years and have two children. Dirce
sees clearly enough what lies ahead, and she knows that she is
doomed. "What cruel star pursues me? All are unjust for me, all
evil" (17r). She begs Nino to let her die so that he and the
children may escape the wrath of the queen when she discovers
the truth. If not, disaster is sure to follow for the whole family.

> Tepido sangue, lacerate membra,
> Ferri taglienti, precipitio, strage,
> Ruine, incendi, spaventose larve,
> Alti muggiti, horribil' ombre, e fiere,
> Sibili, et urli, e fremiti, e latrati,
> Miserandi stridori, e quanto in somma
> Esser può di terribile, e di brutto
> Giù ne l' Inferno, odo nel sonno, e veggio [19v].

I hear and see in my sleep warm blood, mangled limbs, sharp swords,
headlong fall, slaughter, ruins, fires, fearsome specters, deep bellowings,

horrible and cruel ghosts, hisses and howls and roars and barks, pitiful
shrieks, in short as much of the terrible and hideous as can exist down
in hell.

Nino tries to assure his wife that her fears are idle, but when she
leaves he confides in his friend Simandio that he, too, is horrified
by his mother's plans.

When Semiramis learns that Nino and Dirce are married, and
have been married for seven years, she explodes in a frenzy of rage.
"I will pluck out Dirce's heart with my own hands, and before
that I will kill her children before her eyes" (25r). She believes
that her son is a weakling, that he has betrayed her and his heritage.
Therefore she must assert her rights.

> E chi può contrastarmi? e chi s' oppone
> A l' ira grande, al giusto sdegno mio?
> Chi d' obedirmi negherà? chi fia,
> Che per lui contra me si mova? Quale
> Minima squadra di soldati? quale
> Soldato privatissimo conosce
> Altri che me obedire? Io sola
> Gli assoldo, e reggo, e li punisco, e premio.
> Ecco la prova de la mia possanza.
> Gite, e prendete, o miei soldati, hor hora
> Nino, e 'l tenete [29r].

And who can resist me? Who opposes my great wrath and just indignation? Who will refuse to obey me? Who will make a move against me?
What smallest squad of soldiers, what lowest private knows anything else
but to obey me? I alone enroll him, rule him, punish and reward him.
Behold the proof of my power. Go and arrest Nino, O my soldiers, now,
now, and hold him fast.

Nothing that Himetra says and no argument of the good priest
Beleso can soften the queen's resolution to punish the traitors,
for, like Cinthio's Sulmone and Groto's Berenice, she is a Senecan
tyrant who maintains that kings and queens are above morality
and law. Nevertheless, like Sulmone, she pretends to listen to
reason and promises to become reconciled with her son's family.
She orders Simandio to fetch Nino, Dirce, and the children. "I
wish to see them all and to pardon them all. Indeed I have pardoned them; and I want to renew the nuptials today with a feast
worthy of a great king" (34v). All save Dirce are overjoyed by
this good omen and the chorus delivers an ode of thanksgiving.

Not unexpectedly, for Manfredi followed the pattern faithfully, the fourth act opens in gloom. The author showed some skill in trying to break up the messenger's long report of horrors with insertions of dialogue. Dirce's maidservant, Atirtia, discloses to Nino, Simandio, and the chorus what has happened offstage.

Nino: She is dead, it may be? O miserable me, and how? She is dead? Tell me, that I may not delay to follow her.
Atirtia: She is dead; and dead by the hand of the queen.
Nino: O wicked woman.
Atirtia: And your children are also dead by the same hand.
Nino: O my Star, O Fortune, O Fate, O God, why do you tolerate it? O Heaven, why do you not open and rain thunderbolts? [42r].

The girl describes the slaughter. Semiramis, accompanied only by a soldier and Atirtia, led her daughter-in-law and grandchildren to an underground room. There she confronted Dirce, who was shaking with terror. "Why, O Dirce, are you afraid? You should have been afraid when you were so bold and so proud as to try to become the Lady of Assyria" (43v). After considerable talk, and after tying up Dirce, the queen seized the little girl and cut her throat, saying to the mother, "This is the first sign of my love for my grandchildren" (45v–46r). Then turning to the little boy, who had run to Atirtia for protection, she said, "Behold, daughter-in-law, the second sign of my trust, of my love for you" (46r). Despite the frantic pleadings of the mother, Semiramis plunged her dagger into the child's breast. At this point Dirce stopped trembling and cried out, "O wicked mother, O beast, O fury, may heaven loathe you, if there is still pity above; or if the gods still care for us, may the punishment that so wicked a deed deserves overtake you there. . . . You a daughter of a goddess? The gods do not create children unfit to live. The sharp rocks of Caucasus bore you, and Hyrcanian tigers were your nurses" (47r).[27] The infuriated queen rained dagger thrusts upon her daughter-in-law, who died gasping "O Nino!"

The last act is devoted to Nino's revenge; but here again Manfredi strove to make the tragedy something more than another messenger's report. He injected another discovery, namely, that Dirce was Semiramis' daughter, Nino's half-sister. Therefore the wretched Nino, who was so horrified at the prospect of incest with his mother, has to contemplate the fact that he has been living

---

[27] Another one of the numerous echoes of *Aeneid* 4.365–367.

in incest for seven years. This discovery makes him all the more anxious to punish his mother. And he does so, striking her down with a dagger. Then he goes to the room where the corpses of his wife and children lie and does away with himself. A messenger and the faithful Simandio report these last deaths. The chorus concludes with a brief ode in sonnet form on the enmity of Fortune.[28]

---

[28] Two late tragedies of blood by Paolo Bozi recently came to my attention and are perhaps worth mentioning. The first, La Eutheria (Venice, 1588), is a dull imitation of Orbecche that ends with the deaths of all the principal characters. The second, Cratasiclea (Venice, 1591), which also ends in the slaughter of all the good people in the play, is even less effective.

Gothic and Romantic Tragedies

Gothic and romantic elements appeared early in Italian tragedies and reappeared time and again throughout the sixteenth century. When Rucellai wrote *Rosmunda,* about 1515, he was doubtless influenced by Trissino's interest in the history of the Goths in Italy,[1] though he found his argument not in Procopius but in Paulus Diaconus' *History of the Lombards.* Since *Rosmunda* was highly esteemed by Italian poets and critics, it is not surprising that followers sought tragic stories in the histories of the north. We have already seen, for that matter, that the earliest extant tragedy in Italy, the fourteenth-century Latin *Eccerinus* by Mussato, dramatized the tyrannies of Ezzelino da Romano. Mussato's play is close to a morality and it has no love affair; but partly owing to the growing influence of *novelle* and romances, and partly because women were becoming more important in real life and in literature, the sixteenth-century dramatists exploited romantic love in both comedy and tragedy, in Roman tragedies, in tragedies of blood, and in Gothic tragedies.

Of course there is no sharp dividing line between tragedies of blood and what I call Gothic and romantic plays. Some of the plays discussed in the preceding chapter might have been discussed

[1] Trissino was starting his long heroic poem *L'Italia liberata dai Goti,* based on Procopius.

here and some of the following are also tragedies of blood and revenge. Moreover, Cinthio's *Orbecche* served as a model for nearly every kind of Italian tragedy save the religious play. There was a tendency, however, during the second half of the century to explore other sources than classical history and mythology and an increased emphasis upon romantic love affairs. Again Cinthio was partly responsible, for most of his tragedies and tragicomedies were dramatizations of his own *novelle* that were exotic and romantic.

CESARI'S *ROMILDA*

Cesare de' Cesari, doubtless following the lead of Rucellai, selected a melodramatic tale from Paulus Diaconus and dramatized it in 1551 under the title of *Romilda*. His play is conventional in structure and style, and it shares the fate of most contemporary Italian tragedies in being short on action and long on lamentations by heroine, nurse, and chorus. In fact, it is very like the author's *Scilla*.[2]

According to the account in Paulus,[3] Cacano, or Calcano, king of the Bavarians, invaded northeast Italy and killed Gisulfo, Duke of Friuli. The duke's widow, Romilda, and her eight children took refuge in a castle, which was besieged by the enemy. Romilda saw Calcano riding around the walls and fell in love with him. She sent a messenger offering to surrender the castle if Calcano would marry her. Thereupon the Bavarians entered the citadel, sacking, burning, and taking prisoners. Romilda's sons, after desperate maneuvers, managed to escape. Her daughters concealed the raw flesh of chickens in their bosoms, which soon stank so abominably that the Bavarian soldiers would have nothing to do with them. The duchess was handed over to twelve soldiers, who brutally violated her.

Cesari changed some details, softening some and making others more sensational. For example, he omitted the picturesque stratagem of the daughters, but had the cruel king put out the eyes of the two older girls and throw them in prison. The sons are still hiding in the castle when the play ends. The duchess dies in the last act, a disillusioned martyr to tyranny. Cesari used an old nurse in the usual way and substituted a *bailo* (tutor) for

---

[2] See above, p. 180.
[3] 4.12 (54v–56r in Lodovico Domenichi's Italian translation of 1548).

the customary wise counselor. There is a small cast of only five characters plus two daughters who have small parts. There is no prologue and no supernatural agent.

The tone of *Romilda* is set in the opening lines, a soliloquy by the heroine.

> Chi desia di saper quanto fortuna
> Questo nostro mortal misero stato
> Veloce giri, la dolente historia
> Oda de le mie pene, et indi impari
> Quanto meglio sarebbe a un' infelice
> Non esser nato, e se pur nato a pena
> Che questa vita gliapre al pianto gliocchi,
> Gli chiudesse la morte.

Whoever wishes to know how swiftly fortune spins this miserable mortal life of ours, listen to the story of my afflictions, and thence learn how much better it would be for the unhappy one not to be born, and if indeed born, that death should close the hardly opened eyes which this life [has already filled] with tears.

GROTO'S *HADRIANA*

In his second tragedy, probably influenced by the tragicomedies of Cinthio, Luigi Groto turned from the bloodthirsty horrors of *Dalida* to the romantic, pathetic story of Romeo and Juliet, which he doubtless knew from the *novelle* of Luigi da Porto and Bandello. He placed the scene in his home town of Adria, but in ancient Adria, which was at war with ancient Latium. In his dedication (1578),[4] the author again disclaimed equality of his heroine with those of Trissino, Rucellai, Cinthio, and Speroni. He also admitted that she fell short of Sophocles' daughters in art, of Euripides' in passion, of Seneca's in maxims, but he maintained that she yielded to none in dignity.

In the prologue, which is of the detached Cinthian type, the author promised to draw from the spectators an "Etna of sighs and a sea of tears," for they will behold the "most faithful and the most unhappy lovers that Love's arrow ever transfixed." He compared his hero and heroine with Aeneas and Dido, with Pyramus and Thisbe, with Leander and Hero.

The play, which is far too wordy for the most part, is con-

---

[4] There were at least eight printings of *Hadriana* between 1578 and 1626. I have used the Illinois copies of 1583 and 1599, both printed at Venice, and both carelessly printed.

ventional in structure and style. There are two choruses, one of Adrian ladies, the other a semi-chorus of priests that appears briefly toward the end of Act 4. Groto handled the main chorus in the Cinthian manner: it takes no part in the dialogue until the fourth act, when the messengers begin to bring reports of calamities. There is the usual nurse, and a good counselor, of course. Instead of Friar Lawrence, Groto used a magician, for his characters are pagans, not Christians. There are no supernatural agents, however, no goddesses or Furies, no ghosts.

Hadriana herself opens the play, confiding in her nurse. When she admits that she has not only fallen in love with Latino, the enemy prince, but has already spent the night with him, the nurse delivers a discourse on famous women, for example Medea, Scylla, Hypsipyle, who were betrayed by their lovers. The princess, however, refuses to give up Latino. Bad news arrives early, with the entrance of the first messenger, who says that Latino has mortally wounded Hadriana's brother. Thereupon the lamentations begin. The queen mother has lost a son, Hadriana a brother and probably a lover.

Latino makes his first appearance with a long soliloquy in the second act. He has stolen through the Adrian lines to see his mistress and to explain that he unknowingly killed her brother in battle. The two lovers enjoy some minutes together, and 379 lines, before they are interrupted by the nurse. Then, after many complaints and protestations of fidelity, Latino goes back to his camp.

Complications arise, as they should in a neoclassical drama, in the third act, when the queen tells her daughter that the king has chosen a husband for her. Hadriana refuses to accept her father's choice, insisting that she be allowed to mourn her brother's death for a year. When her father enters, a violent altercation follows. The king finally delivers an ultimatum: Hadriana must choose between the marriage bed and a sepulcher. The distraught princess is left to the consolation of the magician, who is a kind man and an able one. He promises to give her a powerful sleeping potion and to send a letter to Latino so that the prince may rescue his mistress from the tomb in which she will be laid. The timing must be accurate, for the potion will lose its power after sixteen hours. Hadriana agrees to the stratagem.

Mago: But tell me, will you not be horrified of so many dead?

Hadriana: If this course will give me my Latino, I would not only be un-afraid to sojourn among the dead but among the lost souls in hell [3.3].[5]

In Act 4, the inevitable messenger reports to the chorus that Hadriana is dead. Then comes the *commos,* with nurse, chorus, and then the king and queen joining in mourning. The queen's lamentations are the most extravagant; she often breaks into rhyme, as was proper for highly emotional speeches.

> Qual sarà quell' Oreste.
> Quell' Atreo, quel Thieste,
> Qual sarà quella rea,
> Quella Progne, or Medea,
> Chi mi divida dal mio amato seme? [4.4].

What Orestes, what Atreus, what Thyestes, what wicked Progne or Medea, who would part me from my beloved offspring?

The last act of *Hadriana* is somewhat unusual among neoclassical Italian tragedies because in it the scene changes several times between the city of Adria and the enemy camp.[6] Like virtually all learned Italian dramatists of the sixteenth century, Groto care-fully preserved an economy of time—little more than the sixteen hours of the sleeping potion—but was freer with the scene than most. The magician soon learns that his artful plan has gone wrong, for his messenger has not been able to deliver the letter to Latino. Latino himself appears in his camp. He has learned of Hadriana's death from a messenger sent by the nurse, who was not informed of the drug. Latino decides to take his own life, but not before he has seen the body of his mistress. In the fifth scene he has again slipped into Adria and into the royal palace. He sits onstage with the lifeless body of Hadriana in his lap. He drinks poison and delivers his swan song of ninety-seven lines. Then, as the poison begins to work, he feels the heartbeat of the corpse.

Hadriana wakes up and the two lovers soon come to an under-standing about the letter that failed to arrive. Then Latino con-fesses that he has taken poison. He urges Hadriana to marry the Sabine prince her parents have chosen for her. Hadriana replies, "Ah, my lord, and do you believe I can do this? Do you suppose

---

[5] A similar bravery is exhibited by Elfenice in *La donna costante,* a comic treat-ment of the Romeo-Juliet story, also printed in 1578. The author, Raffaello Borghini, may have known Groto's play, or vice versa.
[6] But cf. Trissino's *Sofonisba* above, p. 54.

that I am so fickle a woman?" She puts his head on her breast
and stills his arguments.

Hadriana	Siate certo, signor, del morir mio
	Subito dopo voi, come del vostro.
Latino	Ahi, ch' io perdo la vista, e la favella.
	Già spasma il core, e giunge al fine estremo.
Hadriana	Deh Signor mio, non mi lasciate ancora.
	Restate ancora un poco.
Latino	Ahi, ch' io non posso.
	Date, e prendete homai l' ultimo bacio,
	L' ultimo abbracciamento, o cara sposa,
	O quanto quanto poco
	Ci siam goduti in terra.
Hadriana	Ci goderem per sempre in altra parte.
	Aspettatemi pur senza dimora.
Latino	O terra, o stelle, o Luna,
	Per non vi riveder mai più vi lascio.
	Sposa, restate in pace, l' alma mia
	Va donde venne pria.
Hadriana	Ahime, ch' egli si more, io son qui sola.

Hadriana: Rest assured, my lord, of my death immediately after yours.
Latino: Alas, I am losing my sight and my speech. Already my heart
faints and comes to the last beat.
Hadriana: Pray, my lord, don't leave me yet. Stay a little.
Latino: Alas, I cannot. Now give and take the last kiss, the last embrace,
O my dear wife. O how very little we have enjoyed each other on earth.
Hadriana: We will enjoy each other forever in another place. Expect me
without delay.
Latino: O earth, O stars, O moon, I leave you, never more to see you.
Wife, rest in peace; my soul returns whence it came.
Hadriana: Aye-me, he is dying, and I am here alone.

This scene is the high point in the play and good theater, not
unworthy of comparison with the death scene in Shakespeare's
Romeo and Juliet. Hadriana must share honors with Dolce's
Marianna, and possibly with Guidoccio's Mathilda and Veniero's
Hidalba,[7] as the most attractive heroines in Italian tragedy of
the sixteenth century.

Hadriana now longs for death. When she sees Mago approaching, accompanied by a minister of state, she decides to feign being
poisoned. The magician mourns with her over the unfortunate

---

[7] See below, pp. 241–245, 252–258.

accident of the lost letter: "O unlucky lovers, O cruel fate!" Hadriana
tells him that she has already drunk poison, asks him to bury her
with Latino, and to have their story inscribed on marble inside the
tomb. Shortly thereafter she dies. "Wait for me, husband, I follow
you." The minister examines the body and cries, "Ah me, she
was not poisoned." In the last scene, a messenger and the chorus
mourn the ruin of the royal family.

MONDELLA'S *ISIFILE*

It was against the rules of sixteenth-century neoclassical drama
to base a tragedy on contemporary events, for ancient history was
the proper basis.[8] Nevertheless, several Italian poets were tempted
by one phase of contemporary history that was of vital consequence
to their own country, namely, the life-and-death struggle of Christian and Turk. About 1548, Daniele Barbaro wrote a tragedy that
tried, without much success, to dramatize certain events in Hungary
following the death of John Zapolya in 1540.[9] The Turks' capture of
Famagusta, capital of Cyprus, in 1571 was even closer to home,
at least to Venetians, and in 1579 a "new tragedy" entitled *Irene*,
by Vincenzo Giusti, was printed at Venice with a dedication by
the critic Francesco Sansovino, who called the play a worthy
representative of its kind.

The *argomento* of *Irene* remarked that the "subject of the present tragedy is drawn from events partly true and partly feigned."

---

[8] The argument of Angelo Leonico's *Il soldato, tragedia* (Venice, 1550) was
supposedly based on an actual event in Padua. In this scandalous affair a soldier
tried to seduce a young wife, but was repulsed. Thereupon he sought revenge
for his wounded ego; he told the husband that his wife was having an affair
with Captain Bologna and produced a servant to testify that he saw the lover
enter the window of the wife's bedroom. The husband and his brother-in-law
killed the wife and mortally wounded the innocent captain.

Leonico's play has middle-class characters speaking more or less familiar
dialogue. Servants have prominent roles. As such it is bourgeois drama, reflect-
ing in part some of the earlier rhymed tragedies and anticipating, it may be,
later realistic tragedies. Giovan Mario Crescimbèni, author of the *Istoria della
volgar poesia* (1698), would not allow it the name of tragedy, maintaining that
its characters belonged to comedy (see Allacci, p. 729). Nevertheless, the
author was a follower of Cinthio and tried to arrange his play in the neoclassical manner. The prologue has a ghost rising from Acheron. The action starts
just before a supper at which the villainous soldier tells the host that his wife
is an adulteress. The death of the wife and the bloody brawl in the supper room
are reported by servant-messengers. The dialogue is mostly in unrhymed verse.
Doglio includes a slightly revised text of *Il soldato* in his book.

[9] Neri (pp. 108–111) gives an account of this unprinted work.

Probably Sansovino approved of the play because its feigning was in the ancient poetic manner and because its form was Grecian, that is, divided into episodes instead of acts. Since there are five episodes, they might as well have been called acts. The only use of actual history was the framework of the plot. The Turkish commander in Cyprus had violated the terms of surrender and put the Venetian governor to death after shameful mistreatment. Giusti substituted ancient Salamis for Famagusta, an ancient king of Cyprus for the Venetian governor, and ancient Armenians for the Turks. Both Cyprians and Armenians are pagans. An oracle of Apollo has a role in the action.

The very first speech in *Irene*, delivered by a priest of Venus, indicates the tone and directions of the tragedy: "Menacing fate and dire accidents are to man what a furnace is to gold, because they purge him of earthly passions and render him in the test honorable and upright." If the principal characters, namely the king and queen, their young son, and a courtier, are not purged of earthly passions they are at least freed from all cares and temptations of the flesh, for every one of them meets a violent death. The king goes to the Armenian camp outside the walls to surrender the city. There the brutal enemy king has him tortured to death. An Armenian soldier dashes the young prince against a rock before the eyes of the father. The queen, Irene, who has the largest role, and who was probably patterned after Trissino's Sophonisba, laments and mourns with nurse and chorus throughout much of the play. In the last episode the Armenian king sends her a present, a vase containing the mutilated head of her husband and the hands of her son. Thereupon Irene retires to her bedroom and kills herself with a sword. The only remarkable feature of this pedestrian play is a messenger's report in the last episode that outdoes the messenger's report in Cinthio's *Orbecche* for lurid details. The description of the mutilation and flaying of the Cyprian king, who stayed alive for two hours, is pretty horrifying.

Giusti published another tragedy at Venice nine years later (1588), namely, *Almeone*. This second play was based on the ancient Theban cycle of myths and is without distinction.

Francesco Mondella, author of *Isifile* (1582), must have known Giusti's *Irene*, for he used the same plot with only minor changes, and he also made his tragedy "approach the manner of the ancient poets."[10] He did use Turks and Italians, but his Italians are pagans calling upon Jove, Juno, and Venus for the help that never arrives. The hapless viceroy of Salamis (Famagusta) is perhaps closer to Aeneas than to a sixteenth-century Venetian.

Isifile, however, is not Grecian in form. For the most part it is an imitation of Cinthio's *Orbecche* with an echo from the story of Tancred and Gismonda thrown in for good measure. There is no prologue, but the whole first act is devoted to supernatural characters. Juno, who is still punishing the descendants of Aeneas, the father of Italy, to pay off her old grudge against Venus, orders the Furies to fill the Turkish commander with cruel rage and treachery. The ghost of a former king of Cyprus, ousted from the throne by his long-suffering subjects, adds his plea for vengeance. The chorus of Salamian women offers its first ode to the goddess of love.

The action, or the talk about the action, proceeds in the conventional way. The viceroy, Datamo, offers to surrender the besieged city if the terms are honorable. Mustafa, the Turkish general, agrees to Datamo's terms and receives the Italians in a pavilion outside the walls. The heroine, Isifile, young wife of the viceroy, does not appear until the second scene of the third act. Then she injects the first ominous anticipation of disaster; she tells the nurse that she has had a bad dream in which a fierce beast invaded a flock and devoured two pet lambs of the shepherdess. As we have seen, such a dream had already become shopworn by 1582.[11] The bad news arrives on schedule in Act 4, when a messenger informs the chorus that the Cyprian realm has been turned over to "Athamases, Thyesteses, Atreuses, and fierce Scythians." The whole act is a pretty slavish imitation of the fourth act of *Orbecche*. According to the messenger, the Cyprians were no sooner received in the Turkish camp than they were seized and bound. Then the sons of the viceroy, along with a brave soldier named Lisimoco, were slaughtered. The viceroy's hands were cut off. Although verbose, the account is spirited and comparable to the better narratives in Italian tragedy.

---

[10] *Isifile* (Verona, 1582), p. 83.

[11] Isifile's dream may have been suggested by Anna's dream in Cinthio's *Didone*, but cf. the heroine's dream in *Orbecche*. See above, pp. 102, 108. Moreover, the queen in Giusti's *Irene* also has a bad dream preceding the disaster to her family. Actually this use of a dream appeared in Pistoia's *Filostrato e Panfila* (1508).

In the last act a Turkish messenger brings greetings from Mustafa to the *viceregina*. Isifile receives him surrounded by her ladies in waiting, and the chorus stands by. After the proper compliments, the Turk says, "He also gives you this superb golden vase that holds a sacred liquor, which immediately rids the man who drinks it of grief and every suffering." When Isifile asks about her sons and husband she is assured that she will soon see them. She does; she lifts the veil from the vase and sees the heads of her children and the hands of her husband. The messenger adds that there is also poison in the vase. Isifile retires into the palace. An old man reports that the viceroy has been executed on the piazza, his body stripped by the Turkish soldiers and then hanged on the yardarm of an Italian ship. A maidservant from the palace reports the last indignity offered to the Italians: Isifile has been seized by Mustafa before she could drink the poison, shackled, and put on a ship bound for Byzantium.

Mondella's style is elevated, allusive, and often ornate. It suffers little, however, by comparison with the tragic style of his master Cinthio. Many sentiments in *Isifile* are in the traditional Senecan manner. An example of one of the better passages is the following from a soliloquy by the brave and loyal Lisimoco.

> Quando rimiro ben l' instabil Sorte
> Come soglia innalzar l' huomo sovente
> Da basso stato ad alti aurati Seggi;
> E ch' in un punto poi girando il perno
> De la volubil Rota il cacci al fondo,
> Di spavento s' imgombran queste membra,
> E di stupor inarco ambo le ciglia [p. 26].

When I consider well how slippery Fate is wont to raise man from a low estate to lofty golden thrones, and then, spinning the axle of the fickle wheel, plunges him in an instant to the bottom, my limbs are overwhelmed with fear and I knit both my brows in amazement.

FULIGNI'S *BRAGADINO*

Bragadino, by Valerio Fuligni, published at Pesaro in 1589, is poor theater, but it should be given some notice here because it represents a protest against the generally approved method of dramatizing history in the sixteenth century. In both *Irene* and *Isifile* the authors tried to convert contemporary history into classical tragedy, substituting ancient Salamis for Famagusta, feigned characters for the contemporary Venetians and Turks, and pagan manners for Christian. Fuligni objected to this feigning and paganizing. He believed that he could make a "noble tragic poem" out of the action at Famagusta without altering the time, the events, the characters, or the religion of the people engaged. He saw in the heroic defense of Famagusta the best kind of subject matter for Italian tragedy. As his chorus says,

> O Cavalieri, o Duci, o Latin sangue
> Gloria d' Italia, et di Christiana gente [2.4].

The Venetians and Greeks in Fuligni's play are devout Christians who appeal to the Christian God for help and comfort in their anguish. Captain Martinengo, for example, when he hears that Venetian officers are being slaughtered, cries, "O Holy Jesus, how canst Thou tolerate such foul outrages on earth?" (3.3). The protagonist Marcantonio Bragadino, the brave Venetian governor who was flayed alive, glories in being a Christian. He defies the Turkish commander to do his worst: "The greater the torment, therefore, that you wreak on frail and mortal me, the greater will be my glory" (4.4). Fuligni also used Christianity to emphasize the barbarity of the heathen enemy. When Mustafa is gloating over his helpless prisoner he says to Bragadino, "Where is that foolish Christ in whom you trust, who comes not now to pluck you from danger?" (3.3).

It must not be supposed, however, that Fuligni thought of his play as a *rappresentazione sacra*, for he followed the neoclassical rules and models. He was unwilling, for example, to dispense with the pagan machinery that had adorned neoclassical Italian tragedy for a century. There are still allusions in *Bragadino* to pagan mythology, especially to ancient criminals and monsters, such as Atreus, Thyestes, Athamas, Nero, Scylla, Polyphemus, and the cannibalistic Laestrygones. His Turks are as conversant with Greek mythology as are his Greeks and Venetians. Pagan mythology generally represents evil as opposed to Christian good. Moreover, Fuligni did not entirely abandon Senecan fatalism; Martinengo says to the chorus, "No one should consider himself well off while he lives and dwells on earth" (3.1).

A poorly constructed play, *Bragadino* is for the most part a series of declamations and reports by messengers. Three messengers are needed in the last act, and other characters serving as messengers operate in every act. Ironically, the best scene in the play is one involving two Turks, the commander Mustafa and the aga of the Janizaries. While Fuligni's Italians usually express thoroughly conventional sentiments, the two Turks engage in a lively debate about vital moral issues brought out in the campaign. The aga is a brave and honorable man who believes that a brave and honorable foe like Bragadino should be treated with courtesy and humanity; he is genuinely concerned about "conscience, God, friendship, and common honor" (4.3). He remonstrates with Mustafa, urging him to avoid giving the Turks a bad name in Europe. Mustafa rebukes him for his presumption and for his unpatriotic attitude; but the aga sticks to his convictions. "Ah, by God," he says, "do not acquire a name for foul cruelty and for worthless trust." For a moment or two the play comes to life only to subside into the dreary round of complaints and lamentations.

VERLATO'S *RODOPEIA*

Leonoro Verlato's *Rodopeia* (1582) represents another borrowing from the story of Tancred and Gismonda with an added debt to Cinthio's *Orbecche*. The author transferred the scene from Salerno to ancient Byzantium. Verlato was more of a Modern than Mondella, however, and he increased the emphasis on romantic love. He retained the Cinthian ghost of the king's murdered wife, but made her merely a reproach to her tyrannical husband, not an avenging spirit. The dead queen appears only briefly in the third scene of Act 2. The chorus takes no part in the dialogue until the last act, when it has a prominent role. In the detached prologue, the author admitted that he was not inspired by Aeschylus, Sophocles, or Euripides, nor by Seneca, nor, for that matter, by sententious Italian tragedy, but rather by Ovid. Moreover, his appeal, he said, was primarily to the tender feelings of the ladies in his audience. In other words, he increased the romantic eroticism, the cult of the feminine soul, that he found in Cinthio's tragedies and tragicomedies. The result is a long uneven play with some highly theatrical scenes.

The hero, one Sinibaldo, Prince of Greater Armenia, loses no time in expressing the spirit of the drama about to unfold.

> Ecco un gradito, e sconsolato Amante
> Porger soggetto, e novo essempio al Mondo
> Di felice mestitia: ecco a me pure
> Rendere Amor quel che Fortuna ha tolto:

Che se ben questa da la vera altezza
Di Prencipe m' abbassa a dimostrarmi
(Amareggiando il mio felice stato)
Un povero, e negletto Giardiniero:
Sotto ruvide spoglie Amor sovente
Mi leva al sommo Ciel de le sue gioie,
E mi riposa nel suo Paradiso [1.1].

Behold a worthy disconsolate lover presenting a subject and a new example of happy woe. Behold how Love renders me what Fortune has taken away. If Fortune debases me from the true loftiness of a prince (embittering my happy state) to show me as a poor, unkempt gardener, Love often raises me in coarse garments to the highest heaven of his joys, and puts me in his paradise.

The prince is passionately in love with Rodopeia, only daughter of Ismaro, the king of Thrace. He is disguised as a gardener so that he may meet the princess when she walks in the palace garden. Even now Armenian ambassadors are due in Byzantium to ask for a marriage between their prince and Rodopeia. The outlook is therefore favorable save for one thing: Sinibaldo has just had a bad dream in which he found himself leading a white lamb through a labyrinth, trying to find a way out; before he could find a way he was assailed by a fierce tiger that tore his heart out. Sinibaldo confides his hopes and fears in a companion named Aronte, Prince of Lower Armenia.

The heroine opens the second act confiding in Serinda, who is a woman gardener and also in love with Sinibaldo. Rodopeia already knows that her lover is a prince; but Serinda warns her that her father will nevertheless have no mercy on a secret love affair. When her father first appears he is discussing a projected match between his daughter and the prince of Athens. When he informs Rodopeia of his plan she balks, protesting that she does not want to marry, that she does not want to leave home to become another Philomela. Ismaro, who is a tyrant, orders his daughter to prepare for the wedding.

In the third act, Serinda tells Sinibaldo that the princess must marry the Athenian prince. The only solution for the lovers seems to be an elopement, and the two Armenians lay their plans for one. In the fourth act, Serinda, her love for the gardener repulsed, betrays him to the king, who spies on the lovers in the garden. Of course Ismaro is enraged and, despite the pleading of his counselor, resolves to punish the interloper.

Sinibaldo is arrested and brought before the executioner. Then follows a very realistic scene that overstepped the approved boundaries of neoclassical tragedy. Tigrane, the executioner, would be at home on the Elizabethan stage. In his hardboiled efficiency he resembles Bosola in the *Duchess of Malfi* though he lacks the complexity of Webster's character. For a sixteenth-century Italian character he speaks little; his forte is action.

Sinibaldo: What do you wish to do to me? What outrage is this?
Tigrane: Our king has charged me to pluck out the heart and soul from your breast in punishment for your reckless foolhardiness [4.6].

When Sinibaldo learns that Rodopeia has also been arrested he tells Tigrane to do with him what he pleases but to spare the princess.

Sinibaldo: It is all my fault, or indeed love's.
Tigrane: I don't know what love may be, nor do I want to know; but I promise you on my honor that if she has to die by my hands, I will pluck the soul from her heart so fast (console yourself on that score) that she will scarcely be aware of her death.

Sinibaldo's pleas are all in vain, and Tigrane dispatches him then and there, and on the stage.

Tigrane: Soldiers, collect a little of his blood in this vase. O how fresh and rosy it is. . . . A little is enough. Hold this wound well open, for I want to remove the heart from the breast. Behold, I have uprooted it. O what a fine heart!

In the last act there are more deaths and much lamentation and repentance. Now Serinda repents her betrayal of Sinibaldo and her kind mistress. Ismaro still rationalizes his treatment of the lovers, but he begins to feel the prick of conscience before the end. Rodopeia is in a pitiful plight, but she summons spirit enough to defy her father. "My unhappy bridegroom has been wrongly, most wrongly killed; therefore there will never be a time or anything else that could make me repent of a chaste love" (5.3). Ismaro hands her the vase and bids her lift the veil. She does so and sees the heart of Sinibaldo. Then follows a *commos* as the princess and chorus mourn together.

Ismaro is more or less satisfied for the moment, as he discloses to Tigrane. "If you indomitably opened his breast with the sword and removed the heart of the presumptuous and treacherous son of the king of Armenia, I have removed every joy from my daughter with only a glimpse of that lewd fellow's uprooted heart; whence she hates herself and being alive." Tigrane congratulates him. Ismaro admits that he would be glad to have Tigrane dispatch his daughter, too, if he could be sure of a worthy heir to the throne. Nevertheless, the tyrant now begins to feel some stirrings of remorse and he is in no proper state of mind to receive his prospective son-in-law, the prince of Athens. The ceremonious greetings are interrupted by a hysterical servant, who reports that Rodopeia has suffocated herself. Then at last the full tide of remorse sweeps over Ismaro.

> Ah figlia troppo amante, e troppo iniqua,
> Son queste, oimè, queste le nozze sono,
> Ch' in vece d' Imeneo, morte dispensa?
> Ah Prencipe d' Atene, ecco ch' è tolta
> Da la mano crudel di morte avara
> A voi la moglie, a me l' unica figlia [5.6].

Ah daughter too loving, and too recreant, is this, aye-me, is this the marriage that death in place of Hymen allots? Ah Prince of Athens, behold how the cruel hand of greedy death has robbed you of a wife, me of an only daughter.

The Armenian Aronte has not taken the death of Sinibaldo tamely, and now he demands satisfaction. The prince of Athens accepts his challenge. A ring of Greek and Thracian knights is formed and the two princes fight a duel onstage. Both are killed, and onstage. Ismaro realizes that he is responsible for all the tragic deaths: "And I as bereaved husband, bereaved father, the cruel cause of so many dead." He asks the knights and the women of the chorus to prepare the funeral rites. The play ends with a final lament from the chorus.

MASSUCCI'S COSTANZA

La Costanza (1585), by Niccolò Massucci, a native of Recanati in the Italian Marches, was introduced to an elite audience in the Roman palace of Scipione Gonzaga, prince of the Empire, later cardinal, patron of art, friend and protector of Torquato Tasso. In his dedication of the printed tragedy to Gonzaga, Massucci said, "I have compelled myself with every endeavor to preserve the unity of action, the [high] social standing of the tragic characters, the well-nigh indispensable obligation to weave the knot of episodes and to develop the denouement in order to move pity and horror, and to introduce the chorus and its *canzoni* on the basis of the discussions that I heard [in your house]."[12]

The scene is Palermo when it was a Norman city. The chorus is male, made up of young Sicilian gentlemen. There is no prologue. And there is no division into acts, for Massucci was a Grecian, a disciple of Trissino and a devoted Ancient.[13] In large part *Costanza* is an imitation of Sophocles' *Oedipus Rex*, especially in the last two episodes, which are far and away the best in the play.

When the play opens, the ruler of Sicily, Ruberto, is fretting over the precarious state of his realm, harried on one side by the king of Naples and on the other by the king of Sardinia. The Sardinian king is demanding the return of his daughter Costanza, who had been carried off by Ruberto's only son, Ricciardo, now reported killed in a fight with pirates. Ruberto will not give up the beautiful young princess, for he now wants to marry her himself in order to strengthen his throne and, it may be, to satisfy a resurgence of desire in his old body. His counselor doubts that Costanza will ever love an old man; but the king believes, or wants to believe, that she cannot resist the attractions of sharing a throne. The counselor takes a gloomy view of the whole prospect; he sees Palermo becoming another Thebes, ruined by dissension. The chorus believes that all Sicily is doomed.

Costanza does not appear until the third episode. By this time she knows the king's plan and, despite the prudent advice of her nurse, refuses to accept it. Although not yet married to Ricciardo, she has given him her heart and has no intention of betraying his ghost: "You will sooner see the sun at midnight in the midst of the stars; sooner the Sicilian shore will be joined with the Italian shore" (p. 31). The chorus, which overhears the debate since it is a *coro fisso* that remains onstage throughout the play, cries, "Ruberto loves Costanza! O amazing in a king so wise! Love spares no one." Costanza suspects that the king's main motive is lust. Moreover, she believes that Ricciardo is still alive, for she has had a dream in which she lost a fine jewel he gave her and then recovered it. Therefore she remains impervious to all argu-

---

[12] *La Costanza* (Florence, 1585), A3r.
[13] His comedy, *Il Velettaio* (Florence, 1585), an imitation of ancient Roman comedy, was divided into the customary five acts. It is in verse, for the author believed that all drama should be in verse.

ments in favor of the king. "Neither shackles, nor chains, nor long-drawn-out hunger, nor any force will conquer my loyalty" (p. 38). She will kill herself or emulate the daughters-in-law of Aegyptus, who slew their bridegrooms on the wedding night. The male chorus comments,

> Non ha più crudel fera
> O la Libia, o l' Hircania
> D' una femmina irata,
> Quando è rapita d' amorosa insania [p. 39].

Neither Lybia nor Hyrcania has a fiercer beast than an angry woman when she is ravished by love's madness.

A *cameriere* of Ricciardo enters to inform Costanza that his master is still alive and close at hand, hiding until he finds out how matters stand. Costanza leaves to find her lover while the Sardinian ambassador and Ruberto's counselor continue to wrangle over the disposal of the princess.

Ricciardo himself appears onstage. His *cameriere* tells him that Costanza is still true to him, but then confounds him with the news that the king plans to marry her. From this point on the action quickens and becomes pretty good theater.

Ruberto enters in a flurry. He tells the counselor that he has just found a strange man in Costanza's apartment and killed him. He explains that he started to kill Costanza also, but thought better of it and decided to send her back to her father. Then a servant tells the king that his son is still alive and in Palermo.

Ruberto: Where did you see Ricciardo?
Servant: In Costanza's rooms.
Ruberto: Ricciardo in Costanza's rooms?
Servant: I saw him there. I unseen by him. . . .
Ruberto: Aye-me, what brief joy your announcement brings [pp. 68–69].

After further questioning Ruberto begins to sense what has happened. "But I fear, aye-me wretched, that in seeing my eyes may have been too blind." Then turning to the servant, "And that you who believed you were bringing me good news may be the messenger of the most horrible, of the cruelest, tidings an unhappy father could receive" (p. 70). Ruberto now fancies that he sees the ghost of his son before him. The ghost, however, is only one of his own sergeants bringing more bad news, namely, that Ricciardo is alive but mortally wounded. Ruberto rushes offstage and

the chorus cries, "O unlucky old man! O senseless love, where
have you led him?"

The last episode, the seventh, introduces a messenger who repeats much of what has already been disclosed but in greater detail,
adding an account of the pathetic death of Ricciardo with Costanza
bending over him. His report is interrupted by the entrance of
a second messenger who reports further calamities. Costanza has
poisoned herself. Then the king, he says, seized some bodkins from
Costanza's veil and put out his own eyes. The king himself soon
appears, a dreadful spectacle, crying,

> Ah Ciel crudele, ah Terra
> Iniqua: ah gente vile,
> Perchè non m' obedite?
> Datemi la mia spade,
> Che questa oscura notte è poca pena
> A la mia sceleranza.

Ah cruel heaven, ah wicked earth, ah ignoble people, why don't you obey
me? Give me my sword, for this dark night is slight punishment for my
villainy.

The chorus is overwhelmed with pity for the old man, who begs
them to lead him to some precipice so that he may leap to his
death, or to drown him in the sea, and to turn the realm over to
an enemy who will surely be a better ruler than he has been.
Ruberto is led away still begging for death. The chorus ends the
play with a brief comment on the instability of mortal life. Although
somewhat closer in sentiment to the conclusion of Seneca's
Thyestes, Massucci's last chorus probably owes something as well
to the ending of Sophocles' great tragedy:

> Therefore wait to see life's ending ere thou count one mortal blest;
> Wait till free from pain and sorrow he has gained his final rest.[14]

TASSO'S *TORRISMONDO*

A much more celebrated imitation of Sophocles' *Oedipus*, and
the best-known Gothic tragedy in the sixteenth century, is Torquato Tasso's *Il re Torrismondo*, first printed at Bergamo, Mantua,
Turin, Ferrara, Verona, and Venice in 1587,[15] but written earlier,

---

[14] Storr's translation in the Loeb Library. Some classical scholars nowadays consider this final chorus in *Oedipus Rex* spurious; but the sixteenth century apparently accepted it.
[15] I have used the 1587 Bergamo and Verona printings in the Illinois library,
along with the text in vol. 2 of the *Opere* printed at Pisa in 1821.

perhaps started as early as 1573, right after he finished his dramatic masterpiece, the pastoral *Aminta.*

As is well known, Tasso was plagued throughout his literary life by the quarrel between Ancients and Moderns, between classicism and romanticism. By 1587 the classicists had won and Tasso was brought into subjection, though no Aristotelian criticism could wholly stifle his romantic instincts and his genius for lyric expression. In the dedication of *Torrismondo* to Vincenzo Gonzaga, Duke of Mantua, the author remarked that his noble patron would find "some things to imitate, others to shun, others to praise, others to blame, others to delight, others to sadden. And you will be able with your most profound discretion to purge the mind and temper the passions in such wise that the grief of others will be occasion for your pleasure, the rashness of others for your sagacity, and misfortunes for your prosperity." Tasso had studied Aristotle's *Poetics* long before 1587 and he was determined to obey the rules.[16]

Giulio Guastavini, a defender of Tasso in the quarrel with the academicians, wrote an *argomento*[17] of *Torrismondo* in which he tried to show that the tragedy answered the requirements of Aristotle. The plot, he said, "is not simple but involved, containing discovery and reversal of fortune. The tragic characters are between good and bad, rather leaning toward good, particularly Torrismondo, who is the principal character and gives the tragedy its name, and by whom above all fear and pity are aroused, who falls into misery, not through vice or malice, but through rashness or human frailty." The discovery, Guastavini maintained, is of the superior kind recommended by Aristotle, arising inevitably from the action. Therefore *Torrismondo* is like Sophocles' *Oedipus Rex*, which "in the judgment of everyone has held the scepter over all the tragedies ever written in whatever language."

Tasso's tragedy, then, is conventional; its mechanics rather strictly conform to the neoclassical mold. The unities are observed. The chorus, which is not prominent, is used mainly for rhymed odes at the end of each act, but it does take a small part in the dialogue of every act save the last. Tasso's chorus should have some of the best lines in the play—the choruses in *Aminta* are delightful—but its speeches are marred by gloomy clamor about pagan gods, goddesses, Avernus, Acheron, and Styx.

---

[16] In a letter to Scipione Gonzaga on May 22, 1576, Tasso said, "In order to give myself more confidence I have re-read Aristotle's *Poetics.*"
[17] See *Opere* (1821) 2.7–8.

The romantic argument was drawn from the Gothic past of northern Italy. Rosmonda, daughter of the king of the Goths, was fated by the stars to cause the death of her brother Torrismondo, heir to the throne. Therefore the king connived with a nurse to send his daughter to Dacia in care of a trusty servant. To forestall trouble with the queen mother, the nurse's baby was substituted for the princess. After a while the king died and Torrismondo took the throne. Meanwhile the true Rosmonda had been captured by Norwegian pirates and handed over to the childless king of Norway, who named her Alvida after his own dead daughter. The king of Sweden, Germondo, who was an enemy of Norway, fell in love with Alvida and asked his friend the king of the Goths to help him. Torrismondo went to Norway and won Alvida. Because of the enmity with Sweden he did not reveal that he was courting the princess for his friend Germondo. Alvida naturally assumed that she was the affianced bride of Torrismondo. On the return voyage the Gothic ship was wrecked and the two young people forced to share the same tent on shore until they were rescued. Torrismondo could not resist the willing passion of the beautiful Alvida, who regarded him as already her husband. When the two arrived at Arana, capital of the Goths, the full impact of his treachery to Germondo struck Torrismondo.

These events, of course, lie outside the play proper, which begins a few hours before the misunderstanding between hero and heroine is cleared up. The nurse, addressing Alvida, opens the first act in the elevated style recommended for neoclassical tragedy.

> Deh, qual cagione ascosa, alta Regina,
> Sì per tempo vi sveglia? et hor, che l'Alba
> Nel lucido Oriente a pena è desta,
> Dove ite frettolosa? e quai vestigi
> Di timore in un tempo, e di desio
> Veggio nel vostro volto, e ne la fronte?

Pray, what hidden cause, exalted Queen, wakes you so early? And now that dawn is scarcely awake in the clear Orient, where are you hurrying? And what marks of both fear and desire do I see on your face and brow?

Alvida explains that she is tormented at night by bad dreams and fearful visions, for she has been upset by the strange behavior of her husband-to-be. She cannot understand why the marriage ceremony has not been performed. "Already since we arrived the sun has plunged into the bosom of the ocean twenty times, and still

there is delay. And meanwhile—I must speak or hold my tongue—
I, alas, waste away like fresh snow on a sunny hillside." The nurse
tries to cheer her, but, when left alone onstage, expresses her own
distrust of fickle Fortune.

Torrismondo soon appears, and he is more unhappy than Alvida,
for remorse is gnawing him.

> Ahi, quando mai la Tana, o 'l Reno, o l' Istro,
> O l' inospite mare,[18] o 'l mare vermiglio,
> O l' onde Caspe, o l' Ocean profondo,
> Potran lavar occulta, e 'ndegna colpa,
> Che mi tinse, e macchiò le membra, e l' alma?
> Vivo ancor dunque, e spiro, e veggio il Sole?
> Ne la luce del mondo anco dimoro?
> E Re son detto, e Cavalier m' appello?
> La spade al fianco io porto, in man lo scettro
> Ancor sostengo, e la corona in fronte? [1.3].

Alas, when will the Don, or the Rhine, or the Danube, or the unfriendly
sea, or the Red Sea, or the Caspian, or the ocean deep ever be able to
wash away the dark and shameful guilt that stained and tainted my limbs
and soul? Do I still live, then, and breathe, and see the sun? Do I still
dwell in the light of the world? And am I still known as king, and do I
call myself knight? Do I still carry sword at my side and hold scepter in
hand, a crown on my brow?

Then, in 309 lines, the young king pours out his confession of what
happened on the journey from Norway. (Great poet that he was,
Tasso was no exception among the long-winded dramatists of
his day.) The good counselor tries to console him; but Torrismondo, who is a good man and a man of honor, is inconsolable:
"He [Germondo] is deprived of a mistress, and I of a friend and
also at the same time of my honor. How will we be able to live?
Alas, cruel fate!" He does not yet know how much crueler fate
will be before the day ends.

The counselor offers a ray of hope, a possible way out of his
dilemma. Why cannot the king offer his friend Germondo the
hand of his sister Rosmonda?

In Act 2, a Swedish messenger announces the arrival of Germondo, now in the Gothic capital to claim his bride. Torrismondo
is desperate; as he says, the coming of his friend is worse than
the great stone hanging over Sisyphus. Rosmonda (the false
princess) appears, soon followed by the queen mother, who gives

---

[18] The "unfriendly sea" is the Black Sea. Cf. Euripides' *Andromache* 793.

her a lecture on the duties of royalty and bids her prepare to receive her royal suitor.

Rosmonda is unhappy in her exalted role and longs for a humble life. By the third act she has made up her mind that Fortune has played a shabby trick on her. "The time is nigh," she says, "to reject your false braveries and your counterfeit gifts" (3.2). Torrismondo does his best to make Germondo welcome. Alvida, however, assures Torrismondo that she is all his; she wants nothing to do with Germondo, who is unwelcome for several reasons. For one thing, the Swedish prince has always been a deadly enemy of her father.

In Act 4, the counselor, in a carefully wrought speech appealing to Germondo's friendship with Torrismondo, points out the political advantages of uniting Sweden with the Goths and proposes that he marry his friend's sister instead of Alvida. Germondo acknowledges that he puts nothing higher than friendship and therefore is willing to accept the change in brides.

The politicians, however, have not reckoned with Rosmonda, who now discloses her true identity to Torrismondo.

Torrismondo: Are you not the only daughter of [Queen] Rusilla?

Rosmonda: I do not boast of being the only or even the daughter of the queen of the fierce Goths.

Torrismondo: Indeed you are Rosmonda, and my sister.

Rosmonda: I am another Rosmonda, another sister.

Torrismondo: Now explain this talk; explain these bewildering perplexities.

Rosmonda: My mother was your nurse, who then nursed Rosmonda [4.3].

Before the young king can grasp the truth Rosmonda has to tell him how her mother and the old king conspired to get rid of the true Rosmonda for fear of the prophecy.

Now Torrismondo, who is honorably bound to ferret out the whole truth, as appalling as it promises to be, summons a soothsayer. This wise man, like Sophocles' Teiresias, is reluctant to reveal what he knows, but he does say that the king's sister is still alive. Torrismondo next summons an old servant, who tells more of the story, for it was he to whom the old king entrusted the baby princess. He does not know what happened to her after she was captured by Norwegian pirates. At this point, a Norwegian messenger is announced. This visitor brings news that the king of

Norway is dead, leaving Torrismondo his heir. Frontone, the old Gothic servant, recognizes the messenger as one of the pirates who captured the Gothic ship. When he asks him what became of the baby girl, the Norwegian replies that she acquired a noble father. Then Torrismondo, like Oedipus, cries out, "Aye-me, I tardily understand, and I understand too much, and I am fearful of knowing yet again too much." The messenger confirms his apprehension when he says that the Norwegian king adopted the foundling and gave her the name of his dead daughter, Alvida.

At last Torrismondo sees the whole truth.

> Oimè, che troppo alfin sì scopre! ahi lasso!
> Qual ritrovo, o ricerco altro consiglio? [4.6].

Aye-me, at last too much is revealed! Ah, alas, why should I find or seek other counsel?

Germondo wants to help, but Torrismondo cannot bring himself to tell all that has happened.

When the last act opens Alvida does not yet know the truth. She has heard that her "father" is dead and she now believes that her lover is faithless. She is determined to die rather than marry Germondo. In the fourth scene, a *cameriere*, acting as messenger, tells the chorus that both Alvida and Torrismondo have killed themselves. He describes the deaths in detail.

When Torrismondo found Alvida mortally wounded he told her that she was his sister and expressed the hope that her wounds would not be fatal. But it was too late.

> [Alvida] disse:
> O mio più che fratello, e più ch' amato,
> Esser questo non pò; chè morte adombra
> Già le mie luci.
> Dapoi ch' ella fu morta, il Re sospeso
> Stette per breve spatio: muto, e mesto
> Da la pietate, e da l' horror confuso,
> Il suo dolor premea nel cor profondo.
> Poi disse: Alvida, tu sei morta; io vivo
> Senza l' anima? e tacque.

Alvida said, "O my more than brother, and more than beloved, this cannot be, because death already darkens my eyes." After she was dead, the king stood in suspense for a short time; mute and despondent with pity, bewildered by horror, grief crushed his heart to its very depths. Then he said, "Alvida, you are dead; shall I live without my soul?" And he fell silent.

Then, says the messenger, after writing a letter to Germondo, Torrismondo drove his sword into his breast.

The *cameriere* delivers the letter to Germondo and explains what has happened. The queen mother finally learns the truth. She and Rosmonda are engulfed in tears. Germondo offers to become a son to the queen; but she is inconsolable. She is led off-stage wailing, and Germondo cries,

> Ahi lacrime, ahi dolore,
> Passa la vita, e si dilegua, e fugge,
> Come giel che si strugge.

Alas tears, alas sorrows! Life passes, and vanishes, and flees like frost that melts away.

ZINANO'S *ALMERIGO*

Gabriele Zinano published a *Discorso della tragedia* at Reggio-Emilia in 1590, perhaps in answer to Nicolò Rossi's *Discorsi intorno alla tragedia* (1590), which defended the traditional prescription that tragedy must be based on historical truth.[19] Zinano was a disciple of Cinthio, who, it may be recalled, argued and practiced that fiction is not only permissible in tragedy but can be more effective than history in moving pity and terror. Zinano himself argued that excessive pity and terror, such as may be raised by true events, are painful rather than pleasurable, that a feigned tragedy like *Orbecche* will move the passions more moderately and hence give more pleasure than do the "true" tragedies. He also argued against the Aristotelians who advocated sad endings. "Aristotle," he said, "proves that the finest plots are of those [characters] that are close to executing some atrocious deed and then because of a discovery do not do it" (p. 9). It is true that Aristotle, in *Poetics* 14, says, somewhat inconsistently it may be, that the very best tragic situation is one like that in Euripides' *Cresphontes,* in which Merope starts to kill her son but discovers his identity in time to spare his life, and in the same author's *Iphigenia in Tauris,* in which Iphigenia stops just before she kills her brother. The supporters of tragedy with a happy ending and of tragedy with a feigned plot, from Cinthio to Zinano, found this passage in the *Poetics* most gratifying.

Zinano was more concerned, however, with establishing the

---

[19] See Weinberg, pp. 667–672.

validity and superiority of the fictitious plot than with promoting a happy ending, and he found support in the commonly accepted belief that all poetry is imitative (i.e. creative) and verisimilar (i.e. like the truth, but not fact). "If poetry is imitation, tragedy ought also to be imitation. If poetry is imitation of feigned matter, tragedy also ought to be made of feigned matter, and consequently to be feigned. If the characteristic of poetry is verisimiltude and not truth, why make truth the subject of tragedy? If the poet acquires that name of invention (I do not consider etymology), if invention is of feigned matter, why restrict the tragic poet to true matter?" Zinano's logic sounds convincing. "If history narrates things as they are and poetry as they ought to be, where tragedy was true would it not be history and not poetry?" (p. 12).

Like Cinthio, then, Zinano believed that tragedy as well as comedy could use fiction. Like Cinthio, he disagreed with the traditional prescription of historical actions for tragedy because the deeds of princes are always well known and hence credible. But, said Zinano, are they? No, many deeds of the princes of Persia, Tartary, India, China, Ethiopia, and America are unknown to even the wisest men in Italy, and the deeds of northern princes, like those of Scotland, are little known to Italians. But, he said, even with royalty closer to home it is allowable to use feigned actions because the poet must always make some changes when he tangles and untangles the complications of his plot. And finally, Zinano did not overlook the loophole in *Poetics* 9, where Aristotle commends Agathon's tragedy *Antheus,* in which the author invented both the incidents and the characters.

Zinano practiced what he preached in his own tragedy of *Almerigo,* also published at Reggio-Emilia and perhaps in the same year, 1590.[20] Upon reading the argument of this complicated drama of over 5,000 lines one would expect a tragicomedy or even a romantic comedy rather than a neoclassical tragedy. There is a sensational bloodthirsty ending, however. The last act, in which all the deaths occur, is entirely devoted to messengers who bring their reports to the chorus. Like Cinthian tragedy and tragicomedy, *Almerigo* is exotic and spectacular; in the cast of twenty there are five full-dress ambassadors from Tartary, Muscovy, Arabia, Egypt, and Persia.

---

[20] There is no date on the title page and no colophon, but the dedication is dated 1590.

Almerigo, heir to the throne of Spain, attracted by the fame of the Turkish princess Elvira, goes incognito to Constantinople. During his absence his father the king dies. When a faithful servant tells his fiancée Rotilda, daughter of the French king, where Almerigo is, she cuts off her hair, dresses in men's clothes, and goes to Constantinople, accompanied by three young French knights and, apparently, by a chorus of elderly Spanish gentlemen. The complications develop in the Turkish capital. Elvira returns the Spaniard's love, but her father decides to marry her to the Sophy of Persia. Therefore an elopement is planned with the aid of the ever-available nurse. A long-lost sister of Almerigo turns up in Constantinople. Rotilda discloses her identity to Almerigo, who promises to love her "as a sister." But Rotilda's feelings are more than sisterly and she betrays the elopement to her attendant French knights. In the dead of night, on his way to the rendezvous at a temple, Almerigo encounters three "men" who seem to be barring his path. He draws his sword and cuts down all three—Rotilda, his sister, and Elvira. A sudden ray of moonlight discloses the face of his third victim, who is not yet dead. The frantic Spanish prince is seized by the French knights, who throw him in a den of wild beasts and inform the emperor of the attempted elopement. When the tigers and panthers refuse to harm Almerigo, the emperor has his eyes put out. The mortally wounded Elvira drags herself to her lover's side for a last meeting. Thereupon the emperor has both his daughter and Almerigo thrown to the tigers and panthers.

These hair-raising actions are reported by messengers, to be sure, for the author was not so extreme a Modern that he abandoned all classical decorum. *Almerigo*, in fact, has less action onstage than do many neoclassical tragedies, and contains more long, tedious speeches than do most.

Romantic love is the essence of the play. Debates on love are repeatedly exhibited. In the very first scene, when Formindo, the trusty servant, expresses the feeling that they are engaged on a wild-goose chase, Rotilda answers him with spirit. "Love was my counselor," she says, "Love the teacher who seemed to speak to my heart. A royal maid, I have already led you safely through a thousand perils and a thousand horrors. . . . Love commanded, so I followed."

Love is all-powerful for at least four acts. Rotilda, unknown in her disguise to Almerigo, lectures him on his duty to return to Spain. Almerigo admits that he is ashamed of his conduct, but he cannot withstand the beautiful eyes of the Turkish princess. When Formindo lectures him on his lost honor, he remains unmoved. Even the nurse holds forth on the power of love: "He [Love] curbs the bold, he makes timid hearts undaunted in the midst of weapons and fears, he renders the foolish wise and the wise foolish, he makes the base-born magnanimous, the rustic gentle, the fickle constant, and the most lecherous lovers continent" (2.3). When Elvira makes her first appearance she, too, is feeling the overwhelming force of love. "What new thoughts and desires sprout new forms in my heart? What do I think? Am I perhaps in love? What stupor possesses my mind? What makes my limbs tremulous and reverent before the flash of two comely eyes? Is it perhaps a deity that hides in them?" (2.4). And so it goes, I am tempted to say, *ad nauseam.*

Elvira's rhapsodies are perhaps the most extravagant in a play full of Petrarchan sentiments, but Almerigo's raptures are not far behind. "O Elvira, O Elvira, your beautiful foot does not touch the ground because it is a divine foot, and your delicate senses indeed should not have painful objects, or rude objects, or fearful objects" (3.1).

Once in a while, however, Zinano showed that he was able to write straightforward dialogue that sounds almost natural. Moreover, he sometimes wrote such dialogue for crucial scenes, for example, for the scene wherein Almerigo learns that Rotilda is in Constantinople.

Formindo: Rotilda is in this country.
Almerigo: And who induced such a maid to come here?
Formindo: Love. Through a thousand troops and a thousand sails Love enabled her to plough the seas and roam the lands.
Almerigo: And what kind of love?
Formindo: True love, sacred love, modest love, a chaste lover's love, a wife's love.
Almerigo: For whom is so much love?
Formindo: For you yourself.
Almerigo: O day full of marvels! [3.1].

When Formindo points out that Rotilda is his affianced bride,

Almerigo replies, "My father promised her; I promised Elvira."

There is no love in the last act, which is one long wail of anguish. Since the chorus, as usual, is eager to savor every shuddery detail in the messenger's report of the death of hero and heroine, the play ends in horror.

> *Choro* Che segui?
>
> *Nontio* Che segui? ah tanto horrore
> Tratto gli occhi han da l' horrida mistura
> Del sangue al terren misto, e un membro a l' altro,
> Co' i corpi intieri, e morti, e i semivivi,
> Ch' eran presenti, si stordito m' hanno,
> Ch' io non sò, s' io sia vivo, se nò in quanto
> Senso ho a le doglie, e s' io mi volgo al cielo,
> Il cielo istesso lagrimoso parmi.

Chorus: What next?

Messenger: What next? Ah, my eyes have distilled so much horror from the ghastly mixture of blood mingled with earth, of limb with limb, of whole bodies, the dead, and the half-dead that were exhibited, I am so stupified, that I do not know if I am alive, if I am not out of my senses from grief, and if I turn to the sky it seems to me that heaven itself is full of tears.

MIARI'S *PRENCIPE TIGRIDORO*

Il Prencipe Tigridoro, by Alessandro Miari, another poet at Reggio-Emilia, was printed in 1591. Like Zinano, Miari also wrote pastorals and, according to the prologue, turned from shepherds and nymphs to the "royal loves and deeds of princes." Moreover, he also used a fictitious plot in his tragedy, which combined imitations of the story of Merope (and doubtless the Italian Merope plays), Sophocles' *Oedipus Rex,* and Tasso's *Torrismondo.* Miari's argument is almost as sensational as Zinano's in *Almerigo,* and in addition to the exploitation of romantic love there are themes of friendship and filial piety. Here again was material for tragicomedy; but the star-crossed lovers, friends, and parents were destined to suffer ruin. Senecan fatalism was still a potent force in 1591. As one of the few survivors at the end says—he is the Assyrian prince Agesilao—"It never behooves us mortals on earth to praise the day until nightfall" (p. 116). And the chorus of priests of Apollo comments on the tragedy in the same vein:

> Difficile è schivare
> Ciò, che destina il cielo

In noi egri mortali,
Che poco, o nulla vale
Contra celeste forza human sapere [p. 81].

It is hard to avoid that which heaven allots to us weak mortals, for human knowledge is of little or no avail against celestial power.

Artabano, brother to Belo, ancient king of Assyria, usurped the throne when his brother died, setting aside the claim of his nephew Agesilao. Artabano had no children living. Some years before he became king his wife had had a dream that she would give birth to a son who would some day kill his father. Artabano had ordered a soldier named Tissaferne to drown the baby in the Tigris. The wife died in childbirth. Now living at the court in Ninevah is a beautiful exile from Cilicia named Florinda. Agesilao is in love with her. So is the king, who has exiled his nephew, thereby disposing of a rival in love as well as a claimant to his throne. Agesilao's mother, Aspasia, widow of the former king, is still living at the court, though Artabano is planning to have her exiled, too.

The play proper opens just as the exiled Agesilao has secretly returned to Ninevah accompanied by a comrade-in-arms named Tigridoro, Prince of Tarsus. Trigridoro had been happily married to the daughter of the Cilician king, but pirates had carried away his wife and killed his children. He had been wandering over Asia Minor looking for traces of his wife when he fell in with Agesilao, who once save his life. Now Tigridoro has come to help his friend assassinate Artabano. He introduces himself to the Assyrian king as a bearer of good news, namely, that Agesilao is dead. Tigridoro says that he killed him in a duel fought in Mesopotamia, and he produces a head to prove it. The king is as delighted as Aspasia is heartbroken.[21] Artabano refuses to let the mother have the head. "Take the hideous head, O my servant," cries the king, "and for its mockery and my satisfaction exhibit it aloft today so that it is seen by all the people" (p. 28). Then he invites the stranger to make himself at home in the palace. Tissaferne, who is now a general, enters into a conspiracy with Aspasia and Tigridoro to kill the tyrant. Tigridoro explains to the dowager that her son is not dead but is in hiding near the city.

In the third act, Tigridoro meets Florinda and is startled by her

---

[21] These details were suggested by the Merope plays. See my *Tragicomedy*, pp. 101–122.

resemblance to his missing wife. As a gallant knight he offers her his services. After some talk she discloses that she is the wife of the prince of Tarsus. A happy reunion of the faithful couple follows. Then Tigridoro resumes his plan to kill the king and put his friend Agesilao on the throne. He finds himself in a painful dilemma, however, in which love threatens friendship. If he keeps his newly recovered wife, he must betray his friend, who loves her; if he hands Florinda over to Agesilao, as the knightly code of honor demands, he must betray his wife.

In the fourth act, Tissaferne brings bad news to Aspasia and the chorus. The conspirators have bungled the assassination of Artabano, who was only wounded and now is demanding an explanation. Tigridoro has told him that he was the adopted son of Assyria's old enemy, the king of Cilicia. He has also related the circumstances attending his rescue from death by exposure on the banks of the Tigris. Both Artabano and Tissaferne have realized that the prophecy is being fulfilled. As the dying king said, "The son has killed the father, for you are my son, who was not drowned in the Tigris" (p. 80). Then he told Tigridoro about his wife's dream. He pardoned his son and appointed him his successor on one condition, that he seek revenge on Agesilao and Aspasia. Tigridoro has promised to carry out the dying man's wishes.

Then another complication arises. Tigridoro's aunt, who is living in the palace, informs him that his mother (her sister) actually gave birth to twins, to a girl as well as to a boy, that Tissaferne, too kindhearted to drown the babies as ordered, had left the girl in a forest. At this point Florinda cries out, "Alas, I foresee disaster ahead for me" (p. 89). And Tigridoro cries, "Why did not Jove shatter my head on that day the prince of Tarsus bound us with Hyman's ill-omened knot?" (p. 90). The ugly crime of incest is heaped upon their other troubles.

In the last act, Aspasia is reunited with her son Agesilao, but the two have little time to enjoy their happy change of fortune. A messenger reports that Tigridoro has killed himself with the same sword he used on his father, though not before a farewell speech in which he renounced his right to the kingdom and his right to live. "If you, O father, were not worthy to rule in Belo's stead, could I your son, also unworthy, usurp the empire that rightly belongs to his son and my dear friend, Agesilao?" (pp. 109–110). Then the chorus asks, "What did Florinda do?" Florinda, says the messenger, promised to obey her husband's request to marry Agesilao. But she cannot go through with it. Nor does Agesilao now want her to, for he is both horrified and heartbroken by the tragic turn of events. All of his sufferings, ironically enough, have been brought on him by such noble virtues as love, friendship and filial piety. A knight soon brings news that Florinda is dying, poisoned by her own hand. Agesilao goes to hear her dying speech, in which she explains that death is best for her. She urges him to live and rule the kingdoms of Assyria and Cilicia. The chivalrous Agesilao is crushed by her death coming so soon after the death of his best friend.

> Florinda è morta; al corpo immortal tomba
> Fia il mondo, a l' alma eterno albergo il cielo.
> Il cielo, anima bella, hoggi t' accolga,
> E teco quella de l' amico accetti [p. 126].

Florinda is dead. May the world be an everlasting tomb for your body, heaven an eternal abode for your soul. May heaven welcome you today, beautiful spirit, and with you may it receive the spirit of my friend.

GUIDOCCIO'S *MATHILDA*

Giacomo Guidoccio's *Mathilda* was printed at Treviso in 1592, with several commendatory verses in Latin and Italian comparing the author with Trissino and Tasso, with Sophocles and Euripides, and remarking that "you follow the doctrines that the Stagyrite teaches." Actually Guidoccio was a pretty devoted follower of Cinthio and he carried on the romantic eroticism launched by the author of *Orbecche, Arrenopia,* and *Epitia.* The argument of *Mathilda* owes something to the Romeo-Juliet story, possibly something to Groto's *Hadriana.*

Guidoccio's tragedy hardly squares with all the Aristotelian doctrines, but it preserves the unities of action and time. The ghost who delivers the prologue, and who is anxious to see the completion of his revenge on one of the characters, remarks that his leave from hell extends only to sunset. The locale is Granada, but the scenes apparently move about within the city, from room to room within the palace and to the inner citadel or keep. The chorus (ladies of the court) follows the pattern set by Cinthio, but Guidoccio drastically reduced its role. His chorus delivers short odes of ten lines (combining *endecasillabi* and *settenarii*) at the end of each act save the last; it takes a small part in the dialogue of Acts 3 and 4, a somewhat larger part in the dialogue of Act 5, when it listens to the reports of messengers. I know of no learned Italian tragedy in the sixteenth century that reduces the chorus to so few lines, though Angeli's *Arsinoe* and Villifranchi's *Altamoro* make little use of the chorus.

The ghost of the prologue is one Gernando, a jilted suitor of Cleria, younger daughter of the king of Granada. Now he has returned to witness his revenge. "Day is already near, the day that should be as dear to me as it will be grievous and bitter to others." Cleria is not the heroine; she has a subordinate role to her older sister Mathilda, who opens the play with her nurse. As might be expected, she is lamenting the evils that beset Granada, and, as might be expected in a romantic tragedy, she attributes all these evils to love. Her laments are usually unrestrained, but elegantly expressed.

> Ahi che senz' occhi piango, e senza lingua
> Mi dolgo, e non ho voce, e pur io grido,
> Ugualmente mi spiace vita, e morte,
> Perchè amor dà la morte in dolce vita,
> E dolce morte poi detta è la vita
> Trasformata in crudele, e doppia morte [p. 6].

Alas, I weep without eyes, and complain without a tongue, and I have no voice and yet cry out; life and death equally offend me, for love brings death to sweet life and sweet death is then said to be life transformed into cruel and double death.

The nurse agrees with her: "Aye-me, this tyrant Love has no restraint and no law."

Women deliver most of the exposition. Mathilda and Cleria had been brought up at Granada with Clorindo, Prince of Sicily, and both girls fell in love with him. He had chosen Mathilda and was her lover until he was called home to help defend his country. Meanwhile, Ordauro, Prince of Scotland, had chosen Mathilda for his bride. When Mathilda confessed to her father, a much kindlier parent than Juliet's tyrant, that she was already "married" to Clorindo, the king sent ambassadors to Scotland offering Cleria in place of Mathilda. But the fierce Scot refused to accept a substitute and declared war. When the play opens Granada is already besieged by a Scottish army. The situation is desperate, rendered more frightening by Mathilda's dream in which she heard a terrible voice crying, "Fly, Mathilda, fly, for Ordauro has captured the

city!" (p. 12). Then came a vision of her father's mangled corpse
and of herself overtaken by a wild beast that tore at her breast.
Moreover, Mathilda knows that a crisis is at hand, for today her
father is going to make a sortie outside the walls.

Cleria first appears in the second act. She is as mournful as
her sister and more hysterical. Now she is terrified at the prospect
of the sortie, for she will probably lose either a father or a lover.
Despite Ordauro's refusal to accept her, she is in love with him; in
fact, he is the "life of her life." She is more romantic than Cesari's
Scilla and Romilda, and she has also had a dream. Cupid appeared
to her just before dawn and spoke: "O Cleria, don't sleep but get up,
get up, for today must be the last day of Ordauro's life; and make
yourself ready to celebrate the nuptials of Mathilda and Clorindo
with tears" (p. 23). Then, informing her that he was avenging the
death of her old suitor Gernando, he ordered her to dry her eyes
—"no eyes, but fountains, rather swift torrents, of tears" (p. 24).[22]

The king of Granada leads his troops outside the walls. Soon
his squire brings word that the sortie has been destroyed, the king
taken prisoner. The nurse reminds the despairing Mathilda that
Clorindo is on the way with a Sicilian army to raise the siege;
but Mathilda refuses to be consoled. A Scottish messenger enters
bearing a gift from Ordauro.

Mathilda: Aye-me, what do I see? Aye-me!
Messenger: You see the head of your father, who foolishly was less trust-
worthy than he should have been.
Mathilda: O father, O dear father, O head, O dear head, O traitor Ordauro, O wretched Mathilda, what will you do now? Do you want to see
your own death in this lifeless head as in a clear mirror? . . . Envious
death has put out your light, beloved father, and left me instead, poor
daughter, everlasting cause for bitter sorrow [pp. 47–48].

The messenger tells Mathilda that his prince still wants to marry
her; but she spurns the outrageous offer.

The royal counselor, now in charge of the besieged city, brings
news that the enemy is inside the walls. He urges Mathilda to run
to the keep. The chorus begs Cleria to join her sister. But Cleria

---

[22] Cf. Hieronimo's well-known "O eyes, no eyes, but fountains fraught with
tears" in Thomas Kyd's Senecan and Italianate *Spanish Tragedy.* This Petrarchan figure was virtually a commonplace in sixteenth-century Italian,
French, and English poetry. Ben Jonson's ridicule of Hieronimo's lament, in
Every Man in His Humor, has become as celebrated as the original.

refuses to move; she has the romantic notion that she can protect the others from the fury of the enemy. The last act of *Mathilda* is good theater, skillfully contrived and well written. Mathilda drinks a cup of poison just before Clorindo's tutor arrives with news that the Sicilians have routed the enemy and raised the siege. He brings a present from his master—Ordauro's head. Now Mathilda feels the full spite of her unlucky star: "I was born mortal, and my stepmotherly destiny renders me immortal" (p. 63). She tells the tutor that she has already drunk poison.

Clorindo soon appears. Mathilda rallies to greet her lover; she urges him to live and to see her buried in a tomb with the following inscription:

> Qui la figlia d' Ancrisio estinta giace
> Mathilda, e fu sua sorte,
> Che morendo provò due volte morte,
> La prima co'l veleno
> Da se stessa si diede,
> E la seconda fu di rio dolore
> Che le cagionò amore.
> Ma fu felice poi,
> Che in braccio al suo Clorindo,
> Chiuse morendo gli occhi a gli anni suoi [p. 69].

Here Mathilda, daughter of Ancrisio, lies dead, and it was her fate that in dying she tried death twice, first with poison which she gave herself, and a second time from harsh grief that love brought her. But she was happy then, that in dying she closed her eyes on her years in the arms of her Clorindo.

Clorindo has no thought beyond joining his mistress in death: "O happy day, when I lose the sun in order to follow you, my sun." Drawing his sword over the protests of his faithful *bailo*, he cries,

> O dolce vita mia,
> O mio diletto bene,
> Non affrettate tanto
> Questa partita amara,
> Aspettate, ch' io vengo.
> Tu dolcissima bocca
> Prendi gli ultimi baci,
> Gli ultimi amari baci,
> Baci non più d' amor, ma ben di morte [pp. 70–71].

O my sweet life, O my beloved, do not hurry so much this bitter parting;

wait, for I come. Most sweet mouth, take the last kisses, the last bitter kisses, no more love's kisses, but death's indeed.

Neither Mathilda nor Clorindo dies onstage, however.

The nurse, ignorant of the latest disaster, rejoices in the relief of Granada, but her joy is soon cut short by a weeping messenger who says that Mathilda is dead. A *cameriera* adds that Clorindo is also dead, by his own hand. Cleria is still alive; but the *cameriera* says that she "scorns every counsel and cursing heaven calls on death."

ANGELI'S *ARSINOE*

According to the dedication written by the printer (Federico Abirelli), *Arsinoe* (1594), by Nicola degli Angeli, was esteemed by the leading *letterati* of Venice and Padua "one of the most excellent [tragedies] that have been written for many centuries." These *letterati* must have been conservative critics who defended the doctrine that tragedy should be based on the true history of great rulers. Angeli's play has a historical basis. Arsinoe, the heroine, was the daughter of Ptolemy I of Egypt, the Arsinoe who married Alexander's general Lysimachus, King of Macedonia. When her husband died, Arsinoe ruled alone. Then Macedonia was attacked by Ptolemy Ceraunus from Crete. Arsinoe held out in the citadel of Cassandrea and refused to surrender until Ptolemy promised to marry her. Angeli's tragedy begins at this point.

Although the argument of *Arsinoe* was based on ancient history, the long complicated play is a "new" tragedy incorporating many features developed by Cinthio, Speroni, and Tasso. Incest is prominent, and it contains other echoes of *Oedipus* and *Canace*. Love is all-important. A second heroine, in the manner of tragicomedy and comedy, is disguised as a boy throughout the whole action. The chorus of old men has no connection with the plot and takes no part in the dialogue; it merely moralizes at the end of each act save the last.

The action begins with a dialogue between two royal counselors, one of them an honest, fearless man, the other a sycophant. The honest counselor, Aristonico, does not trust Tolomeo and his brutal soldiers and recommends continued resistance. The other counselor argues that love will save the day, "love, which always unites and does not divide, which always preserves and does not destroy."[23] Aristonico disagrees. Even when the queen's secretary, Dione, reports that Tolomeo has signed a treaty preserving the inheritance of Arsinoe's sons, he suspects treachery.

At this point an old friend of Dione from Crete appears with a strange tale. The visitor, an innkeeper in Crete, relates how one night an old gentleman, accompanied by a boy, came to his inn with a story of escape from Egypt and shipwreck near Crete. The boy, said to be an unwanted son of Ptolemy I, was left with the innkeeper, who raised him as his own son. Later the king of Crete met the youth, took a fancy to him, and brought him to the palace, where he became an accomplished knight and finally the commander of the Cretan army. He also became the lover of Orinthia, only child of the king. He (Tolomeo) led an expedition against Corcyra (Corfu) and took it. Then he attacked Macedonia. Meanwhile Orinthia had gone on a pilgrimage to the island of Delos.

Orinthia herself appears before the end of the first act. Disguised as a page, she has come from Delos to find her lover Tolomeo, who is about to marry Arsinoe. She asks Dione to get her an audience with the queen, whom she wants to warn against the treachery of Tolomeo. She also wants to punish her faithless lover: "I would like to tear out his heart with this hand, to devour his entrails and flesh with these teeth. Ho there, who supports my revenge on so fierce a tyrant? Who offers me sword, noose, fire? Ah, alas, where is Love taking me?" (16v).

Arsinoe, who does not enter the scene until the second act, receives the page and listens to the story of the base-born Tolomeo, son of an innkeeper, who is waging war on Macedonia without permission of the Cretan king, who won the heart of the Cretan princess and then betrayed her. Arsinoe does not believe Orinthia; she cannot believe that a genuine princess would appear in public dressed in such clothes, and therefore she must be an imposter in league with her kinsman Dione to betray the city to the enemy. The queen orders Orinthia, Dione, and the innkeeper arrested. Since news has just arrived that her father is dead, Orinthia is now the queen of Crete.

Another character appears before the end of the second act to assume an important role. This character is Perinto, an Athenian

---

[23] *Arsinoe* (Venice, 1594), 6v.

cavalier, who is friendly to Arsinoe but believes Orinthia's story. Orinthia evades arrest but finds herself completely frustrated. "O my unhappy plight; Love, unjust tyrant!" (34v). She still loves Tolomeo although she hates him, and she is willing to use any means to prevent his marrying Arsinoe. She and Perinto enter into a conspiracy with two Cretan spies (officers in Tolomeo's army) to capture the *rocca* (citadel) by a ruse. Perinto says that he can bribe the keeper to give up the keys.

The president of the Macedonian senate and the senators are brought on the stage in the fourth act. Aristonico continues to warn against Tolomeo, "this captain, surely the son of larceny and envy, among his thievish warriors" (43r). The queen continues to be bedeviled by her own indecision.

The last act is highly theatrical, with several discoveries and reversals of fortune. The unstable queen now opens the gates to the Cretans. Tolomeo enters and makes a pretty speech, protesting that his main goal all along has been the benefit of Arsinoe and her two sons. All he wants for himself is her person. "Behold, then, before your Highness not a conqueror but one conquered. The crown of Macedonia is yours and your sons'. I shall always be a minister of your hints and commands" (54v). The queen and the young princes are delighted at this happy turn of events. Then follows a good dramatic scene between Arsinoe, Tolomeo, and the page.

> *Orinthia* Questa corona, traditore, è mia.
> *Tolomeo* Di gittar tu corona ardisci?
> Questo colpo t' ancida.
> *Orinthia* Orinthia anciderai?
> Anciderai Orinthia?
> Mi riconosci traditor pergiuro?
> *Tolomeo* Io feritor, ferito?
> Io micidial già morto?
> Così rintorce Amor i colpi, e impiaga
> Con l' armi de' begli occhi? Hor questo ferro
> Non più di Tolomeo si cinga al fianco [55v].

Orinthia: This crown, traitor, is mine.

Tolomeo: Do you dare cast down this crown? May this blow kill you.

Orinthia: You will kill Orinthia? Will you kill Orinthia? Do you recognize me, perjured traitor?

Tolomeo: I the wounder am wounded? I the killer am already dead? Does

Love thus parry blows, and wound with beautiful eyes for weapons?
Now may this sword of Tolomeo no more gird his side.

Arsinoe, who witnesses this exchange, is now forced to believe that
the page is truly Orinthia, Queen of Crete.

Thanks to Perinto, the *rocca* is captured. Arsinoe is betrayed.
Tolomeo brutally informs her that she will be a servant to his
queen Orinthia, that her two sons must be executed. Soon Perinto
reports to Tolomeo that he has seen two soldiers with drawn swords
overtake the queen and the young princes. Now more discoveries
and reversals occur. Tolomeo asks the Athenian if he ever heard
that the king of Egypt had a feeble-minded elder son. Yes, says
Perinto, he had heard that the boy was lost at sea. Tolomeo then
asks him if Arsinoe is the sister of the lost Egyptian prince. Yes,
says Perinto. Tolomeo, in the manner of Oedipus, cries, "Already
I feel in my breast (O cruel fate) my soul and heart fearful and
trembling" (60r). He summons the innkeeper and demands the
truth. He now realizes that he has killed his nephews and almost
married his sister. Now he begins to lament and to call for punishment of himself: "I already feel all the infernal Furies besieging
my heart" (62r). One of the Cretan officers reports that Orinthia
has tried to kill herself but failed. Now she has taken command
of the Cretan army and plans to kill Tolomeo. All the Cretans
desert Tolomeo to follow Orinthia.

The play ends rather abruptly with a messenger's spirited
report of the brutal butchering of the two young princes before
the eyes of their mother Arsinoe.

VILLIFRANCHI'S *ALTAMORO*

Giovanni Villifranchi's *Altamoro*, a long, tedious tragedy that
combines blood and revenge with romantic love, was carelessly
printed at Florence in 1595. Neri dismisses it as an "imitation of
Torrismondo." It is somewhat reminiscent of Tasso's tragedy in
having incest and an Oedipus-like resolution, but the similarity is
superficial. If Villifranchi followed Tasso, he made many alterations in his model. Torrismondo unwittingly falls in love with
his own sister. In Villifranchi's play, a young prince has unwittingly
fallen in love with his own sister and, to add further complications,
the father of the young lovers falls in love with the girl (his own
daughter) and kills his young rival (his own son). In the resolu-

tion, the father grieves over his ignorant killing of the son, and the self-blinded daughter goes into exile with her mother for guide.

The scene of *Altamoro* is Naples. The king of Naples, Altamoro, has defeated the king of Sicily (who opens the play as a ghost seeking revenge), and now has fallen in love with one of his prisoners, the Sicilian princess Arontea. His wife, Isandra, jealous of her younger rival, has another prisoner released and brought to the palace, that is, a young African prince named Dornando, who is the lover of Arontea. Altamoro, insane with jealousy, confronts both prisoners in the dungeon, taunts them, then cuts out Dornando's eyes, his tongue, his lips, and finally his heart. Arontea, who returns Dornando's love, is so shocked by this inhuman deed that she seizes a sword hanging on the wall and gouges out her own eyes. In the fourth act, a soothsayer informs Altamoro and Isandra that Dornando and Arontea are their own offspring, long presumed lost at sea but actually rescued and adopted by royalty in Africa and Sicily. When Isandra sees her mutilated daughter she assumes that Altamoro has also perpetrated this horror. Therefore she stabs him. All of these gruesome deeds are faithfully reported by messengers.

The brief summary above suggests that Villifranchi was probably more indebted to Cinthio's *Orbecche* than to Tasso's *Torrismondo,* and it is true that *Altamoro* is like *Orbecche* in several ways. The ghost rising from hell to open the play, the torture and killing in the dungeon, the behavior of the tyrannical king, the behavior of the good counselor, the behavior of the queen when she thinks that she is avenging her daughter, the long detailed reports of the messengers, all point to Cinthio's first tragedy. Altamoro is nothing like the chivalrous Torrismondo, but he is very like Cinthio's Sulmone. Isandra's stabbing of her cruel husband may well have been suggested by Orbecche's stabbing of her cruel father. The only contributions of Tasso, probably, were romantic love, incest arising from shipwreck, and the Oedipus-like resolution. But romantic love, incest or the threat of incest, shipwreck, and mistaken identity were common property in Italian comedy and tragicomedy and by the end of the sixteenth century *Oedipus Rex* was as popular as *Thyestes* and *Medea.*

Although *Altamoro* is not a good play, it is instructive in showing us many of the faults that beset Italian tragedy of the Renaissance. In fact, Angelo Ingegneri, when he set down his rules for playmaking in 1598,[24] must have had tragedies like *Altamoro* in mind as examples of what to avoid. In the first place, Villifranchi's plot is unduly extended and obscured by superfluous soporific dialogue and soliloquies. Ingegneri said that a dramatist is not a lyric poet; but for four acts Villifranchi tried to be one, and most of the speeches in *Altamoro* swarm with far-fetched conceits and mythological allusions. Villifranchi violated another rule of Ingegneri in bringing a ghost onstage. Villifranchi's chorus is used in the very way Ingegneri disapproved of; that is, it takes no part in the action but merely sings *canzoni* at the end of each act.

In the diction, the worst feature of *Altamoro*, the author even disregarded the advice of his master Cinthio. In the *Discorsi*, it may be recalled,[25] Cinthio condemned the "Spanish" manner of writing, such as, "Thus the billows of my conceits, issuing from the fountain of my heart and entering the sea of your profound virtue, lose their straight course in the waves of your praises." There may not be anything quite so bad as this in *Altamoro*, but some of the speeches are not much better.

In the first scene of Act 3, Isandra promises to bring Dorando to Arontea:

> Lieta dunque l' attendi, e posa in porto
> Del bel seno di lui la stanca nave
> De le tue belle membra, e di pensieri.

Then await him joyfully, and put the weary ship of your beautiful arms and of your thoughts in the harbor of his noble bosom.

Even the nurse is not exempt from this conceited mannerism. In trying to calm the queen she says, "May the blowing winds of your sighs neither swell you on high nor submerge your bark of life" (1.4).

When Altamoro, who is a tough, middle-aged tyrant, makes love to Arontea in front of the prison grating, he sounds like a sonneteer.

> Io t' amo, e queste fredde mura il sanno,
> I t' amo, e queste dure pietre il sanno,
> I t' amo, e questi feri algenti il sanno,
> La terra, il mar lo sa, l' Inferno, Il Cielo
> Lo sa [1.3].

---

[24] See below, pp. 279 ff.
[25] See above, p. 81.

I love you, and these cold walls know it; I love you, and these hard stones know it; I love you, and these cold iron bars know it; the earth, the sea knows it, hell, heaven knows it.

Arontea rejects his love. She clamors for release so that she may visit the tomb of Dornando, whom she believes to be dead, so that "I may bathe the hard stone with living tears, and my kisses will be as hot as his bones are cold."

Villifranchi's messengers indulge in even more extravagant language than do Cinthio's; at least they are even fonder of Senecan mythological-geographical allusions. Typical is the speech of the messenger who has just witnessed the appalling death scene in the dungeon:

> Io nel gelato Reno,
> A le nevi di Borea, a ghiacci algenti
> N' anderò de Rifei gelidi monti,
> A Caucasi, et a Caspii, et ad entrambe
> Le Tane, solo per armar di gielo
> Il petto; et arrezzar gli occhi dolenti
> A fieri simolacri; Ah sei più Giove? [4.1].

I will go to the freezing Rhine, to the snows of Boreas, to the cold ice of the frigid Scythian mountains, to the Caucasus, to the Caspian, to both the Dons, solely to arm my breast with frost and to shade my smarting eyes from savage images. Ah, do you still exist, Jove?

In fairness, however, it must be said that occasionally, though only occasionally, Villifranchi showed that he could write dramatic dialogue that has some resemblance to natural speech. The queen's lament in the last act is certainly acceptable although it sounds like many another tragic lament. Isandra is brooding over the horrible death of her son, the blinding of her daughter, and her own stabbing of Altamoro.

> Angolo non rimiro, ov' io non scorga
> Le membra del mio figlio;
> Luce non vedo, che non rappresenti
> Le tenebre perpetue di mia figlia?
> Voce non odo, ch' io non creda quella
> Di loro, e del consorte,
> Che mi chiamano al mio castigo eterno? [5.2].

Do I see any corner where I do not perceive the limbs of my son? Do I see any light that does not represent the everlasting darkness of my daughter? Do I hear any voice that I do not believe is theirs, or my husband's, which call me to my eternal punishment?

VENIERO'S *HIDALBA*

Maffio Veniero, Venetian patrician, archbishop, anti-Petrarchan poet, who wrote poems in the Venetian dialect, wrote one of the better Italian tragedies of the Renaissance. Neri and Bertana pass over *Hidalba* (1596)[26] with scarcely more than brief mention, but Ingegneri, in 1598, singled it out for praise along with Trissino's *Sofonisba,* Speroni's *Canace,* Torelli's *Merope* and *Tancredi.*[27] Although Ingegneri may have been anxious to mention these particular poets because they were patricians, his praise of *Hidalba* was doubtless honest enough because the play actually does fit most of his recommendations for a good tragedy and avoids most of the faults he condemned. While *Hidalba* is hardly unique among sixteenth-century tragedies in Italy, since its form and style are somewhat reminiscent of Aretino's *Orazia* and since the author followed the fashion of using an ancient model (i.e. *Antigone*), it is nevertheless unusual in being devoid of revenge, devoid of sensationalism, and devoid of bombast.

The argument of *Hidalba* is Gothic in the sense of being northern. After long wars the king of Friesland patched up a peace by marrying the sister of his enemy the king of Denmark. Two children were born, Armilla and a boy. The Friesian king never became reconciled with the Danes, however, and just before his death willed that in the event of his son's dying without issue the crown must descend to his niece Hidalba, not to his daughter Armilla. The son did die without issue and the Friesians prepared to crown Hidalba, who had no desire to be queen but was urged to accept the throne by her father, Isandro. Armilla, who was fond of her cousin and never meant any harm to her, nevertheless distrusted Isandro. She was supported by the commander-in-chief of the army, an able and ambitious man named Tarpace, and she promised to marry him if his troops won her the throne. Tarpace seized the city and stopped the coronation ceremonies. Hidalba was willing to give up the crown she never wanted, but her father and husband persuaded her to accept the support of the president of the royal council. Civil war broke out. Tarpace killed Isandro and Hidalba's husband, Atirsi. News of her father's death

---

[26] Allacci lists four printings: Venice, 1596; Bologna, 1597; Venice, n.d.; Venice, 1623. The Illinois copy is the first printing (Venice, 1596).

[27] *Della poesia rappresentativa,* in Guarini's *Opere* 3.522.

was brought to Hidalba, but her husband's death was concealed from her. Hidalba mourned for her father and asked permission to bury his body. At first Tarpace refused to let her have the body for burial but later sent a corpse to her. When she examined the bier, assuming that it contained her dead father, she discovered the body of Atirsi, her beloved husband. Meanwhile the president roused the common people, attacked Armilla's forces, and killed Tarpace. Armilla fled the city. Hidalba retired to her apartment with the body of Atirsi, picked up the dead man's dagger, and plunged it into her heart.

The play is carefully constructed. There are twenty-seven scenes, only one of which (5.4) seems tedious. The most crucial scene comes near the end of Act 4, when Tarpace shows Armilla an intercepted letter in which Hidalba yields to her father and gives the president permission to renew the civil war. Then Armilla allows Tarpace a free rein and more bloodshed is inevitable. The catastrophe, foreshadowed in the fourth act, as Ingegneri recommended,[28] follows in the last act. There are no long soliloquies, and what soliloquies there are seem to be delivered in the presence, and apparently in the hearing, of the chorus, which is a *choro fermo* (fixed chorus) that evidently remains onstage after it enters at the close of Act 1. Veniero used the chorus in accord with the advice of Horace and the practice of Sophocles, as Ingegneri recommended; his chorus, made up of women sympathetic with Hidalba, takes a major role in the dialogue.

Although there are four deaths among the principal characters, *Hidalba* is not a tragedy of blood and revenge. The word "revenge" *(vendetta)* occurs only twice in the play. Hidalba uses it in the last act (5.2), but only after she is all but prostrated by Tarpace's refusal to let her have Isandro's body. Then she asks the gods to avenge this shameful treatment of the dead by punishing the general. Armilla is not vengeful; she never becomes reconciled to the necessity of doing away with her cousin although she does not balk at having Isandro and Atirsi killed in battle. Tarpace is not a cruel man; he is a soldier and adopts the only practical means of insuring Armilla's possession of the throne. He refuses to allow burial of Isandro's body because permission would indicate a weakness of resolution in his party and the fickle commons would

---

[28] See below, p. 280.

be easily swayed by any sign of weakness or of strength. The president is not vengeful; he believes that Hidalba should have the throne. The messengers are never hysterical, but report disasters in calm, matter-of-fact speech. There is no ghost rising from hell to demand blood and vengeance.

Veniero's powers of characterization were not remarkable, but the characters in *Hidalba* are better conceived and better portrayed than the average in Italian tragedy. The author obeyed the prescriptions of Aristotle and Horace as interpreted by sixteenth-century scholars; he made all his characters consistent from first to last act and he made them observe the recommended decorum of age, rank, and sex. The heroine, *modesta Hidalba*, is credible and attractive. She desires only peace and the love of husband and father. Deprived of this love, she has no wish to live. She is a gentle, kindhearted lady and only under the most extreme provocation does she use anything but gentle speech. Her strongest language comes when she faces Tarpace, who had killed her father and now refuses to give up the corpse for honorable burial.

> Empio, iniquo, immodesto, aspetta, aspetta
> Il premio di tuoi merti; il cielo è giusto [5.2].

Wicked, ungodly, shameless, wait, wait for the recompense you deserve; heaven is just.

The most unusual feature of *Hidalba* is the diction, which is the simplest, I believe, in any Italian verse tragedy of the century. Senecan fatalism is sometimes expressed, usually by the chorus, but there is little or no Senecan rhetoric. I have found no mythological allusions in the play, and the only specific reference to one of the gods appears in the choral ode at the end of Act 3.

> Gonfia, Nettuno il mare,
> E con l' acque il terren confond, e mova:
> E sian gli huomini iniqui esca de pesci.

Swell the sea, Neptune, mingle and stir the land with the waters, and let evil men be food for fishes.

When she is depressed the heroine may express Senecan sentiments, but she never harps on them. In the second act she grows weary of her father's persistent nagging and begs him to leave her alone in a speech that may echo Seneca's Hippolytus.

> Padre mio, caro padre, accetta in bene
> I miei poveri detti, e i miei ricordi.

> Diam tempo al tempo: et un volta credi,
> Che chi non regna anchor vive e riposa:
> E meglio chi sta lungi da le Corti
> Respira di quest' aria, e mira il Cielo:
> E più risplende a le campagne il sole,
> Che ne i palazzi, e ne i reali alberghi [2.6].

Father, dear father, kindly accept my poor words and my memories. Let us mark time; and for once believe that he who does not reign yet lives in repose; and it is better to live far from courts and breathe this air and see the sky; and the sun shines more in the fields than in palaces and royal dwellings.

Isandro, exasperated by his daughter's lack of worldly ambition, cries, "It is a fault to nourish their faults with our misfortunes." Hidalba replies, "They may be faults, but they are not sins" (2.6). Anserte, an old man and Hidalba's confidant, sometimes indulges in Senecan fatalism, but never in Senecan rhetoric, as, for example, in his moralizing on the sudden death of Isandro.

> Vedi che duro termine raffrena
> L' humana ambitione.
> Vedi, e vediamo noi,
> Che 'l mondo altro non è, che cieca polve,
> Un baleno gli honor, la fama un tuono [3.6].

You see that a hard end curbs human ambition. You see, and we see, that the world is none other than blind dust, honors a flash of lightning, fame a rumble of thunder.

The figures of speech in *Hidalba* are almost always easy and restrained. From the very opening of the play Hidalba believes that she is wrong in taking the crown from her cousin Armilla. Moreover, she has a premonition that some dark evil is threatening her and her husband.

> Come il Sole a mortali
> I matutini suoi pallidi lumi.
> Temo di me, ma più d' Atirsi io temo.

As the sun [sends] its pale early-morning light to mortals. I fear for myself, but I fear more for Atirsi.

Anserte, who tries to calm her fears, pursues the same figure briefly.

> Che, se l' errante caso
> Assale un dubbio petto,
> Si teme d' ogni incontro,
> Et ogni nube, che compar nel Cielo,
> Par, che gli apporti un mortal tempesta.

If errant chance assails a doubtful breast, it is afraid of every encounter, and every cloud that appears in the sky seems to bring it a deadly storm.

The closest thing to a conceited play on words, and one of the few passages that seems to be inconsistent with the author's anti-Petrarchan style, appears in a choral ode at the end of Act 4.

> Duolsi; e la doglia ha in essa
> Morte; e morte ha il dolor: piange morendo,
> Misserissima figlia, e muor piangendo.

She grieves; and grief is her death, and death is her grief: dying she weeps, most wretched daughter, and weeping she dies.

It must not be supposed, however, that Veniero's characters never express tragic emotions, for sometimes they do, though they make small use of the traditional ornaments of the grand style. The chorus repeatedly expresses alarm for its mistress Hidalba. After news of the *coup d'état* of Tarpace and Armilla, it cries,

> O sposo afflitto, o tormentata figlia,
> O giorno oscuro, o sollevato Regno,
> O d' ardite speranze animo franco [2.6].

O afflicted husband, O tormented daughter, O dark day, O insurgent realm, O free spirit of daring hopes!

Anserte, who feels Hidalba's grief almost as much as she does, has a good opportunity to indulge in high-flown allusions to ice-bound Scythia and the frozen mountains of Caucasus, but instead he says,

> Vattene, fuggi pur sola, e dolente
> Ove notitia d' huom mai non arrive:
> E dove vuoi fuggir? se teco porti
> Tai piaghe aperte del tuo duol nel core?
> Chi ti riceverá? qual lido ignoto,
> Qual cieco bosco, o solitario monte? [3.6].

Go, flee alone and wretched where no notice of man ever reaches. And where do you want to flee if you carry with you such open wounds of grief in your heart? Who will receive you, what unknown shore, what dark forest, or lonely mountain?

Hidalba, as expected, is the most emotional character and she carries the chief burden in the tearful last act. When she sees her husband's body on the bier she faints. She recovers to reproach Armilla, but her thoughts keep returning to her husband.

> E tu diletto sposo,
> Ecco, che liete nozze

Ci ha mantenute il cielo.
Che scetri, che corone
Faranno ambe felici.
Sarà la regia nostra un duro sasso,
Il letto nuttial la terra ignuda:
E i lumi per le feste a pena spenti
Fian per l' esequie tue di nuovo accesi [5.3].

And you, beloved husband, behold what joyful nuptials heaven has held for us. What scepters, what crowns will make both of us happy. A hard stone will be our palace, the bare ground our nuptial couch; and the coronation lights scarce-spent will be newly kindled for your obsequies.

One of the most remarkable examples of restrained speech under strong provocation to indulge in bitter recrimination and threats of revenge is Armilla's remark when she realizes that the coronation ceremonies are about to begin, that her rightful claim to the throne has been set aside.

Hor mio fratello è morto, e io rimango
Figlia sol die miserie unica herede.
Et hoggi è il dì, che s' incorona Hidalba:
Ond' io me ne starò sprezzata, e vile
Spettatrice del fasto e pompa altrui [1.3].

Now my brother is dead, and I, an only daughter, remain sole heir of miseries. And today is the day that Hidalba is crowned; whence I shall stand a despised and lowly spectator of the pride and pomp of others.

Perhaps Tarpace's speeches are most characteristic of Veniero's style; certainly they are realistic and natural, more proper, it may be, to comedy than to neoclassical tragedy. When Armilla promises to marry him if he helps her, he accepts the pact without any bluster or any grandiose appeal to Mars or Bellona.

De l' arme arbitro io solo; hor sequa, hor corra
Danno, ruina, e morti; al fin l' aquisto
E la gloria e maggior, ch 'l danno e 'l rischio [1.3].

I alone assume the authority of arms; now may danger, ruin, and death come running; in the end profit and glory are greater than danger and hazard.

When Armilla refuses to include Hidalba among the enemies that must be destroyed, Tarpace says,

Fia virtù la pietà, se accorta fia:
Ma poco accorta è la pietà dannosa [4.3].

Mercy may be a virtue if it be politic; but if mercy is little politic it is harmful.

Some of the conversation between Tarpace and his lieutenant would be at home on the comic stage. The soldiers have been keeping watch on Hidalba's headquarters, and Tarpace remarks,

> Hai tu veduto il moto
> E 'l modo di fuggir, c' han fatto questi?
> Che quando ci han veduti,
> Ogn' un parea, c' havesse
> A caminar sul foco? [2.7].

Did you see the bustle and the way they fled, how, when they saw us, everyone seemed to have to walk on fire?

If more Italian poets had adopted the methods of Veniero and Aretino, the whole character of Italian tragedy in the sixteenth century would have changed, and doubtless for the better. Aretino and Veniero, however, remained almost alone as poets who sought to bring the same kind of reality to Italian tragedy that Ariosto, Machiavelli, Aretino, Cecchi, and Grazzini brought to Italian comedy. Even the introduction of prose into Italian tragedy was unable to save it from pedantry and affectation, as I shall try to show in the next chapter.

XI

Prose in Italian Tragedy

At the beginning of the sixteenth century the learned dramatists in Italy faced a difficult problem: they wished to write like the Ancients and yet preserve verisimilitude, which demanded the appearance of reality. When they changed from Latin to Italian the demand for realistic dialogue became even more acute. The logical solution, if one were a naturalist, was prose, the language of everyday life, and some of the comic playwrights soon accepted this solution. The first *commedia erudita* in prose was Publio Filippo Mantovano's *Formicone,* first performed at Mantua in 1503.

There was no unanimous acceptance of prose as the proper medium for comedy, however, and many playwrights were of two minds about it. After all, both Terence and Plautus wrote in verse and both Horace and Aristotle apparently regarded verse as necessary for all drama. Certainly neither Horace nor Aristotle recommended prose. Ariosto published a prose version of his *Cassaria* in 1508. Twenty years later he turned it into unrhymed verses called *sdruccioli* (ending in dactyls). Giraldi Cinthio refused to accept prose as proper for either comedy or tragedy. Lodovico Dolce could not make up his mind on whether comedy should use verse or prose; he wrote in both mediums. Even in his comedies written in verse, however, he tried to produce a conversational style. The prologue to his *Il marito* (1545) says:

"Comic verse ought to please him who likes verse because it is altogether easy and flexible, and whosoever prefers prose will find it similar to prose, because he will not know whether it is prose or verse." The comic dramatists did not settle the issue, but continued to use verse in some comedies although the majority were written in prose. Nevertheless, the tendency in the second half of the century was toward a more conversational style in all drama. In his best tragedy, *Marianna*, Dolce promised his audience that it would find "no haughty words or weighty epithets, but smooth discourse and pure, easy speech."

The tragic dramatists were not troubled at first by any such dilemma, for it was almost unthinkable that tragedy could be written in anything but verse and in the high style. Horace and Aristotle agreed that the language of tragedy must be elevated above common speech. The ancient models, Seneca, Sophocles, and Euripides, were poets whose poetry rivaled in majesty the grand style of Virgil and Homer. It was almost unthinkable that tragedy could be written in prose, but not quite; there was Cicero, whose authority was as formidable as that of Horace and Aristotle, whose prose orations and essays rivaled in majesty and elegance the finest poetry of the ancient dramatists and epic poets.

As the "new" drama developed, and as Italian dramatists grew more confident of their powers, it was inevitable that sooner or later some writer would experiment with prose in a tragedy. In 1550, Cavalcanti's *Giuditio,* that criticism of Speroni's *Canace* which explored many dramatic theories and practices, mentioned the idea of prose in tragedy. One of the speakers in the dialogue asks why the writers of vulgar tragedies should not go a step further than unrhymed verse and write their plays in prose. The Florentine (35r) dismisses the query by pointing out that Aristotle considered verse an essential part of tragedy. Toward the end of the century there was considerable critical agitation of the possibility of using prose in all drama. In 1592, Agostino Michele, a Modern and himself the author of a tragedy written mostly in prose, published a *Discorso,* "in which, contrary to the opinions of all the most illustrious writers on the art of poetry, it is clearly shown how comedies and tragedies can be written in prose with much praise." Michele argued that prose had already been successfully used in comedy and that it would also be suitable for tragedy. New times demand new customs. Aristotle himself described the changes that both comedy and tragedy went through in finding the right kind of diction for dialogue. Prose is more verisimilar (lifelike) than verse and will serve the modern audience better than artificial verses, which are removed from everyday speech. In 1600, Paolo Beni, a learned and able critic, published a *Disputatio*, "in which it is shown that it is better to release comedy and tragedy from the fetters of meters." Beni's argument in favor of prose in the theater was based on Horace's "to teach and to delight" and on the assumption that the popular audience is unlearned and therefore unable to understand anything save plain language, that is, prose.

These attempts by critics to establish prose as the proper language for tragedy as well as for comedy did not pass unchallenged. Faustino Summo, a Grecian who attacked both tragedy with a happy ending and pastoral tragicomedy, tried to refute the arguments of Michele and Beni.[1] Summo had no quarrel with the necessity of verisimilitude in the drama, but his interpretation of verisimiltude differed from Michele's and Beni's. As an Aristotelian Grecian, Summo believed that verisimilitude in comedy and tragedy meant not so much a mirror of life as an idealization of life, not what is but what ought to be. Poetry is speech raised above everyday speech and for that very reason is more delightful than prose.

Even before the publication of Cavalcanti's *Giuditio* and over forty years before the critical wrangles between Michele, Beni, and Summo at least one learned Italian wrote a so-called tragedy in prose. About 1546-47,[2] a long play in Italian prose called *Tragedia intitolata Libero Arbitrio* appeared. The author was Francesco Negro Bassanese, a Benedictine who left the order, crossed the Alps to Strasbourg, returned to Italy a militant Protestant and anti-Trinitarian. He ran a humanistic school at Chiavenna (near Lake Como) for a while, moved to nearby Tirana, and thence to Poland, where he died. His play was translated into French at Villefranche in 1558, into Latin at Geneva in 1559, and then into English as *A Certayne tragedie written first in Italian,*

---

[1] See the ninth discourse in *Discorsi poetici* (Padua, 1600) and *Risposta in difesa del metro nelle poesie, et nei poemi, et in particolare nelle tragedie e comedie* (Padua, 1601).
[2] Neri (p. 126, n. 2) says that the first edition, which he had never seen, was printed in 1546–47. Allacci lists a 1549 printing. The Illinois copy is the second edition of 1550.

by F.N.B. entituled Freewyl, and translated into Englishe, by
Henry Cheeke.[3]

Negro's play is not a right tragedy, nor a true morality, but a
hybrid, partly neoclassical and partly medieval. It owes something,
it may be, to the popular sacre rappresentazioni, but more to the
Latin school drama known as the Christian Terence. It has five
acts divided into scenes. It starts in medias res, on the day that
news of the Protestant rebellion in Germany reaches Rome. All
the scenes take place in a Roman piazza, and apparently all the
action happens in one day. Nevertheless, the characters do suggest
a morality; some are realistic, some supernatural, some allegorical:
for example, a pilgrim Fabio, a steward Felino, a notary Trifone,
a barber Bertuccio, the apostles Pietro and Paolo, the archangel
Raphaele, a king Libero Arbitrio, a secretary Discorso Humano, a
royal steward Atto Elicito (Unlawful Act), and Signora Gratia
Giustificante (Lady Grace Justifying).

The apostle Paul explains to the barber, the real hero of the
play, why he is witnessing a tragedy: "But do you know, Bertuccio,
in what way this fellow [Free Will] is king? I wish to tell you;
in the same way as are the kings of tragedies performed in theaters,
for many times a very poor and very mean man appears there in
the dress and form of a king and makes a show of having very
great power and dominion, but everything is nevertheless fabulous
and counterfeit" (O3v). In other words, the play exhibits the downfall of a king, albeit a false king. Free Will has a small role; he
appears in only one scene (2.1).

Negro's Free Will is actually more like comedy than tragedy.
It is written in conversational prose, makes a hero out of a humble
barber, and contains some humor in addition to many satirical
thrusts at the pretensions and vices of the papacy and Roman
clergy. Negro's chief model may well have been Pammachius, by
Thomas Naogeorgus (Kirchmeyer), a tragoedia nova in Latin verse,
first printed at Wittenberg in 1538. This first edition has a poem
by the author addressed to "Doctor Martin Luther, notable professor of sacred literature." Kirchmeyer's play is a violent attack
on the papacy. It has realistic, supernatural, and allegorical characters, such as a servant named Dromo, Satan, Peter, Paul, Anti-

---

[3] The Short-Title Catalogue gives [London, 1589], but the date is disputed.
The English translation is lively but not always accurate.

christ (Pammachius), and Truth. A few samples from Negro's play will illustrate the Italian's use of satire and humor.

Diaconato, master of the household of Master Clergy and the only subtle character in the play, is fond of irony. He offers the steward an etymology of the word *cardinal*, which he explains as the creeping in of extra letters into *carnal*. The four cardinal virtues, he says, are "rapine, ingratitude, sodomy, and apostacy" (C7). And he speaks of the pope's maintaining his cardinals and other high clergy in "all the pomp, triumph, pride, grandeur, play, pleasure, sport, wantonness, delicacy, and Sybaritic and Sardanapalus lives as cannot be imagined in this world" (D1). Of course these luxuries are no longer considered sins or vices in the clergy, though they are still sins and vices in the laity. Diaconato advises the steward, however, to stifle his doubts about the church. "Do you not see," he says, "that if we should not trust in the divine theologians and sacred canonists, who hold fast the monarchy of the pope with their arguments, a good part of us would have to make our living with a mattock in hand?" (N5). When Diaconato says good-by to the pilgrim there is the following exchange.

Diaconato: Then as you please, go with *buona ventura.*

Fabio: I don't want to go with Bonaventura, nor with Scotus, nor with Thomas Aquinas, the monkish grasshoppers, but with Morgan Corse, skipper of the brigantine.

Diaconato: You never forget your quips, M. Fabio. But go with God [D2].

Amonio, a chancellor, explains to the barber that the terms "obedience," "poverty," and "chastity," directives for all monks, constitute a rhetorical figure called *antiphrasis,* that is, "when, either in jest or for some other reason, we use a word in the opposite of its original sense" (F3). The barber Bertuccio (Ape), a cousin of the famous Pasquino, is a comic figure for the first three acts as he mutters objections to himself while listening to the discourses of the Roman churchmen, but becomes serious when Peter and Paul expound the Christian doctrine to him in the last two acts.

Negro's argument runs as follows:

Signor Free Will, son of Signora Reason and of Signora Will, prince of human operations, was brought by means of the scholastic theologians to dwell in Rome, where, being made a Christian papist and moreover a most invincible king by the pope, he received from his holiness the crown of the kingdom of good works. Afterwards, by means of Signor Unlawful Act, master of his household, having earned a marriage with Signora Congruous, he begat by her Signora Worthy.[4] And so living happily with his family in his kingdom for a long time, he extracted by means of imposts on merit a very large quantity of treasure. At length understanding through letters from King Ferdinand [the emperor] brought by Dr. Eck[5] about the rebellion of many of his subjects, he labored with the pope to make some provision for such disorder. But while they went about this, Signora Grace Justifying, sent from Heaven to earth by God to make it good, secretly beheaded the king. And the pope, finally exposed as the true Antichrist, received from God the sentence to be destroyed little by little with the divine word.

The heart of the theological argument advanced by the author is found in the third and fourth acts. The name of Free Will, says Paul, "was invented by the devil to make the world believe that his power is greater than that of the Lord God, he being able to do good and evil as he wishes and God unable to do anything but good and no evil (O3). As Raphael later adds, Free Will is arrogant and presumptuous, challenging the omnipotence of God.

Negro's purpose was religious propaganda, not the arousal and relief of pity and fear. Nevertheless, as I have already mentioned, he preserved several mechanical features of neoclassical tragedy. The climax of the action, that is, the destruction of Free Will, was contrived in the approved manner: the evil king is executed offstage and his death is reported, first by rumor and then at first hand, by Grace Justifying, who performed the deed herself in the same way as "Judith did to Holofernes."

There is no questioning Negro's acquaintance with classical and neoclassical drama. He knew that he was not writing a popular *sacra rappresentazione*. It should be emphasized, however, that the popular religious plays underwent considerable modification in the sixteenth century when they were written by playwrights trained in the learned comedy or tragedy. And religious plays, although considered old-fashioned and somewhat vulgar, continued to offer entertainment at carnivals and continued to attract the attention of some learned playwrights.[6] Anton Francesco Grazzini and Giovanni Maria Cecchi, masters of the *commedia erudita*, also

---

[4] As the author explains, *Gratia de congruo* and *Gratia di condigno* are scholastic terms meaning merit acquired by honest behavior and merit acquired by duty and reason.

[5] One of Luther's most formidable opponents.

[6] Doglio (pp. lvii ff.) argues convincingly that the tragic dramatists of the *riforma cattolica* exerted a significant influence on Italian tragedy. Many of these reform plays were in Latin.

wrote *commedie spirituali*. Luigi Groto, author of learned tragedies, comedies, and pastorals, was the author of *Lo Isach, rappresentation nova*, first published at Venice in 1586. Grazzini, Cecchi,
and Groto brought the religious play up to date; that is, they gave
it the form of neoclassical drama.

Giovanni Francesco Alberti's *Oloferne* (Ferrara, 1594) provides a
good late example of the Italian biblical tragedy arranged according to Aristotelian rules and neoclassical practice. The unities of
time and place are strictly observed. The author added a love affair
to the well-known Old Testament story of Judith and Holofernes.

The best neoclassical biblical play by an Italian, so far as I know,
is Gironimo Giustiniano's *Iephte* (Parma, 1583), as good a tragedy
as the "pagan" dramas by Cinthio and Dolce. It is Grecian in form,
that is, arranged as prologues, episodes, and choruses. The unities
are carefully preserved. The characters, especially Jephthah, his
wife, and daughter, come to life. There is genuine pathos in some
of the scenes between father and daughter, and the last words of
the daughter, just before she goes offstage to be sacrificed, are
worthy of comparison with the celebrated farewell address to the
Sun by Racine's Phèdre (see below, p. 285):

> Et tu della mia vita ultimo giorno;
> Ch' ancor sereno io veggio, ecco, ti lascio.

And thou, the last day of my life, which, I see, art still calm and clear, lo,
I leave thee.

In 1586, at Florence, there appeared a *tragedia spirituale* entitled *David sconsolato*, which provides another good example of
what happened to many religious plays in Italy in the second half
of the century. The author was Pier Giovanni Brunetto, a Franciscan
friar and a learned man. His *tragedia spirituale* is not very different from other learned Italian tragedies which make no claim to
religious spirituality. In other words, *David sconsolato* is not a
history but a tightly constructed play. It has the usual prologue,
which is delivered by a nameless adulterous son of David,[7] who
has risen from "Avernus" to witness the disaster brought on his
father's house by the revolt of Absalom. David is the central figure,
a tragic hero, and all the scenes point toward his heart-rending
lament in the last act—"O Absalom my son." Although the char-

---

[7] This seven-day-old infant may have been suggested by Canace's nameless infant in the first scene of Speroni's *Canace*. See above, p. 119.

acters make a point of separating the God of Israel from Jove, Mars, Apollo, and Pan, classical allusions crop up from time to time. Just before his suicide, for example, Achitophel indulges in a complaint that seems more appropriate to a classical tragedy: "Aye-me, what river, either Don, or Nile, or furious Tigris, or fierce Rhine, or gold-rich Tagus, will be able to cleanse the blood of my cause?" (p. 104). Achitophel hangs himself onstage. Such death scenes, however, are far from rare in the learned tragedy. Brunetto's versification is conventional, largely eleven-syllable *versi sciolti* with some unrhymed *settenarii* and rhymed choral odes.[8]

More interesting, and more to the point in this chapter, is Giambattista Velo's *Tamar, attione tragica rappresentata nella Città di Vicenza dalla Compagnia Nuova l'anno M.D.LXXXVI,*[9] which might be called a prose rival of *David sconsolato*. Every element in *Tamar* is strictly neoclassical save the dialogue, which is all prose. The prologue is in eleven-syllable *versi sciolti* and unrhymed *settenarii,* the choral odes in the same measures.

Velo's use of prose in a "regular" tragedy was apparently accidental rather than calculated. According to the address to the reader appended to the printed version, the author was reluctant to have his tragedy published in its original form, and he explained that he used prose only because the play had to be written in a few hours and because some of the actors could not handle verse. Every literate person knows, he admitted, that "tragic matter ought to be written in verse."

The argument of *Tamar* was based on ancient history, that is, on the history of the ancient Hebrews. Velo was not a good dramatist, or he was too hurried, and he contented himself with a close following of the biblical account, merely supplying missing dialogue and dutifully compressing the events into a single day, the scenes into a single scene before the royal palace in Jerusalem. In other words, he adopted the approved method of contemporary tragic dramatists. Moreover, he tried to alter the emphasis of the

---

[8] *David sconsolato* offers an instructive comparison and contrast with George Peele's *Love of David and Fair Bathsabe, with the Tragedy of Absalon,* which appeared about the same time or only a few years after 1587. The English play has no division into acts; it begins with the love affair of David and Bathsheba and proceeds through the death of Uriah, the rape of Thamar, the stabbing of Amnon, the revolt and death of Absalom, to the mourning of David.
[9] Published at Vicenza in 1586.

biblical account and of most plays on the subject, for he chose to write a *Tamar*, not a *David*.

The tragedy in the biblical account is David's loss of a beloved son. Velo tried to shift the spotlight to Thamar, whose tragedy is the loss of a beloved brother, the brother who had avenged her honor by killing her ravisher. The sixteenth-century Thamar finds herself in a tragic dilemma: she will be left desolate if her father is killed in the civil war; she will be left desolate if her brother is killed. "If I had this life from my father, yet from my brother I have recovered my honor, than which there can be no more precious jewel on earth" (3.3). The change was doubtless dictated by the Italian fashion in tragedy, the fashion set by Cinthio, whose protagonists were always women jealous of their honor. Velo was not successful, however, for his Thamar is scarcely more prominent than Bathsheba or David or Absalom, and not so dramatic a character as Achitophel. Velo failed to keep the spotlight squarely on his heroine.

The prologue, spoken by the ghost of Amnon, who has risen from hell to witness revenge for his own death, harks back to Seneca's *Thyestes*, Cinthio's *Orbecche,* and a host of preceding Italian tragedies. Amnon, it may be recalled, was killed by Absalom for ravishing their sister Thamar. The ghost has leave until sunset, so the action must be completed in a single day.

The opening speech of the queen Bathsheba talking to her nurse expresses a sentiment already shopworn by 1586:

Bene, ahi lassa, conosco, che alcuno felice, o beato chiamar non si può; mentre in questo carcere di miserie si trova [1.1].

I know truly, alas, that no one can be called happy or blessed while he is still in this prison of miseries.

Bathsheba says that she was formerly the happiest and most exalted of women, but now she is the most unfortunate, a "model of the instability of these worldly riches and honors." The nurse coaxes her to unburden her mind of grievous pangs, and so the queen proceeds to deliver the exposition.

Tamar follows the normal pattern of Italian tragedy. Most of the events take place outside Jerusalem and have to be reported. Absalom chooses the strategy of Chusai (one of David's henchmen) over that of his counselor Achitophel, who then hangs himself. The rebel forces are beaten and Absalom killed. News of his death is brought to Jerusalem by Chusai in the last act. When David asks about his son, Chusai replies, "Absalom (and I am sorry to say it) has arrived at that end to which every mortal is eternally destined" (5.2).[10] David mourns. A maiden reports that Thamar is dying. The old nurse had performed a mercy killing; she had given Thamar a cup of wine with poison in it. Thamar is brought onstage for the death scene.

David: Deh figliuola cara come mi voi lasciare? come presto ne vai.
Tamar: Altro non posso: Io vo.
David: Ohimè.
Tamar: Restate in pace: a Dio.
Donzella: Ohimè, Signora nostra.
David: O cuore, o cuore sopra tutti addolorato: o padre, o padre ne i figli più d' ogn' altro infelice, et in che stato ti trovi? [5.4].

David: Dear daughter, pray, how can you leave me? How soon you go.
Thamar: I cannot do otherwise. I go.
David: Aye-me!
Thamar: Rest in peace. Good-by.
Maiden: Aye-me, our mistress.
David: O heart, O heart more sorrowful than all others, O father, O father more unhappy than any other in his children, and in what state are you now?

The chorus ends the play with a short ode.

In my judgment, Velo's play suffers no disadvantage by being written in prose, for to most modern ears prose is preferable to mediocre verse. Velo used both chorus and messenger in the Cinthian manner although the messengers always speak prose and the chorus speaks prose unless it is delivering an ode at the end of an act.

A fair specimen of Velo's poetic chorus is the following extract from the ode at the end of Act 2.

> Questa vita mortal che a tanti, e tanti
> Mali soggiace ogn' hora,
> (Quasi Nave tra l' onde, e venti posta)
> Par che giammai si fermi
> In un stato medesimo; e i giorni, e l' hore,

[10] The *Bibia volgare* (Venice, 1566) reads: "Alqual rispondendo Chusi disse, i nemici del mio Signor re, et tutti quelli si levano contra di esso in male siano fatti come il putto."

E i mesi, e gli anni sono
Sempre penosi, e sempre
L' un mal succede all' altro. . . .

It seems that this mortal life, which submits every hour to so many many
evils (like a ship placed between waves and winds) never stays still in
the same order; and the days and hours and months and years are always
painful, and always one evil succeeds another.

Velo made his chorus follow the prescription of Horace: it favors
the good characters and gives them wholesome counsel. Thus the
women of the chorus try to comfort Bathsheba, who is convinced
that ruin is imminent:

Dopo il bene il male; et dopo il male, il bene succeda però nelle pro-
sperità si deve temere; et nella avversità sperare [3.2].

After good evil; and after evil good may succeed; therefore one should
fear in prosperity, hope in adversity.

The servant who reports the suicide of Achitophel is reminiscent
of the Senecan-Cinthian messenger. He has worked himself into
a frenzy of grief and horror; but he never offends decorum by
alluding to Greek mythology in a Hebraic setting.

Dove ne vado ahi lasso? come da me fia raccontata si dolorosa nova? con
quali parole esprimer potrò sì horribile successo? che solo a ramentarlo
tutto d' horrore pavento [3.4].

Alas, where am I going? How may I recount such grievous news? With
what words will I be able to express such a horrible event? For in merely
recalling it I am overwhelmed with horror.

Like the messengers in *Thyestes* and *Orbecche,* he expresses himself pretty well after he warms to his work; he regales the chorus
with a detailed account of Achitophel's hanging himself from a
beam in his study.

Four years after Agostino Michele argued in print for prose
tragedy his *Cianippo* was published at Bergamo.[11] This play is in
prose throughout excepting the choral odes at the end of Acts
1–4, which are in rhymed and unrhymed *settenarii.* Michele made
extensive use of two choruses (one female, one male); one or another, or both, of them appears in every scene save one (4.3),
which is a soliloquy by a courtier. The choruses always speak
prose when engaged in dialogue. Even the prologue, delivered by
Bacchus, is in prose.

---

[11] *Cianippo tragedia di Agostino Michele,* Bergamo, 1596.

The use of prose, however, is Michele's only departure from the approved course of neoclassical tragedy. As he acknowledged in his address to the reader, he found his argument in ancient history, in the nineteenth section of Plutarch's *Parallel Histories of Greeks and Romans,* the gist of which runs as follows. Cyanippus of Syracuse neglected sacrifices to Bacchus. Whereupon the god made him drunk. In his drunkenness he ravished his only daughter Cyane. Later, when a plague broke out in the city and the Pythian oracle recommended the sacrifice of an incestuous person, Cyane stabbed her father and then killed herself.

Michele did his best to transform this sensational but meager story into a lofty tragedy with complex plot. He elevated Cianippo to the throne of a great kingdom and surrounded him with a counselor, high priest, courtiers, *cameriere,* and a chorus of men. Ciane became a princess provided with a faithful nurse and a chorus of sympathetic women. He created some motivation for the outlandish behavior of the characters and created scenes of recognition and reversal of fortune. Ciane discovers the identity of her ravisher —the crime was committed in a dark underground passage—by means of a ring that fell to the ground in the struggle. When she learns that her own father is her betrayer she assumes that he deliberately violated her to prevent her joining the virgin votaries of Diana. After she has mortally wounded him she learns that he unwittingly attacked her while under the spell of drunkenness. Then she repents and turns upon herself as the "most wicked murderess that ever was of an innocent man" (37r).

Ahi me misera, ahi me infelice, che strana et horibile metamorfose ha in me veduto l' universo? poichè per esser stimata pia, in un momento empia son rimasta.

Alas miserable me, alas unhappy me, what strange and horrible metamorphosis the universe has beheld in me, since in trying to be esteemed pious I am left in a moment impious.

Ciane's suicide becomes a more or less inevitable solution of a hopeless situation and the princess stabs herself with the same bloodstained dagger she had used on her father. Her death is offstage. Although Cianippo is stabbed onstage, he is carried into the palace to die. Michele was careful to preserve classical decorum throughout the tragedy.

At first glance it looks as though the author has violated the

classical economy of time, for his play begins *ab ovo,* with the
sinister promise of Bacchus that Cianippo "will prove to be in
future ages a tragic subject no less famous and no less celebrated
than Oedipus." Nevertheless, Michele crowded all the events (the
drunken frenzy of the king, the outbreak of the plague, the assassination of the king, and the suicide of Ciane) into one day. The
parallels with Oedipus appear in the third and fourth acts, when
Cianippo is trying to find the cause of the plague, that is, the
incestuous person who has called down the punishment of the gods.

Since *Cianippo* is conventional Italian tragedy of the sixteenth
century in subject matter, structure, and characterization, the most
interesting feature is the style. Even here, however, Michele offered
no startling innovations beyond the mechanical change from verse
to prose, for he still tried to write in the elevated style long recommended for tragedy. His aim in turning from verse to prose
may have been greater verisimilitude, or a more natural speech,
but he was unwilling to go so far as did Ruzzante (Angelo Beolco),
an early naturalist in comedy. After a few plays in verse, Ruzzante,
in the late 1520's, turned to prose, even to peasant dialects, because prose was more natural, because prose could be less literary
than verse. Apparently Michele did not share Ruzzante's distrust
of literary styles in the drama.

Consequently the author of *Cianippo* usually wrote in rather
elaborate Ciceronian periods that are carefully balanced, often
antithetical, often rising to amplifications. The speech of the characters is anything but naturalistic. Even in crucial scenes, wherein
the authors of verse tragedy often wrote straightforward easy dialogue, Michele was busy with his artful rhetoric. The best dramatic
dialogue in the play comes late in the fourth act, when Ciane learns
from the high priest who the owner of the ring is, that is, who her
ravisher is. The following passage is not bad dialogue, yet it certainly bears the mark of contrivance.

Sacerdote: Dirollovi volontieri perch' è conoscente vostro.

Ciane: Io lo conosco?

Sacerdote: Non sol lo conoscete, ma con sommo ossequio lo riverite.

Ciane: Ahimè io lo riverisco?

Sacerdote: Anzi che non pur lo conoscete, e lo riverite, ma non men che
voi stessa l' amate.

Ciane: Ahimè misera, ahimè infelice io l' amo?

Sacerdote: Cianippo padre vostro, e Re vostro, ha l' annello come suo a me chiesto, et allui da me l' annello, come suo, è stato restituito [30v].

Priest: I will tell you willingly because he is an acquaintance of yours.

Ciane: I know him?

Priest: Not only do you know him, but you revere him with the highest respect.

Ciane: Alas, I revere him?

Priest: In fact, not only do you know him and revere him, but you love him no less than you love yourself.

Ciane: Aye-me miserable, aye-me unhappy, I love him?

Priest: Cianippo your father, and your king, has asked me for the ring as his, and the ring has been returned by me to him as his.

The nurse, who loves Ciane and always takes her part, is profoundly shocked by the news of the rape, and bursts into a wail of anguish. After the first broken ejaculations, however, she settles down into balanced periods.

Che cosa orribile odo io? ohime infelice. Ditemi, dolcissima figliuola mia, come? quando? dove? da cui? Oh cielo, perch' acconsenti a malvagità sì grave? O terra, perchè sì abbominevol mostro patientemente sostieni? [13v].

What horrible thing do I hear? O me unhappy! Tell me, sweetest daughter, how, when, where, by whom? O heaven, why do you assent to such noisesome wickedness? O earth, why do you suffer patiently such an abominable monster?

Even in her last speech, after the death of Ciane, when the old woman is in despair, she carefully preserves her artful periods.

Ah dolcissima figliuola mia già queste poppe vi diedero per tributo il latte; hor quest' occhi vi consacrano le lagrime, e tosto queste vene vi conduceranno in sacrificio il sangue. Vi diedi il primo cibo nella vita vi darò l' ultime esequie nella morte [40r].

Ah sweetest daughter, these breasts once gave you their milk in tribute; now these eyes hallow my tears for you, and soon these veins will bring my blood in sacrifice for you. I gave you the first nourishment in your life, I will give you the last funeral rites in your death.

Two more extracts from *Cianippo* will sufficiently illustrate Michele's prose style in tragedy. It matters little what character we choose, for they all speak more or less alike, from the god Bacchus down to the nurse and *cameriere*.

The formal style appears at the very beginning, in the prologue spoken by Bacchus.

Sopportar dunque più non debbo, che la mia Deità dal mondo tutto perch' è buona amata, perch' è possente riverita, perch' è giusta temuta sia, da te solo Cianippo hor vilipesa, biasmata, calpestata. . . . Son io forse di minor grado fra gli Dei in cielo, od a loro d' inferior possanza fra gli huomini in terra? la mia gratia non ti è stata cara, non ti è stato grato il mio amore, ti sarà nimica la mia ira, e ti sarà avversario il mio furore, e provarai tuo mal grado quanto possa giustissimo sdegno d' un Dio contra la vana et sciocca alterezza d' un huomo mortale [1v–1r].

Therefore I ought no longer to tolerate that my divinity, which is well loved by the whole world, mightily revered, justly feared, should now be despised, reproached, trampled upon by you alone, Cianippo. . . . Am I perhaps of minor rank among the gods in heaven or with less power than theirs among men on earth? My favor has not been esteemed by you, my love has not been acceptable to you; my wrath will be your enemy, and my fury will be your adversary, and despite yourself you will show how much the most righteous scorn of a god may be able to do to the vain and stupid pride of a mortal man.

Another characteristic passage comes from a speech by the counselor to the high priest.

Come la Natura ha sciolto ogni legame al mio pensiero; affine che liberamente dir io vi possa, che Bacco non con la guerra come Marte, non con la pestilenza come Diana, non con la sterilità come Cerere, non co' l fulmine come Giove, ma solo col vino punir ci puote [4r].

Since nature has loosed every bond from my thought, so I may freely tell you that Bacchus cannot punish us with war as does Mars, not with pestilence as does Diana, not with barrenness as does Ceres, not with the thunderbolt as does Jove, but only with wine.

It cannot be said that prose made a big splash in the now well-charted sea of Italian tragedy; but in the next century it became the accepted medium for tragicomedies as well as for comedies, and it reappeared in tragedy. The opposition to prose in tragedy continued, however, headed by Aristotelians who kept repeating the same arguments advanced in the sixteenth century by Cavalcanti and Summo. For example, Giovanni Battista Filippo Ghirardelli, a Roman *letterato* whose name has been kept alive by Corneille's favorable mention of him in the *Discours de la tragédie*,[12] offered a prose tragedy, *Costantino*, at Rome in 1653.[13] His play was vehemently attacked by the conservative critics. Ghirar-

---

[12] Corneille, referring to Italian writers of tragedy, spoke of "un de leurs plus beaux esprits, Jean-Baptiste Ghirardelli."
[13] The Illinois copy is the second edition (Rome, 1660), which contains the author's defense of prose tragedy.

delli answered with a *Difesa dalle opposizioni fatte alla sua tragedia del Costantino* in 1660. The leading argument of the enemy,
according to the *Difesa* (p. 34), was that "Aristotle in the definition of tragedy had established verse as an essential part."

Ghirardelli's long wearisome play (189 pages) is written entirely in prose. There is no chorus. The plot is extremely complicated. The argument was based on a shameful episode in the
life of Constantine the Great, namely, the emperor's jealousy of
Crispus, a son by his first wife, whom he had put to death. The
Italian playwright introduced numerous complications in a manner more reminiscent of tragicomedy than of Roman tragedy.
For example, he introduced Constantine's first wife, presumed
dead, disguised as a man. Crispus is disguised as one Varus and
is madly in love with Valeria, daughter of his father's enemy
Mazentius, a rival emperor. Valeria pretends to be estranged from
her father and comes to Constantine's camp in order to stir up
rebellion among his troops. Afranius, Mazentius' general, appears
disguised as a common soldier. Constantine's second wife, Fausta,
falls in love with her stepson Crispus, who never has a chance to
survive this formidable array of friends and enemies. Whose
tragedy emerges from this plethora of complications it is hard to
determine; but the author maintained, in the *argomento*, that
Constantine was "destined in the drama to arouse wonder (*maraviglia*) in theaters with the representation of an Augustus once
dreadful to the universe, then because of human pride become
the sport of Fortune and the Fable of Buskins."

Costantino was no better calculated to win a large following for
prose tragedy than were *Tamar* and *Cianippo*. It is not a good
play by any standards, Aristotelian or modern. Contrary to the
hopes of its exponents in the late sixteenth and early seventeenth
centuries, prose did not bring greater verisimilitude to Italian
tragedy. As Bertana (p. 217) has said, "The invading prose did
not rejuvenate or revive our theater; in fact, it increased, if that
was possible, its pallor and weakness. The fact is that short lines
merely became long, certain singsongs and cadences broke down,
but the rest remained unchanged; the subjects, the dramatic coin-
cidences, the situations, the passions, the characters, the episodes,
the style were always what they were before."

XII

Italy's Contribution to Tragedy

There is no doubt about the importance of Italian influence on Renaissance drama outside Italy. It is extremely difficult, however, when studying this influence, to separate Italian plays from *novelle*, histories, and dramatic theory, and this difficulty faces students of both French and English drama. It is clear that French and English playwrights borrowed much from the Italians, but what they took from *novelle* and histories and criticism and what they took directly from plays is far from clear.

In France, Italian models were apparently more numerous for comedy and tragicomedy than for tragedy. An important predecessor of Molière and the man who naturalized the *commedia erudita* in France, Pierre Larivey, adapted no less than twelve Italian comedies into French prose between 1579 and 1611. Tasso's *Aminta* and Guarini's *Pastor fido* were well known in France, and Jean Mairet, in the preface to his *Sylvanire* (1631), acknowledged that he had arranged his tragicomedy in the classical-Italian pattern of *prologue, protasis, epitasis,* and *catastrophe*: "This division is according to the order of Terence's comedies, which Tasso and Guarini have punctually observed." (It was Giraldi Cinthio who introduced the Terentian order into tragedy as well as into tragicomedy.) Mairet also followed the Italians as models of style: "I have taken the modern Italians as models and followed their example as much as I could in the propriety of matter and words, avoiding their obstrusive and vicious affectation of conceits [*pointes*] and antitheses . . . supporting my reasonings by *sententiae* and proverbs, and above all never straying from my subject to indulge in the description of a wilderness or a brook." As Lancaster has said, Mairet experimented with the rules, "but the experiment worked."[1] These rules were the Italian dramatic rules, which had been worked out in accord with the authority of Horace and Aristotle and with the practice of Terence and Seneca. Mairet's masterpiece, *Sophonisbe* (1634), the first strictly "regular" French tragedy, firmly established the rules in France. And *Sophonisbe* owed much to Trissino's *Sofonisba*, which had been twice translated into French during the preceding century, into prose by Mellin de Saint-Gelais about 1559, into verse by Claude Mermet in 1585.

It seems, then, that the principal Italian stimulus to neoclassical French tragedy, the tragedy that culminated in the plays of Corneille and Racine, came from the Grecian Trissino, not from the more productive Giraldi Cinthio and his followers. Cinthio's *Orbecche* was the most important tragedy in the sixteenth century, but its author was mainly known outside Italy for his *novelle*, which provided the plots of *Orbecche* and his tragedies with a happy ending. I can find no evidence that *Orbecche* served as a model for any French dramatist although some of its techniques appeared again and again in French tragedy.

The story of Italian influence on Elizabethan drama is parallel to that in France. In England also there is more evidence of Italian models in comedy and tragicomedy than in tragedy. Several Elizabethan-Jacobean playwrights, major and minor, professional and academic, made use of Italian comedies, for example Ben Jonson, George Chapman, John Marston, Anthony Munday, Abraham Fraunce, Walter Hawkesworth, Samuel Brooke, George Ruggle, Thomas Tomkis.[2] Tasso's *Aminta* and Guarini's *Pastor fido* were also well known in England and helped to shape English pastorals and tragicomedies. In tragedy, however, there are few examples of English adaptations or translations from the Italian. George Gascoigne's *Jocasta* (1566) was a translation of Dolce's

---

[1] *History of French Dramatic Literature in the Seventeenth Century* (Baltimore, 1929–42) 1.754.
[2] See my *Italian Comedy in the Renaissance*.

play. Cupid's speech in the prologue to *Gismond of Salerne* (1567–68) was taken from Dolce's *Didone*, but there is no evidence that the authors knew Pistoia's *Filostrato e Panfila;* they probably found their argument in Boccaccio's *novella*. Then there is William Alabaster's Latin *Roxana* (1632), an adaptation of Groto's *Dalida*. So far as I know, that is about all we can be sure of. I have found no evidence that English dramatists imitated either Trissino's *Sofonisba* or Cinthio's *Orbecche*.

Every student of Elizabethan drama, nevertheless, knows that English tragedy between Gascoigne and Shirley is teeming with Italian plots, characters, and stylistic devices. We speak glibly of "Italianate" plays although we never define "Italianate" with any precision. The Italian influence is there, however. Vernon Lee, in her essay "The Italy of the Elizabethan Dramatists,"[3] has written eloquently and perceptively of the fascination exerted on our puritanical forefathers by the "splendid and triumphant wickedness of Italy." And, she says, "The dramatic grandeur, the pschological interest, the mysterious fascination of Italian crime impressed most of all the men whose work was with the dramatic and psychological—the Elizabethan playwrights. The crimes of Italy furnished the subjects of nearly half of the tragedies written in the reigns of Elizabeth and James I." The Italian Rébora agrees in the main with Lee: "The profound art and poetry of the greatest among the Elizabethans gathered this enormous vitality of sentiments and of passions, good and evil, from Italy."[4] Fredson Bowers, who knows Elizabethan tragedy as well as anyone, is more restrained but hardly less emphatic: "Italian stories and characters, in especial, dominated the Elizabethan tragic stage and had a profound effect on the type of play produced."[5]

Elizabethan tragedy was largely Italianate, but the contribution of Italy came more, it may be, from *novelle*, histories, and hair-raising stories brought home by English travelers than from a study of the plays of Trissino, Aretino, Cinthio, Speroni, and Groto. Nevertheless, we cannot altogether discount the plays and the Italian actors who performed them, for some Elizabethans did know something about Italian tragedy. The members of the *commedia dell' arte* included England as well as Paris in some of their

[3] In *Euphorion* (1884).
[4] P. 205.
[5] *Elizabethan Revenge Tragedy*, p. 47.

tours, and they occasionally played tragedies as well as comedies. Hieronimo's play within a play in Kyd's *Spanish Tragedy* is an Italianate tragedy with an "Italian dame" as heroine. When Balthazar suggests that a comedy might be more suitable for amateur actors, Hieronimo replies,

> A comedy?
> Fie, comedies are fit for common wits:
> But to present a kingly troop withal,
> Give me a stately-written tragedy,
> *Tragedia cothurnata*, fitting kings,
> Containing matter, and not common things.
> My lords, all this must be performed
> As fitting for the first night's reveling.
> The Italian tragedians were so sharp of wit,
> That in one hour's meditation
> They would perform anything in action [4.1].

There is no doubt about the admiration of Elizabethans for Italy and Italian art, but one thing that has bothered literary historians and critics is the inferior quality of sixteenth-century Italian tragedy as compared with the best Italianate tragedies of England and France. Perhaps this phenomenon should not vex us, for the theater has always provided numerous examples of good plays based on poorly written stories and of good plays that are remakes of earlier greatly inferior plays. Shakespeare alone provides enough examples of this practice to convince us that the quality of the source or influence may not affect the quality of the finished product. In Italian literature, for example, Boccaccio was a first-rate writer of prose; but Boccaccio's stories, while repeatedly used by the best Elizabethan poets, including Shakespeare, were probably not so eagerly read as those of Bandello, who was scarcely a second-rate writer. Creizenach has suggested as much: "Particularly in the blood and vengeance tragedies we can constantly realize how the [Elizabethan] poets' imaginations had been fired by those tales treating of a 'bellissima vendetta,' which Bandello especially relates with such grim enjoyment."[6] Even so, some explanation of the seeming paradox of poor Italian *novelle* and tragedies contributing to good English tragedies may be in order, and I shall try to show why Italian tragedy of the Renaissance was inferior to the English and French and then why it nevertheless

---

[6] *Geschichte des neueren Dramas* (Halle, 1909) 4.223.

was necessary to the development of great tragic dramatists like Shakespeare and Racine.

Twentieth-century Italian critics have been ready enough to admit that their countrymen's tragedies in the sixteenth century cannot match the best English and French tragedies of the seventeenth. I have already quoted Rébora's acknowledgement that there is nothing in seven centuries of Italian drama that can boast of a scene "so pathetic, so intensely human, so exquisitely poetical" as the death of Webster's Duchess of Malfi. Bertana (pp. 104–105) explains the sterility of the Italian tragic dramatists as the result of accepting the "double yoke of imitation and the rules," that is, the slavish copying of Seneca or Euripides or some earlier Italian poet and the painstaking observance of the Aristotelian rules. This yoke, Bertana believes, condemned the Italians to emphasizing plot and neglecting characterization. Aristotle had said that there can be a good tragedy without characters, but none without a plot. Bertana believes that the Italians followed this dictum too carefully, and consequently their characters lack individuality and, what is worse, psychological depth.

Since it may be unfair to compare Italian tragedy, which was so shackled, with Elizabethan tragedy, that was free to use or to reject the ancient models and rules, I propose to examine a French tragedy that was composed under neoclassical restrictions closely resembling those confronting the Italian playwrights of the preceding century. I have chosen Racine's *Phèdre*, which has been generally esteemed a masterpiece of its kind. That Racine worked with the same models and the same rules that the Italians used can be readily demonstrated.

In 1598, Angelo Ingegneri, who had taken part in the celebrated production of *Oedipus Rex* in the Teatro Olimpico at Vicenza, published an essay entitled *Della poesia rappresentativa e del modo di rappresentare le favole sceniche discorso*,[7] in which he laid down rules for writing and producing Italian plays. He was mainly interested in pastoral tragicomedies,[8] for he believed that these could be more economically produced than either tragedies or comedies, but his remarks on composition hold for tragedy

---

[7] I have used the version printed in vol. 3 of Guarini's *Opere* (Verona, 1738). References are to page numbers in this volume.
[8] Ingegneri was the author of a pastoral, *Danza di Venere* (Vicenza, 1584), and a tragedy, *Tomiri* (Naples, 1607).

as well as for tragicomedy. Like Giraldi Cinthio and Guarini, Ingegneri was a Modern who nevertheless had great respect for the Ancients; he believed that the *Gran Maestro Aristotile* had provided the basic precepts of dramatic art and that Sophocles' *Oedipus Rex* was the best model for tragedy. A brief summary of Ingegneri's own precepts will indicate the framework of learned dramatic theory in Italy at the close of the sixteenth century.

PLOT. The action of a tragedy should be clear and straight-forward, neither unduly extended nor superfluous, "nor tiring [the audience] with tedious laments, with thoughts that are difficult and long stretched out" (p. 504). The solution of the complex plot should be indicated in the fourth act, the full effects exhibited in the last act. *Concatenazione* of scenes *(liaison des scènes)* is necessary, and the stage should never be left empty. Modern dramatists have often erred here; but the Greeks, especially Sophocles, have shown how the scenes should be articulated. The unities of time and place—of course they were not called "unities" in 1598—should be carefully preserved. (Ingegneri was a disciple of Castelvetro, whom he referred to several times.) The span of time exhibited onstage should be limited to a "natural day, that is, twenty-four hours," and the poet would do better if he made the elapsed time of the action correspond to the actual time needed for performance, that is, "four or five hours" (p. 486). Ingegneri spoke disapprovingly of a tragedy about Sophonisba in *ottava rima* —he had read it but forgotten the author's name[9]—in which the scene shifted from Cirta to Carthage, Numidia, Rome, Egypt, and "various parts of the world," and in which the characters "ferried about from one place to another at their pleasure" (p. 510). In other words, there should be unity of place.

CHARACTERS. The number of speaking parts should not exceed twelve, and these, if invented, should conform to the customs of their country, if historical, to recorded facts. All characters should be verisimilar. All characters should observe decorum. Ingegneri was opposed to introducing supernatural characters on the stage; he maintained that he had never seen a ghost that was not ridiculous. And even more ridiculous was bringing on "infernal spirits to scare the children" (p. 488).

THOUGHT AND DICTION. All speeches in the dialogue should be part of the texture of the plot, not merely witty or figurative

---

[9] Doubtless Galeotto Del Carretto. See above, p. 39.

conceits; for a banquet of sweets soon becomes nauseating. A dramatist is not a lyric poet. Soliloquies, especially in many modern plays, said Ingegneri, are sometimes of such length and of so little verisimilitude that "he who could sleep all that time, and wake up at his pleasure when the other scenes in dialogue come, I believe would feel much more delight" (p. 499). Even short soliloquies are only tolerable when they occur in remote localities, when the time is at night, or when the speaker is extremely agitated.

CHORUS. Ingegneri was no admirer of the tragic chorus, at least of the way it had been used by many poets, both ancient and modern, who introduced it only at the end of an act, hunting up a "canzone to be sung (as is usually said) for the love of God" (p. 490). The tragic chorus should observe verisimilitude and decorum, in accord with the advice of Horace and the practice of Sophocles. Pastorals and comedies need no chorus because "these two kinds of poesy imitate private actions" (p. 493).

Ingegneri based his rules on the best ancient and sixteenth-century theory and practice. The French rules for the seventeenth-century stage were based on the same sources. As Bernard Weinberg (p. 1093) has remarked, Ingegneri's precepts "would not differ materially from those of a French theorist of 1675." Racine's Phèdre was first produced in 1677. And Racine also accepted the "double yoke of imitation and the rules."

Racine's invention was comparable to that of the Italian tragic poets. By his own admission, in the preface to Phèdre, he found his subject matter in Euripides' Hippolytus, Seneca's Phaedra, Plutarch's biography of Theseus, and Virgil. Although he did not acknowledge any debt to earlier French versions of the play, it has been shown by various scholars that he also borrowed some details from earlier French dramatists.[10] His principal models, however, were Euripides and Seneca. That Racine tried to obey

---

[10] So far as I know, Racine was not acquainted with Italian versions of the story. Actually the story of Phaedra was not a favorite in Italy during the sixteenth century. Allacci lists only one Fedra and two Ippolitos that were printed in the sixteenth century, and one of these is Dolce's translation of Seneca's tragedy. There were several Ippolitos in the seventeenth century, some of them musicals. Italian translations of Racine's Phèdre appeared in 1736 and 1738. Giuseppe Baroncini's Tragedia (Lucca, 1552), since it appeared rather early, should be mentioned here. It doubtless owed much to Seneca's version of the Phaedra story, for the situation and the treatment are Senecan. The queen in the play loves her stepson Flamminio, who is the lover of her daughter. The queen betrays the lovers to the king, then kills herself. Baroncini's prologue is delivered by the Fury Alecto.

the Aristotelian rules is evident from his statement about the heroine, who, he believed, "has all the qualities that Aristotle requires in the hero of tragedy, and which are proper for arousing compassion and terror."

PLOT. Racine adopted the Italian method of adding further complications to a classical plot; in this instance a second love affair (Hippolytus and Aricie) was added to the main triangle of Phaedra-Hippolytus-Theseus. Giraldi Cinthio had recommended and practiced this Terentian technique in his tragedies with a happy ending, for example *Antivalomeni, Arrenopia, Epitia.* We have seen numerous examples of the "double plot" in Italian tragedies, such as Tasso's *Torrismondo,* Valerini's *Afrodite,* Zinano's *Almerigo,* Miari's *Prencipe Tigridoro,* Guidoccio's *Mathilda,* and Angeli's *Arsinoe.* Racine was eminently successful in maintaining classical unity, for the love affair of Hippolytus and Aricie was fused to the main action by the common political issues involved.

The plot of *Phèdre* is so carefully wrought that there are no superfluous scenes or characters. The nurse, for example, who was often a mere confidante in Italian tragedy, a comforter and sometimes a check to the heroine, is a key figure in the action; it is Oenone who precipitates the denouement by misrepresenting the behavior of Hippolytus; that is, she tells Theseus that his son actually made love to Phaedra. Aricie is part of the plot, and an important part, for it is she who arouses Phaedra's jealousy. Hippolytus' tutor also takes an active part, and he doubles as a messenger in the last scene. Incidentally, he is the only messenger in the play.

The over-all structure of *Phèdre* squares with Ingegneri's recommendation that the solution of the complex plot be indicated in the fourth act and its full effects exhibited in the last act. Moreover, there are no long expository speeches in Acts 1 and 2. The *action tragique* begins as soon as Phaedra begins to speak. Racine's exposition is made to seem like action, as in the best Greek tragedies, as in Sophocles' *Oedipus Rex.* Shakespeare achieved a similar happy result in the exposition of his great tragedies *King Lear, Othello, Hamlet,* and *Macbeth.* Racine accepted the rule of *liaison des scènes.*

The unities are scrupulously observed in *Phèdre.* The tightly woven plot assured unity of action. Unity of time is emphasized in Theseus' command that Hippolytus leave Troezen before sunrise of the next day. Since there is evidently no shift of scene from the area before the royal palace, there must be a strict unity of place. Governing all is a restraint and economy that the Italian dramatists admired in ancient Greek tragedy but seldom mastered in their own compositions.

CHARACTERS. In fabricating his plot Racine followed the path marked out by the Italians and the French disciples of the Italians. In portraying his characters he left the Italians far behind, for the principal distinction of *Phèdre* is the masterly psychological analysis of character, not only in the heroine but in the other characters as well.

Racine said that he made his heroine less culpable and more noble than the Phaedra of Euripides and Seneca. Phaedra, as he saw her, was caught in the toils of destiny, tainted by the blood of her mother Pasiphaë (who fell in love with a bull). She had a horror of the illicit passion that seized her, and her crime was a "punishment of the gods rather than an action of her will." Nevertheless, she does not attribute all her troubles to Venus or to a malignant star, as do so many victims in Italian tragedy; there is no such simple explanation for her plight. As Racine said, "Phaedra is neither altogether guilty nor altogether innocent." As she tells the nurse, her hands are not guilty of any crime but she cannot say the same for her heart:

> Grâces au ciel, mes mains ne sont point criminelles.
> Plût aux Dieux que mon coeur fût innocent comme elles! [1.3].[11]

Instead of whining at length over her plight, Phaedra tries to come to terms with herself. She examines herself and recoils from what she finds: "J'ai conçu pour mon crime une juste terreur" (1.3). When, driven by a relentless passion, she discloses her love to Hippolytus, she detests herself as she does it: "Je m'abhorre encore plus que tu ne me détestes" (2.5). The pity and terror aroused in this tragedy are not induced by a goddess or a Fury or a star, or by any outside force; they come from within the characters themselves.

Perhaps the most impressive achievement of Racine in this play, as compared with preceding Italian tragedies, is the skill

---

[11] Cf. Euripides' *Hippolytus* 317.

with which he wrought his characterizations within the limitations set by classical and neoclassical rules. Greek tragedy, Seneca's tragedy, and Italian tragedy for the most part allowed very little physical action onstage, little or no physical violence onstage, and no long span of time in which to show change or development of character. Consequently the neoclassical poet, if he wished to make his characters more than masks or traditional types, had to show dramatic conflict as an inner struggle, a struggle in the minds or souls of his characters. Accepting these limitations, Racine turned inward; the tragic struggles in *Phèdre* rage inside the heroine, and also inside Hippolytus, Theseus, and Aricie, even inside Oenone the nurse. Racine could use little physical action and no violence onstage, but he made up for this lack by creating his own kind of *action tragique*. Possibly he profited by observing the failures of the Italians, as Jean Mairet, in his *Sophonisbe*, profited by the failures of Trissino. I do not know. One thing is certain, however, and that is, Racine was a far better Grecian than the Grecians in Italy.

There are no supernatural characters in *Phèdre*, no god or goddess, no Nemesis, no Fury, and no ghost, though both Aphrodite and Artemis appear in his Greek model (Euripides' *Hippolytus*). Phaedra repeatedly refers to Venus, Theseus asks Neptune to punish his erring son, and a sea-monster is said to be the cause of the runaway that wrecked Hippolytus' chariot and killed the driver; but all of these supernatural beings are outside the play. Moreover, the sea-monster could be explained, if need be, as an aberration of the tutor's excited imagination. Racine followed the advice of Aristotle on the use of supernatural mechanism better than did most of the Italian Aristotelians; he resolved his plot by natural and probable means, by the actions of human characters.

THOUGHT AND DICTION. The sentiments in *Phèdre* may not always appeal to readers outside France, but the diction, to anyone who has some understanding of the language, is beyond criticism, perfect among its kind. The sound is always an echo to the sense. There is nothing in sixteenth-century Italian tragedy to compare with Phaedra's speech at the close of the third scene in Act 1, the speech beginning "My wound is not a recent one" (*Mon mal vient de plus loin*), in which she describes to Oenone her long and fruitless struggle to overcome her infatuation for her stepson. This speech is a superb analysis of the physiology and the psychology of love. There are no platitudes here about the madness of love, but the disease itself.

I have often called attention to the Italian playwrights' dependence upon mythological allusion to elevate their thought and diction. In so doing they were usually following the example of their favorite model, Seneca, and usually with indifferent success. There are mythological allusions in Phèdre; but Racine invariably humanized these and made them seem to be natural expressions of particular characters in particular situations. Theseus' invocation of Neptune in the fourth act seems natural, for the sea-god was his special patron. Moreover, Theseus does not ask the god to hurl his son into the sea; he asks him to stifle the young man's shameless lust: "Étouffe dans son sang ses désirs effrontés" (4.2). The great speech of Phaedra in the sixth scene of Act 4, wherein she imagines that she descends to the lower world to face her father Minos, who passes sentence on the mortal sinners brought before him, seems to be a natural outburst of this particular woman in her particular dilemma. One of Phaedra's early speeches, very shortly after she first appears onstage, introduces us to the daughter of Pasiphaë, who was in turn the daughter of Helios the Sun:

> Noble et brillant auteur d'une triste famille,
> Toi, dont ma mère osait se vanter d'être fille,
> Qui peut-être rougis du trouble où tu me vois,
> Soleil, je te viens voir pour la dernière fois [1.3].

Nothing could better prepare us for the sad fate of this heroine. There is an immediacy here that transcends classical mythology and brings home to us the réalité of Phaedra's passion.

Several times I have noted that the Italian tragic dramatists occasionally abandoned the high-flown style and wrote simple speeches in crucial scenes. When they did, however, they were apt to be paraphrasing some better writer such as Virgil or Boccaccio. Crucial speeches of Cinthio's Antony and Cleopatra, for example, almost invariably suffer by comparison with parallel speeches of the same characters in Shakespeare's play. The same unfavorable comparison has been made between Pescetti's Cesare and Shakespeare's Julius Caesar. Racine understood the effectiveness of simple, straightforward speech when the character faces a momentous event. There is a good example of this technique in the last act of *Phèdre*, when Theseus, who is all but overwhelmed by grief for the death of his innocent son and by regret for his own cruel treatment of that son, sees Phaedra approaching. He says, "Mais, Madame, il est mort, prenez votre victime" (5.7).

Ingegneri condemned the extensive use of soliloquies, especially long ones, but allowed them a place in tragedy, especially when the speaker is extremely agitated. There are only four soliloquies in *Phèdre*, all of them short save one (4.5), which is only twenty-one lines long. All express great agitation of spirits. In 3.2, Phaedra appeals for vengeance to Venus, who has hitherto been unable to reach the unfeeling Hippolytus, or so Phaedra believes. In 4.3, Theseus curses his son, who, he believes, has committed incest. In 4.5, Phaedra expresses amazement at the news that the cold-blooded Hippolytus is in love with Aricie; she is amazed and then jealous. In 5.4, Theseus feels his first doubt that Hippolytus is guilty of incest.

CHORUS. There is no chorus in *Phèdre*. Racine did use a chorus in *Esther* and *Athalie;* but the chorus was going out of fashion in France. We have observed that the chorus in Italian tragedy declined in importance between Trissino's *Sofonisba* (1515) and Guidoccio's *Mathilda* (1592) and that Ingegneri, writing in 1598, was hardly an enthusiastic advocate of the tragic chorus.[12] Like

---

[12] Early in the seventeenth century some Italians expressed dissatisfaction with the tragic chorus. For example, Angelo Gabrieli, whose *Ciro, Monarca di Persia* was printed at Venice in 1628, abolished the chorus in the interest of greater verisimilitude. Since princes, he argued, do not "reveal the secrecy of their treaties in public piazzas, it would seem to me very unseemly to make a Persian monarch appear in a feigned public courtyard in the presence of a fixed chorus."

There are always exceptions to general tendencies. Giovanni Angelo Lottini's *Niobe* (Vicenza, 1595), for example, is a kind of throwback. Although the tragic chorus was dwindling in Italy by 1595, Lottini made much of two choruses, male and female, in this feeble dramatization of the ancient myth of Niobe, whose pride in her large family was humbled by the gods. The play is mostly a long lament in a variety of long and short lines, rhymed and unrhymed.

An earlier *Tragedia* (Venice, 1575) by Claudio Cornelio Frangipani is old-fashioned in a different manner from Lottini's. In Frangipani's "Tragedy" a quarrel between Pallas and Mars is resolved by Mercury with a command from Jove. There are two choruses, which join the characters in singing the praises of Henry III of France, in whose honor the masque—it is like a masque—was presented. The author justified his title of "Tragedy" by maintaining that he had returned in practice to a drama older than that recommended by Aristotle, namely, to the form practiced by Thespis. This earlier Greek form, of course, emphasized the chorus.

Shakespeare, Racine compensated somewhat for the loss of the classical chorus by writing lyrical passages in the dialogue.

More than once I have suggested that Italian playwrights like Cinthio, Dolce, and Speroni cannot sustain comparison with Shakespeare, Marlowe, and Webster because they were not as good poets as these Englishmen. The test of poetry, however, is not an infallible test in the theater, nor in evaluating Italian tragedy of the sixteenth century. Torquato Tasso was a first-rate poet, certainly comparable to the best Elizabethan dramatists and to Racine. But Tasso was not a first-rate tragic dramatist, and his failure in the theater cannot be attributed entirely to the double yoke of imitation and the rules. Racine accepted the same yoke, or, it may be, assimilated the same yoke. John C. Lapp, in a good book on Racinian tragedy, says, "The point that I shall try to make in the following pages is not that Racine's genius bowed gracefully beneath the yoke of superimposed rules . . . but rather that he assimilated and transformed dramatic convention so as to produce a drama particularly his own."[13] Lapp acknowledges that Racine was also an imitator; he points out that in the great confession scene in *Phèdre* (2.5) "Racine's dramatic and poetic inspiration are almost wholly Senecan."[14] The French poet surpassed his ancient model, to be sure. The truth is that Racine beat the Italians at their own game; he fashioned better neoclassical plots. Furthermore, he was a great master of characterization and a great stylist.

Despite conscious efforts to do so, the Italians did not wholly succeed in modernizing their neoclassical tragedies. (The comic dramatists did better.) Racine did. The Italians remained imitators of Seneca, Euripides, Sophocles, Virgil, and Ovid in the sense of copyists. Racine was an imitator in the sense of emulator; he stole from the Ancients but he made their riches his own. *Phèdre* is a thoroughly French play although its events and characters are Greek. The Italian tragedies are not thoroughly Italian, but still bear the marks of the Ancients.

In 1701, the able English critic John Dennis contended that ancient tragedy, for example *Oedipus Rex*, was superior to modern tragedy (both French and English) for two reasons: it was more

---

[13] *Aspects of Racinian Tragedy* (Toronto, 1955), p. 36.
[14] *Aspects of Racinian Tragedy*, p. 173.

regular, it was more religious.[15] Some readers today may question the statement that ancient tragedy was religious; but it is true. John Jones, in a recent book on Aristotle and Greek tragedy, says, "Embedded in the plays, and especially in Aeschylus's, are forms of prayer and ritual cries and invocations with a religious significance which the audience must have taken immediately."[16] Dennis greatly admired Racine because the French dramatist carefully observed the rules. He considered him inferior to the Ancients, however, in the second qualification, religion, though Racine did use religion in such plays as *Esther* and *Athalie,* which were drawn from *l'écriture sainte.* Although Dennis had read some Tasso, he apparently did not know Italian tragedy of the sixteenth century. Had he known it, he would surely have called it inferior to Racine's, for, despite its virtue of regularity, most of it had no religion at all, either pagan or Christian.

In breaking away from the popular *rappresentazioni sacre* the neoclassical dramatists of Italy also broke away from the Christian religion, at least in tragedy. In their eagerness to imitate the Ancients the Italian tragic poets adopted the gods of ancient Greece and Rome, but not the ancient religions. It may be recalled that Albertino Mussato made some use of classical theory and practice in his *Eccerinus* (c. 1315); he divided his tragedy into five acts, and he used messengers, chorus, and Senecan rhetoric. These classical trappings, however, are mechanical, and the tragedy, although written in Latin, is Italian and Christian. Mussato did not copy Seneca or Virgil or Ovid any more than did Dante. Italian tragedians in the fifteenth and sixteenth centuries did not follow the example of *Eccerinus;* they copied Seneca, Virgil, and Ovid. Consequently the religious feeling of Mussato and Dante was all but lost in neoclassical tragedy.

Ugo Betti (1892–1953), the leading tragic dramatist of twentieth-century Italy, believed that religion, or at least moral convictions on good and evil, on justice and injustice, must be present in tragedy. In his essay on "Religion and the Theater,"[17] he argued that the twentieth-century theater, and this is certainly true of his

---

[15] *Advancement and Reformation of Modern Poetry,* in *Critical Works of John Dennis,* ed. Edward N. Hooker (Baltimore, 1939) 1.200.
[16] *On Aristotle and Greek Tragedy* (Oxford, 1962), p. 61.
[17] See *The New Theatre of Europe,* ed. Robert W. Corrigan (New York, 1962), pp. 322–332.

own theater, was again returning to religion. He believed that the twentieth-century theater was closer to the "passionate Middle Ages" than to the "brilliant and tolerant Renaissance." Betti evidently recognized the nonreligious character of most Italian tragedy in the Renaissance.

While nearly all of the Italian poets of the sixteenth century subscribed to the moral function of tragedy, and while they usually provided plenty of moralizing in good counselors and chorus, sometimes in hero or heroine, they did not try to make their tragedies of blood and revenge and lust religious in any more than a superficial way. As we have seen, astrology was more important than religion in tragedy. In Dante's *Commedia* it is divine love that moves the stars. In sixteenth-century Italian tragedy it is the stars that move love, or lust. Time and again the Italian characters lay the blame for their mishaps and their misdeeds on the stars.[18] They almost never invoke the Christian deity, the only one that their authors could have believed in, and the only code of conduct that they faithfully follow is that of honor.

This non-Christian quality in Italian tragedy was more aesthetic than irreligious, for the humanists who wrote plays could be good Catholics and still write pagan plays. The generally accepted standard for tragic poetry was the practice and theory of the Ancients, that is, Seneca, Euripides, Sophocles, and Aristotle. Outside the writers of sacred drama—and religious plays continued to appear throughout the century,[19] especially in southern Italy— there were few who objected to paganism in tragedy. Valerio Fuligni, author of *Bragadino* (1589), who tried to substitute Christianity for the customary Jove, Venus, Mars, and Apollo, must be regarded as an exception among the learned dramatists. And even among the writers of sacred plays Seneca and Aristotle were influential. Cortese Cortesi of Padua, author of *Giustina, Reina di Padova*, published at Vicenza in 1607, warned his readers that one who makes too much of Aristotle seems to forget that he is a Christian. Nevertheless, he admitted that the reader would occa-

---

[18] There are always exceptions, of course. Dolce's Herod, for example, blames only himself for the cruel deaths of his wife and children: "I do not have to lament me of Fortune, because I myself was my own evil instrument." See above, p. 176. While Dolce did not get his argument from the Bible, the story of Herod is closely related to the Bible and therefore to religion.

[19] Doglio (pp. lvii ff.) rightly reminds us that the Counter Reformation in Italy encouraged the composition of religious plays, some of which were tragedies.

sionally find in his work "Fortune, Chance, Stars, Fate, Destiny, or
other like terms. . . . Ancient usage has already made these
inseparable from common speech, or at least . . . from poetical
compositions."[20] The notice to the reader of Giambattista Della
Porta's *L'Ulisse, tragedia* (Naples, 1614) offered a similar warning: "The present tragedy is performed by noble characters, and
therefore if you find within it these terms, fate, destiny, chance,
fortune, force, and the necessity of stars, gods, and the like, it has
been done to conform to the customs and rites of the Ancients.
But, according to the Catholic religion, these things are all vanity,
because the paramount and universal cause, every consequence and
event, must be attributed to blessed God." Della Porta's play,
based on Homeric legend, is frankly pagan.[21] Cortesi's, however,
is a *tragedia spirituale;* the heroine is an early Christian martyr
executed by the Romans in the first century.

---

[20] *A discreti e cortesi lettori l' autore,* pp. 12–13.

[21] One of the leading comic playwrights of the time, Della Porta wrote at least
two tragedies, *Giorgio* (1611) and *Ulisse.* The latter is a conventional play,
with a conventional plot. Neptune, baffled in his numerous attempts to destroy
Ulysses, turns for help to the inferno; he summons Cerberus, Megaera, and
the ghosts of the suitors slain at Ithaca. Ulysses senses disaster, for his dreams
have been troubled by warnings of evil. He has already sent Eumaeus to
consult the oracle of Apollo, which predicts that Ulysses will die by the hand
of his own son. Naturally Ulysses assumes that Telemachus will be his killer.
He has Telemachus arrested and exiled. But he has overlooked Telegonus, a
son by Circe. Telegonus invades Ithaca, fails to recognize his father, and kills
him in combat.

Della Porta's tragic style is hardly distinguished, but he could write good
dialogue and some passages are lively and natural. The following exchange
(p. 32) between son and father will illustrate the author's better efforts.

Telemaco	O con quanta allegrezza, e gioia vengo A riveder l' amata Itaca mia.
Ulisse	La tua non sarà mai, mentre, che vivo.
Telemaco	E riveggia 'l mio Rè. *Ulisse* Non dice padre.
Telemaco	A cui desio dal ciel la vita lunga.
Ulisse	Dice, che a lui gli par lunga la vita, Perchè co'l suo desio misura il tempo.

Telemachus: O with how great joy and delight I come to see my beloved Ithaca
again.
Ulysses: [aside] It will never be yours while I live.
Telemachus: And I shall see my king again. *Ulysses:* [aside] He doesn't say
"father."
Telemachus: For whom I crave from Heaven a long life.
Ulysses: [aside] He says that to him my life seems long, because he measures
time by his desire.

Here in this lack of religious feeling, this lack of moral conviction, lies another reason for the failure of Italian tragedy to measure up to the English and French. This failure, however, cannot be explained by the Italian preference for pagan arguments and characters over Christian. The characters in Shakespeare's *Hamlet* are Christians while those in *King Lear* are pagans, yet *Lear* is a greater tragedy. It is also a moral play, even a religious play. Lear swears by Apollo and Jupiter, but he undergoes as profound a moral and religious regeneration as any Christian in the last two acts. In the last act, when the chastened old tyrant has recovered from his fit of madness brought on by his own bad temper, he says to his youngest daughter,

> Upon such sacrifices, my Cordelia,
> The gods themselves throw incense.

And Lear is not the only character in the play who upholds morality and religion. Besides Cordelia and Kent, there is the good Duke of Albany. When a messenger reports the death of the wicked Duke of Cornwall, Albany cries,

> This shows you are above,
> You justicers, that these our nether crimes
> So speedily can venge!

Racine, in the preface to *Phèdre*, subscribed to the moral function of the dramatic poet. The theater of the Ancients, he remarked, "was a school where virtue was no less well taught than in the schools of the philosophers. After all, Aristotle wished to give rules to the dramatic poem, and Socrates, the wisest of philosophers, did not scorn to lend a hand to Euripides' tragedies. It is to be hoped that our works may be as sound and as full of useful instruction as were those of the Ancients." Racine maintained that he tried to make his heroine more virtuous than the Phaedra of Euripides and Seneca.

Raymond Picard, a recent editor of Racine, says that one interpretation of *Phèdre* argues that a biological and religious fatality makes the heroine an innocent victim and reduces the tragedy to a "kind of theological pantomime, where the strings that manipulate Phaedra, sacred marionette, will be visible to the eyes of the experienced spectator."[22] Picard does not accept such an inter-

---

[22] *Oeuvres completes de Racine* (Paris, 1951) 1.759.

pretation. Moreover, he believes that *Phèdre* is more human than theological, more humanistic than Christian. Calling the play humanistic—and most of the sixteenth-century Italian tragedies were humanistic—is not necessarily calling it irreligious or amoral. Phaedra may believe that she is a victim of Venus and of the family curse, but she does not believe that she is a helpless, irresponsible victim. She knows that she has broken, in thought if not in deed, the moral code of her society and the laws of her religion, and that she has incurred the vengeance of the justicers above. No one, I should think, emerges from a reading of *Phèdre* without realizing that he has had a moral and religious experience, an experience similar to that of reading *King Lear,* but hardly similar to that of reading *Orbecche* or *Canace.* Fuligni's *Bragadino* is full of pious Christian moralizing, but it is a poor play. Religious and moral feeling may help to make a good tragedy great; they cannot rescue a poor tragedy.

Perhaps the inferiority of Italian tragic poets, when compared with Shakespeare and Racine, can best be summed up by admitting that Italian tragedy of the Renaissance seldom if ever exhibits the enlargement of the human spirit. Great tragedy, whether ancient Greek, English, or French, does. The Italian heroes and heroines often meet death heroically, often with stoical resignation, but they seldom if ever emerge better human beings in the last act than they were in the first act. In great tragedies, heroes and heroines do.

Nevertheless, Italian tragedy in the Renaissance, for all its obvious defects, did contribute much to the theater of western Europe. Specifically it fostered a close-knit complex plot and, especially in England, an emphasis on revenge, blood, and lust, ghosts and supernatural characters, prophetic dreams, elaborate laments, an attempt to out-Seneca Seneca, and a standard pattern of verse forms.

The most important contribution of the Italians to the Renaissance theater was a complex plot with discoveries and reversals of fortune, often an intricate plot involving several threads of action, such as several love affairs and several revenges. The genesis of this Italian type of plot lay in the Horatian-Aristotelian rules and the practice of Terence, and Giraldi Cinthio first set the pattern in both theory and practice. The Italian plot, and the neoclassical French plot also, observed the unities of time and place. The Elizabethan poets usually ignored or paid little heed to these last two unities, but the better ones respected the more important unity of action, even when they used subplots. In *King Lear*, for example, the subplot of Gloucester and his two sons comes together with the main plot of Lear and his three daughters in Act 4 and the two plots are perfectly fused in the last act. Classical economy was not ignored in Elizabethan England, as Ben Jonson's preface to *Sejanus* and Webster's preface to the *White Devil* testify, although even admirers of classical economy like Jonson and Webster could not break down the popular taste for once-upon-a-time plays or revive the tragic chorus. Histories remained the people's choice on the London stage at least until the advent of Fletcherian tragicomedy. While Jonson and Webster doubtless learned economy from the Ancients, they could also have learned it from the Italians, and probably did.

Elizabethan tragic poets not only rivaled the Italians in devising intricate plots but sometimes surpassed them. There is no Italian tragedy more intricate or so skillfully executed as Middleton's *Women Beware Women*, Beaumont and Fletcher's *Maid's Tragedy*, Ford's *Broken Heart* and *'Tis Pity She's a Whore*.

In surveying the Italianate tragedy of revenge in England it is impossible to separate the influence of *novelle* and Italian histories from that of Italian tragedy, especially when we recall that many Italian tragedies of revenge, such as *Orbecche* and the Tancred-Gismonda plays, were based on *novelle*. It is also impossible to separate Italian influence from that of Seneca's *Thyestes* and *Medea*, which served as models for Italians and Englishmen alike. Bowers found that "Revenge tragedy [in England] was created by a perfect fusing of Seneca and the Italianate."[23]

Shortly after Cinthio's *Orbecche* (1541) Italian playwrights, including Cinthio himself, began to combine love or lust with revenge. It is perhaps a coincidence or perhaps a natural development of catering to the populace, but the English playwrights also introduced sexual passion into revenge tragedy and developed it to the point where it all but superseded revenge. I have already called attention to *Gismond of Salerne* (1567–68) as the first tragedy of love on the English stage. It was also a tragedy of revenge. Love or lust is not the main force in the *Spanish Tragedy*,

---

[23] P. 267. Bowers insists that the theme of "blood-revenge" was more Teutonic than Roman or Italian.

certainly not in *Hamlet,* but it became more and more prominent
in such plays as *Women Beware Women,* Webster's *White Devil,*
the *Maid's Tragedy,* Ford's tragedies, and Shirley's *Cardinal* (1641).
The culmination of the Italianate tragedy of revenge and lust was
surely Ford's *'Tis Pity She's a Whore,* in which sexual passion has
pushed revenge to a subordinate position although revenge is still
a driving force in the action.

In the decay of the Italianate tragedy of revenge, especially
when it was written by amateurs, all sorts of excesses in blood
and lust turned the English stage into a gangsters' slaughterhouse.
I am thinking especially of Goffe's *Orestes,* which I shall discuss
later, and of William Heming's *Fatal Contract* (1630–38), in which
rape and torture vie with the sword and poison for attention, in
which a maiden ravished by a prince disguises herself as a eunuch
and sets out to outdo all earlier revengers, save possibly Vendice
in Tourneur's *Revenger's Tragedy,* by wiping out a whole royal
family. Least tragic but bloodiest of all is the fifth act of Sir
John Suckling's *Aglaura* (1637), in which no less than seven leading characters, including a king, the king's brother, the crown
prince, and the heroine, meet death in or about a cave. As though
to demonstrate that this slaughter was merely a slavish copying
of the blood-lust-revenge play, attended by no genuine feeling for
tragedy, the author later obliged Charles II by writing another
last act with a happy ending for all the characters. Again we
may have a coincidence, but the Italian tragedy of revenge went
through a similar degeneration between *Orbecche* and Decio's
Acripanda or Manfredi's *Semiramis.*

Ghosts and Furies in Renaissance tragedy doubtless go back to
Tantalus and the Fury in the first act of Seneca's *Thyestes.* The
Italians, however, made more use of these supernatural agents
than did Seneca, and the Elizabethans used them almost as much
as did the Italians. The ghost is actually not a prominent feature
in Seneca's tragedies.

The messenger also goes back to Seneca, who used him to describe gory and supernatural events offstage. Cinthio considered
the messenger one of the most important characters in tragedy and
emphasized his role, as did many of his followers. Since the Elizabethans could show death and torture on the stage, they were not
so dependent on the *nuntio,* but they often used him. Nuntius in

the second act of Chapman's *Bussy D'Ambois,* for example, would have been at home on the stage in Ferrara.

Tragic drama has no monopoly on prophetic dreams and visions of disaster, but such phenomena became commonplace in Italian tragedy, beginning[24] with Orbecche's dream of a fierce eagle that attacked two snow-white doves and their brood (i.e. Sulmone attacking his daughter's family) in the fourth act of *Orbecche.* A host of imitators followed suit. There are similar dreams and visions in Elizabethan tragedy although they are not so numerous as they are among the Italians.

The Italian tragic poets, all save a few anti-Petrarchans, were fond of writing elaborate laments for their harassed heroes and heroines, and many of these laments are full of conceits. It was this sort of thing that Mairet objected to and tried to avoid. Elizabethans sometimes wrote tragic laments that are similar to the Italian.

Another characteristic of Italian tragedy that became almost a commonplace was trying to out-Seneca Seneca, that is, trying to surpass the horrors of *Thyestes* and *Medea.* The basis for this ambition probably lay in Seneca himself, for in *Thyestes* 56–57 the Fury urges Tantalus to outdo the "Thracian crime" (i.e. the rape of Philomela and the vengeance of Procne). The Italian revenger often promises to make Atreus, Medea, and Procne seem tame by comparison. Elizabethan playwrights occasionally imitated this device.

Trissino introduced the formal pattern of versification in Italian tragedy and Cinthio confirmed it in both practice and theory. This pattern was unrhymed verse for most of the dialogue, rhyme for choruses and for some passionate or sententious speeches in the dialogue. Shakespeare's *Romeo and Juliet* is a good illustration of this Italian pattern; in this early work the dialogue is mostly blank verse while rhyme is used by the chorus, occasionally by the lovers, and by Friar Lawrence in some of his sententious speeches. Other poets than Shakespeare also used the pattern. Blank verse, corresponding to eleven-syllable *versi sciolti,* became the principal medium of Elizabethan tragedy.

Since it is scarcely feasible here to examine a large number of

---

[24] Actually beginning, it may be, with Pandero's dream of blood in Pistoia's *Filostrato e Panfila* (1508).

English tragedies for illustration of Italianate practices, I have selected four representative plays for this purpose. These are Kyd's *Spanish Tragedy* (1592), the most popular Elizabethan tragedy; *'Tis Pity She's a Whore* (published 1633), John Ford's masterpiece; *Hoffman* (c. 1602), a minor but fairly important tragedy by Henry Chettle; Thomas Goffe's *Orestes* (published 1633), an academic tragedy written by an Oxford divine. In discussing the Italianate qualities of these four plays I cannot possibly discriminate very often between the influence of *novelle* and the influence of tragedies. No one can. But I have selected qualities that could have come from the Italian plays, qualities that are especially prominent in the Italian tragedies of the sixteenth century.

There has been too much emphasis on Seneca in interpreting the *Spanish Tragedy*. Seneca contributed much to the play, as he did to most tragedies of the sixteenth century, but no more than did the Italians. Kyd's plot is Italianate. Seneca's plots are never complicated; but the *Spanish Tragedy* is made up of intrigues and counterintrigues. Lorenzo conspires to murder Horatio so that Balthazar may have his mistress, the beautiful Bel-Imperia. Then Hieronimo conspires with Bel-Imperia to avenge the death of his son by murdering Lorenzo and Balthazar. Lorenzo is the arch-schemer, the subtle Machiavellian villain, and he is the Italianate character who breaks into Italian in the third act.

> E quel che voglio io, nessun lo sa,
> Intendo io; quel mi basterà [3.5].

And no one knows what I want; I know, and that will be enough for me.

Old Hieronimo has never been a schemer, but after his son's death necessity and the desire for revenge force him to become cunning. After he becomes cunning he, too, breaks into Italian.

> Chi mi fa più carezze che non suole,
> Tradito mi ha, o tradir mi vuole [3.14].

He who offers me undue blandishments has betrayed me, or wants to betray me.

The ghost of Andrea, who opens the play with Revenge, at first glance seems to hark back to Tantalus in *Thyestes*. But Andrea is no Tantalus; he is much closer akin to the Italian ghosts that rise from hell in prologue or first act to witness revenge on their enemies. Seneca's character has no desire to revisit Argos and watch

his cursed offspring commit more crimes; he comes reluctantly, pro-
testingly, hounded by the Fury, who gives him no choice. Andrea
does not know at first why he has been brought back to earth.
Revenge soon explains why.

> Then know, Andrea, that thou art arrived
> Where thou shalt see the author of thy death,
> Don Balthazar the prince of Portingale,
> Deprived of life by Bel-Imperia:
> Here sit we down to see the mystery,
> And serve for chorus in this tragedy.

From then on Andrea watches the net slowly draw around Balthazar with all the impatience and satisfaction of Cinthio's Selina
or Groto's Moleonte, Asinari's Duke of Capua, Turco's Selambria,
Valerini's Adonis, Cesare Della Porta's Armilla, or Decio's Orselia.

There are two instances of prophetic dreams or premonitions in
the *Spanish Tragedy*. The Viceroy of Portugal has dreamed that
his son Balthazer is or will be killed. His attendants try to assure
him that the young man has only been captured and may be alive.

> *Viceroy*   But now Villuppo, say,
>   Where then became the carcass of my son?
> *Villuppo*   I saw them drag it to the Spanish tents.
> *Viceroy*   Ay, ay, my nightly dreams have told me this [1.3].

Bel-Imperia is troubled by a premonition that her servant Pe-
dringano will betray her and Horatio.

> *Horatio*   What means my love?
> *Bel-Imperia*   I know not what myself:
>   And yet my heart foretells me some mischance [2.4].

The parallel here between English and Italian is not quite satisfactory, for the English premonitions are vague while the Italian
characters always see a bird of prey or a wolf or a tiger, some
realistic slaughter of themselves or of their loved ones.

The laments in the *Spanish Tragedy* are more apt than not to
be Italianate. Heronimo's notorious "O eyes, no eyes, but fountains
fraught with tears" goes back ultimately to Petrarch, not to Seneca.
Another speech by Hieronimo in 3.7 is as good an example of
Italianate lament as the more celebrated one. The whole speech
is characteristic of the full-blown style, but a selection will suffice
for illustration.

> The blustering winds, conspiring with my words,
> At my lament have moved the leaveless trees,
> Disrobed the meadows of their flowered green,
> Made mountains marsh with spring-tide of my tears,
> And broken through the brazen gates of hell.

Kyd's tragedy was written in what had already become the standard pattern of diction. Most of the dialogue is in blank verse. The love scene between Bel-Imperia and Horatio in 2.4 is partly in rhyme.

> Horatio   Now that the night begins with sable wings
>   To overcloud the brightness of the sun,
>   And that in darkness pleasures may be done,
>   Come Bel-Imperia, let us to the bower,
>   And there in safety pass a pleasant hour.

There is some rhyme in Hieronimo's lament over the body of his son in 2.5.

> O earth, why didst thou not in time devour
> The vild profaner of this sacred bower?
> O poor Horatio, what hadst thou misdone,
> To leese thy life ere life was new begun?

Hieronimo's wife Isabella, who soon goes mad, also uses some rhyme.

> What world of grief—my son Horatio!
> O where's the author of this endless woe?

The choruses are in blank verse and rhyme. The dumb shows were doubtless suggested by the Italian *intermezzi,* which were usually used in comedies, occasionally in tragedies.

Chettle's *Tragedy of Hoffman* is an Italianate tragedy of revenge and lust. Hoffman, whose father had met foul play, sets out systematically to kill all the people responsible for the admiral's death, and he nearly succeeds. When he can he uses a red-hot crown of iron, the instrument used on his father, to destroy his victim. Hoffman meets his own death, however, when he falls in love with the Duchess, mother of his first victim. He realizes that lust has come between him and his revenge.

> [I] had only three [more] to offer to the fiends,
> And then must fall in love [L2].[25]

---

[25] Page references are to the London edition of 1631. I have modernized spelling and punctuation.

There are two examples of prophetic visions of death in the play. Otho, the first victim, has miraculously survived shipwreck, but he is far from happy since he fears that death is still imminent.

> Another trouble grieves my vexed eyes
> With ghastly apparitions, strange aspects
> Which either I do certainly behold
> Or else my soul, divining some sad fate,
> Fills my imaginary powers with shapes
> Hideous and horrid [B2].

An Italian playwright would have described these hideous apparitions in detail. Just before what he hopes will be his final triumph Hoffman also senses disaster.

> But I can tell thee somewhat troubles me,
> Some dreadful misadventure my soul doubts,
> And I conceive it with no common thought,
> But a most potent apprehension [K3].

Like the Italian revengers, Hoffman promises to outdo Atreus, Procne, Oedipus, and Medea.

> Come image of bare death, join side to side
> With my long injured father's naked bones;
> He [Otho] was the prologue to a Tragedy,
> That if my destinies deny me not,
> Shall pass those of Thyestes, Tereus,
> Iocasta, or Duke Jason's jealous wife [C2].

To the Italian Rébora it seemed that the "process of [Elizabethan] absorption of the culture and the moral crisis of Italy reached its saturation with John Ford." He explains: "From the formal literary imitations of the third quarter of the sixteenth century, with so much of Seneca, of academic discussion, of artificial classicism, we have arrived now at an author who represents for us, as perhaps none other, the grievous collapse of the Italian ethical conscience in an abyss of unchecked passions, of unchained impulses, of gloomy sorrow, with an art altogether new."[26] And he adds, "Ford is the [Elizabethan] author most profoundly impregnated with Italian mentality and sentiments." Rébora considers 'Tis Pity She's a Whore Ford's masterpiece and "one of the most ferocious and at the same time most passionately poetic tragedies that have ever been written."

---

[26] Pp. 213–214.

As mentioned earlier, lust overshadows revenge in Ford's great tragedy, yet revenge is there driving these lustful characters to ruin. The plot is complicated and very skillfully made. Giovanni, who loves his sister Annabella, has rivals. Soranzo is courting Annabella with her father's approval, and marries her in Act 4. When he discovers that his bride is already pregnant, all his thoughts turn to revenge. Grimaldi is another suitor. When he is thwarted and beaten by Soranzo's servant Vasques, he too seeks revenge. Hippolita, a castoff mistress of Soranzo, pretends to be reconciled to his marriage with Annabella, then tries to poison him but succeeds only in poisoning herself. Hippolita's cuckolded husband also seeks revenge on Soranzo, who in turn is mad for revenge on Annabella and then on Giovanni after Vasques discovers who the father of the unborn child is. Annabella's maid Putana is rewarded for disclosing the secret of the child by having her eyes put out and then by being burned to death.

The last act rises to an Italianate climax of hate and blood. Soranzo has but one thought now:

> Revenge is all th' ambition I aspire;
> To that I'll climb or fall: my blood's on fire [5.2].

And a little later:

> Soranzo   'Tis well: the less I speak, the more I burn,
>   And blood shall quench that flame.
> Vasques   Now you begin to turn Italian [5.4].

Vasques congratulates himself on his own astute handling of his master's cause: "I rejoice that a Spaniard outwent an Italian in revenge." But the Spaniard scarcely surpasses Giovanni, who, like Tancred, presents Annabella's bleeding heart to her husband, expressing a favorite sentiment of the Italian revengers; that is, he has rivaled Atreus and other tyrants in his bloody deed.

> The glory of my deed
> Darkened the mid-day sun, made noon as night [5.6].

G. F. Sensabaugh has called attention to the description of Annabella that Giovanni gives to his confessor. He remarks that the young man speaks "like a sonneteer."[27] So he does, and like an Italian sonneteer or like an Italian playwright who imitated the sonneteers.

---

[27] *The Tragic Muse of John Ford* (Stanford, 1944), p. 158.

> View well her face, and in that little round
> You may observe a world's variety;
> For color, lips; for sweet perfumes, her breath;
> For jewels, eyes; for threads of purest gold,
> Hair; for delicious choice of flowers, cheeks;
> Wonder in every portion of that throne.
> Hear her but speak, and you will swear the spheres
> Make music to the citizens in heaven [2.5].

The closest bond between Ford and the Italians is the moral anarchy that drives his melancholy characters to their doom. Sensabaugh argues that Ford's dramatic laws were different from those of Sophocles and Shakespeare since his were scientific rather than ethical, "modern" rather than traditional. He points out that while Giovanni is willing to pray to escape the god of vengeance he nevertheless resigns himself to incest because he believes that the "fates have doomed" him. In other words, Giovanni had more faith in astrology than in religion or ethics. Ford's dramatic laws may have been derived in part from the clinical discussions of sex in Burton's *Anatomy of Melancholy;* they were certainly very like those of the sixteenth-century Italian poets.

Thomas Goffe's *Tragedy of Orestes,*[28] acted by students of Christ Church at Oxford sometime after 1616, according to Bowers, "presents perhaps the most consciously contrived succession of horrors and bloody incidents of the whole Elizabethan period." Bowers believes that aside from Seneca's *Agamemnon* the author's models were the *Spanish Tragedy,* Marston's *Antonio's Revenge, Hamlet, Macbeth,* and Tourneur's *Revenger's Tragedy.* I would add Groto's *Dalida* or possibly Alabaster's *Roxana,* a Latin imitation of *Dalida* that had been well known in academic circles since 1592.

Goffe's play, which begins with the homecoming of Agamemnon, presents a parade of avenging executioners. Deaths occur frequently and all of them onstage. In the first act, Aegisthus and Clytemnestra stab Agamemnon as he lies in bed. In Act 4, Orestes stabs the parasite Misander, then, disguised as a physician, gains entrance to the royal bedchamber, stabs the child of Clytemnestra and Aegisthus before the eyes of its parents, smears the infant's blood on them, offers them cups of the blood, and then slowly stabs them to death. In the last act, Strophius (father of Pylades) dies of grief and exhaustion, Electra commits suicide, Orestes

---

[28] Published at London in 1633.

goes mad and stabs the corpses of Strophius and Electra. Finally
Pylades and Orestes kill each other.

Aegisthus appeals to the Furies to help him in his revenge.

> But now begin, thou black Eumenides,
> You handmaids of great Dis, let such a flame
> Of anger burn me as doth Etna's forge.
> On fury, on, our hate shall not die thus [1.2].

This plea sound very like that of Groto's Berenice, who was trying
to outdo Clytemnestra.

O dreadful daughters of gloomy night . . . you Tisiphone, you Alecto,
you Megaera, O as many damned souls as inhabit hell, come to me
and arm me with savage rage, with a desperate and burning heart
[*Dalida* 2.3].

Clytemnestra's exhortation to Aegisthus, as he strikes the first
blow at Agamemnon, is certainly in the spirit of Italian tragedy,
in the spirit of Sulmone in *Orbecche*, of Berenice in *Dalida*, and
of many other Italian revengers.

> Wound him, Aegisthus, kill him not at once.
> We'll be true tyrants; let him feel he dies [1.4].

After Agamemnon dies, riddled with wounds, Clytemnestra cries
in exultation:

> Now I am Clytemnestra right, now I deserve
> To add one more to the three Furies, now
> Do I count this more than my nuptial night.

Compare Berenice's triumphant cry after she has killed Dalida
and the children.

Now I am a woman, now I am strong, now I am Queen, now I wear the
crown worthily. This is the way to repay injuries with interest [*Dalida*
4.3].

Aegisthus is no less triumphant than his partner in revenge.

> Methinks I now go equal with the stars
> And my proud head toucheth the highest pole.
> Hark, Hell applauds me, and methinks I hear
> Thyestes[29] tell me I have done enough.

Agamemnon's bloody ghost appears in the fourth act, crying,
"Why flags revenge?" The ghost of Hamlet's father probably

---

[29] Aegisthus was a son of Thyestes and therefore had an old score to settle with
the son of Atreus.

suggested the situation, but Orestes' reply to his father is certainly Italianate although its decoration does sound like the early Marlowe.

> Great Agamemnon's Ghost, I will bedew
> Thy hearse with blood instead of brinish tears,
> And build a pile up of their murdered trunks
> To burn thy marrowless consumed bones [4.7].

In the second act, a messenger reports the ominous presence of Orestes and Pylades to Aegisthus. He uses the characteristic Italianate flourishes of horror and amazement.

> Were my mind settled, would the gelid fear,
> That freezeth up my sense, set free my speech,
> I would unfold a tale which makes my heart
> Throb in my entrails: when I seem to see't [2.5].

There is one example in *Orestes* of the prophetic dream or vision which is always a prelude to bloodshed. This example is more Italianate than any other of the kind that I can recall. In the fifth scene of Act 1 Orestes enters, "as from his bed, unbuttoned in slippers, a torch in hand."

> What horrid dreams affright me? I see naught
> That I should fear, and yet methinks I fear.
> Mine eyes scarce closed, my busy fancy saw
> A sight that dashed all comforts of the day:
> Methought my Father lying in his tent,
> Hateful Achilles for his wronged love
> Comes in with Briseis, and they two let forth
> Streams of fresh blood from out his aged side,
> With that his echoed shriek did make me wake.

Finally, one of the most Italianate speeches in Goffe's play comes from Clytemnestra's father, Tyndarus, when he finds the slaughtered bodies of his daughter, son-in-law, and grandchild. Turning to Orestes, he cries,

> Was this thy deed?
> Thy silence say 'twas thine; what Tanais,
> Tygris, or Rhenus, or what flowing sea,
> Should wash thee in the salt Meotis stream,
> Or Tethis at full tide o'rflow thy bank,
> Still would the spots of murder stick on them [5.1].

There are many parallels in Italian tragedy to this speech. One of the best, and one that could have been known to Goffe, is from

Torrismondo's speech in the third scene of Act 1 of Tasso's *Torrismondo:*

Alas, when will the Don, or the Rhine, or the Danube, or the unfriendly sea, or the Red Sea, or the Caspian, or the ocean deep ever be able to wash away the dark and shameful guilt that stained and tainted my limbs and soul?

If the sixteenth-century Italians had contributed nothing more to Elizabethan tragedy than a well-articulated complex plot, they would have made a major contribution. And the good plot came from the tragedies rather than from the *novelle.* Giraldi Cinthio, for example, always reworked the plots of his own *novelle* when he dramatized them, condensing the action and increasing the dramatic suspense. The Elizabethan playwrights might have learned to turn their rambling histories into more compact dramas by following the example of Terence and the rules of Horace and Aristotle. All of them doubtless studied Terence in school. Few of them, however, studied Aristotle's *Poetics.* Moreover, they did not have to go through this toilsome process of improving their native drama, for the Italians had already done the job, bequeathing a well-made modern plot to the European theater in both their learned tragedies and comedies and in their *commedia dell' arte.*

In addition to the all-important gift of a well-made plot, the Italian tragic dramatists contributed other valuable qualities to Renaissance tragedy, not the least of which were royal dignity, elegance, and sophistication. Kyd's Hieronimo would not be satisfied with any play save a "stately written tragedy" in the Italian manner. In the first half of the sixteenth century and during most of the second half the only stately written tragedies in Europe were the Italian. While mysteries, farces, and histories were being performed in northern Europe by what Boileau called troops of silly pilgrims, Italians in Florence, Venice, Rome, Ferrara, Mantua, and other towns were seeing or reading tragedies by Trissino, Aretino, Cinthio, Dolce, and Speroni that seemed at the moment to rival the compositions of Seneca, Sophocles, and Euripides. It is not too much to say that the Italians showed French and English playwrights that it was possible to write native tragedies that might rival the best efforts of the ancient Greeks and Romans.

Selective Bibliography

Allacci, Lione, *Drammaturgia di Lione Allacci accresciuta e continuata fino all' anno MDCCLV*, Venice, 1755.

Apollonio, Mario di, *Storia del teatro italiano*, vol. 1, Florence, 1954.

Bertana, Emilio, *La tragedia*, Milan, [n.d.].

Berthé, Louis, *J. B. Giraldi*, Paris, 1920.

Bowers, Fredson Thayer, *Elizabethan Revenge Tragedy* (1587–1642), Princeton and Gloucester, 1940, 1959.

Cavalcanti, Bartolomeo, *Giuditio sopra la tragedia di Canace e Macareo, con molte utili considerationi circa l' arte tragica e di altri poemi con la tragedia appresso*, Lucca, 1550.

Ciampolini, Ermanno, *La prima tragedia regolare della letteratura italiana*, Florence, 1896.

Cinthio, Giraldi, *Discorsi . . . intorno al comporre de i romanzi, delle comedie, e delle tragedie, e di altre maniere di poesie*, Venice, 1554.

————, *Le tragedie di M. Gio. Battista Giraldi Cinthio, nobile Ferrarese*, Venice, 1583.

Cloetta, Wilhelm, *Beitraege zur Litteraturgeschichte des Mittelalters und der Renaissance*, vol. 1 (*Komoedie und Tragoedie im Mittelalter*), vol. 2 (*Die Anfaenge der Renaissance Tragoedie*), Halle, 1890, 1892.

Crocetti, C. G., *G. B. Giraldi ed il pensiero critico del sec. XVI*, Milan, 1932.

Cunliffe, J. W., *Early English Classical Tragedies*, Oxford, 1912.

D'Ancona, Alessandro, *Sacre rappresentazioni dei secoli XIV, XV, e XVI*, 3 vols., Florence, 1872.

————, *Origini del teatro italiano*, 2 vols., Turin, 1891.

Denores, Iason, *Discorso . . . intorno a que' principii, cause, e accresci-*

menti, che la comedia, la tragedia, e il poema heroico ricevono dalla philosophia morale, e civile, e da' governatori delle republiche, Padua, 1587.

————, Poetica . . . nella qual per via di definitione, e divisione si tratta secondo l' opinion d' Arist. della tragedia, del poema heroico, e della comedia, Padua, 1588.

Doglio, Federico, Il teatro tragico italiano, Parma, 1960.

Ebner, J., Beitrag zu einer Geschichte der dramatischen Einheiten in Italien, in Muenchener Beitraege zur romanischen und englischen Philologie 15 (1898).

Flamini, Francesco, Spigolature di erudizione e di critica, Pisa, 1895.

Gasparini, Giammaria, La tragedia classica, Turin, 1963.

Horne, P. R., The Tragedies of Giambattista Cinthio Giraldi, Oxford, 1962.

Kennard, Joseph Spencer, The Italian Theater, vol. 1, New York, 1932.

Morsolin, Bernardo, Giangiorgio Trissino, Vicenza, 1878.

Neri, Ferdinando, La tragedia italiana del cinquecento, Florence, 1904.

Rébora, Piero, L'Italia nel dramma inglese (1558–1642), Milan, 1925.

Rucellai, Giovanni, Le opere, ed. Guido Mazzoni, Bologna, 1887.

Signorelli, Pietro Napoli, Storia critica de' teatri antichi e moderni, vol. 5, Naples, 1813.

Speroni, Sperone, Canace, tragedia del Sig. Sperone Speroni, alla quale sono aggiunte alcune altre sue compositioni, et una apologia, et alcune lettioni in difesa della tragedia, Venice, 1597.

Summo, Faustino, Due discorsi, l' uno intorno al contrasto tra il Signor Speron Speroni e il Giudicio stampato contra la sua tragedia di Canace e di Macareo . . ., Padua, 1590.

Teatro italiano antico, 10 vols., Milan, 1808–12.

Teatro italiano, vol. 1 (Le origini e il rinascimento), ed. Silvio D'Amico, Milan, 1955.

Trissino, Giangiorgio, La poetica, [Parts 1–4], Vicenza, 1529, [Parts 5–6], Venice, 1563.

Weinberg, Bernard, A History of Literary Criticism in the Italian Renaissance, Chicago, 1961.

Zinano, Gabriele, Discorso della tragedia, Reggio, [1590].

Index of Italian and Latin Tragedies

Index of Names

The genesis and development of Italian tragedy and its important contributions to English and French drama are traced in this companion volume to the author's *Italian Comedy in the Renaissance*.

It discloses that the French theater of Corneille and Racine and the Elizabethan theater of Shakespeare and others owed a great deal to the Italian playwrights. Although they were not as successful as their colleagues, the Italians showed French and English playwrights that it was possible to write native tragedies that might rival the best efforts of the ancient Greeks and Romans.

As in his earlier book, Professor Herrick examines the major plays of the period and offers analyses of plot, character, and style. He flavors his detailed account with selections of dialogue. Most of the quoted material is given in the original Italian, with English translations.

Modern tragedy had its beginnings in Italy, the cradle of all the modern arts, and in Latin, the language of high style. Seneca was the model — in fact, for nearly three centuries humanists in Italy and elsewhere regarded him as the best model for tragic writers.

Tragedies in the fourteenth and fifteenth centuries were based either on contemporary or recent history, or drawn from ancient Roman or Greek history or classical mythology. Sixteenth-century playwrights continued to exploit these sources, but added romantic love from Italian novels.